HOLY FIRE

In His Image

BOOK ONE

HOLY FIRE

In His Image

DR. KEVIN L. ZADAI

Unless otherwise indicated, Scripture quotations are taken from the New King James Version. Copyright © 1982 by Thomas Nelson, Inc. Used by permission. All rights reserved.

Scripture quotations marked (KJV) are taken from the King James Version. Public domain.

Scripture quotations marked (NLT) are taken from the Holy Bible, New Living Translation, copyright ©1996, 2004, 2015 by Tyndale House Foundation. Used by permission of Tyndale House Publishers, a Division of Tyndale House Ministries, Carol Stream, Illinois 60188. All rights reserved.

Scripture quotations marked (AMP) are taken from the Amplified Bible, Copyright © 1954, 1958, 1962, 1964, 1965, 1987 by The Lockman Foundation. Used by permission. www.Lockman.org

Scripture quotations marked (AMPC) are taken from the Amplified® Bible (AMPC), Copyright © 1954, 1958, 1962, 1964, 1965, 1987 by The Lockman Foundation Used by permission. www.Lockman.org

Scripture quotations marked (NIV) are taken from the Holy Bible, New International Version®, NIV®. Copyright © 1973, 1978, 1984, 2011 by Biblica, Inc.™ Used by permission of Zondervan. All rights reserved worldwide. www.zondervan.com The "NIV" and "New International Version" are trademarks registered in the United States Patent and Trademark Office by Biblica, Inc.™

Please note that Warrior Notes publishing style capitalizes certain pronouns in Scripture that refer to the Father, Son, and Holy Spirit, which may differ from some publishers' styles. Take note that the name "satan" and related names are not capitalized. We choose not to acknowledge him, even to the point of violating accepted grammatical rules. The author and Warrior Notes have made an intentional decision to italicize many Scriptures in block quotes. This is our own emphasis, not the publisher's.

Cover design: Virtually Possible Designs

Warrior Notes Publishing
P O Box 1288
Destrehan, LA 70047

For more information about our school, go to www.warriornotesschool.com. Reach us on the internet: www.Kevinzadai.com

ISBN 13 TP: 978-1-6631-0048-1

DEDICATION

I dedicate this book to the Lord Jesus Christ. When I died during surgery and met with Jesus on the other side, He insisted that I return to life on the earth and that I help people with their destinies. Because of Jesus's love and concern for people, the Lord has actually chosen to send a person back from death to help everyone who will receive that help so that his or her destiny and purpose are secure in Him.

I want You, Lord, to know that when You come to take me to be with You someday, I sincerely hope that people remember not me but the revelation of Jesus Christ that You have revealed through me. I want others to know that I am merely being obedient to Your heavenly calling and mission, which is to reveal Your plan for the fulfillment of the divine destiny for each of God's children.

ACKNOWLEDGMENTS

In addition to sharing my story with everyone through the book *Heavenly Visitation: A Guide to the Supernatural,* God has commissioned me to write over sixty books and study guides. Most recently, the Lord gave me the commission to produce the *Holy Fire* series. This book addresses some of the revelations concerning the areas that Jesus reviewed and revealed to me through the Word of God and by the Spirit of God during several visitations. I want to thank everyone who has encouraged me, assisted me, and prayed for me during the writing of this work. Special thanks to my wonderful wife, Kathi, for her love and dedication to the Lord and me. Thank you to a great staff for the wonderful job editing this book. Special thanks as well to all my friends who understand what it is to live in the *Holy Fire* of God and how to operate in this for the next move of God's Spirit!

CONTENTS

Salvation Prayer

INTRODUCTION

When Jesus visited me, He warned me that a season of testing was coming to the earth and that many people were not ready due to their lukewarmness. Then I noticed that others were able to persevere in times of trouble and persecution. What was it that distinguished those who were prepared and those who were not? The answer is the baptism of the holy fire from the altar of God.

Jesus was the Son of Man, not just the Son of God, so His life, recorded in the Word of God, is an example to us. His life is written to help us to walk in the same fire of the Holy Spirit that He did. When you are baptized with holy fire, it paralyzes the devil and empowers you to function in your calling as a chosen one.

As you read this book, I pray that you become more intimately acquainted with the Holy Spirit, who is a flame of fire, so that you may walk on the highway of holiness.

Blessings,
Dr. Kevin Zadai

1

FIRE FROM THE ALTAR

He will baptize you with the Holy Spirit and fire.
—Matthew 3:11

Holy fire is not physical fire; it is a spiritual fire from the other realm. There is an altar in Heaven, and there is a heavenly host around the throne room that are flames of fire.

And concerning the angels, He says, 'Who makes His angels winds, and His ministering servants flames of fire (to do His bidding).

—Hebrews 1:7 AMP

3

According to the Bible, angels are ministering spirits that are flames of fire, and they will touch us from the other realm, which is what we want.

We can see and touch so many things here on earth. We can see and touch each other; however, there is so much more around us that we do not see. We cannot see in the spirit realm because we fell in the garden. Our physical eyes do not see everything, and our ears no longer hear everything around us.

Science has found that we only see a tiny fraction of the electromagnetic spectrum or visible light—an estimated .0035 percent.[1] However, all these other spectrums are around us, and if we could see into them, we would see the angels, all the heavenly hosts, the saints, and all these different things going on around us.

The devil gets nervous when we talk about the holiness of God, the highway of holiness, and the fire from the altar because he was once intimately acquainted with these. He could walk on those fiery stones, see the throne of God and be with God. As it says in Ezekiel 28, he was in the Garden of Eden and was an anointed cherub that covered and protected. But now that he has been cast out, he no

---

[1] "Visible Light: Eye-opening research at NNSA," National Nuclear Security Administration, October 17, 2018, https://www.energy.gov/nnsa/articles/visible-light-eye-opening-research-nnsa.

longer has access to these things. However, through Jesus Christ, now *we* do.

Jesus did not die for angels, cherubs, seraphim, teraphim, or Nephilim. He died for us, human beings, and through Jesus, we have been introduced to the Holy Spirit, Who is a flame of fire. He is a beautiful Person who brings us into all truth and touches us with holiness, for we are to be holy as our Father God is holy.

BAPTIZED WITH UNQUENCHABLE FIRE

John the Baptist met Jesus in person when Jesus was introduced to him at the Jordan River. However, John and Jesus first encountered each other when they were each in their mother's womb. Interestingly, when Mary was visiting Elizabeth, their babies jumped within their wombs when they got close (Luke 1:39-45). This encounter shows that God has started life in the womb, and when the baby Jesus and baby John met, they knew each other.

At the Jordan River, John announced that he recognized Jesus and said, "Behold! The Lamb of God who takes away the sins of the world!" (John 1:29). Then John said,

> *I indeed baptize you with water unto repentance, but*
> *He who is coming after me is mightier than I, whose*

sandals I am not worthy to carry. He will baptize you
with the Holy Spirit and fire. His winnowing fan is in
His hand, and He will thoroughly clean out His
threshing floor, and gather His wheat into the barn;
but He will burn up the chaff with unquenchable fire.

—Matthew 3:11-12

John explained that the Holy Spirit would baptize us with fire. When a Christian or any person is introduced to heavenly fire, satan knows that his grip on those people will become less and less as the fire of God starts to influence them. The fire of God burns out the chaff and gets rid of the things in our lives that are flesh hooks within us from satan. Jesus said,

I will no longer talk much with you, for the ruler of
this world is coming, and he has nothing in Me.

—John 14:30

The ruler of this world, satan, had nothing to hook himself within Jesus's flesh. I often think about this because Jesus walked as a man and said that about satan. Jesus was the Son of Man, not just the Son of God, and the signs, wonders, and miracles that He did in front of us were recorded because He was doing them to help us. So I want to relay to you that it is possible to put to death the misdeeds of the body by the power of the Spirit. Paul explained this in the book of Romans.

> *For if you live according to the flesh you will die; but*
> *if by the Spirit you put to death the deeds of the body,*
> *you will live.*
>
> —Romans 8:13

We can be baptized with fire from the altar of God, which will paralyze satan. He does not want any of us walking in that fire and putting to death the misdeeds of the body. He wants us to be lukewarm at best, which is why Jesus was very upset about the lukewarm Christians (Revelation 3:16). When Jesus visited me, He specifically warned me about what was coming to the earth and that He was done with lukewarmness. He warned me about what would happen in a season of testing; He showed me that people were not ready for it due to their lukewarmness.

As born-again believers, we should regularly reflect on the fact that Jesus has helped us through everything and that we are the church of the living God. We are the remnant, and we have an edge because of that. In the Bible, people who encountered and were baptized with the fire of God could persevere in times of trouble and persecution. They were the remnant church, the ones that grew the church. The disciples of Jesus eventually became apostles, turning the world upside down. They went out and did exactly what Jesus told them to do, producing disciples as well.

> *Jesus told me that the secret to a Christian life was the holy fire of God that comes from the sapphire stones mentioned in Exodus.*

Jesus wants us to be more aggressive toward the enemy than we are today, which is why I am talking about holy fire because holy fire is very aggressive. In other words, it changes you and causes changes in your life. You might say, "Well, I'll get to that," and you procrastinate as we sometimes do. Suddenly, an emergency will arise where it must be done, which is when we diligently get it done. Because of the holy fire, we make decisions about matters we usually wouldn't.

Jesus told me that the secret to a Christian life was the holy fire of God that comes from the sapphire stones mentioned in Exodus.

> *Then Moses went up, also Aaron, Nadab, and Abihu,*
> *and seventy of the elders of Israel, and they saw the*
> *God of Israel. And here was under His feet as it were*

a paved work of sapphire stone, and it was like the very heavens in its clarity.

—Exodus 24:9-10

When you encounter that sapphire floor and holy fire, you make decisions you usually would put off. I could do many things at once, so I procrastinated, always trying to navigate what I needed to do. But I have changed because I realized I just need to do things immediately and be very productive. As I pray for other believers, many are supposed to write books and poetry. Some are supposed to be practicing their musical instruments. Others are supposed to use their voices and start doing broadcasts, even if it is from their cell phones. Still, others are supposed to begin ministering to people and then connect with us.

When you get baptized with that holy fire, you will want to function in your calling and, as a chosen one, do a specific task on earth at this time. The adversary, satan, does not want people to be motivated, and he certainly does not want them to be productive. If you write your poetry, book, or songs and create worship music or do a broadcast, you will destroy what he is doing in people's lives. You will paralyze him which is why he doesn't want you to be productive.

The war around you causes you to want to cower in fear and hold back from your calling. When you start to get baptized with this holy fire, satan will sometimes discourage you from moving forward because he knows you are gaining momentum in the Spirit. He knows that you will be able to pray effectively to help others. He will fight against you, come at you, and oppose you.

> *However, when He, the Spirit of truth, has come, He will guide you into all truth; for He will not speak on His own authority, but whatever He hears He will speak; and He will tell you things to come.*
>
> —John 16:13

Remember, the Holy Spirit works with us, bringing us into all truth. When we have the Bible open and meditate on the Word of God, that Word is a heavenly substance. It is not just words and letters on the page; it will actually jump out at you and become dimensional through the Holy Spirit. The Holy Spirit is continually giving us life. He is the breath of God, and He breathes life into the pages of Scripture so that it becomes dimensional. Then the Word of God becomes living and ignites something within you.

TO WILL AND TO DO FOR HIS GOOD PLEASURE

Therefore, my beloved, as you have always obeyed, not as in my presence only, but now much more in my absence, work out your own salvation with fear and trembling; for it is God who works in you both to will and to do for His good pleasure.

—Philippians 2:12-13

This passage tells us that we are supposed to work out our salvation with fear and trembling, which is what you do when you submit to the Holy Spirit. This releases an ignition inside you, and you are working out everything that has to do with you through the power of the Holy Spirit. The Lord is working with you, producing the manifestation in your life.

Today, many people have certain belief systems but are not fully convinced about many truths in the Word. You present facts to them, but they read, watch the news or videos, and measure them up. Other people make decisions based on their emotions and past experiences. However, the Word of God is the absolute truth. The Word of God was in existence before anything else. The revelation and truth in God's Word are beyond anything you can see, think, hear, or comprehend. Most people accept what they see and hear because they do not have a mindset of faith.

> *Now faith is the substance of things hoped for, the evidence of things not seen.*
>
> —Hebrews 11:1

The Lord wants us to take the substance of the things hoped for and have the title deed of what we believe for, which is what faith is. Faith is that substance. Faith is what we cannot see physically but have in our spirits. Hebrews 11 talks about how faith is the substance that allows you to pray into your future and receive the answer before you see or hear it in the natural.

In the same way, you seek out your salvation with fear and trembling. You are not seeking salvation if you are already saved. In other words, Paul is saying that we must seek out everything that has to do with what Jesus Christ obtained. You might need some deliverance or financial provision. The Lord might need to convince you that He wants to prosper you in everything you do. You might need healing. Getting saved does not mean you were physically healed, delivered, or financially prosperous according to God's plan. You work out that salvation with fear and trembling, and the holy fire is a key to this. The manifestation of that holy fire comes because we yield and take it by faith.

THE MANIFEST POWER OF HIS HOLY FIRE

We all have an imagination. When we think about our favorite food or person, this warm feeling suddenly comes over us. It is almost as if we are actually eating our favorite food or with our favorite person, even though we might not have seen them for a while. It becomes real because our emotions, wills, and even the chemicals in our bodies respond to our imaginations, adding to that experience of what we are thinking.

I think about the holy fire, and the fact is that right now, angels are on fire up there in the throne room of God. An altar in Heaven is full of fire right now. I see the angels and the altar on fire. I see the seraphim there, and they are big, and flames of fire are circling over the Lord and the throne room saying, "Holy, holy, holy." These experiences are real and happening in Heaven now (Isaiah 6:1-4).

Think about the coals on that altar where Isaiah was in the throne room of God. He saw one of the seraphim go over with the tongs, take one of those hot coals from the altar, and touch his lips (Isaiah 6:6–8). Many coals on that altar are available now, and the hand of an angel could touch your lips with one of them. I imagine these things. I picture the sapphire floor and the holiness of God, the beautiful blue sapphire stones, the white flames, and everything going on in Heaven right now. By picturing these things, that manifestation in my own life becomes a reality.

> *If then you were raised with Christ, seek those things which are above, where Christ is, sitting at the right hand of God. Set your mind on things above, not on things on the earth.*
>
> —Colossians 3:1-2

As I picture Heaven, the people around me are completely unaware of what is happening there and within my mind, and suddenly, they start to feel the Lord moving! I take my reality, my spirit, and I am thinking and meditating on the things above where Christ is seated at the right hand of God. When I start doing what Paul told the Colossians to do, it suddenly becomes real in my body, mind, and spirit. It is almost as though I am there; I believe I *am* there because that is the more real realm. Now people around me start to sense something is happening, but they cannot comprehend it with their minds.

> *As Christian warriors and disciples of Christ,*
> *when we start to yield to the other realm, that*
> *realm begins to emanate from our spirits.*

As Christian warriors and disciples of Christ, when we start to yield to the other realm, that realm begins to emanate from our spirits. When a group of people yields to the Spirit of God in an environment together in a meeting, God will start moving among them because He has free reign over those people. At that point, even unsaved people will begin to feel the shift to the heavenly realm.

I always allow my mind to picture the good and acceptable things in God's perfect will (Romans 12:2). When the holy fire starts to burn, it wants to manifest. All kinds of things can start happening in meetings: People get touched by God, begin to repent, and experience the power of God. We have seen demons leaving people, and even witches who had come to disrupt the service, have gotten saved and delivered, all because the heavenly realm has touched them, and there is a manifestation.

We want Christian believers to understand that there is a baptism of fire, and you will have the same things happen to you! As the holy fire manifests inside you, you will help and teach people. As people around you start to feel and yield to that manifestation, they will get saved, healed, and delivered. You could be operating in the gifts of the Spirit as well, giving them words of knowledge and words of wisdom and praying over them with tongues and interpretations.

> *When the Day of Pentecost had fully come, they were all with one accord in one place. And suddenly there came a sound from Heaven, as of a rushing mighty wind, and it filled the whole house where they were sitting. Then there appeared to them divided tongues, as of fire, and one sat upon each of them. And they were all filled with the Holy Spirit and began to speak with other tongues, as the Spirit gave them utterance.*
>
> —Acts 2:1-4

WAGE WAR WITH YOUR PROPHECIES

Jesus promised us that the day of Pentecost would come. One of the manifestations that happened on the day of Pentecost was that people saw tongues of fire on the disciples' heads, which is another symbol of the Holy Spirit. You can be baptized with that fire even now. God wants to fan those coals inside you, all the gifts in you by the laying on of hands, and the prophecies that have been spoken over you. God wants you to declare those words over your life and wage good warfare with them. Paul told Timothy,

> *This charge I commit to you, son Timothy, according*
> *to the prophecies previously made concerning you,*
> *that by them you may wage the good warfare.*
> —1 Timothy 1:18

Remember that Jesus has already paralyzed satan. He has made a show of him openly and has destroyed the devil's works.

> *And having disarmed the powers and authorities, He*
> *made a public spectacle of them, triumphing over*
> *them by the cross.*
> —Colossians 2:15 NIV
> *For this purpose, the Son of God was manifested,*
> *that He might destroy the works of the devil.*
> —1 John 3:8

Jesus was sent back to do this and has already done it. Now we are still here, and Jesus is in Heaven, and He sent us the Holy Spirit. The Holy Spirit wants us to enforce the fact that Jesus made an absolute fool out of satan and defeated him. He made a show of satan openly and triumphed over him through the cross.

YIELDING AND BEARING FRUIT

> *I say then: walk in the Spirit, and you shall not fulfill the lust of the flesh. For the flesh lusts against the Spirit, and the Spirit against the flesh; and these are contrary to one another, so that you do not do the things that you wish. But if you are led by the Spirit, you are not under the law.*
>
> —Galatians 5:16-18

As Christians, we must learn to yield to the Spirit and not the flesh, remembering that there are many manifestations of the Spirit. Paul also tells the Galatians about the fruit of the Spirit.

> *But the fruit of the Spirit is love, joy, peace, longsuffering, kindness, goodness, faithfulness, gentleness, self-control. Against such things there is no law.*
>
> —Galatians 5:22-23

Aside from the fruit of the Spirit, there are the works of the flesh. Paul tells us,

The acts of the flesh are obvious: sexual immorality,
impurity, and debauchery; idolatry and witchcraft;
hatred, discord, jealousy, fits of rage, selfish
ambition, dissensions, factions, and envy;
drunkenness, orgies, and the like. I warn you, as I
did before, that those who live like this will not
inherit the kingdom of God.

—Galatians 5:19-21 NIV

Paul differentiates what spirit operates based on what is coming forth in the flesh. When you see someone acting a certain way, Paul tells us to pay attention and look at the spirit behind all that. He gives us a list of the works of the flesh, one of which is witchcraft. Some of the fruit of the Spirit are love, peace, and joy. So you can judge and see the manifestation of each spirit in a person.

As warriors of Christ, we must manifest the fire from the altar in Heaven daily. As a result of that heavenly fire, the angels are sent to ignite and minister to us. We need to be ignited, and we need to manifest that. Even the floor in Heaven is holy. When God came down on the mountain in Exodus 24:10, He stood on a sapphire platform in front of Israel. That is the same sapphire stone on the throne room floor in Heaven with white-hot flames coming out of it, and that can touch us. We can walk on these even though it is in the spirit because Heaven has no limitations. As believers, our spirits are not held back by the limits of our flesh and minds.

Holy fire ignites you because it is already burning hot. For example, after you preheat the oven to 450 degrees in preparation to bake, when you open the door to put in the food, a blast of hot air suddenly emerges. That heat was in there the whole time, but the door was closed. You had turned the knob on and didn't feel anything different until you opened the door. Then, suddenly, what was in there touched you when it came out. That heat from the oven affects you; if you let it, it could heat the whole room and your whole house. The manifestation I am talking about permeates you and everything around you, so look for that and use your imagination. The Holy Spirit in us is joined to the Lord, so our spirit is joined to the Lord, and we become one with Him in spirit (1 Corinthians 6:17).

Our flesh is just the house we live in here on earth. We can be one with the Lord and be married to Him, yet our flesh will want to do something different. It is as though the flesh is another person, and this is because it is not redeemed. It needs to be disciplined, told what to do, and corrected constantly, or it will do what it wants. Your body did not change from one day to the next when you were born again. It stayed the same. Why? Because the body is not touched by the spiritual encounter of the born-again experience you had.

> *But if the Spirit of him that raised up Jesus from the dead dwell in you, he that raised up Christ from the dead shall also quicken your mortal bodies by his Spirit that dwelleth in you.*
>
> —Romans 8:11 KJV

Your spirit is made new, but your body does not respond. You must start to meditate on the Word of God, image the Word, pray in the Spirit, and build yourself up in your most holy faith (Jude 1:20). Then suddenly, that same power that rose Jesus from the dead will begin to quicken your mortal body, as Paul tells us. When you are born again, you are joined to the Lord in one Spirit with Him. That is the born-again experience, and the fire of God is of the same substance.

The fire of God can be transferred, and you can experience that in your spirit, and I have that happen all the time. I am burning up inside at times, but I am not physically hot. Other times, I get physically hot because of what is happening in my spirit. It is coming out with overflowing life, peace, and joy, and all these things are flowing out. However, your body might be in pain or hungry. Your mind might not be on the things of God, but your spirit gets ignited because something is happening in the Spirit that is affecting you.

If you learn to yield to the Holy Spirit and follow what I am explaining, you can take that experience, and it will start affecting your mind, will, and emotions. Suddenly, your soul will side with your spirit. Then together with your body, you put to death the misdeeds of the body by the spirit. You rule and reign from your heart, and you no longer let the flesh rule you. You no longer allow your thoughts, emotions, and all the other things inside you that are contrary to the Word of God to rule you.

2

JOINED WITH THE LORD

But the person who is joined to the Lord
is one spirit with Him.
—1 Corinthians 6:17

The Holy Spirit in us is joined to the Lord, and our spirit is one with the Lord through the Holy Spirit. We become one with Him in Spirit. The same holy fire that the Holy Spirit, the Father, and Jesus have is in your spirit. On the day of Pentecost, tongues of fire came upon those in the upper room, and there were other manifestations of the Spirit (Acts 2:1-4). In the same way, when we are baptized with holy fire, we also have a fire within us and upon us, which begins working in our lives.

You need to keep the fear of the Lord in mind daily (Proverbs 9:10). Think about the fear of the Lord, the holiness of God, and how He is greater and holier than us. Yet the Lord wants us to be in His glory and be unified with Him; He longs for us to walk in and experience His love. To get this from our spirit into our flesh and mind, we need to meditate on it. We need to pray it out, think about it, and then we can walk it out during our day. The holy fire needs to come out from our spirit, and we cannot just wait for it to come upon us.

I have heard people say, "I want to go to that service because I always feel the presence of God there." However, the days of going from one meeting to another to get a spiritual high are over. Those days are done. Jesus wants you to walk in this all the time as an individual believer. Even if you cannot get out of your house because of what is happening in your area or life, you can experience God's presence anywhere. You don't have to have a certain apostle or prophet come to town or attend a specific meeting. The Lord wants you to walk in this; in these end days, we will all walk in this.

> *You prepare a table before me in the presence of my enemies; you anoint my head with oil; my cup runs over. Surely goodness and mercy shall follow me all the days of my life; and I will dwell in the house of the Lord forever.*
>
> —Psalm 23:5-6

RECEIVE EVERYTHING GOD IS OFFERING

If you look at the different revivals and moves of God, they have all emphasized certain subjects. We get to where we are almost an expert on each topic, but then the next move of God emphasizes something else. At the end of this age, we need to be exposed to everything. I want to sit at the table and receive everything God offers us. Why not? Why wouldn't the Lord set a table before us in the presence of our enemies? Why wouldn't He give us everything in this last move? I am talking about the love of God, power, gifts of the Holy Spirit, faith, healing, deliverance, and all the different moves of God we have gone through.

The Lord wants the apostles, prophets, pastors, teachers, and evangelists to minister to the body in the last days. He wants the disciples to be ministered to, and He wants the body of Christ to rise up and become the ready bride so that Jesus can come back and get her. We will be mature and unified in the faith because the fivefold ministry of the church will do its job.

Holy fire will move us into what God has for us. When I was on the other side, I saw that certain things were written about us that never came to pass, which bothered me. God wants so many things; He even announces them, and then they don't come to pass at times.

We try to ignore these kinds of discrepancies, never even discussing them. But what if God's intention is made known, and we are supposed to operate in faith and start implementing those things?

For one thing, we are supposed to be distribution centers for prosperity and wealth to help others. We are supposed to be distributing healing. We are supposed to be praying for people and helping them get the healing that God wants them to have. Demons shouldn't be able to speak through Christians. They should not be able to influence Christians, but they do. People need deliverance and need to understand and experience expelling demons. Yet in so many instances, God's will is not being done.

No Christian should be in debt; the financial system is a trap. We are supposed to stay out of debt, but how many people are debt free? Jesus suffered and died for our sins, but how many people don't feel forgiven even though they say they are Christians? But they are still dealing with guilt and shame.

How many babies were killed today in their mother's womb? That would never be right because Psalm 139 clearly says that the Lord knew us before we were born. He watched us being formed in our mother's womb and has already named us! God's will is not always done, and because of that, we need to allow the holy fire to work in our lives so that we engage God in His perfect will.

DON'T LOWER THE BAR!

Once we know God's perfect will, even if it doesn't happen right away, even if there is a war and a fight to accomplish it, we must stay in there. We cannot lower the bar and change our doctrine because we face problems. We have to say that God is true, and every man is a liar (Romans 3:4). I will stand in faith, no matter what happens.

You must realize that you must stand firm if things have been stolen from you. You cannot lower the bar and say God must have wanted that. God has already told you, He doesn't want these negative things to happen. If He tells you, "This is what I have chosen; this is what I want," then you must stand on that. When problems come, it is not God's fault. It means there is a war down here, we are in a broken world, and we will have to adjust. We must take a stand and believe God's Word, regardless of our circumstances.

A highway shall be there, and a road, and it shall be called the Highway of Holiness. The unclean shall

not pass over it, but it shall be for others. Whoever
walks the road, although a fool, shall not go astray.

—Isaiah 35:8

I saw in Heaven that if we walk in holiness and get on that highway of holiness in Isaiah 35, we will experience the will of God. We will start to see a holy fire in our lives burn up that chaff, and suddenly, we can hear more than we could before. Our spiritual ears are cleaned out, our eyes are healed, and we can see into the Spirit. We get discernment. We start to discern the truth in God's Word and become excited about serving Jesus, no matter what's happening in our lives.

Many people are in churches and do not hear God's Word because the leadership, the ministry, and the church are afraid of offending people. They are fearful of telling the truth because it might affect the church's finances or their relationships with the government, town, or city. The fivefold ministry of the church is supposed to speak the truth, no matter what. But sometimes, the leaders have a hireling mentality where they no longer minister because they are called and chosen. They are mainly there for convenience and good intentions but fear reprisal.

But mark this: There will be terrible times in the last days. People will be lovers of themselves, lovers of money, boastful, proud, abusive, disobedient to their parents, ungrateful, unholy, without love, unforgiving, slanderous, without self-control, brutal, not lovers of the good, treacherous, rash, conceited, lovers of pleasure rather than lovers of God having a form of godliness but denying its power. Have nothing to do with such people.

—2 Timothy 3:1-5 NIV

The Lord showed me that satan extracted certain words from our vocabulary, which we hardly use anymore, such as the blood of Jesus, holiness, and the cross. We fear offending people or seeing them leave our church or organization because we speak the truth. The truth is that it offended people because of their lukewarmness. Lukewarm people only want to hear what's easy or convenient. Paul was telling Timothy this when he spoke about the end days; he said people would be lovers of themselves.

For the time will come when people will not put up with sound doctrine. Instead, to suit their desires, they will gather around them many teachers to say what their itching ears want to hear. They will turn their ears away from the truth and turn aside to myths.

—2 Timothy 4:3-4 NIV

Paul warned Timothy about what would happen in the last days. People would not tolerate sound doctrine. Sound doctrine is the truth—the absolute truth—that is in Heaven. If you are a true apostle, prophet, pastor, teacher, or evangelist, you will speak the truth, and you may offend people. What you say could be interpreted as political, or they could categorize you; however, what you are saying is what God wants. People also get offended when words don't come to pass because they fail to understand that a war is going on in the spirit.

DON'T BACK OFF

God has shown that He wants people healed and delivered. He wants you to have a God-fearing government. However, satan won't sit back and let these kinds of people get into office. When godly people get into leadership, satan starts losing control. Godly people don't focus on money or control, but on helping people.

> *You take the holy fire at the altar within yourself,*
> *and then you present that to people—the reality of*
> *God's holiness and high standard of excellence*
> *for every area of life.*

When you have holy fire in ministry, you continually want to help people because you want to get the truth out there, no matter what. Many people get offended in the last days because they do not want to hear the truth. Yet when you sit and talk with them about their problems, you observe that their lack of faith is not helping them. At that point, you must take the truth that is in Heaven and give it to them. You take the holy fire at the altar within yourself, and then you present that to people—the reality of God's holiness and high standard of excellence for every area of life.

> *"For I know the plans I have for you," declares the*
> *Lord, "plans to prosper you and not to harm you,*
> *plans to give you hope and a future."*
> —Jeremiah 29:11 NIV

You cannot back off deliverance or the fact that the Lord wants you to prosper. God does not want you to wake up and fail or lose money every day. He has a plan for you to succeed, prosper, and be in good health, even as your soul is prospering (3 John 1:2). God's plan for you is that every place your feet tread is your sphere of influence. God will cause everything you lay your hands on and touch to prosper, which is how God's personality is. We may offend people who say they don't believe in healing, deliverance, or prosperity, and they go down the list of the gospel message to negate each blessing. However, do not back off the message because they need you to be strong and stick to God's standard.

Some people do not want you to talk about the crucified life because the crucified life is all about putting the flesh and your will under the control of the Holy Spirit. If you do that, the holy fire will burn in you. Healing and deliverance will flow, and what is acceptable to the Lord in Heaven will manifest, which is what you want.

> *Righteousness and justice are the foundation of*
> *Your throne; mercy and truth go before Your face.*
> —Psalm 89:14

Some people will stop giving to the church or an organization because they are offended and don't want you to talk about specific topics anymore. However, you must speak about it if it is part of the Bible. What you believe comes from the throne of God, and God's throne is established with truth, righteousness, and justice. You cannot negotiate or compromise what God has set up. God has already established His throne, and will not change His personality for you. God is who He is, and He was who He was long before we even existed. God knows better than we do.

> *You must keep the standard of the holy fire and keep it very hot because Jesus hates lukewarmness.*

Rebellious people will not accept the Word of God, and you may have to let them leave your life. You must keep the standard of the holy fire and keep it very hot because Jesus hates lukewarmness. He does not want people to live lukewarm lives; He loves it when people are hot. Jesus doesn't want anyone to go to hell, and He loves everyone, but if you're going to be a friend of God, then you must be willing to hang out with Him.

I guarantee that you won't get cold around Jesus. There will be flames and an atmosphere of life in every situation. The Jesus I encountered is full of joy and life, and He is a problem solver. He wants to resolve people's issues and take care of you, but will you let Him? Many people in churches and groups will not allow the fivefold ministry to teach them correctly because that would mean that they would have to change. They would have to get red hot like the altar in Heaven.

GOD'S FRIENDS LIKE IT HOT

Some of us are the remnant, yet we find ourselves in churches with a lukewarm atmosphere because leadership has compromised the message. These churches have not allowed people to experience the holy fire, the fiery sapphire in Heaven, because they have not experienced it. Some people will leave the church because it's lukewarm. Half of the people will tell the pastor they need to tone it down or they will leave, then the other half will say to the pastor that if they don't heat it up, they are going. Everyone is threatening to leave, and you cannot please them all.

The Lord has taught me that you will only please about 60 percent of the public in any situation when you take a stand. So, you must ensure that people are on board with the Word of God for the right reason. Some people can be offended by what you wear, what you know, or anything you say or do. The Lord has taught me how to operate so I can get at least 80 percent in agreement instead of 60 percent. When you listen to the Holy Spirit, He will give you instructions so that you may keep as many people as possible.

So many people involved with our ministry worldwide want that one true God. They sincerely want to serve God and live that sanctified, crucified life. I am called to help and encourage those people, and I am fine with that. I don't care about the goats, tares, and unwise virgins because I am looking at Gideon's army, an army that was whittled down from tens of thousands to three hundred (Judges 7). They defeated the enemy that night because they were chosen and were all 100 percent on board with God.

So many leaders are compromised because they fear losing people, but they lose half their people anyway because the remnant does not want a lukewarm message. A weak message will not cut it in our times with all this warfare going on. So many leaders are pressured to talk about what makes people feel good. Did you ever notice that a feel-good message seems to go away the minute the devil rears his head and starts to talk to you or when you encounter warfare? That is when you know you will need more than a feel-good message. So what would that entail?

> *For the word of God is living and powerful, and sharper than any two-edged sword, piercing even to the division of soul and spirit, and of joints and marrow, and is a discerner of the thoughts and intents of the heart.*
>
> —Hebrews 4:12

That kind of message would require fiery hot words from the throne room of God. With that holy fire, you can blast the devil so that people discern that the Spirit of God is a sword to separate the soul and the spirit. People can now discern between the flesh and the Spirit of God, which is what we need. I only have a few really on-fire people I can watch and listen to because they are few and far between. Certain teachers don't compromise but only a very few. I would rather just listen to the Bible.

THE CRUCIFIED LIFE BRINGS HOLY FIRE

As an on-fire believer—a warrior—you need to speak the truth in love, stay in that fire, and love people. You know what Jesus went through for us. He was crucified, but He wasn't crucified so that we could have a feel-good message, a feel-good mindset, and kind of skirt through life, barely making it. Jesus did not die for that. He died so that we could be set free and have life, not just life but life more abundantly!

> *The thief does not come except to steal, and to kill, and to destroy. I have come that they may have life, and that they may have it more abundantly.*
>
> —John 10:10

Jesus has already labeled your enemy. He said the thief comes to steal, kill and destroy. So wherever you see stealing, killing, and destroying, you can label that as the enemy, remembering he is a thief. When the enemy or the government steals from us, I label that. Jesus comes to give us life more abundantly. So immediately, you can discern that there is a separation there.

When these problems happen, I immediately run to God, as King David did. David would run right to God whenever anything went wrong or messed up. However, when anything went wrong for King Saul, or he messed up, he would try to fix it himself. He even went to the witch of Endor instead of running to God (1 Samuel 28:7-19). King Saul was not a seeker of God and did not respond very well to the trouble that happened to him.

> *Then Jesus said to His disciples, "If anyone desires to come after Me, let him deny himself, and take up his cross, and follow Me."*
>
> —Matthew 16:24

We, however, have learned how to deny ourselves, pick up our cross, and follow Jesus. When we walk in that crucified life, we encounter His power because we are crucified with Him. You can rise up and declare, "I have been crucified with Christ; it is no longer

I who live, but Christ lives in me; and the *life* which I now live in the flesh I live by faith in the Son of God, who loved me and gave Himself for me" (Galatians 2:20, emphasis added).

You cannot take the gospel and water it down to make it feel good because it will never be right. If you try to tone down addressing the demonic, people will stay bound, which should not happen with Christians. We should always be rough with the devil and push back. Always command him to leave, expelling demons and driving them out.

We should never entertain demons or back off the message and try to manage them. No, we don't manage devils; we don't talk to them except to address them and drive them out. We must deal with this in our minds, wills, and emotions because we will not accept compromise. The holy fire we encounter on this earth is from another realm, which drives out demons.

It is the same with healing. Many of you are dealing with pain in your body and need healing in your emotions. Backing off the message will not help. You will not resolve your pain by saying, "Well, you know, it must be God's will to stay in pain." You are trying to rationalize or justify the fact that nothing has happened, which is an exercise in futility. You are trying to sort it out and process it in your mind. What if God never intends for you to allow compromise in your life? Because that is the truth.

In the dispensation we are in right now, in this end-time scenario, the real test is that we still have to stand firm like never before. A feel-good message will not help you. Your body and mind must come in line with your spirit. You are to be set apart from the world so that people can see that God is with you in this life and world. But you are not supposed to be part of the world. You are only visiting here. You have been crucified with Christ, and it is no longer you who lives but Christ who lives in you.

3

KNOW THE TRUTH

And you shall know the truth, and the truth
shall make you free.
—John 8:32

In the book of Revelation, Jesus warned us not to be lukewarm (Revelation 3:16). Right now, we are in a time of testing that will reveal if people are lukewarm or not. In the teaching of the ten virgins, the five unwise virgins did not make it to the wedding because they were not ready, and their lamps were burning out (Matthew 25:1-13). These virgins were saving themselves for marriage and were preparing to meet the groom. Yet they never made it to the wedding and never encountered what they were waiting for because they weren't ready.

The five wise virgins who were ready were not allowed to help the five unwise virgins who were not. If they had tried to help, they wouldn't have had enough oil. The holy fire burning hot within us reveals the truth, and the truth sets us free. The Spirit of the Lord gives us freedom as He is the Spirit of truth; He teaches us reality from God's perspective (John 16:13).

In the Old Testament, the children of Israel went to Egypt because God sent Joseph there ahead of time to preserve them (Genesis 45:7-9). When Pharaoh was warned in a dream about the coming famine, Joseph told him the interpretation of the dream and then helped him (Genesis 41:1-36). God had orchestrated everything. The favor of Pharoah upon Joseph allowed Joseph to bring his father and his brothers down to Egypt, where it was safe and had plenty of grain available.

After Joseph passed away, the next Pharaoh of Egypt did not remember Joseph or his people. Over the following four hundred years, the population of the children of Israel grew, but they became enslaved because they were not Egyptians. The people of Israel were put in Goshen, which was a suburb of the metropolis. God remembered them, and when it came time for deliverance and all those plagues were unleashed upon the Egyptians, God protected them (Exodus 8:22, 9:26).

That is a type and shadow of what is happening today. Egypt is a type of the world, and Goshen is a type of the remnant church of Christ. The remnant was extracted from Egypt through God's mighty deliverance at the Red Sea. However, the journey to Canaan should have taken the Israelites only a few weeks but instead took forty years (Numbers 32:13). During that time, God tested them in the desert and showed them what was in their hearts. God was faithful and kept His covenant and His Word to His people, but the children of Israel did not acknowledge it and were not thankful.

God protected Israel in Goshen for forty years in the desert and could not renege on His covenant because He had given them His Word. Even though the Israelites in the desert were unbelieving and stiff-necked, and God's wrath burned against them, God still sent an angel to guide them (Exodus 32). God had warned them that the angel He sent would not tolerate their sin or unbelief, and they should not provoke him. (Exodus 23:20-24.) Unfortunately, a whole generation who did evil in the sight of the Lord died in the desert, except for Joshua and Caleb. They were chosen to take the new generation into the promised land.

OBEDIENCE WELCOMES THE HOLY FIRE

Therefore, as the Holy Spirit says: "Today, if you will hear His voice, do not harden your hearts as in the rebellion, in the day of trial in the wilderness, where your fathers tested Me, tried Me, and saw My works forty years. Therefore I was angry with that generation, and said, 'They always go astray in their heart, and they have not known My ways. So I swore in My wrath, 'They shall not enter My rest.'"

—Hebrews 3:7-11 AMPC

The book of Hebrews warns us not to be like the children of Israel, who did not enter the promise through unbelief.

Let us, therefore, be diligent to enter that rest, lest anyone fall according to the same example of disobedience.

—Hebrews 4:11

We must do everything we can to labor to enter that rest and not be like the Old Testament people. In order to teach us God's ways, Hebrews shows us parallels between the New Testament believer and the children of Israel in the Old Testament. Everything in the Old Testament is to help us, so we can now look at this example and know that we should be burning hot for God. We should be learning from everything that happened in the Old Testament.

Samson is another example in the Old Testament. After his hair had been cut off, he wokc up as before, but he did not know that the Spirit of the Lord had left him (Judges 16:20). It is frightening that Samson had so much power but did not notice it was gone. Becoming dull and cold, Samson was no longer on fire for God.

The same thing happened in Sodom and Gomorrah when the angels went down to get Lot and his family out of Sodom after talking to Abraham (Genesis 19). Interestingly, the city's men did not discern that God's angels were angels. They called out to Lot and told him to send out the men so they could have sexual relations with them. The men of the city were so far gone that they didn't even know that those men were heavenly angels. They could not discern anything special about those individuals, which proved how depraved they were.

At the end of this age, we are fighting similar battles. Churches will disappear where the gospel message is not being preached and people are not being helped, but those churches that are on fire will not disappear. Just as Jesus talked about pulling lampstands from the churches in Revelations, lukewarm churches will suddenly no longer be operating (Revelation 2:5). The seven churches in the book of Revelations were all in northern Turkey, then were gone like a puff of smoke. A couple of them are now Islamic mosques, and the rest are rubble, which was never God's will. Jesus was trying to encourage them when He said, "He who has an ear, let him hear what the Spirit says to the churches" (Revelation 3:22).

SET AFLAME IN THE SECRET PLACE

Today, we dwell in the secret place, the special place described in Psalm 91. It is a place of intimacy, of being on the mountain with God in the cleft of the rock. Moses wrote Psalm 91, which came from his encounter with God in the cleft of the rock (Exodus 33:19-23). He said that if you are in that secret place of the Most High, none of these things will touch you—no diseases, demons, or evil will befall you, and no arrows will come in and kill you. He wrote from the revelation he received from his encounter with God. Moses was fiery hot and was not lukewarm at all. He experienced the fire of God and the glory of God, as he was face to face with Him on the holy mountain (Exodus 33:11).

We don't know everything that happened there on Mount Sinai, but we can catch glimpses through the Scriptures. The Israelites were afraid to go up on the mountain because the top of it was on fire with thunder and lightning. Yet Moses walked right into it (not just once but a couple of times) and was engulfed in the fire for forty days.

> *Press into getting on fire for God, maintaining that fire, and staying in it!*

When Moses finally came down from the mountain, his face shone with so much light, and he had to cover his face so that the people were not frightened (Exodus 34:28-30). Moses's level of spirituality was based on his environment, and it was hot. He knew that everything about God was life and truth. Press into getting on fire for God, maintaining that fire, and staying in it!

> *And the glory which You gave Me I have given them,*
> *that they may be one just as We are one.*
>
> —John 17:22

In the New Testament, we have been given the glory of God. Jesus said we would share the same glory He and the Father shared. John 17 describes how we share the same love, unity, and glory that Jesus and the Father do. Jesus prayed for us to have all that. Pursue feeling the fire and holiness of God and allowing it to change you. We, believers, are now set apart and can now learn from and be transformed by the stories in the New and Old Testaments.

But as He who called you is holy, you also be holy in all your conduct, because it is written, "Be holy, for I am holy."

—1 Peter 1:15-16

People do not understand who lucifer was, nor that satan is no longer allowed to experience the holiness of God. He used to walk on those fiery stones on Mount Zion, the mountain of God. Now, we have been invited into the holy of holies to walk on these fiery sapphire stones.

But you are a chosen generation, a royal priesthood, a holy nation, His special people, that you may proclaim the praises of Him who called you out of darkness into His marvelous light.

—1 Peter 2:9

We are to be holy as God is holy because we are now His heirs—the sons and daughters of God. Goshen is a type and shadow of this secret place where the remnant church dwells. Yet we are to enter the promised land, experiencing provisions and benefits in the land of the living.

The Spirit Himself bears witness with our spirit that we are children of God, and if children, then heirs— heirs of God and joint heirs with Christ, if indeed we suffer with Him, that we may also be glorified together.

—Romans 8:16-17

I am not waiting until I get to Heaven to experience the things of God because I have discovered that we can experience them here. The Word of God will always be true, so you must come to a point where you listen to it. If you don't want to believe the Word of God, you have a bigger problem than I can help you with. I am all for speaking the truth and implementing it in your life. Some people want to argue about the Word, and even if they win the argument, they would not necessarily go to Heaven. They may still reject the truth. Live your life fiery hot, speak the truth in love, and let God do the rest.

SIDE WITH GOD AND BECOME HOT

Many people do not understand where lucifer came from and that he experienced the height of holiness and the holy fire. He was created beautifully and beyond description.

You were the seal of perfection, full of wisdom and perfect in beauty.

—Ezekiel 28:12

He had the number one seal on him; that is how highly regarded he was. God established satan on His holy mountain, where he experienced holy fire, which is why he constantly tries to get people to be lukewarm. He wants people to get mixed into this world by compromising and yielding to all the desires of the flesh.

So, because you are lukewarm and neither cold nor hot, I will spew you out of My mouth!

—Revelation 3:16 AMPC

The churches that support compromising doctrine or lukewarmness will be spewed out of Jesus's mouth, just like the seven churches were in Revelation 1-3. If God pulled the lampstands of these seven churches, it wouldn't be fair if He did not deal with all the churches in the same way. The message may have been harsh to those people, but they didn't make it when they should have been thriving. I believe that Jesus was investing in them and trying to help them.

When satan fell, he became a middleman between God and man. Because of his corrupt merchandizing, he corrupted his sanctuary

(Ezekiel 28:16). Now, on earth, we have many corrupt systems, such as financial, government, and health care systems. They are corrupt because satan is the god of this world.

The devil is very aware of how God operates in His kingdom. He knows that he must get us to sin and compromise so that we lose the blessing of God that allows us to participate in His kingdom. Adam and Eve were in a very powerful covenant with God and were one with Him. Sadly, satan convinced Adam and Eve to side with him instead of God. You must think about that and choose not to allow this corruption because God has given us everything through Jesus Christ. Now is the time to preach the gospel and the Word of God, and then He will confirm His Word with miracles, signs, and wonders following (Mark 16:20). We help people and give them the good news, and when we do not water it down, it becomes a fire.

When I speak absolute truth from Heaven, I feel the fire; even if people don't like it, I feel God's pleasure. I sense God siding with me because I am siding with Him, and we are one. There is unity in His love and glory. However, I don't feel that unity, glory, or love when I back off because God does not want me to shrink back. We must listen to what He is saying and do only that; otherwise, we start to leave Him.

I do not pray for these alone, but also for those who will believe in Me through their word; that they all may be one, as You, Father, are in Me, and I in You; that they also may be one in Us, that the world may believe that You sent Me.

—John 17:20-21

In our victorious life in Christ, He is causing us to triumph because we are siding with Him, staying in His glory, love, and unity. In John 17, Jesus prayed for all who would believe and those who would come after and participate. He prayed that their prayers would be answered. Jesus prayed for us to experience the same glory, unity, and love as the Trinity. We are to live in that place with Them, which can be accessed anytime, anywhere. The victorious life is living in God's fiery, fiery, hot Spirit in the flames that come from His throne. Even the angels are flames of fire who minister to us from the fiery stones and altar (Hebrews 1:7).

THE EXPRESSION OF THE HOLY SPIRIT

The early church understood the gospel message and preached it effectively because they heard it from Jesus and the disciples. Then satan rose worldwide and had a heyday, influencing people and persecuting Christians. Paul persecuted Christians, and after becoming a Christ-follower, he also became a target of persecution. Many Christians were killed during this period and had to flee and leave everything. The truth was setting them free, but it also caused division. I am urging you to separate yourselves now. Do not wait, having to be set apart by force eventually. The gospel's message is potent because we are already separate from the world.

On the day of Pentecost, when they were all together, the Holy Spirit came, and they experienced manifestations of the power of God (Acts 2:1-13). The Holy Spirit came with a mighty rushing wind and flames of fire on their heads. The disciples were baptized in the Spirit and began to speak in other tongues that they did not know. At that time, many people in Jerusalem had come from different regions to offer sacrifices. They knew it was a miracle when they heard these Jewish people speaking in their distinct languages.

Physical manifestations, such as wind, fire, and then utterances in tongues, took place. The Spirit of God was on them so strongly that they acted drunk. Peter stood up, apologized, and said, "For these are not drunk, as you suppose, since it is only the third hour of the day. But this is what the prophet Joel spoke" (Acts 2:14-21, Joel 2:28-32). I imagine they were high on God, full of joy and laughter, which was a manifestation. They were in one accord that day, experiencing the wind, fire, utterance, and joy to the point that they appeared drunk, but these are all manifestations of God's power. They were experiencing the other realm and were in the world, but they were not of it (John 17:14-16).

When you yield to and are baptized in the Holy Spirit and fire, you will experience the other realm. You need to see these manifestations in your life to become bold. We need to stay in line with what God is doing. The early church was set apart and did great exploits for God (Acts 2:42-43). Those who know their God will do mighty exploits (Daniel 11:32). The power of God fell on the day of Pentecost because they obeyed Jesus. Jesus told them that He was going to the Father and would send another like Him, and He did (John 14:12, 16-17). Jesus said that the Helper, the Spirit of Truth, would be with us forever and never leave us. We know that the Holy Spirit will never leave us, no matter what happens, and His presence will release a manifestation of God's power.

The Holy Spirit that came on the day of Pentecost has not changed. He is still the same Person, so why would He back off and tone down if He came at the beginning with such power and expression? We have somehow compromised as a church, as leaders, teachers, and students. Not only should the message be the same, but also the manifestations, because the Holy Spirit does not change. I think about this daily; if the manifestation is not happening in my life and

I am not seeing others catch it, I must be backing off because I know God is not backing off.

> *When we are on fire and produce fruit in keeping with repentance, then we can hand off the baton to the next generation with fire from the altar.*

I am sure you have known people who have backed off. I have even told others, "I remember when you were so on fire for God." When you talk to them, you find out what happened, and they struggle with processing it. They may have been attacked, pressured, persecuted, or kicked out of their church. And because they didn't properly process these events, they lost their edge. What happens then is that the church gets robbed.

Think about people like Smith Wigglesworth, who saw thirty-seven people raised from the dead. If he had backed off, then the standard of our faith would have been affected. We don't see nearly the same number of people raised from the dead today. He was a plumber, not even a minister for much of his life, yet he did more for God than most people. He was on fire for God and never let his flame dim. Aren't you glad that he didn't compromise and back off? We need that standard, and now we must be the standard for the next generation. When we are on fire and produce fruit with repentance, we can hand off the baton to the next generation with fire from the altar.

4

THE THRONE OF GOD

In the year that King Uzziah died, I saw the Lord
sitting on a throne, high and lifted up, and the train
of His robe filled the temple.

—Isaiah 6:1

Many revelations were given to us by the prophets, like Isaiah, who saw the Lord high and lifted up and described the throne room of God, along with others like Daniel, Ezekiel, and John. These men of God saw mighty things and wrote about them in the Bible. God instructed Moses in detail on how to make all the different implements of the tabernacle, including the ark of the covenant. The Lord said,

And see to it that you make them according to the pattern which was shown you on the mountain.

—Exodus 25:40

God wanted it a certain way because it was an exact image of what is in Heaven (Hebrews 8:5). The ark of the covenant and the mercy seat are precise reproductions of what is in Heaven.

And the cherubim shall stretch out their wings above, covering the mercy seat with their wings, and they shall face one another; the faces of the cherubim shall be toward the mercy seat.

—Exodus 25:20

The cherubim in Heaven are huge with very long wings; they are on each side of God and cover Him on His throne. Picture God sitting in the middle of the mercy seat in Heaven, seated on His throne. The reality is that the cherubim cover Him. Moses replicated that portion of the throne room on earth. Psalm 91:4 says, "He shall cover you with His feathers, and under His wings, you shall take refuge," but this does not mean that God has wings or feathers; His cherubim that cover Him do, and God is enthroned in the midst of them. We can be in the midst of God and encounter all these realities.

The Throne of God

He who dwells in the secret place of the Most High
shall abide under the shadow of the Almighty.

—Psalm 91:1

Psalm 91 describes the shadow of the Almighty and the proximity to Him on His throne. The light projected from the face of God is so intense that the wings are covering Him to block that intense glory, protecting those around Him. It is not a shadow as we understand it here on earth because there are no shadows in Heaven, but there are greater and lesser degrees of everything in Heaven, including light.

Scripture describes many types of celestial beings, which are not all the same. The cherubim are different from the angels. The angels are ministering spirits; they are messengers that appear as mere men, but they are not and can come to you in different forms. For the most part, the angels who come to you do not need wings to get around because they are flames of fire (Hebrews 1:7). They are faster than the speed of light and have to slow down so you can see them. At the speed of light, they can travel about 7.5 ten times around the earth in one second.[2] That is how fast they are.

---

[2] "How 'Fast' is the Speed of Light?" NASA.gov, accessed January 14, 2023, https://www.grc.nasa.gov/www/k-12/Numbers/Math/Mathematical_Thinking/how_fast_is_the_speed.htm.

Above it stood seraphim; each one had six wings:
with two he covered his face, with two he covered his
feet, and with two he flew.

—Isaiah 6:2

The seraphim have six wings and function in God's throne room. Their wings cover their face and feet, and they fly above God, calling out, "Holy, Holy, Holy, is the Lord of hosts, the whole earth is full of His glory" (Isaiah 6:3). The glory revealed in the Old Testament has also been revealed through Jesus Christ in the New Testament. The fulfillment of the Old Testament is Jesus, Who is a better covenant with better promises.

HOLY AND SET APART

Think about the glory between the cherubim on the mercy seat of the Holy of Holies in the tabernacle. Consider how God chose to come and dwell between the cherubim. Certain aspects of the Holy of Holies were essential to God. The dwelling place of the Most High is the hottest spot in Heaven, where God is enthroned between the cherubim. Moses appointed Aaron, his brother, as the first high priest to oversee the tabernacle (Exodus 28:1-2).

> The dwelling place of the Most High is the hottest spot in Heaven, where God is enthroned between the cherubim.

Then He said, "I will make all My goodness pass before you, and I will proclaim the name of the Lord before you. I will be gracious to whom I will be gracious, and I will have compassion on whom I will have compassion."

—Exodus 33:19

Moses asked God to show him His glory (Exodus 33:18-23). God put Moses in the cleft of the rock and told him that when He passed by, Moses would see His goodness and that God would proclaim His name to him. God was going to announce His name and reveal His characteristics to Moses, which, according to Hebrew scholars, is God's name. God told Moses His name, then afterward, only the high priest knew it. The name would be whispered to the next in line when it was time for a new high priest.

God's name was only spoken once a year inside the Holy of Holies, in front of the mercy seat. The high priest had to come in wholly set apart before making the sacrifice in the Holy of Holies (Leviticus 16:1-34). He had to be dressed in a certain way and could not show any skin except his face. Everything had to be performed in a particular way with the blood of a perfect, unblemished lamb. The high priest would come in, sprinkle the blood on the mercy seat and announce the name of God, which only he knew. If the high priest did everything right, the sacrifice was accepted, and Israel's sins were forgiven for another year. He would do whatever else was required and then go back out. The high priest could only go in and out of the Holy of Holies when he was instructed to.

God made a way and set a pattern, then Jesus came and fulfilled it all in the New Testament. I think about how I can go into the holy place whenever I want. People ask me, "How often can I take communion?" This is like asking, "When can I pray?" or "How often can I pray?" I just say, "Yes," because there is no limit now, and you should not do it as a formality. If you can enter and take communion several times a day, you should do that because it is not wrong to take communion all the time. But it is wrong to do it without discerning the Lord's body and what it means. It is the same with prayer; you don't pray just to say you prayed. You pray because you know God hears and wants to answer your prayers; this is when you know that you are effective in prayer.

There are no shadows in Heaven, yet you can stand in that secret place in the shadow of the Most High. There is a place where you are so close to the cherubim, and God enthroned; you are protected from the full glory of God coming from His face, just like Moses experienced.

> *But He said, "You cannot see My face; for no man shall see Me, and live."*
>
> —Exodus 33:20

You cannot see God and continue to live in your body. Your body is fallen and cannot handle the full glory that emanates from God's face. If you did see it, you would be transformed into an eternal mode that could not be undone. It is this way in Heaven right now.

DWELLING IN THE HOLY OF HOLIES

> *I beseech you therefore, brethren, by the mercies of God, that you present your bodies a living sacrifice, holy, acceptable to God, which is your reasonable service.*
>
> —Romans 12:1

Here on earth, God has made provision through Jesus Christ for us to go to that mercy seat. The blood of Jesus is there, so you don't have to present blood again; you offer yourself as a living sacrifice. Paul told the Romans to present themselves as a living sacrifice, wholly acceptable unto God. It is your reasonable and daily service because your spirit is always before God.

> *All believers should live in the reality that they will live forever and never leave Jesus.*

In Heaven, your name is written in the Lamb's Book of Life, and the blood of Jesus has forgiven all your sin. All believers should continually walk in the reality that they will live forever in Heaven and never leave Jesus. This is my reality; I will experience all these things every day, no matter what.

Think about being in that secret place right now, so close to the throne that you can see the cherubim and their wings reaching up on each side of God. You cannot see the Father's face, but bright light comes from His body as He sits in a timeless realm. Suddenly, you see the glory of God brighter than any flame. You can see Jesus and the angels as you look at the altar. You can see the six-winged seraphim and the flames. You can see where the cherubim's wings cross in front of God and on the other side of Him and how they block His face. What emanates from Him is much brighter than anything else around the Father, confirming that God would have that highest standard.

Psalm 91 says that when you are in the secret place of the Most High, you will not get sick, and the devil will not take you out. None of these terrible things will happen to you. Angels will be assigned to you because you are close to the Lord. You are not just visiting the Most High, but you have made Him your dwelling place—your habitation.

Many Christians are disqualified from encountering God's best because they do not want to make the Most High their habitation. Many believers do not want to live there; they just want to visit. They only desire an encounter or a revelation. However, many others are past that point now. As warrior disciples, students of Christ, and part of the remnant, we are past having a revelation and an encounter. Visitation is fine, but we should mature so that we become residents of Heaven. We live in Heaven; our spirits are just here visiting.

When we have this revelation, we become much more productive as we finish our lives here on earth. Our bodies and our finances are healed. Our minds, wills, and emotions are healed because we experience the eternal realm. We are not waiting until we reach Heaven to enact certain gifts in our lives. I want to be exposed to those in my spirit and walk them out here.

> *And there I will meet with you, and I will speak with you from above the mercy seat, from between the two cherubim which are on the ark of the Testimony, about everything which I will give you in commandment to the children of Israel.*
>
> —Exodus 25:22

In Exodus 25:17-22, God gave Moses explicit instructions on preparing a place where God could meet with him, and it was to be a replica of what is in Heaven. Moses implemented God's plan, which included many details and secrets from God. However, we engage at a much higher level in the new covenant than they did.

THE NEW AND LIFE-GIVING WAY

> *And so, dear brothers and sisters, we can boldly enter Heaven's Most Holy Place because of the*

blood of Jesus. By his death, Jesus opened a new and life-giving way through the curtain into the Most Holy Place. And since we have a great High Priest who rules over God's house, let us go right into the presence of God with sincere hearts fully trusting him. For our guilty consciences have been sprinkled with Christ's blood to make us clean, and our bodies have been washed with pure water.

—Hebrews 10:19-22 NLT

Think about what the high priest in the Old Testament experienced. Jesus opened a new and living way for everyone to enter the Holy of Holies by His blood. As believers, we are now of a higher order than the high priest. I like to remind people what Jesus said when He spoke of John to the multitudes.

For I say to you, among those born of women there is not a greater prophet than John the Baptist, but he who is least in the kingdom of God is greater than he.

—Luke 7:28

In other words, anyone who has ever lived previously was below John. Up until that point, John the Baptist was the greatest in the kingdom. He was greater than Abraham, Elijah, and everyone in the kingdom. In Luke 7:28, Jesus stated that the "least in the kingdom of God is greater than he," meaning that every believer from then on is greater than John the Baptist. This truth could take a lifetime to process.

When you begin to understand and encounter subjects such as the holy fire, the heavenly sapphire, the highway of holiness, and "Be ye holy, for I am holy," you are essentially in habitation at the throne of God (Isaiah 35:8, 1 Peter 1:16). You are at a place by the cherubim where the wings are casting a lesser degree of glory; no demon can touch you or talk to you. Nothing is coming at you, no arrows or disease can touch you, and you can trample on serpents and scorpions and have power over the enemy (Luke 10:19).

Angels are assigned to you because you are as close as you can get; you couldn't handle the glory coming from the Father's face if you were any closer. I don't know, but maybe when we get to Heaven, a time will come when we can see God's face. However, when you are there, you realize you don't know how anyone, even those out of the body, could handle the face of God. I did not see God's face, but what I did experience was much more than I could take.

THE END OF EVIL'S PROSPERITY

So much evil is in this world, and the people perpetuating it do not seem to be scathed. They seem to live forever in their wickedness, almost as if they arc immune to misfortune. Yet Christians are encountering cancer and all these other problems, and it seems as if they must fight for everything they believe in while evil seems to prosper.

I saw in Heaven that these evildoers' days of prosperity were coming to an end. Until now, satan has been protecting them because they are his and have given themselves over to him, but their hour of judgment is coming. However, if we run into the most Holy Place, we should be able to receive our healing, deliverance, prosperity, and everything that God has bought for us through Jesus Christ. We should be able to obtain that, but such a war is going on to stay healthy and keep our finances up.

If you abide in Me, and My words abide in you, you will ask what you desire, and it shall be done for you.
—John 15:7

Jesus answered and said to him, "If anyone loves Me, he will keep My Word; and My Father will love him, and We will come to him and make Our home with him."

—John 14:23

Jesus said to him, "If you can believe, all things are possible to him who believes."

—Mark 9:23

Why wouldn't the gospel include these benefits? If you love the Lord, your God, and obey Him, why wouldn't He answer you? You can ask whatever you desire, and it will be done for you. If you believe, nothing is impossible for you. It seems too good to be true. Then you see the wicked, who murder people, steal from, and cheat people, living to a nice old age. There seems to be no justice because they take advantage of people in their nation by doing wickedness and prospering. David wrote about this in the Psalms.

But as for me, my feet had almost stumbled; my steps had nearly slipped. For I was envious of the boastful, when I saw the prosperity of the wicked.

—Psalm 73:2-3

The day is coming when wickedness will not prosper and no longer occur. We can pray and ask God to take care of these situations because whatever we bind on the earth is bound in Heaven. We can bind, loose, make decisions, and bring in the kingdom of God because Jesus said that the least from now on in the kingdom is greater than John. As the church of Jesus Christ, the gates of hell cannot prevail against us (Matthew 16:18). That is a church abiding in the shadow of the Most High, a hot church full of flames from the altar and on fire for the Lord.

> *Assuredly, I say to you whatever you bind on earth*
> *will be bound in Heaven, and whatever you loose on*
> *earth will be loosed in Heaven.*
>
> —Matthew 18:18

Many of the angels' names in the Bible—Gabri-el, Micha-el, and other names, such as Isra-el—have the letters *EL*[3] in them, which is the shortest name of God. It is almost as though God implanted His name in these names. If God made lucifer, called satan, and he was the epitome of perfection, then that must not be his original name (Ezekiel 28:12). Before he fell, lucifer would have had God's name within his name too.

---

[3] "H410 - 'ēl - Strong's Hebrew Lexicon (kjv)." Blue Letter Bible. Accessed 1 Feb, 2023. https://www.blueletterbible.org/lexicon/h410/kjv/wlc/0-1/

Strong's Concordance tells us that *lucifer* is the Hebrew name *hêlēl*,[4] meaning "bright and shining one of God." So the original word wasn't *lucifer*; the name *lucifer* is a Babylonian god not found in the original text. In the original text, helel has *el* in his name. That confirmed what I suspected: that lucifer was not his original name. God created him perfectly until iniquity was found in him; he shone brightly and was appointed as an overseer of the garden of Eden.

The Nephilim were the fallen ones, fallen angels that did not keep their proper domain but left their abode and are in chains now (Jude 1:6). The Nephilim influenced the sons of God to go into the daughters of men (Genesis 6:4). Nimrod built Babylon. In Hebrew, his name means "one of the mighty ones" (Genesis 10:8).[5] He was one of the hybrids that the Nephilim influenced. That hybrid race had to be destroyed because it resulted from a union between the fallen angels and the daughters of men. There are three different entities here: the Nephilim, the sons of God, and the daughters of men.

Babylon was built by satan through Nimrod. In the New Testament, the mystery Babylon is mentioned in Revelation 17:5. Nimrod had

---

[4] "Lexicon :: Strong's H1966 – hêlēl," Blue Letter Bible, accessed August 5, 2022, https://www.blueletterbible.org/lexicon/h1966/kjv/wlc/0-1/.

[5] "H1368 - gibôr - Strong's Hebrew Lexicon (kjv)." Blue Letter Bible. Accessed 1 Feb, 2023. https://www.blueletterbible.org/lexicon/h1368/kjv/wlc/0-1/

to be stopped because he built the first walled cities and ruled over people (Genesis 11:1–9). Some scholars believe he was the first to capture and keep people inside the city, not to protect them but because he was a dictator. God had to come down and stop him from building the tower of Babel.

5

ADDRESSING THE SPIRITUAL FIRST

I will ascend above the heights of the clouds, I will be
like the Most High.' Yet you shall be brought down to
Sheol, To the lowest depths of the Pit
—Isaiah 14:14-15

When Isaiah and Ezekiel prophesied, it seemed as though they were prophesying to a physical king, prince, or nation, but they were also addressing the spiritual entity behind the physical. We can see these alternating word usages in Isaiah 14:4–17 and Ezekiel 28 when there is a switch from the word "prince"[6]

---

[6] "H5057 - nāḡîḏ - Strong's Hebrew Lexicon (kjv)." Blue Letter Bible. Accessed 1 Feb, 2023. https://www.blueletterbible.org/lexicon/h5057/kjv/wlc/0-1/

to "king,"[7] two different Hebrew words. You might not pick that up in some translations, but there is a parallel. Prophets can address the spiritual as well as the physical. However, the spiritual is the top priority and is addressed first, and then the physical manifestation happens later but in between is warfare.

> *Those who see you will gaze at you, and consider you, saying: "Is this the man who made the earth tremble, who shook kingdoms, who made the world as a wilderness and destroyed its cities, who did not open the house of his prisoners?"*
>
> —Isaiah 14:16-17

Isaiah shows us that in the end, lucifer falls to the ground; everyone will see it and wonder how this could be the person who caused all the nations to fall and the cities to burn. Isaiah was exposing what was happening behind the scenes. When you first read it, Isaiah appears to be talking about the physical rule of a nation and king.

A prophet speaks from the realm of the spirit, but he addresses two realms: the physical and the spiritual. A lot will happen between the time a person speaks from that realm until the manifestation occurs.

---

7 "H4428 - melek - Strong's Hebrew Lexicon (kjv)." Blue Letter Bible. Accessed 1 Feb, 2023. https://www.blueletterbible.org/lexicon/h4428/kjv/wlc/0-1/

We also see that certain things do not happen because of warfare. Jesus prophesied and said what God wanted, but it did not always occur. For example, He said, "O Jerusalem, Jerusalem, the one who kills the prophets and stones those who are sent to her! How often I wanted to gather your children together as a hen gathers her chicks under her wings, but you were not willing!" (Matthew 23:37).

Jesus told the people of Israel that they did not discern their day of visitation (Luke 19:44). We see this happening today with nations and individuals. How many people have heard the Word of God, rejected it, and will go to hell if they do not repent? As believers, if we do not apply all that we know and do not allow the Lord to work in our lives, we might not see His word come to pass in our lives. What could God accomplish if you yield a little more today than yesterday, and what would that mean in eternity?

> *God's perfect will isn't being done because people chose not to accept it, but that does not change God's heart or what He wants.*

When I was in Heaven, I saw perfection and God's plan. There I saw the United States speaking as one nation; however, they were not encountering what God wanted on earth. God's perfect will isn't being done because people chose not to accept it, but that does not change God's heart or what He wants. What happens then is that when the prophet speaks, fewer people understand his words. We can see where the Word is being stolen, and we must stand up.

THE FIRE PRODUCES A BETTER CROP

The prophet releases the Word, just like in the parable of the sower (Matthew 13:18–23). The Word is sown in all four soil types, but only one yields a return, which is 25 percent. Now, that soil type doesn't always produce a hundredfold return. Instead, some of the returns were thirty, sixty, and one hundredfold. The holy fire can touch you, and to the degree you become hot and productive and do what God wants you to do, you have either a thirty, sixty, or hundredfold return—providing that your soil has been properly cultivated.

Taking care of your soil requires you to get rid of the hard soil, the rocks, and the thorns and chase away the birds that come to steal the seed. You must do everything you can to cultivate your heart because Jesus said that the soil represents men's hearts. If you do, you can affect how much of a return the Word of God has in your life. In a service of one hundred people, the parable says that only twenty-five people have the proper soil to receive the Word. Then you must divide those into three different percentages: thirty, sixty, or a hundredfold return.

If you want the fire, the heat must be turned up in your life. When I was in Heaven, I realized how much we are affected by God's holiness, His presence, His glory, His Word, the fire from the altar, and the sapphire floor. His holiness, the heat of the Holy Spirit, and that fire that burns eternally will burn out every imperfection. I realized that satan (lucifer, helel) was the epitome of perfection and that he walked on those sapphire stones. He is no longer permitted to walk there, but now we can.

I was given this revelation of the holy sapphire in Heaven when I saw Jesus standing on this beautiful floor. Those blue sapphire stones were glowing, on fire with white flames rising through them, and Jesus bid me to walk to Him on those stones. In Exodus 24:10, God Himself came down on a platform of sapphire stone that He stood on in front of the elders in Israel.

I have been a Christian for over forty years, and I think about those first twenty years and how I was never told any of this. Every day since my heavenly encounter has been a shock of revelation from the Word of God. I can deal with circumstances in this life differently now because of what I know. I have had forty years of dealing with my heart and my soil and then the return of that Word. It is alarming how long it took for me to start seeing the soil producing a hundredfold return from the Word of God, and I think about it all the time.

PARALLEL REALMS

You were the anointed cherub that covers with overshadowing [wings], and I set you so. You were upon the holy mountain of God; you walked up and down in the midst of the stones of fire [like the paved work of gleaming sapphire stone upon which the God of Israel walked on Mount Sinai].

—Ezekiel 28:14 AMPC

Our enemy used to walk on Heaven's holy floor of sapphire stones. He understands more about what has been given to us through Jesus Christ than some Christians, which shouldn't be the case. As Christians we should know more about our Father than the adversary. The enemy has fallen, and through Jesus Christ, he has openly been shown to be a fool in front of the whole world (Colossians 2:15). Jesus triumphed over him on the cross and destroyed the works of the devil (1 John 3:8).

Isaiah saw how lucifer had fallen and prophesied to both the physical and spiritual realms. Similarly, Ezekiel 28 speaks to both realms as Ezekiel addresses the *prince* of Tyre and the *king* of Tyre. He was addressing the future and the millennial reign. Isaiah described him as the one who caused the nations to be destroyed and cities to be burned (Isaiah 14). Isaiah and Ezekiel saw the same thing, and we can glean from their prophecies. You cannot just read them on the surface as though they were merely referring to some war between kings of the past and their nations.

> *Behind the scenes, a whole other world is operating at a higher level with good and bad entities working and warring, and we must not forget this.*

We can see a similar two-realm prophecy with Daniel, who was hauled off from Israel to Babylon with his people and dealt with captivity by a Babylonian king (Daniel 10). When Daniel prayed, the angels came, and he saw that higher entities influenced the world powers. He saw the archangels fighting with kings and princes. If you look, you will see that some kingdoms hadn't even come into power yet, but they did after God dealt with the King of Persia.

You are dealing with many people and activities during your day: conversations, interactions, working, homeschooling your kids, driving, going to the grocery store, or dealing with your family. But behind the scenes, a whole other world is operating at a higher level with good and evil entities working and warring, and we must not forget this. Ezekiel addressed the physical Prince of Tyre, who was there at the time. However, this King of Tyre does not seem to be recorded in history, and from the prophecy, you can tell that it is not about a physical king.

> *You were the seal of perfection, full of wisdom and perfect in beauty. You were in Eden, the Garden of God.*
>
> —Ezekiel 28:12-13

There was never a king like that. Also, Tyre was an actual city that existed, but there is no way that Tyre was in Eden, the garden of God. Ezekiel is talking about a particular being in the garden of God, a being full of perfection and the epitome of perfection. All of these wonderful stones were in and on them, and there were timbrels and pipes within them.

> *You were the anointed cherub who covers; I established you.*
>
> —Ezekiel 28:14

You cannot be a physical king and be a cherub because a cherub is a spiritual being with wings. These spiritual beings are at the throne of God. They are not angels as we know them, as there are different types of these beings.

> *You were on the holy mountain of God; You walked*
> *back and forth in the midst of fiery stones. You were*
> *perfect in your ways from the day you were created,*
> *till iniquity was found in you.*
>
> —Ezekiel 28:14-15

We know that this king of Tyre would not have been on God's holy mountain. This king was corrupted and cast to the ground. It is obviously helel; he was over sanctuaries, but he corrupted them because of his iniquities. It doesn't seem possible for a being so perfect to become corrupt, but his iniquities were because of his trading or merchandising. God destroyed him by bringing fire from within him. If you become lukewarm, compromised, and corrupted, you can experience what Ananias and Sapphira did (Acts 5:1–11). Due to sin, you could suffer a premature death by being exposed to this level of the holiness of God.

All who know you among the people are astonished
and appalled at you; you have come to a horrible end
and shall never return to being.

—Ezekiel 28:19

You must understand that everyone on the earth will see that this being, satan, is judged in the end (Isaiah 14:12-17). Everyone will behold this and wonder that this was the person who brought people to their knees and destroyed nations and cities. Remember, the prophet is pronouncing and talking about two different people. One was a physical ruler living in a physical city named Tyre. The other is a spiritual entity operating behind the scenes in the spirit, affecting the natural ruler over Tyre at the time.

You see all the corruption in governments on earth now taking place and wonder why there is no justice. The common people are sometimes overcome because upper-level entities can usurp authority by affecting the ruling class within the government. If the church, the body of believers, does not take authority by binding and loosing, items are taken from the people, and justice does not rule. There is killing, stealing, and destroying because the thief is actually in charge of that nation, and these entities are willing and able to influence the physical leader. You will see both good and evil kings and good and bad governments, which all have to do with what is discussed here. The dynamics of the dual kingdoms are where you have the spiritual and the physical realms.

FOCUS ON TRUTH AND HOLINESS

But we speak the wisdom of God in a mystery, the hidden wisdom which God ordained before the ages for our glory, which none of the rulers of this age knew; for had they known, they would not have crucified the Lord of glory.

—1 Corinthians 2:7-8

Paul said if the rulers of this world had known, they would never have crucified Jesus. In doing so, they fell into a trap. God overcame these so-called rulers, these hierarchical fallen ones, who were ruling on many different levels. The little I know and what I have seen is shocking enough for me not to talk about because there is so much more we don't know.

However, I know that the only way to usurp authority over them is to enforce what Jesus has already done; Jesus has already literally destroyed the works of the devil, openly making a fool of him and triumphing over him on the cross. We must focus on the blood, the cross, Jesus's name, the highway of holiness, baptism with the Holy

Spirit and fire, and the things of God because these are the only things that have defeated these entities.

We must reinforce what has already been done. We are not inventing a ministry or a subject, pushing an agenda, or talking about conspiracies and the events behind the scenes. Some of these activities are valid, but if you focus on them, you are not giving people solutions or the answers they need. If you are always looking for that kind of thing, you can get concerned and into fear. But if we talk about the blood of Jesus, minister the gospel, and expose the enemy, using the spiritual weapons of our warfare that Paul talks about in Ephesians 6, then we are offering solutions to problems.

We are giving people tools and the ability to be warriors. We must focus on the tools and the truth God has given us instead of the conspiracy theories because they can be overwhelming. You could keep talking about all the activities going on in secret, and your concerns may all be valid, but talking about those subjects doesn't help people. They will still have to go home after the conversation and deal with issues in their own homes and lives. We have solutions, and we walk in the Spirit. We live in the Spirit and wage war with the weapons of righteousness and truth we have been given.

6

THE ANOINTED CHERUB WHO COVERS

You were perfect in your ways from the day you were
created, til iniquity was found in you.
—Ezekiel 28:15

In the garden of Eden, helel was given the ability to rule as a caretaker and overseer. He was a covering cherub and a guardian. Today, we would liken him to private security for Eden. Ezekiel 28:18-19 explains that satan had sanctuaries and other places where he had overseeing capability, but he was found trading and merchandising. He had inserted himself as a middleman, which is how the world system is set up now.

If you and I wanted to trade, buy, or sell something to each other, we could just agree and do the transaction. However, whether under the guise of protection or regulations, the government and different entities in our world system have inserted themselves into trading, buying, and selling as middlemen. On the surface, they say they need to monitor these activities to protect you and make it look like they are covering you. However, they are ultimately trying to control you and make money. That person or government entity does not need to be otherwise involved.

If you have an agreement between two individuals, you can make a transaction, but when all these regulations and other entities become involved, it becomes corrupt. You then have to pay them for their services when you are already paying taxes for them to serve and protect you. They are not there to make money from you and certainly not to control you. We are supposed to control the government; the government should not control us. They are not supposed to tell us what we can believe or do. The people have hired them, and in a free society, a democracy, we elect officials to oversee us and take care of matters; they work for us.

By inserting himself into certain situations, helel corrupted all of the world's systems. If you and I were going to negotiate a deal, we would need someone to broker it. Why did we need this third party to be involved? If I were to hand you money to exchange goods or services, I would not need anyone else involved. I would give you the money in exchange, and then we would agree, having a contract between ourselves. A corrupt system where you must go through a third party creates a false need for something. Then they set it up so you cannot pay for it outright and have to borrow money. The situation becomes expensive, so you constantly depend on other entities to be involved, which is just corrupt.

We should work and earn income, not be overburdened by taxation. We should be able to buy a house outright, have it built, and pay someone to do that. Instead, it is almost impossible for most people to purchase a home because they are overtaxed and not paid a fair wage, so they have to borrow money. Then the loan has such a high rate of interest that it takes you years and years to repay it. And when you pay it back, it's three times more than if you initially paid for it with cash. This whole system is corrupt and was set in place by satan.

YOU DON'T NEED THE MIDDLEMAN

By inserting himself into these situations, lucifer corrupted them through his trading. His multitudes of iniquity were in his trading and merchandising (Ezekiel 28:18). He did it by creating an artificial need for a middleman. Another example is health care which is too expensive because you must have insurance. The insurance system is corrupt because it supports a problem and meets its needs. Instead of getting you well, medical professionals often prescribe medicine to take away the symptoms. You will have to take medication for the rest of your life. God's will is for us to be healed, and there should be a solution. Yet this system creates the need for other people and entities to control you.

The Holy Spirit has ways to lead and guide you into the truth so that you will not be dependent on these middlemen that insert themselves into situations. Remember, they create a problem to solve and create a need in your mind to involve them. You must allow the Lord to lead and guide you out of these situations so that you depend only on Him. When He provides for you, you don't need the middleman.

> *Owe no one anything except to love one another, for*
> *he who loves another has fulfilled the law.*
> —Romans 13:8

God wants you out of debt. As Paul said, he wants you to pay for products outright and not owe any man anything except love. Even in the old covenant, when you loved the Lord your God, obeyed Him, and did all that He commanded in the law given to Moses, then all these blessings would come upon you (Deuteronomy 28).

You must choose this day who you will serve (Joshua 24:15). Will you be obedient and love the Lord your God, putting His Word before you? If you do, God will prosper you in everything you do and take sickness away (Exodus 15:26). You will lend to many nations but not borrow from any. The fear of the Lord will come upon all the other nations because of you, and they will be afraid of you. If your enemy came against you one way, he would have to flee before you in seven directions (Deuteronomy 28:1-14). These are some of the promises in God's covenant with Israel.

> *But as it is, Christ has acquired a [priestly] ministry which is more excellent [than the old Levitical priestly ministry], for He is the Mediator (Arbiter) of a better covenant [uniting God and man], which has been enacted and rests on better promises.*
>
> —Hebrews 8:6 AMP

In the new covenant, God has made all His promises through Jesus Christ; it is a better covenant with better promises. So wouldn't that be even better than the promises in Deuteronomy 28? I don't see many Christians operating in the old covenant today, let alone the new covenant. People will argue with you and say, "Well, that is the Old Testament." So I say, "Okay, so we are supposed to be sick and poor and have problems with devils in the New Testament." Then their response is, "Whatever God wants." However, God has already revealed what He wants. He has already given us an old covenant and then fulfilled it in Jesus. Then He gave us a new covenant through the blood of Jesus based on better promises, according to the Word of God. It is a better covenant with better promises, so it must be better than Deuteronomy 28.

If you are not living in the promises of Deuteronomy 28, you could go back and just love the Lord your God and place that law before you; love Him and obey what He says. You can at least benefit from the old covenant. But, no, you don't need to settle because, through the blood of Jesus, we have much more than that, and it should be a lot greater. The Lord is not taking away healing and prosperity in the new covenant; that would be against Scripture.

PARTNERS AND PARTAKERS

He who has My commandments and keeps them, it is he who loves Me. And he who loves Me will be loved by My Father, and I will love him and manifest Myself to him." Judas (not Iscariot) said to Him, "Lord, how is it that You will manifest Yourself to us, and not to the world?" Jesus answered and said to him, "If anyone loves Me, he will keep My word; and

*My Father will love him, and We will come to him
and make Our home with him."*

—John 14:21-23

God intervened because hclel, lucifer, literally inserted himself to bring people into bondage. God said that if we love Him and obey Him, He will come and live with us. If God took away sickness in the old covenant, then certainly, through the stripes that Jesus took on His back and the blood of Jesus, He gives us all the previous benefits plus all the new and better benefits through the new covenant (Isaiah 53:5). The new covenant would supersede and be overwhelmingly greater than the old covenant.

Logically, why would Jesus, God's only Son who shed His blood for us, be less than when He hadn't yet come, and the people were still under the law? Why would the blood of goats, lambs, and animals be a more beneficial sacrifice than the blood of Jesus? That would never happen because Jesus destroyed the works of the devil, and He gave us these precious promises.

> *As His divine power has given to us all things that
> pertain to life and godliness, through the knowledge
> of Him who called us by glory and virtue, by which
> have been given to us exceedingly great and precious*

promises, that through these you may be partakers of
the divine nature, having escaped the corruption that
is in the world through lust.

—2 Peter 1:3-4

Peter picks up on the fact that we can be partakers of the divine
nature through these precious promises. We can be partners with
God, which is so much greater than in the Old Testament, when we
were under the law, servants of God, and we had to obey or else.
Now we are considered partners and partakers of that divine nature.
We can escape the corruption in the world, which is the result of
lucifer's corruption of the sanctuaries through his merchandising.

> *Now we are considered partners and partakers of*
> *that divine nature, and we can escape the*
> *corruption in the world.*

Since helel was made perfect, when he fell, he fell in a huge way
and is now corrupt. However, he knows what holiness is and what
it is like to be on the mountain of God and be the epitome of
perfection. He was right there to see God and operate as an overseer
of the garden. Helel was an ambassador and called to cover Eden
(Ezekiel 28:14). How tragic to know all that he knew and then fall.

He knows about holy fire, the highway of holiness, and the sapphire platform (Isaiah 35:8, Exodus 24:10).

The real children of God, made in His image, are the heirs of God, which helel could never be. We are human beings, joint heirs with Jesus and heirs of God (Romans 8:17). Since he was created as a cherub, helel was not made in God's image. We are the only ones that Scripture says were made in the image of God (Genesis 1:27). A strategy of satan is to prevent people from talking about holy fire, the highway of holiness, the Holy Spirit, or the holy angels. He doesn't want you to know about the throne of God, the flaming sapphire floor, and sons of God who have the authority to trample on serpents and scorpions and over all the power of the enemy (Luke 10:19).

Satan does not want you to know anything I am telling you, and he will do his best to corrupt the system to hide the truth from you. If you begin going toward God and seeking His face, satan will create lying signs and wonders to discourage you and stop all these things from being added to you (Matthew 6:33). He tries to shut you down; however, he can, such as theft, disappointment, and trauma. His goal is to stop you from thinking that God is a good God. Only you know better.

The Word of God teaches the truth and sets us free; the Spirit of God enforces that within us. The Holy Spirit is enforcing the covenant and blessing right now. He is implementing all that God has ever said or will ever say. Everything established in Heaven can be set on this earth through yielding to the Spirit of prayer and saying, "Thy kingdom come. Thy will be done on the earth as it is in Heaven" (Matthew 6:10). As human beings, we need to proclaim that with our mouths because we are ambassadors now, far above satan and every evil spirit. We have been exalted above all those because we have been bought by the blood of Jesus (Ephesians 2:6).

When we get to Heaven, we will be restored to a position above the angels and even Adam and Eve because we are new creations in Christ; this means that we are a species that has never existed before (2 Corinthians 5:17). It is hard to fathom, but we will see satan being judged. The fire will come and consume him; he will be turned to ashes and will be no more (Ezekiel 28:18-19).

While here on earth, we must realize that the system we live in, the worldly system, is not God. God would never kill babies, steal from people, or set Himself up as a dictator. He would never set people above us as dictators who would steal from us, kill or destroy us, or want a government to control us. God would never allow that to happen. So we can see that this world is corrupt, and God is not in control of it because so much damage is being done instead of life being given.

> *For the Lord is good; His mercy is everlasting, and*
> *His truth endures to all generations.*
>
> —Psalm 100:5

When Jesus came, He healed people and did not make people sick. He drove devils out and didn't call devils to go into people. Jesus gave to people and never took from them. He told people the truth that set them free. As believers testifying that our God is good, we must communicate this to everyone. Today, nations cry out for godly leadership, which is on God's heart. However, corruption comes in, unjust balances exist, and possessions are stolen.

The church must stand up and fight, bind the devil, and continue to stand firm so that God can judge and rule righteously within our lives. We must grasp that the god of this world, small *g*, is in charge of this world, and his system is corrupt. He was corrupted, so his sanctuary was defiled because of the multitude of his iniquities and the iniquity of his trading (Ezekiel 28:16-17).

> *The church must stand up and fight, bind the devil, and continue to stand firm so that God can judge and rule righteously within our lives.*

You must always be aware of what binds you. Be aware of when you need to depend on someone to broker a deal for you. Be cautious when you are told to take medication, borrow money, or pay a particular person. Be aware that this kind of system is not in Heaven; it is part of the world's corrupt system.

YOU ARE GOD'S POSSESSION

The god of this world, "the prince of the power of the air," as Paul called him, is in charge and is the spirit that works in every unsaved person (Ephesians 2:1-3). So anyone who is not saved, not born again, cannot say no to the devil. They will continually be bombarded and overcome by these evil spirits, which is the work of the prince of the power of the air. A Christian can resist the devil because they have the born-again experience. Their spirit is set apart as holy unto God. It has become a new creature (2 Corinthians 5:17). A Christian cannot be taken over to the point of possession because possession is ownership. The devil cannot own a Christian.

However, they can be controlled or manipulated by the devil; it is up to that person and whether they choose to say no.

People in the world do not have any power to resist the devil because he is too strong for them. They do not have God's power and life in their spirit because they don't have that experience of being born again as a new creation. You can build yourself up as a Christian and say no to the devil.

As satan cannot occupy the same territory as the born-again human spirit, the idea of possession is usually wrong. The word often used in Scripture is the Greek word *daimonizomai*[8], which translates as "demonized" or "to be under the influence of a demon." Scripture refers to proximity and domains; the word does not have anything to do with ownership as we think of it. It has to do with how much of the devil you have relinquished your authority to, communicated with, and given over to him. The devil cannot do anything unless we give him authority verbally and by our actions.

In Him you also trusted, after you heard the word of truth, the gospel of your salvation; in whom also, having believed, you were sealed with the Holy Spirit

---

[8] "G1139 - daimonizomai - Strong's Greek Lexicon (kjv)." Blue Letter Bible. Accessed 1 Feb, 2023. https://www.blueletterbible.org/lexicon/g1139/kjv/tr/0-1/

of promise, who is the guarantee of our inheritance until the redemption of the purchased possession, to the praise of His glory.

—Ephesians 1:13-14

A human being is made in the image of God, so even an unregenerated man, in their fallen state, can be retrieved through the born-again experience. Demons cannot come into the spirit of a born-again person because they are sealed. An evil spirit can only influence a Christian in their body and soul, which is their mind, will, and emotions. Because of this, Christians can get sick and be deceived. In their minds and emotions, they are attacked and disappointed. Christians can experience negativity in their souls because we are comprised of three parts: spirit, soul, and body. Possession is impossible for you as a Christian because you would have to undo your salvation and tell the Lord you don't want to be saved anymore. You would have to go back and hand yourself over to satan. If you were to say that, you could be sure that Jesus would fight for you because He said He would leave the ninety-nine to go after the one (Matthew 18:11-14).

If people have problems with evil spirits, I ask, "How much have you given over to the devil? Are your problems because you have yielded to him?" The devil cannot do certain things unless you permit him. Of course, attacks and curses are also at work, but they don't take away from the blood of Jesus and the name of Jesus. They do not get to the point where you are powerless because that would be against what Jesus has already done through the Word of God.

SUBMIT TO GOD, RESIST THE DEVIL

At one point, satan was perfect, and he knew what it is like to be perfect; he knows that you are perfect as a new creature in Christ. He will attack you in every way possible, and you must not give in, no matter what you encounter. This is for every Christian; you must use the name of Jesus and the blood of Jesus to push satan back because he knows he will have to leave. The people in the world do not have this ability. When dealing with an unsaved person, they must first get saved. You will be fighting all their battles for them if they are not saved. They will not be able to fight independently, which will be a losing battle. Lead people to repent and receive salvation, then teach them to submit to God, resist the devil, and the devil will flee from them (James 4:7).

If the devil is not fleeing from you, you have not submitted to God or resisted the devil. God cannot lie—if He told us to submit to Him, resist the devil, and he will flee from us, then that must happen! We know it is not God's fault if it doesn't happen. If something is not working, it is not God's fault. As remnant warriors, we must realize that we cannot fall back. We cannot go back and retrench; we must keep moving forward. If God has established something in His Word and circumstances are contrary, we must continue to push the devil out. We cannot let him push us out. We are not powerless, and it is impossible for him to win because of what God has already established with us.

When satan was walking on those fiery stones in Heaven, he had this false sense of being like God. It got to the point where he could not discern that he wasn't God because he had all these wonderful encounters. During my Heaven encounter, I saw those beautiful fiery sapphire stones and had such an amazing feeling in that atmosphere. If any iniquity were found in you, it could twist that feeling, and you would be quickly judged.

GOD'S TREE IN THE GARDEN

Adam and Eve were not supposed to eat from the tree of the knowledge of good and evil in the garden (Genesis 2:17). People often ask why God would even put that tree there to tempt them. You must understand no temptation was there. The temptation came through the enemy, and if the enemy had not done that in the garden, Adam and Eve would not have even considered eating from that tree. Since Adam and Eve had free will, the enemy suggested that God was keeping something from them and that they would be like God if they ate of the tree. However, they were already like Him, except they could not know good and evil and still choose good. God reserved this only for Himself because He can know all this and still choose good.

We were never meant to know evil. The tree was placed there like a tithe; it was set apart for the Lord and never ours. We were never to eat from it. God put it there to show Adam and Eve they would never be perfect like God. In other words, God reserved that for Himself. They already thought *I am like God, but I am not God.* When they saw that tree, they knew they could not eat from it because they were not God, and it was always before them to remind them. God does this in our lives and with the cherubs, the seraphim, and the different angels He created. They were not allowed to touch certain things or go to certain places. God is reminding everyone that even in this atmosphere of perfection in Heaven, you could be misled, thinking that you are like God. That is what happened to helel.

7

OUR ADVERSARY, THE DEVIL

Be sober, be vigilant because your adversary the devil walks
about like a roaring lion, seeking whom he may devour.
—1 Peter 5:8

The anointed cherub who covered, whose name was helel, became known as lucifer, the devil, or the adversary. He inserted himself into situations and corrupted the whole system here on earth, so now there is a system of debt. When you owe people money, you are manipulated and controlled by that. In the end, when you see the antichrist coming into power, you can see how he controls everything, and if you don't submit and receive the mark of the beast, you will not be able to buy or sell (Revelation 13:16–17).

That was the plan from the beginning: lucifer usurped authority to take control of people, stole humans from God in the garden of Eden, and mankind fell.

Jesus bought us back, so we must not back off. As Christians, we must get out of debt and be aware of situations where we can be manipulated or controlled. Our adversary, satan, tries to create the problem and then is right there to resolve it, but the government was never meant to operate that way. In the United States, the government was never meant to control you. The taxpayers hired individuals—which we refer to as *the government*—to protect us, serve us, and uphold the Constitution.

The Constitution is not about the government; it is about the people, with many provisions to protect us. We are a republic with a constitution, and that Constitution protects us. We pay taxes to the government to keep us secure and protected. The federal and state governments use various resources to serve and manage us effectively. But corruption has come in, and satan has set up leaders to manipulate and control us. It has become all about making money and controlling people. The leadership now makes decisions for people instead of letting them make their own decisions and electing officials to carry out their desires and will.

Jealousy overtook helel when he saw that man and woman were given authority over everything in the garden. If helel was an ambassador and the guardian over the garden, why would God appoint the man and woman to be over everything and keep the garden? Even though this cherub was so close to God in perfection, iniquity was found in him. He saw that man, not him, was made in the image of God, so helel tricked the woman, Eve, into eating from that tree and then giving it to her husband to eat (Genesis 3:1-6).

> The adversary has been hard at work for thousands of years to corrupt the system and enslave people. In contrast, Jesus came to break off bondages and redeem us.

Adam and Eve were tricked into disobeying God, which corrupted them and opened their eyes to good and evil. They then knew all the possible terrible things, whereas before, this would not have even entered their minds. They could know and concoct evil as soon as they ate that fruit. Before that, mankind was never meant to know evil. Adam and Eve were thrown out of the garden, and afterward, they started to deteriorate and eventually died. Corruption came in, then the first lie and murder (Genesis 4:8-10).

The adversary has been hard at work for thousands of years to corrupt the system and enslave people. In contrast, Jesus came to break off bondages and redeem us. He came to give us benefits through the promises of God. If we believe and cooperate with God by believing in Jesus and being obedient, loving, fearing, and serving Him, we will receive the reward of eternal life, and in this life, God will work with us. For those who want to share the gospel's good news and preach the message, God will confirm His Word with signs and wonders following (Mark 16:20). God gave us all the gifts of the Spirit, the fruit of the Spirit, and the fivefold ministry of the church. He gave us the apostle Paul, who wrote the letters to the churches that outline all the benefits of being in Christ, all the "in Him" Scriptures.

When helel fell, he corrupted man and woman because mankind took the place of that perfection as sons and daughters of God. We took the place of being part of God's kingdom at a higher level because we were made in God's image. The fall devastated us, yet Jesus corrected it in the spirit realm. If you implement His covenant through faith and cooperation, you will see manifestations of the covenant in action in your life.

A few Christians around you might participate in that covenant, but others do not. They will tell you that they are Christians, but people often don't understand the meaning of covenant and don't know how to apply it. They do not realize that they must respond to God's Word and enforce certain truths in their lives. You not only have to know the truth, but you need to experience the freedom of that truth by seeing its fruit manifest in your life.

HATE EVIL, HOLD ON TO WHAT IS GOOD

How you are fallen from Heaven, O Lucifer, son of the morning! How you are cut down to the ground, you who weakened the nations! For you have said in your heart: "I will ascend into heaven, I will exalt my throne above the stars of God; I will also sit on the mount of the congregation on the farthest sides of the north; I will ascend above the heights of the clouds, I will be like the Most High."

—Isaiah 14:12-14

The enemy, lucifer, fell; he hates people, including you. He will never change or repent; he can't and will not be redeemed; there is no hope for him. He will continue to wreak havoc by killing, stealing, and destroying (John 10:10). He is a thief and a liar, and he will always do that, no matter what (John 8:44). Even if you cry or laugh, satan does not change. He has no reason to change because he can't, and there is no reward for him. He was in Heaven and fell because, in his heart, he thought he could be God. He was deceived into thinking that he was God. Isaiah 14 says that lucifer had a heart from which he spoke and imagined all these evil agendas. Not only did he corrupt himself from the perfection described in Ezekiel, but we also see that he could get in and corrupt mankind.

> *These six things the Lord hates, yes, seven are an abomination to Him: A proud look, a lying tongue, hands that shed innocent blood, a heart that devises wicked plans, feet that are swift in running to evil, a false witness who speaks lies, and one who sows discord among brethren.*
>
> —Proverbs 6:16-19

> *Love is to be sincere and active [the real thing— without guile and hypocrisy]. Hate what is evil [detest all ungodliness, do not tolerate wickedness]; hold on tightly to what is good.*
>
> —Romans 12:9 AMP

You must hate satan. People say you are not supposed to hate; however, you must hate what God hates. Seven things God hates are listed here in Proverbs, and they are all things that satan has done.

Your enemy hates you, and it is right to hate him; you must hate him. The problem with humanity is that people think that following God means you must love people, and they have a wrong idea of love. However, pure love is to hate evil; you cannot love evil. Our adversary, satan, is evil, and some people are his offspring—he has children.

> *You are of your father the devil, and the desires of your father you want to do. He was a murderer from the beginning and does not stand in the truth, because there is no truth in him. When he speaks a lie, he speaks from his own resources, for he is a liar and the father of it.*
>
> —John 8:44

Jesus said the Pharisees were satan's children and were like their father, the devil, who was a liar from the beginning. Jesus labeled them as a brood of vipers (Matthew 12:34). He said that satan was the head snake and the Pharisees were his children. Jesus called them sons of hell (Matthew 23:15). When the Pharisees and Sadducees came to Jesus's baptism, Jesus said, "Who warned you to flee from the wrath to come?" (Matthew 3:7). In other words, Jesus didn't even want them to repent; they were mocking Jesus because satan mocks God.

You must hate evil, and you must hate what God hates. If a person is propagating evil and has turned themselves over to satan and are his children, you can pray for those people. I am not saying you shouldn't pray for people, but you must see that God hates His enemies and will destroy them. God sees your enemies as His enemies (Exodus 23:22). Yes, Jesus said to love your enemies; I understand (Matthew 5:44). You should pray for them and love them. But what is love?

Pure love is hating what is evil. You hate what God hates, and you cannot stop hating what God hates, especially when you realize that people are in a war and cannot resist evil spirits if they are not saved. You can pray for their salvation, of course, but if they have decided not to turn to God, then in time, they will be judged. Those evil spirits influencing them are already judged, but a person who continues to yield and does not repent faces the same judgment, even though hell was not God's original intent for mankind.

For ever since the creation of the world His invisible attributes, His eternal power and divine nature, have been clearly seen, being understood through His workmanship [all His creation, the wonderful things that He has made], so that they [who fail to believe and trust in Him] are without excuse and without defense.

—Romans 1:20 AMP

Jesus said hell was made for the devil and his fallen angels, his messengers (Matthew 25:41). People were never meant to go to hell, but humans have been pulled into this and still go to hell because they do not repent and accept Jesus. People can find out about God's goodness in many ways, and even creation preaches it. Paul told the Romans that no one who has seen God's workmanship in creation has an excuse or defense. When lucifer fell, he took people with him, so you must hate your enemy. He will never back off, so you must come at him continually because that is what he will do to you. We release people from the bondage of satan by praying for them and preaching the gospel. But if they resist the prayers and the message, they will receive the same judgment as satan because they allow him to be their father. Whether they like it or not, their judgment will happen, even if it is by default. They must choose because being neutral is not an option. You are either in or out with God.

KNOW WHAT YOUR ENEMY IS UP TO

In Isaiah 14:13-14, you can see how satan used the "I" word a lot. Being completely self-centered and deceived, satan was thrown out of Heaven by what he knew about God. The enemy of your soul wants to destroy you, and his knowledge of God helps him to do so. When you know more than he knows, you won't be destroyed. Paul said,

> *Lest satan should take advantage of us; for we are*
> *not ignorant of his devices.*
> —2 Corinthians 2:11

Well, what did that mean? Paul taught his people all the ways that satan works, which is what we should understand. We cannot focus only on the positive aspects of the Word of God because we must know our enemy. We are in a war, and even the military studies their enemy.

At the highest levels of professional competitive sports, they study and know their opponents. I had a family member who played professional football. A week before the game, he was assigned films to watch his opponent play in previous games. He would watch those films repeatedly for hours, studying how the person he would be facing in the game operated until his plays became predictable. Before this, I did not realize that football was like science and used psychology. Instead, I thought that football players practiced, lifted weights, and just played the game; however, they had to learn all the plays available and what an opponent was prone to do in certain situations. I began to think about applying this spiritually to the devil because he is our enemy.

Many aspects of our enemy are still mysteries to us. However, in the Word of God, we can find certain aspects of his personality and modes of operation. God gave satan permission to use his power over all that Job had (Job 1:12). We can list what satan did to Job and his family and study our enemy. When you study satan's attacks on Job, you will find that he could affect the weather because he caused tornadoes. He could influence the enemy armies of the Sabean people to come against Job and his family. The enemy, satan, afflicted Job's body with boils, so we know that he can affect people's bodies. He also killed Job's family members. These were the modes of attack that satan used against Job.

Now we know that the weather can be controlled by satan. We know that he can influence our enemies to come into our borders and attack us. Sickness and disease can come against us because of him. Those close to Job, like his wife, were so disgusted by what was happening that they just gave up. She said to him, "Do you still hold fast to your integrity? Curse God and die!" (Job 2:9). That was a terrible thing to say, and Job would not do it, but it shows that evil spirits can influence people around you.

You must be wise and hate satan and study the facts. The enemy attacked Job through those four different avenues. Be aware of these avenues and seal them up around you so that he doesn't come against you this way. Our enemy, satan, hates people and will never love them, and he will never repent. You must hate what God hates and know your enemy; you cannot back off because it doesn't work.

Evil spirits don't back off just because you back off. They come at you because you are gaining momentum. If you are building yourself up and studying the Word of God, the parable of the sower says that satan immediately comes in to steal the seed of the Word (Matthew 13:3-23). Frequently, in times of study or attending a conference and hearing new teachings, as I meditate and apply them to my life, suddenly, the wildest things happen to me in an attempt to steal the Word. Ironically, these attacks happen through the same avenues that Job experienced. The attacks reveal the enemy's battle strategies. Even though Paul said we are not ignorant of satan's battle strategies or his devices, sometimes it seems as if we are. The treasures in God's Word need to be dug into and understood.

DISCREDITING YOUR ENEMY

God, Who gives life to the dead and calls those things which do not exist as though they did.

—Romans 4:17

> *If the Lord has spoken something and it looks contrary to what is happening, you need to keep speaking what God has said, calling the things that are not as though they were.*

You cannot let anything come out of your mouth that would give your adversary, satan, permission to come in an even greater way. You cannot say anything contrary to what God has said. If the Lord has spoken something and it looks contrary to what is happening, you need to keep speaking what God has said, calling the things that are not as though they were. You will always have to believe what God has said and recognize that what He said is His will. Be firm, bring what He said into this realm, and do not back off even when you get hit.

The enemy, satan, tries to discourage and eliminate you by getting you to back off. It is imperative to watch your words. Speak to your inner man and say, "I am not giving in. The Lord is good, and He is not the one doing these things to me." As you discredit satan and continue to give credit to God, say, "Lord, You will deliver me, and the devil will have to pay back seven times what he has done." Do not opt out with your words.

The next thing to do is start giving. Whenever satan attacks you and tries to break your momentum, immediately look for people to help. You can start giving your time, giving good words, prophesying over people, praying for people, and giving your substance. Even if it is a can of food, whatever you have, go into a giving mode. When satan is stealing, you should do the opposite. You can use these battle strategies when satan is at work, trying to stop you from advancing.

Now satan knows he must get you to agree with your circumstances. By speaking and agreeing with his system and way of thinking, you opt out, just like Adam and Eve did. They opted out of what God had already established with them; satan is always trying to get you to opt out. He tried to get Jesus to opt out in the desert by tempting Him to operate as the Son of God when Jesus came as a Son of Man (Matthew 4:1-11). However, whether He was the Son of God wasn't the question. The temptation was that Jesus had to do everything by the Spirit because the Father told Him what to do (John 12:49). He never did anything on His own (John 5:19). Jesus was only obedient, so He was an example of a person who was submissive to God, the Father, and only did the will of the Father (John 6:38). Jesus had to submit Himself to the Spirit and the Father and only do what He was commanded.

Therefore He says: "When He ascended on high, He led captivity captive, and gave gifts to men."

—Ephesians 4:8

And I will give you the keys of the kingdom of Heaven, and whatever you bind on earth will be bound in Heaven, and whatever you loose on earth will be loosed in Heaven.

—Matthew 16:19

We receive all these gifts Jesus has for us because He did not operate as a Son of God but as a Son of Man. And because of that, the authority was handed back over to us. Jesus took the keys from the devil and gave them to the church; now we have that authority with binding and loosing power. Be encouraged and know that this is how the enemy operates; we cannot let him have his way. We must never back off and allow satan to have authority over us; we must exercise authority over him.

8

MADE IN THE IMAGE OF GOD

Then God said, "Let Us make man in Our image, according
to Our likeness; let them have dominion over the fish of
the sea, over the birds of the air, and over the cattle, over
all the earth and over every creeping thing that creeps
on the earth." So God created man in His own image;
in the image of God He created him; male and
female He created them.
—Genesis 1:26-27

When helel was created, he was a beautiful cherub, the
epitome of perfection. However, when Adam and Eve were
created, they were made in the image of God. We are more than

cherubs because we are human beings made in God's image. We are hated by satan because we have been redeemed, and the authority of the earth and the heavens has been given back to us. We are now seated with Christ in the heavenly realms. He raised us up together with Him and made us sit in the heavenly places (Ephesians 2:4-7).

It started in Genesis when God created man and established boundaries and qualifications. God gave us the specifications of who we are, our function, and everything that has been given to us. Before we were even created, the Holy Trinity knew all this from the beginning and established it. God always wanted someone besides Themselves to talk to and fellowship with. Fellowship is all about communion and the ability to communicate and understand who God is. God is wonderful and all-powerful, and His glory is so strong, but who can stand in His presence (Psalm 24:3-5)?

> *God always wanted to have someone besides Themselves to talk to and fellowship with. Fellowship is all about communion and the ability to communicate and understand Who God is.*

Unfortunately, many people have not perceived why mankind was created. Christians should be able to grasp many of these things because of the Spirit of God and the Word of God, but they don't. The fivefold ministry of the church is supposed to teach these principles and build up the body. Unfortunately, people have compromised, and the Word of God is not being preached; in turn, this has lowered the standard of understanding and revelation in the body of Christ.

I have seen this happen in cycles through the study of Christian history. Renewals and revivals have occurred throughout history, but it was never meant to be that way. We should not need revival or another move of God. We should always be in the move of God because God is always moving. We are the move of God. There are no rewards for being left to ourselves and not pursuing or seeking God diligently. We don't see the revelation and the standard that Jesus Christ established.

Studying our history has allowed me to see the cycles where the fire of God starts to die down, and then another move of God or a revelation of the Word of God comes forth. We fail in these areas because we are not diligent. We should know certain truths, which we knew in times past, but weren't kept in front of us. The Holy Spirit is very powerful and always willing. The teacher of the fivefold ministry should speak from that power and release the Word of life.

BE IMITATORS OF GOD

Therefore be imitators of God as dear children. And walk in love as Christ also has loved us and given Himself for us, an offering and a sacrifice to God for a sweet-smelling aroma.

—Ephesians 5:1-2

Today, we see people in the remnant church who are done because religion has not provided what we need. It was never meant to be this way from the beginning, but Christians fall into these ruts. Then they become part of a denomination or a movement, but that sometimes deteriorates. After studying all this, I found that we don't have a revelation that God is holy (1 Peter 1:15-16). He has called us to be holy, wanting us to be imitators of Him as dearly loved children.

Paul reminds us in Ephesians 5:1 to be imitators of God as His children, but we forget about God's original intent in Genesis 1:26-27. We need to know this. What does it mean to be made in the image of God? It means you are a partner and a partaker; you are so much like Him that there are more similarities than differences.

For if you live according to the flesh, you will die;
but if by the Spirit you put to death the misdeeds of
the body you will live. For those who are led by the
Spirit of God are the children of God.

–Romans 8:13-14 NIV

After being redeemed from a fallen state, the Word of God shows that you need to put to death the misdeeds of the body and have your mind transformed. Then you are to walk in the Spirit, for those led by the Spirit of God are sons of God. Being led means that you are not the leader; the Holy Spirit is, and you conform to the authority of the One Who is leading you. When the Holy Spirit is our leader and leads us into all truth to which we are submissive and obedient (John 16:13). When the Spirit of God leads us, we become qualified as children of God.

We can easily miss the mark when we don't remember God's original intent for mankind and who we are in Him. We judge ourselves in our fallen state by not understanding God's intention for mankind, and we never see the original plan. We then do not interpret our destiny in Christ correctly and set the bar for our goals too low. We must go back to the Word of God and see what is said in Genesis 1:26-27. God made us in His image and then gave us dominion over everything. Everything that was made was given over to us.

After the flood, God reestablished His covenant with Noah (Genesis 9:1-19). God chose Noah and the eight people on the ark when everything on earth was destroyed. God repeated His covenant with them when they exited the ark, and everything started again. God commanded them to have dominion, multiply, and replenish the earth, so God's command continued on the other side of the flood. Later, the Lord told Moses that if the Israelites obeyed God and did what He commanded, all these good things would happen to them. But if they didn't obey, bad things would happen to them (Deuteronomy 28). God set before them blessings or curses, and they would have to choose.

GOD'S GLORIOUS CHURCH

Jesus answered and said to him, "If anyone loves Me, he will keep My word; and My Father will love him and We will come to him and make Our home with him."

—John 14:23

And whatever you ask in My name, that I will do, that the Father may be glorified in the Son. If you ask anything in My name, I will do it.

—John 14:13

The body of Christ is a family, yet how many people do you know who truly understand this and walk in it? Yet the whole church is supposed to be one. We should not have all these denominations interpreting the Word of God differently and everyone broken up into small individual groups. We should be one big body of believers called the bride of Christ, the glorious church built up, and the gates of hell cannot prevail against her (Matthew 16:18).

Maturity and unity of the faith are established when the fivefold ministry of the church is equipping and building us up. We should all believe the Word of God and not cut out parts because it is "not for today." Unless God tells you it's done, it's not done. Paul said that all the gifts would eventually cease because they won't be needed anymore when that which is perfect has come (1 Corinthians 13:8-10). However, we obviously haven't reached perfection, and Jesus has not returned yet.

*And this gospel of the kingdom will be preached in
all the world as a witness to all the nations, and then
the end will come.*

—Matthew 24:14

*If then you were raised with Christ, seek those things
which are above, where Christ is, sitting at the right
hand of God. Set your mind on things above, not on
things on the earth.*

—Colossians 3:1-2

Jesus said that the gospel would have to be preached in all the world, and then the end shall come, and we need to do what He said to do. We are not to focus on the things of this world, earthly things, but on where Christ is seated at the right hand of God. God's original intent for people was to be spiritually minded and set our sights on the heavenly things where we are seated with Him in heavenly realms.

When the Trinity met, they talked about their plans and how they would create this wonderful garden and call it Eden. The name *Eden*[9] means "pleasure"; God was setting man in the "Garden of

---

[9] "H5731 - 'ēḏen - Strong's Hebrew Lexicon (kjv)." Blue Letter Bible. Accessed 1 Feb, 2023. https://www.blueletterbible.org/lexicon/h5731/kjv/wlc/0-1/

Pleasure." They were going to do this wonderful work of creation, and man and woman would be created in the image of God. "In the image of God" meant that man would have his own free will because God has His own will. God always chooses to do good and be who He is.

> *Before we were born, before we were thought of, God planned all the days to be written in our book.*

However, to make mankind in the image of God with free will meant that people would have the ability to choose whether to serve Him. God knew that they would not be God, only an image and likeness of Him. Today, we see many aspects of life veering away from God's plan because of free will and the enemy's work.

> *All who dwell on the earth will worship him, whose names have not been written in the Book of Life of the Lamb slain from the foundation of the world.*
> —Revelation 13:8

At creation, God had already determined that Jesus would be slain, to which He agreed. They planned all this, and the Son of God agreed to come back. Revelation 13:8 says that Jesus was slain from the foundation of the world before you and I were even made. Before we were born or even thought of, God planned all the days to be written in our book (Psalm 139:13-16). God's perfect plan was that we would serve Him even though we had free will. We must choose God every day; if we don't choose and obey Him, circumstances and situations will go wrong, and it will not be God's fault. God created us like Him, but we are prone to do our own thing. Jesus was sent because we fell, but the fall of man was determined before we were even made. Jesus was already seen as slain, which was all in the plan.

GOD DESIRES OUR FELLOWSHIP

In His foreknowledge, God knew what would happen ahead of time, but He still created this world and us. He also preplanned the coming of Jesus. That is how much God loves us and wants fellowship with us. Today's biggest problem is that people do not understand God and His needs, which is to have fellowship with us. When we reject God, it hurts Him more than anything.

When we choose not to have fellowship with God, meet with Him, acknowledge or thank Him, He is so hurt. This happened in the garden of Eden with Adam and Eve and with Moses and the Israelites. God was grieved when the Israelites did not want to meet with Him to come up to the mountain. They were His chosen people, and He had done so much for them. God kept His Word and covenant with Joseph and all the fathers, and after four hundred years of slavery, He delivered them out of Egypt. After God performed many signs and wonders, delivering them, the Israelites did not want to come up to meet Him on Mount Sinai. They were afraid of Him (Exodus 19:9-25). God was so hurt that He set borders on the mountain and said that anyone who touched its borders would die, including the animals. Later, the Lord was still hurt and said to Moses,

> *I have seen these people, and indeed it is a stiff-necked people! Now, therefore, let Me alone, that My wrath may burn hot against them, and I may consume them. And I will make of you a great nation.*
>
> —Exodus 32:9-10

What would cause God to turn on the children of Israel after all He did to deliver them? God was hurt because He knew they should have acknowledged His goodness and plan and thanked and honored Him.

The same thing happened in the garden of Eden; God was hurt that Adam and Eve would talk to a serpent about the tree instead of talking to Him. They knew that God came down to the garden, and they could have spoken to Him about this, and He would have explained it to them. Also, think of Cain after the fall. He was outside the garden, about to sin, when God came to help him, to coach him. God said,

> *If you do well, will you not be accepted? And if you*
> *do not do well, sin lies at the door. Its desire is for*
> *you, but you should rule over it.*
>
> —Genesis 4:7

Yet look what happened—Cain disregarded everything that God said. God came face-to-face with Cain and talked with him, but Cain still killed his brother, hurting God.

The devil, satan, was the wedge that came between God and us. God wanted us to communicate directly with Him; instead, satan became a broker or middleman between us. Religion comes from satan and creates a break in fellowship between God and us. Jesus said to the Pharisees,

> *Woe to you, scribes and Pharisees, hypocrites! For*
> *you travel land and sea to win one proselyte, and*

when he is won, you make him twice as much a son
of hell as yourselves.

—Matthew 23:15

What a terrible thing to say, but Jesus was telling the truth. They were sons of hell, and their converts in that religion made them twice the sons of hell. Religion produces enslavement and bondage.

HE MAKES US HIS DWELLING PLACE

From the beginning, God wanted us to have fellowship and a relationship with Him. Religion has a form of godliness but denies its power (2 Timothy 3:5). Many organizations and people are mocking God today. Having no power, they come against people who believe the whole Bible. They are clouds without rain, who have established themselves against the gospel, the good news, which demonstrates God's power through healing the sick, raising the dead, casting out devils, and preaching jubilee, the year of the Lord's favor (Jude 1:12).

God's favor is a blessing, and He wants to help you in all areas of your life—finances, body, and even your spiritual life—but religion will tell you that is not for today. Religion tells you that God is not interested in people anymore because He has done everything He will do for us, and that is it. But that is not true, which we know by the Word of God.

> *And I will pray the Father, and He will give you another Helper, that He may abide with you forever—the Spirit of truth, whom the world cannot receive, because it neither sees Him nor knows Him; but you know Him, for He dwells with you and will be in you.*
>
> —John 14:16-17

Jesus said He would send us another Comforter like Him who would be with us forever. This was the Holy Spirit, Who came on the day of Pentecost and is still empowering us today. We have not been left powerless because the Holy Spirit has not diminished in any way. In the Gospel of John, Jesus says, "Loving me empowers you to obey my word. My Father will love you so deeply that we will come to you and make you our dwelling place" (John 14:23 TPT).

What's amazing is that not only is the Holy Spirit coming, but Jesus and the Father are coming and dwelling inside us. In essence, Jesus is saying that when we love God as evidenced by our obedience, He and the Father come to make their home in us, which is a byproduct of being the image of God. We are spiritual people who have a spirit; God can dwell in us because God is a Spirit.

> *If you abide in Me, and My words abide in you, you will ask what you desire, and it shall be done for you.*
> —John 15:7
> *And my God shall supply all your needs according to His riches in glory by Christ Jesus.*
> —Philippians 4:19

In John 15:7, Jesus said, "Ask what you desire." He was not referring to your needs. God has already promised to take care of our needs. All our needs are met, which means our desires can also be given to us. Looking back at what Adam and Eve had, Jesus was relaying that He was buying us back to that place of total reliance and provision from God.

However, you must remember that we are not of this world anymore. We are just visiting here, and satan is still the God of this world, even though we are in it. The church must treat satan roughly—he has to be prayed out and forced out. Corruption will continue to happen in our system unless we do something about it, not only individually as Christians but also corporately as the body of Christ.

Then God blessed them, and God said to them, "Be fruitful and multiply; fill the earth and subdue it; have dominion over the fish of the sea, over the birds of the air, and over every living thing that moves on the earth."

—Genesis 1:28

God blessed Adam and Eve and said to them, "Be fruitful," which means producing manifestation so that you will see the fruit. Then they were to multiply, fill the earth, and subdue it. *Subdue* is a strong word, meaning "dominion" and "to be forceful."[10] They were to have dominion over the fish of the sea, the birds of the air, and every living thing on the earth. God gave us dominion and told us to increase, multiply, and replenish. God said this to Noah to reestablish His covenant with the eight from the ark after the flood destroyed everyone on earth.

In Genesis 15:18-21, God made a covenant with Abram and outlined the borders of the land God gave to Abram. The specifications He gave are the borders of the garden of Eden and the same borders Joshua was told to take back in Joshua 1:4. Scholars have indicated that the Garden of Eden covered a vast area in the

---

[10] "H3533 - kāḇaš - Strong's Hebrew Lexicon (kjv)." Blue Letter Bible. Accessed 1 Feb, 2023. https://www.blueletterbible.org/lexicon/h3533/kjv/wlc/0-1/

Middle East of an estimated fifteen hundred square miles.[11] Although the exact size is unknown, this would be similar to the size of the heavenly Jerusalem that comes down from Heaven (Revelation 21:1-16). The original borders extended into other Middle Eastern nations. Israel would have owned all Middle Eastern nations if they had been willing and obedient and done everything the Lord commanded. They would have owned all the oil, and the wealth would have been Israel's.

Through Jesus, God is now expecting to have fellowship with all believers. He wants to see the church enforce what He has always intended for this earth. We are supposed to be waging a good warfare (1 Timothy 1:18-19). That means we should speak the things that are not as though they were (Romans 4:17). We should always say what God wants, even if we don't see it. If someone steals from us, we should put our foot down and say, "That was not God's will!" Then we should command the enemy to pay us back. We are stolen from all the time. This world system constantly steals from your finances and health. Many things in our environment come against our health and against the covenant God has with us. God never intended for our environment to be poisoned. He never

---

[11] Grant R. Jeffrey, *Unveiling Mysteries of the Bible* (New York City: Crown Publishing Company, 2013), 19.

intended for us to pay high interest rates or be controlled by anyone except Himself.

God wants us to own everything because He bought everything for us. He made this world for us, not for the devil, the devil's people, or religion. God made the earth for human beings who loved and served Him. When mankind fell, a remnant was left, a group of people who believe and walk on the narrow path, a path that Jesus said only a few find (Matthew 7:13-14). Jesus questioned whether He would even find faith on the earth when He returns (Luke 18:8). According to the parables of Jesus, we can estimate that only 50 percent of people will make it into the kingdom.

You now know that you have been made in the image of God, yet His intention for us is not always carried out. It is up to you to feed yourself in the Word of God and grow spiritually, building yourself up. We must pray for the fivefold ministers of the church to stand up, do their job, and prophesy over us the things that are not as though they were.

9

ALL THINGS ARE POSSIBLE

Jesus said to him, "If you can believe, all things are
possible to him who believes."
—Mark 9:23

God established us as the authority on the earth, but that authority was stolen from us in the garden. Now, Jesus has bought it back for us. The problem is that the church has not risen, and we are not living out Matthew 16:18, where the gates of hell shall not prevail against the church.

Prayerfully, you have realized you are made in the image of God and that you are a child of God. You are willing to walk in the Spirit, not fulfilling the lust of the flesh (Galatians 5:16). You are allowing yourself to be led by the Holy Spirit and building yourself up in your most holy faith (Jude 1:20).

As you walk with Christ, you will begin to realize that Jesus said you could ask for anything in His name, and it will be done for you, and "if you can believe, all things are possible to him who believes" (John 14:14, Mark 9:23). When this kingdom truth sinks in, you will think, *Why am I not asking for more?* You cannot ask for too much because there is no limit; all the limitations have been taken off. What we have experienced down here is because of this fallen world. However, if we are born again, our spirit does not know defeat or limitations.

> *Behold, I tell you a mystery: We shall not all sleep, but we shall all be changed—in a moment, in the twinkling of an eye, at the last trumpet. For the trumpet will sound, and the dead will be raised incorruptible, and we shall be changed.*
>
> —1 Corinthians 15:51-52

It does not matter what is happening around me because God's Word will always be true. God will always be good; He will always be our provider and a good Father. We know that He will, at some point, allow us to walk over just like Enoch did and to be caught up with Him. Paul said we would be caught up in the twinkling of an eye. The Lord will translate us, but until that happens, we will preach the same gospel that Jesus did and see God manifest, confirming His Word with signs and wonders following (Mark 16:20).

> *And do not be conformed to this world, but be transformed by the renewing of your mind, that you may prove what is that good and acceptable and perfect will of God.*
>
> —Romans 12:2

Mankind was never meant to know evil, which means that we should be in every way transforming our minds by renewing them with the Word of God. We should always be working toward thinking only about the good. We must focus and meditate on the good and acceptable things and the perfect will of God. (See also Philippians 4:8.) We should never be thinking about destruction or the bad things that could happen. We should not be focusing on satan but on God. When we do this, we can be assured that when we pray, God hears us and answers us because that is in the Word of God.

SOWING TO THE SPIRIT

And if we know that He hears us, whatever we ask, we know that we have the petitions that we have asked of Him.

—1 John 5:15

We see that when we pray, God hears us. But God says that you can ask whatever you desire, and it will be done for you because you love and obey Him (John 15:7). So if you love God and follow Him, there is no limit in your prayer life. It is also important to remember that God is not mocked, and a man will reap what he sows (Galatians 6:7). In other words, if you sow to the flesh, you will reap the flesh, and everyone will see that. But if you sow to the spirit, that will manifest. Even if there is a war and it takes a while for it to manifest, at some point, you will see a manifestation of what you sow to the spirit because God will not allow Himself to be mocked.

> *These circumstances in your life cannot keep mocking God, and ultimately, you will reap what you sow; continue to sow into righteousness and justice.*

Eventually, our prayers will be answered if we hang in there and are consistent. If it seems that God doesn't hear or answer you, do not be upset with God. You keep sowing into the spirit, knowing God cannot be mocked. In other words, these circumstances in your life cannot keep mocking God; ultimately, you will reap what you sow; continue to sow into righteousness and justice. I sow into my nation, government, and people because, in time, I will reap what I have sowed. We must continue to stand for our country and each other, the remnant, the body of Christ. We must stand for them, letting God arise so that the Word of God becomes apparent and visible to the world.

ALL THINGS HAVE BECOME NEW

We were not built for failure or for praying and not receiving an answer. Ultimately, we were not made to be away from God. We were created from the beginning to be close to Him, be in His family, and have Him as our Heavenly Father. He is a good Heavenly Father, better than an earthly father because He is God. From the beginning, you were not made to be apart from God or to sin; however, we encounter terrible things because of the fall.

Therefore, if anyone is in Christ, he is a new creature: old things have passed away; behold, all things have become new.

—2 Corinthians 5:17

Remember, if you are a born-again, Spirit-filled believer, you are a new creation in Christ. You were not meant to sin, which means everything old has passed away. Inside your spirit, you have been made the righteousness of God in Christ Jesus, which is the gospel (2 Corinthians 5:21). So now, we cannot be ruled by our bodies or minds because our spirits will rule over them. According to Paul, if we live in the Spirit, we will not fulfill the lust of the flesh (Galatians 5:16).

We were not created to sin, fear, or doubt; it is not part of who we are in the Spirit. We have been inwardly made perfect through the blood of Jesus due to the born-again experience. As a result, we walk in love and the fruit of the Spirit. Outwardly, however, we live in a fallen world, and bodily death has not been overcome. We still have weaknesses in our flesh and minds because our souls are not yet perfected.

As we yield our spirit to the Holy Spirit, we fulfill the desires of the Spirit. We must also have God's mindset so that our thoughts and bodies fall in line with the Spirit. The discrepancies that we see down here are because of weakness. Christ did for us what we could not do in ourselves, which is why we now need to depend on the Holy Spirit (2 Corinthians 12:9). The Spirit of God inside us is the Holy Spirit. He is not just the Spirit of God; He is holy.

As believers, we are equipped with God's holy, written Word and the Holy Spirit and have holy angels around us. We can choose to walk on the highway of holiness, the holy sapphire, and the holy fire. As warriors, we have all these holy things inside and out and all around us. Discrepancies seem to be disappointments and discouragements. Simply put, a disappointment is distance between you and your appointment, and discouragement is distance between you and your courage. We feel discouraged and disappointed because we are in a fallen world, yet even though we are separated from God physically, we are not separated from Him spiritually.

> *But he who is joined to the Lord is one spirit with Him.*
>
> —1 Corinthians 6:17

Paul said that when we join ourselves to the Lord, we are one with Him in Spirit, and we experience fellowship with God within us. If we are going to experience that outwardly, we must allow the Holy Spirit to manifest. We manifest the Holy Spirit through our lips when spiritual thoughts rise from our hearts into our minds. By allowing the Holy Spirit to put to death the misdeeds of our body, we rule and reign and have dominion so that God conquers us from within ourselves. We then begin to encounter Him outwardly in our bodies and minds and see healing, deliverance, and prosperity. The goodness of God overcomes problems.

WALKING IN THE SUPERNATURAL

Or what man is there among you who, if his son asks for bread, will give him a stone? Or if he asks for a fish, will he give him a serpent? If you then, being evil, know how to give good gifts to your children, how much more will your Father who is in heaven give good things to those who ask Him!

—Matthew 7:9-11

Our God is a good God; He will not give us a stone if we ask for bread. He will provide for us so that we triumph over our enemies. The devil will not steal, kill, and destroy and will not take your finances because God will preserve them. All this warfare is going on because satan doesn't want us to operate in what God has for us. The enemy cannot win against us if God is our Father and we operate in the Spirit.

Every day, we pass up so many opportunities to walk in the supernatural. The Holy Spirit has been sent to gird us up, help us, lead us, guide us, be our Advocate, and break curses. The Holy Spirit comes to enforce the blessing so that we walk in the light and see discrepancies, disappointments, and discouragement destroyed—that is all part of our warfare.

The enemies who war against believers are fallen ones, who are evil spirits that were disembodied before the flood. They are not redeemable. These evil entities understand you and work against you, not for you. They know they cannot be redeemed, have no reason to help you, and have no reason to hope. Their destiny has already been proclaimed. God has already cast judgment on them, and they are going to the pit. They are going to the fire, and they hate you (Matthew 25:41).

> *Speak from the other realm and stand on what your Father in Heaven wants to do for you, which is found in the Word of God.*

God wants to lead and guide you into the blessing and His plan for you (Jeremiah 29:11). He wants you to be productive and reap what you sow. He wants you to sow into the spirit. You must not allow satan to steal your crop. However, in your life, you must produce by faith and start to call the things that are not as though they were. It does not matter if you don't see or feel it happen because you must pull it out of the other realm and bring it into this realm from your spirit. Speak from the other realm and stand on what your Father in Heaven wants to do for you, which is found in the Word of God.

God wants to give you health, provision, and deliverance. He will give you His heart, show you His plans, and tell you things to come; when it doesn't happen right, just stand firm. Do not back off because it is not His fault. The enemy steals from people every day, and we must continue to stand against him because he is the thief. God does not steal and does not need to steal to do His work—satan does.

When helel fell, he took a certain number of angels with him under his command (Isaiah 14:12; Revelation 12:9). The sons of God were the godly line on earth. The fallen angels taught the sons of God to sin by interbreeding with the daughters of men, which was against God (Genesis 6). Interbreeding produced a corrupted line that God had to destroy because the serpent's seed had gotten into God's creation. It was so bad that "all flesh had corrupted their way on the earth" (Genesis 6:12). This genetically altered animals, humans, and many other species. God wanted to preserve the bloodline through the godly line of Noah (Genesis 6:8).

> *Knowing that you were not redeemed with corruptible things, like silver or gold, from your aimless conduct received by tradition from your fathers, but with the precious blood of Christ, as of a lamb without blemish and without spot.*
>
> —1 Peter 1:18-19

The Messiah came through a perfect, unblemished human being in the body God gave Jesus. Jesus was the perfect sacrifice, the Lamb without blemish, and His blood was presented to the Father. Now through Jesus's blood sacrifice, we are redeemed.

> *For the law of the Spirit of life in Christ Jesus has made me free from the law of sin and death.*
>
> —Romans 8:2

We must yield to the Spirit to fight against the curse, the law of sin and death. We are responsible for bringing forth through prayer, interceding, and pushing back all the enemy's evil plans. When God came to Adam, Eve, and the serpent after they ate of the tree, He had something to say to each of them (Genesis 3:8-24). The Father presented what would happen and announced certain curses would be put on each of them. God prophesied that the seed of the serpent would eventually bruise the heel of the woman's seed, but that heel would crush the head of the devil's offspring (Genesis 3:15).

This curse revealed to satan that God had the plan to crush him and his offspring, so he went to work to stop it. That is why Cain killed Abel (Genesis 4:1-15). Throughout history, satan has attempted to kill the deliverer in the womb. We see it during the times of Noah, Moses, and when Jesus was born. Each time a deliverer was prophesied, satan attempted to hinder God's plans. This is happening even today through abortion; satan is after the children in the womb, a whole generation. There is an attack on fathers and offspring in the womb, and satan thinks he can somehow trick God so that this prophecy won't come to pass.

CHRIST, OUR MEDIATOR

When Moses received the book of the law, we were forbidden to do certain things (Deuteronomy 31:24-26). Today, the church explains very little about evil spirits, witches, mediums, etc. Yet in Deuteronomy 18:9-12 and Isaiah 47:13-15, God tells us we should not consult astrologers, magicians, or mediums because they are an abomination to the Lord. We are never to consult these evil spirits.

We should go directly to God through our relationship with Him, Jesus Christ, and the Holy Spirit. King Saul went to the witch of Endor to consult with her about what he should do as king (1 Samuel 28:3–25). Yet Samuel had already told Saul that God had torn the kingdom from him and given it to David. We should never consult with witches or astrologers or look to the stars for guidance. These types of foreknowledge are from the fallen ones.

God has created order in everything, but the fallen ones try to reverse-engineer times and seasons. Guidance from the stars is the only thing satan can rely on because he doesn't have a relationship with God. It is forbidden because we have now been given this ability through Jesus Christ to have a one-on-one relationship with God through the Holy Spirit. Whatever causes us to depend upon an individual or a man to get to God is from satan. The devil has been fighting all these years. Now at the end of the age, we finally have the revelation of being in Christ and Him being in us (Galatians 2:20). The only mediator between God and men is Jesus Christ.

For there is one God and one Mediator between God and men the Man Christ Jesus.
                                        —1 Timothy 2:5

The body of Christ is supposed to be built up through the operation of the fivefold ministry of the church, the gifts of the Spirit, and the fruit of the Spirit that God established in Ephesians 4:11-16, 1 Corinthians 12:1-11, and Galatians 5:22-23. When these systems were established in the New Testament church, the body of Christ grew astronomically and exponentially. This tremendous expansion was because of the power of the Holy Spirit and the testimony of Jesus.

10

SPEAKING TO MOUNTAINS

*For assuredly, I say to you, whoever says to this
mountain, 'Be removed and be cast into the sea,' and
does not doubt in his heart, but believes that those things
he says will be done, he will have whatever he says.*
—Mark 11:23

We have allowed God to bring us to the point where we see who we are in Christ. We know we have been made in the image of God and have so much potential for His kingdom. Many of us go through life without knowing these truths and the Word of God. The fivefold ministry of the church is supposed to bring this forth. In these last days, we need to participate in and be partakers of the divine nature, which is accomplished through God's promises.

> *His divine power has given to us all things that pertain to life and godliness, through the knowledge of Him who called us by glory and virtue, by which have been given to us exceedingly great and precious promises, that through these you may be partakers of the divine nature, having escaped the corruption that is in the world through lust.*
>
> —2 Peter 1:3-4

Peter said that we are partakers of the divine nature through the promises given to us, so we must look and see what those promises are. Once we repent and learn to walk in the Spirit, we are given the ability, dominion, and authority to become sons of God (Romans 8:14). Jesus did not teach us to maintain our old way of life until He comes; He never taught us to be passive and sit and wait for God to do something. Most religious people today have this mentality, but the remnant church of Christ should be different. Jesus taught us to be assertive and to step into God's authority as sons.

The remnant church says, "I will inquire of the Lord like David did with the ephod and ask if we shall go to war. Lord, will you give them into our hands?" (1 Samuel 23). The remnant is always ready to go to war; being prepared is part of being on the narrow way. Growing up, I was never taught this in church, and even after I was born again, I wasn't taught these things. I had to go to college to learn from individuals who taught this. While working in the marketplace with God working in me, I also learned many things in my career of thirty years.

> *The remnant is always ready to go to war; being ready is part of being on the narrow way.*

As Christians, we need to have an edge about ourselves, and Jesus will take us there with His teachings and the writings of Paul. However, unless you are diligent to fast, dig into the Word, and pray in the Spirit, you will not know and discover many truths because you are not seriously looking for them. However, God will send you teachers who will teach you God's Word and build you up if you so desire it.

THE REMNANT IS AGGRESSIVE

Assuredly, I say to you, whatever you bind on earth will be bound in Heaven, and whatever you loose on earth will be loosed in Heaven.

—Matthew 18:18

It is puzzling that religious people and even many Christians I have encountered will fight you on the most aggressive truths that Jesus taught. To a point, satan will allow you to believe certain truths as a Christian. However, when you start to get into the more aggressive truths, such as binding and loosing, asking and knowing you will receive, and speaking to mountains, all hell will break loose against you. The attacks will come through people that call themselves Christians, who think they are true believers who believe in God's Word.

For though we walk in the flesh, we do not war according to the flesh. For the weapons of our warfare are not carnal but mighty in God for pulling down strongholds.

—2 Corinthians 10:3-4

Once you figure out that you are supposed to prophesy, be diligent, and command evil spirits to stop and get out of your way, they will.

Jesus talked about speaking to the mountains, but how many Christians do you know that have mountains being removed? (Mark 11:23). In America, big mountains need to be removed because so much is being stolen from us; we need to stand up against these. And remember, no matter what country you live in, you can stand up as an individual anywhere in the world and see mountains removed. I see more people against the message of moving mountains than those who support it. The enemy, satan, knows that once you get to a certain point with God, there is no way that he can control you.

> *For assuredly, I say to you, whoever says to this mountain, "Be removed and be cast into the sea," and does not doubt in his heart, but believes that those things he says will be done, he will have whatever he says. Therefore I say to you, whatever things you ask when you pray, believe that you receive them and you will have them.*
>
> —Mark 11:23-24

Once you figure out that you are supposed to prophesy, be diligent, and command evil spirits to stop and get out of your way, they will. You must command these mountains that satan put in your way, these curses against the Word of God, to be removed and cast into the sea. You must break them and command them to leave. You must be persistent enough to start speaking to mountains and calling the things that are not as they were. Refuse to accept the diabolical antichrist spirit trying to permeate governments and the church. This should not be happening on our watch, but it is.

> *Again I say to you that if two of you agree on earth concerning anything that they ask, it will be done for them by My Father in Heaven. For where two or three are gathered together in My name, I am there in the midst of them.*
>
> —Matthew 18:19-20

If you start standing up against evil, others will say, "I want to be in on that." You now must war in your church and do what God has called you to do. Pray for people, help them, and gather together with others to meet weekly, agreeing in prayer. When believers get to the point where they know they will get what they have prayed for, the devil cannot fight that. The enemy does not want you to set an example for other people to follow. When that happens, he will see a rebellion in his domain and says, "I cannot control these believing Christians."

When you speak to mountains or ask anything, you shall receive, period. And if you believe, nothing shall be impossible! These truths are far beyond most people's thinking. Most people do not even consider them, let alone see them in operation, and satan is happy about that. True believers must start talking to others and let them know that they can believe in God and must get into the Word of God. They must build themselves up and be forceful, take what is in Heaven by authority, and demand that it come to earth. When you do that, all hell will be nervous that you are showing people how to speak to mountains. Not only will you see what will happen in your own life, but suddenly, circumstances will begin to change around you quickly—that is the mark of a true believer.

BEAR FRUIT

When these people eat with you in your fellowship meals commemorating the Lord's love, they are like dangerous reefs that can shipwreck you. They are like shameless shepherds who care only for themselves. They are like clouds blowing over the land without giving any rain. They are like trees in

*autumn that are doubly dead, for they bear no fruit
and have been pulled up by the roots.*

—Jude 1:12 NLT

You will encounter people who have a form of godliness but deny its power (2 Timothy 3:5). They are like clouds without rain. They will say they are Christians, but they don't believe in what the Bible says regarding the life of a believer. So everything is fine until you start to cast out devils, lay hands on the sick, pray in tongues, and raise the dead. Then, suddenly, people whom you thought were believers are not believers. These people will oppose you because they are not of the right spirit, even though they say they are Christians.

We see this example when Jesus corrects Peter for speaking from the wrong spirit in Matthew 16:22-23. Peter told Jesus that He would not die on the cross. You would expect Jesus to correct Peter gently, but Jesus went right at him and said, "Get behind me, satan!" Peter must have wondered what had just happened. He was speaking by another spirit, satan himself, and Jesus showed Peter and everyone around him that this was the wrong spirit.

Something similar happened with Judas. Jesus prayed all night and chose His disciples based on what God told Him (Luke 6:12-16). Yet Jesus still chose Judas, and he could have been fired for stealing during those three-and-a-half years. John knew about it and said that Judas was a thief because he took from the money bag (John 12:6). If John knew that Judas was a thief, don't you think he would have told Jesus, and would it have mattered? Jesus knew anyway, so He let it all happen. Even the best religious people can get trapped, misled, and fall.

Signs will follow the believing ones and upset the religious leaders. For example, Stephen was persecuted for ministering in the power of the Holy Spirit. He wasn't even an apostle; he was a wise, Spirit-filled believer who waited on tables (Acts 6:8-10). The denominational leaders shut him down because the spirit behind that religion was anti-Christ, and they were not believers. They could not discredit Stephen because what came from his mouth was so powerful, and signs and wonders followed him. They had to get rid of Stephen, so they killed him (Acts 8:1-2). It is the same with Jesus and all the prophets. The prophets spoke according to what the Father said, and to stop those words, they were killed, just like Jesus and Stephen.

Therefore I say to you, whatever things you ask when you pray, believe that you receive them, and you will have them.

—Mark 11:24

You begin to make waves when you believe you will receive what you ask for. Jesus told you to speak to mountains and believe for anything. You were told to ask without limitations, and you shall receive. The word for *ask* in Greek translates to "demand."[12] You already know it's God's will. You demand healing to come because you know that Jesus was crucified, and He took stripes upon His back for our healing (Isaiah 53:5).

THE BRIDEGROOM IS COMING

Jesus cursed the green fig tree, which had no fruit (Mark 11:12-25). Even after figs ripen, they can be left on the tree to dry, so either fresh or dried figs will always be available. Jesus was hungry, and seeing the fig tree in leaf, He went to find fruit on it, but there was none. This fig tree in leaf should have had fruit on it.

---

[12] "G154 - aiteō - Strong's Greek Lexicon (kjv)." Blue Letter Bible. Accessed 1 Feb, 2023. https://www.blueletterbible.org/lexicon/g154/kjv/tr/0-1/

This fig tree was an example of a religion having a form of godliness but denying its power. It is like the tares that look like wheat until it is time to harvest (Matthew 13:24-30). These tares never come to fruition, so when it comes time to bear fruit, they have none. During the harvest, the owner has the wheat gathered into his barns, but the tares are bundled and burned. And that is what happened to the fig tree that Jesus cursed; when it came time, it produced no fruit.

Jesus describes the same thing when He teaches about the wise and foolish virgins (Matthew 25:1-13). The ten virgins were betrothed and waiting for their bridegroom. They were supposed to be prepared throughout the engagement period because they didn't know when the bridegroom would come, which was part of the tradition. Five of the virgins were wise, and five were foolish. The foolish virgins did not discern that they were about to be married and needed to get ready. They had only a certain amount of time before the marriage. They did not have to spend a whole lifetime preparing because it was within a specific timeframe. The foolish virgins were not diligent and did not view the occasion of their marriage as important enough to spend that time in preparation.

We are now at that point; the bride of Christ is getting ready. We are getting oil in our lamps, wicks trimmed, and everything ready to operate in darkness. We are being prepared for whatever happens next, even for the moment when we will be taken to be with the Lord. We must be ready—the bridegroom is coming to bring the bride to the marriage supper of the Lamb (Revelation 19:6-9).

RELIGIOUS DOCTRINE IS FRUITLESS

Why did Jesus curse the fig tree in Mark 11:12-14? The idea behind the fig tree is that the tree should always produce fruit and be ready because the tree's purpose is to serve humanity. That tree was commanded to bear fruit. When the tree didn't fulfill its purpose, it was like the religion of the day (Mark 11:12-25). Jesus was always against religion and spoke against the Pharisees and Sadducees because they were not doing what God had ordained them to do. In the same way, the tree was not doing what it was created to do.

Jesus reveals all these truths in the parables to show us that we must produce fruit and be ready. Tares are not wheat (Matthew 13:24-30, 36-43). So they do not act like wheat or do what wheat would do. Likewise, goats are not lambs. Although goats look like lambs, their personalities are entirely different, and they are not submissive (Matthew 25:31-46). Counterfeits are all around us, and we need to discern and be the sheep, the wheat, the fruitful tree, and the wise virgins.

Jesus said that if you believe, you can tell this mountain to be removed and be cast in the sea (Mark 11:23). Cursing the fig tree is an example of speaking to a mountain to be removed. Jesus cursed the fig tree at its roots, and it immediately responded. Jesus said this after Peter noticed that the fig tree had withered. When the fig tree had no fruit, Jesus cursed the tree at the root, a symbol of the religious spirit, which is a form of godliness that denies the power of God (2 Timothy 3:5). Why did he curse it? Because it deceives people, causing many to go to hell.

The devil cannot stop a true believer, so he attempts to incriminate the believer by working to discredit them. If you notice, religion comes against the true believer and tells them that *they* are the ones deceiving people and sending them to hell.

> *You will know them by their fruits. Do men gather grapes from thornbushes or figs from thistles? Even so, every good tree bears good fruit, but a bad tree bears bad fruit. A good tree cannot bear bad fruit, nor can a bad tree bear good fruit. Every tree that does not bear good fruit is cut down and thrown into the fire. Therefore by their fruits, you will know them.*
> —Matthew 7:16-20

Therefore bear fruits worthy of repentance and do not think to say to yourselves, "We have Abraham as our father." For I say to you that God is able to raise up children to Abraham from these stones. And even now the ax is laid to the root of the trees. Therefore every tree which does not bear good fruit is cut down and thrown into the fire.

—Matthew 3:8-10

You will know them by their fruit. We will have fruit that lasts, producing fruit in keeping with repentance. Jesus mentioned fruit often. Jesus cursed the religious system because it did not produce fruit, but the kingdom of God has fruit that lasts. With our authority as true believers, we can speak to mountains, and if we believe in our hearts that what we say with our mouths will come to pass, we will have it. Jesus said that you could do this, and He did not say anything false. By His words, Jesus took off the limits, and now we need to speak to mountains. We need to curse religious doctrine and diabolical religious schemes being entertained in the world, which is anything that has that form of godliness but denies the power. Paul does not want us even to have fellowship with those kinds of people because they misrepresent Him and take people down a path that is a false religion (2 Timothy 3:5).

Casting down arguments and every high thing that exalts itself against the knowledge of God, bringing every thought into captivity to the obedience of Christ.

—2 Corinthians 10:5

Jesus cursed the fig tree and told us to speak to anything standing in our way and anything that exalts itself above the knowledge of God. We need to take it into captivity, speak to it and have it removed. Christ redeemed us from this curse, so we no longer operate in a curse; we are now walking in the power of the Spirit.

WE CAN BEGIN AND END IN THE SPIRIT

Christ has redeemed us from the curse of the law, having become a curse for us (for it is written, 'Cursed is everyone who hangs on a tree').

—Galatians 3:13

Galatians 3:13 is a very popular verse, but I wonder how many believers understand it. Paul was quoting Old Testament Scripture. We have been redeemed from the religious system of the law. Jesus was hung on the cursed tree and became a curse for us so that by faith, we could encounter the blessings of Abraham. Abraham believed in God, and it was credited to him as righteousness (Genesis 15:6, Romans 4:1-22). We believe in Jesus, which is then credited to us as righteousness. Our position is based on the fact that we believe.

How many of us are encountering failure or feeling disconnected even now? Peter had this happen while walking on water because he doubted (Matthew 14:28-31). Jesus immediately confronted him because Peter was doing well until he doubted. Paul said something similar to the Galatians when he asked who cut in on them and stopped their momentum. Paul wanted to know who had bewitched them; after beginning in the Spirit, he questioned if they would finish in the flesh (Galatians 3:1-3). Peter was told to come to Jesus on the water, and he looked at his circumstances and started to sink. Jesus addressed his failure as due to doubt and fear. We need to catch these truths for ourselves. Peter failed in what appeared to be more than we could do. How many of us have walked on water? However, his fear and doubt caused him to sink.

> *Who shall separate us from the love of Christ? Shall tribulation, or distress, or persecution, or famine, or nakedness, or peril, or sword? As it is written: "For Your sake we are killed all day long; We are accounted as sheep for the slaughter." Yet in all*

these things we are more than conquerors through Him who loved us.

—Romans 8:35-37

Rejoice and be exceedingly glad, for great is your reward in Heaven, for so they persecuted the prophets who were before you.

—Matthew 5:12

We are more than conquerors, and all these situations that come against us cannot separate us from the love of God. Jesus said that reward is exceedingly great for believers who endure persecution. So we must realize that there is a reward in that.

But also for this very reason, giving all diligence, add to your faith virtue, to virtue knowledge, to knowledge self-control, to self-control perseverance, to perseverance godliness, to godliness brotherly kindness, and to brotherly kindness love. For if these things are yours and abound, you will be neither barren nor unfruitful in the knowledge of our Lord Jesus Christ.

—2 Peter 1:5-8

Now to Him who is able to keep you from stumbling, and to present you faultless before the presence of His glory with exceeding joy.

—Jude 1:24

Allowing these virtues that Peter spoke of in 2 Peter 1:5-8 to manifest in your life will keep you from being unproductive. The spirit world is constantly moving around us, responding to our words and our prayers. When we pray, proclaim, and prophesy the truth, angels and the Spirit of God are ready to enforce what we declare. However, if we speak doubt, fear, and unbelief, if we adhere to religious spirits, then conversely, those evil spirits are right there to enforce curses because we have permitted them.

Regarding the spirit world, we have been given dominion and authority to speak to our mountains and tell them to be removed. But if we make them permanent, they will stay permanent. Many people don't want to hear this. We must realize and be accountable that our words count because we count. Jesus has given us the keys; we now have authority as God's sons and daughters on earth. We must forbid what needs to be prohibited; if we don't do it, then what is not supposed to be done will be done. We often see this in our lives; in our nation, some individuals are given over to the devil, who seem to have the power.

The real power, however, has been given to the church, and if the church says no, then that is the final authority. We have only seen that happen in history at certain times because believers got together, prayed, agreed, and were in unity, and they forbid it. Whole nations have been changed by one person forbidding. I have seen groups of people who did not even have a high school education but knew how to pray and changed history. We are supposed to be doing this as well.

The in-dwelling power of the Holy Spirit in you wants to give voice through your lips, and you must not back off. The devil does not want you to gain momentum, so you must be persistent and breakthrough.

11

FIRST TO FALL

"How you are fallen from heaven, O Lucifer,
son of the morning! How you are cut down to the
ground, You who weakened the nations"
—Isaiah 14:12

Helel, the devil, was created as perfect, but he was not made in the image of God. He was the epitome of perfection, "the seal of perfection, full of wisdom and perfect in beauty," but he fell (Ezekiel 28:12). Ezekiel prophesied concerning him,

You defiled your sanctuaries by the multitude of
your iniquities, by the iniquity of your trading;
therefore I brought fire from your midst; it devoured
you, and I turned you to ashes upon the earth in the
sight of all who saw you.

—Ezekiel 28:18

In perfection, helel was the cherub that covered Eden. God created man and woman and placed them there in the garden. So even though helel was beautiful and perfect, he was not made in the image of God. God only made man in His image. So what happened to helel? His eyes were opened, and he saw something that caused him to be twisted and perverse. He used the serpent to tempt man because it was more cunning than any beast of the field, and he could manipulate it (Genesis 3:1). Different animals have different personalities and characteristics, some aggressive and some docile. Knowing he could sway her using its characteristics, helel chose to talk to Eve through the serpent. There is a lot of mystery in all this. I would encourage you to do word studies using *Strong's Exhaustive Concordance* and review Ezekiel 28 and Isaiah 14:12-21.

Before helel used the serpent to deceive Eve, he was the first to fall, even though no one tempted him. He probably ate from the Tree of Knowledge of Good and Evil, and his eyes were opened. Since helel was made perfect and no one tempted him, he could not have understood good and evil until then. Adam and Eve fell because they were seduced and deceived, but something happened inside helel; he fell first, was corrupted, and iniquity was found in him (Ezekiel 28:15).

When Adam and Eve were formed, they looked like God and lived in Eden, where helel was guardian. When God made man, He gave them dominion over everything; possibly, helel could see that Adam and Eve looked like God. As a cherub, he did not resemble God. He must have realized that he no longer had a job and would have another assignment because men and women were taking over.

> *Studying the Word of God helps us understand that the whole world system is a result of helel's corruption.*

As mentioned, God told Adam and Eve they were given dominion over everything. I think jealousy and envy were brought into that situation, which produced iniquity in helel. He possibly ate from that tree, which opened his eyes to good and evil because otherwise, evil was not known in the world. There was no evil or way for a man or any being to know evil. Only God could know evil, and He chose not to give that ability to anyone.

God placed that tree in the garden and told them not to eat from it, showing that He was God and they were not. All the created beings—helel, the other animals, and, of course, Adam and Eve, who were made in the image of God—were to stay away from that tree and not eat from it. That tree was placed there because Adam and Eve were created so perfectly that they might have the idea that they were God. The tree helped maintain a clear separation.

Studying the Word of God helps us understand that the whole world system is a result of helel's corruption, which is why we must dive a bit deeper into this subject. He was holy at first and assigned to be over certain sanctuaries or holy places. Still, he became defiled and then defiled those sanctuaries (Ezekiel 28:18). There was iniquity in his trading, and the word there is sometimes translated as "merchandising." Trade and commerce became corrupted when helel came in. He was then judged, and holy fire came out from within him.

At the beginning of the church, a similar event happened with Ananias and Sapphira when they appeared before Peter. The presence of God was so strong in the New Testament church that it was powerful enough to kill them both because they lied to the Holy Spirit. Essentially, that is what happened here with helel. The Lord pronounced through Ezekiel that because he was corrupt, he would be judged, the holy fire would come out from him, and he would be turned to ashes. We do not understand everything because we also know that he was thrown into the lake of fire in the book of Revelation (Revelation 20:10). Although we can't explain it, that is what Ezekiel saw.

THE MIDDLEMAN

When helel saw Adam and Eve, he suddenly knew he was not the chosen one and was not what he thought he was. It is crucial to understand how this works, so it bears repeating. Although we don't know the exact details, he somehow became a middleman in the world system. If you look at what is happening in the world today, you realize that all this regulation is control and manipulation. You cannot buy and sell directly because a middleman always goes between the buyer and seller. That middleman charges you for these so-called services. It might only cost a few dollars to make the product, but they double and triple the price because the middleman distributes it to the vendor. The middleman supposedly needs to check this and regulate that and charges a fee for it. That is how satan became a middleman and corrupted the multitude with his merchandising.

Today, so many extra institutions are involved with the affairs of life, which is how the debt system was developed. People are overtaxed and cannot buy a house on their own with cash because they cannot afford it. Then they are enslaved because they pay their mortgage for thirty years; they end up paying three times what the house is worth by the end of that term. You pay almost all interest for the first twenty-three years of the thirty-year loan. Think about paying three times as much for your house over thirty years when you could have just paid cash for it upfront. It is a debt system. In addition, the banks will not pay you a fair interest rate for holding your money, yet they keep and invest it. The bank makes a tremendous profit off your money, but they don't pay you to use it. So this whole system is corrupt because satan inserted himself into it, and we can see this corruption coming into the entire world.

Today, we are witnessing the god of this world, satan, the prince of the power of the air, enslaving multitudes (Ephesians 2:1-3). At some point in a generation in the future, he will be able to bring forth the son of perdition, the antichrist, and place him in a world-dominating position (2 Thessalonians 2:3-4). However, we will not let that happen while we are still here.

As Christians, we need to understand the goal of the antichrist. By inserting himself into the system, lucifer made himself the middleman so that at some point, you would not be able to buy or sell unless you have a mark (Revelations 13:11-18). You will have to take this mark or maybe put a genetically altered substance in your body, and they will try to control you. God is revealing lucifer's plan to us through the book of Revelations.

The adversary, satan, is very wise, knowledgeable, and understands holiness. He understands the dynamics between God and us; his goal is to separate us from Him and keep us away from Him out of jealousy and envy. He doesn't even want Christians to live long lives because they might start preaching, prophesying, or start walking with God, as Enoch did. So he tries to sabotage Christians, causing problems in their lives.

Yet evil people who follow satan often live a lot longer and seem to prosper in everything they do. If they break the law, they don't seem to get caught. In contrast, a Christian who does something wrong is caught right away, which is the world system. It is a corrupt system with unjust balances, corrupt judges, and a corrupt government. The same thing happens with banks and money. The enemy does not want a country's currency to be based on the gold standard. He wants their currency to float, not be backed by gold, and have no standard. Then a country can inflate its money and keep printing it, so it is eventually worth nothing, which is our corrupt system on earth.

Your enemy, satan, hates holy fire because it motivates Christians to walk in the fullness of God. The holy fire burns up the chaff in our lives so that we walk on that highway of holiness (Isaiah 35:8). We will then see and hear clearly and behave and walk the way we are supposed to. The world will see our witness, and people will get saved.

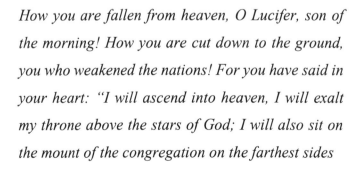

Each day you wake up, no matter what you feel like or what you are going through, you must remember you are being groomed and made ready to walk as a son or daughter of the Most High God.

How you are fallen from heaven, O Lucifer, son of the morning! How you are cut down to the ground, you who weakened the nations! For you have said in your heart: "I will ascend into heaven, I will exalt my throne above the stars of God; I will also sit on the mount of the congregation on the farthest sides of the north; I will ascend above the heights of the clouds, I will be like the Most High."

—Isaiah 14:12-14

As I previously mentioned, the name *lucifer* here was not in the original, and the name is actually *helel*[13] in Hebrew, meaning "shining one." To sum this up, helel was tempted to be God and overthrow Him. Fallen beings are now our enemy and God's enemy, all because of envy and jealousy.

WALKING IN AUTHORITY

Each day you wake up, no matter what you feel like or are going through, you must remember you are being prepared and made ready to walk as a son or daughter of the Most High God. As a child of God, you will be an ambassador on earth for the kingdom of God. Now helel (lucifer or the devil) is out, and you are in, and you are the one who is walking in authority on this earth.

Behold I give you the authority to trample on serpents and scorpions, and over all the power of the enemy, and nothing shall by any means hurt you.

—Luke 10:19

[13] "Lexicon :: Strong's H1966 – hêlēl."

God gave Adam and Eve authority in the garden (Genesis 1:26–30). When Noah came off the ark, God gave him the same covenant and told Noah to go forth, multiply, prosper, and have dominion over everything (Genesis 9:1-17). God made almost the same covenant, word for word, with Noah as He did with Adam and Eve. And now, under the new covenant, Jesus said He gives us authority and power to trample on serpents and scorpions and over all the power of the enemy (Luke 10:19).

> *But to as many as did receive and welcome Him, He gave the authority (power, privilege, right) to become the children of God, that is, to those who believe in (adhere to, trust in, and rely on) His name.*
>
> —John 1:12 AMPC

To those who believe and embrace Jesus, He gives authority, power, and the right to become children of God. As a cherub, helel saw in the garden that he was not made in the image of God. When he saw that Adam and Eve had full authority in the garden, he tried to take humanity away from God, but Jesus came back and changed everything, giving us a better way.

12

FROM THE FOUNDATION OF
THE WORLD

All who dwell on the earth will worship him, whose
names have not been written in the Book of Life of the
Lamb slain from the foundation of the world.
—Revelation 13:8

Have you ever known identical twins? I have, and I couldn't
tell them apart until I was friends with them for a long time.
After a while, I learned specific characteristics that set them apart.
God looks and is a certain way; if He makes an image of Himself,
there are so many similarities that it is hard to tell them apart at

times. In Heaven, I saw that we were made in the image of God and that we looked like Jesus. I saw so many similarities with what was in Heaven. I was in a glorified state in Heaven, without my body, and I saw the future. I was excited that God had made me in His image and that I was more like God than we would ever know here on earth. The spirit behind worldly religion does not want you to know this.

God created man in His image, desiring someone like Him to communicate and fellowship with; however, that came with a liability. In other words, it came with a very high risk. If you give someone a choice in a relationship, they might not make the choice you want them to. However, because you gave them the ability to choose, you must honor their free will.

The Father decided He would make man in His image. We do not fully understand this revelation because we were not taught. People could choose not to serve God at any time. They could decide not to listen to God's words or submit to His authority. Then God would have to let them make their own decisions but always be there and make Himself available.

From the beginning, man disobeyed the simple command not to eat of the Tree of Knowledge of Good and Evil (Genesis 2:15-17). God placed that tree in the garden because of free will and reminded all the beings, including helel, not to eat of it. It reminded them that He was God and they were not. As mentioned, I believe that helel ate from that tree. When he saw that Adam and Eve looked just like God, he became envious and jealous and used the serpent, the most cunning of all the animals, to tempt them. Adam and Eve were separated from God because of what helel did.

BATTLE OF THE BLOODLINES

We can see the battle for the bloodlines through all the lineages in the Old Testament. The flood in Genesis 6 was a battle for the genetics of the human race. The enemy was trying to pervert humans, so they were not fully human, which would disqualify them from being redeemed by the Messiah. The devil also tried to corrupt the Messiah's body through the bloodlines. We see through history that the Messiah was not corrupted, and His genealogy proved to be pure human stock (Matthew 1:1-17).

> *Knowing that you were not redeemed with corruptible things, like silver or gold, from your aimless conduct received by tradition from your*

*fathers, but with the precious blood of Christ, as of a
lamb without blemish and without spot.*

—1 Peter 1:18-19

Under the law of the Old Testament, a family would present a
spotless lamb for sacrifice each year (Exodus 12:5). The spotless
lamb without flaw proved that no genetically flawed animals were
sacrificed. The offering of a blemished lamb was not acceptable.
When Jesus came, if Mary's bloodline had been corrupted with the
hybrid race, He would have been blemished. Then satan would have
been able to say, "I got you. He's not fully human." However, Jesus
came in a perfectly human body and was not corrupted.

We will see this corruption of humanity again. There will be an
onslaught against human beings in these last days because satan will
try to alter people's DNA again. One way or another, satan is trying
to create human hybrids. He could choose to do it through
something injected into people or in our food. Once we know his
plans, we can look at some of what is happening now with medicines
and foods. Hybrid-type seeds and genetically altered injections are
being developed. We must be cautious and investigate because, at
some point, satan will start to use these to change us genetically.
I don't know when that will happen, but I always pray over my food,
medicines, or anything I ingest. If I have a check from the Holy

Spirit about something, I investigate it. Part of satan's plan is trying to mar or blemish what God has made because God made man and woman in His image. That is why satan has planned all these ways to alter a person's identity, even who they are sexually, whether male or female.

Unfortunately, all these things are happening because the antichrist spirit in the world wants to come forth and alter our DNA. He wants to change the way we live and get us off track. You must be very careful about that because God created us in the beginning, in His image, male and female (Genesis 1:27). Adam and Eve were in God's likeness, in His image.

The enemy, satan, tried to corrupt Jesus's bloodline and body, but it did not work because Jesus was fully human. With what is happening today, even if we are born again and Spirit-filled, we must watch and be careful not to take something into our bodies that could alter us. I say that because we don't know what the mark of the beast is, and it could be something that alters your DNA so that you are no longer fully human. If you take that mark, you become ineligible for redemption because you are not fully human anymore. Jesus died for complete, 100 percent human beings. When will we find a generation of people so altered that they are not fully human anymore? They may even have animal or other kinds of DNA in them. Today, they are using reptilian DNA to see if they can alter people so that they live longer. They are even using different animal DNA in experiments on people.

CREATED ON THREE LEVELS

God created us on three levels: physical, psychological, and spiritual. If you start to alter any of those and are not born again and the Holy Spirit does not change you, you cannot inherit the kingdom of God. God made us in His image on three levels. Our bodies, souls, and spirits are all important, but we must be born again to inherit the kingdom of God. We cannot go to Heaven unless we are born again (John 3:3). The Holy Spirit transforms our spirit. If a person is not born again and an evil spirit comes into that person and abides in their spirit, they are also altered and go to hell.

You can also be altered psychologically, either for good or evil. If you are not transformed by renewing your mind (Romans 12:2), then satan, through the media, will alter your mind so that you get off track, and then the psychological part of you—not just your spirit—is corrupted. If your spirit is not born again, you are corrupted, but your soul can also be corrupted. You can have a born-again spirit and a corrupted soul through the entrance of evil spirits, wrong thinking, and wrong information.

Or do you not know that your body is the temple of the Holy Spirit Who is in you, whom you have from God, and you are not your own? For you were bought at a price; therefore glorify God in your body and in your spirit, which are God's.

—1 Corinthians 6:19-20

The image of God is so important because God made us the way He wanted us to be, and we cannot allow ourselves to be altered in any way.

Your body can be altered too. Your body is a temple of the Holy Spirit, so you must discipline and take care of it to fulfill what it is called to do. Whatever you are called to do, your body goes with you. If you allow your body to be altered, you can get to where you are not fully human as before the flood, and you will no longer be in the image of God. Alarmingly, as a society, we can allow biology to alter a person's DNA, but will they be human anymore? At what point would they be a hybrid?

The image of God is so important because God made us the way He wanted us to be, and we cannot allow ourselves to be altered in any way. Our body is the temple of the Holy Spirit, and our soul—our mind, will, and emotions—is to be renewed by the Word of God. Our spirit needs to be born again, filled with the Holy Spirit, and full of the holy fire; we need to walk in that.

The Holy Trinity decided before they made the earth that they would make man in their image, and then they made the earth for us. You can be delivered from an orphan spirit if you understand that God created this whole earth and the garden of Eden for us. God did not need it because He has many worlds and a vast, beautiful realm in Heaven.

God has many other things we do not know about because the universe goes on forever. After all, it is being created at the same speed God spoke it, so there are light-years and light-years of the vast space of creation. We are the only ones made in God's image, and God chose to put man and woman on earth (Genesis 1:26). The Lord clearly showed me that He did not come back and die for aliens or another race, and Jesus is not going to die again.

Jesus was struck and died once for humanity because we were made in His image. Jesus did not die for any other beings and has no other reason ever to do that again. Jesus only died once, and He did it for us. I am trying to show you that we were exclusively chosen to be created. God created everything before He created us. The Trinity decided They would make humans and give them full authority and free will. Churches today are not teaching that we have free will.

THE GOD OF THIS WORLD BLINDS THE MINDS OF UNBELIEVERS

In whom the god of this world hath blinded the minds of them which believe not, lest the light of the glorious gospel of Christ, who is the image of God, should shine unto them.

—2 Corinthians 4:4 KJV

It is startling how people will say that God is in control, yet all this killing, stealing, and destroying is happening on earth. Paul says that is happening because the *god* of this world, small *g*, who is satan and the prince of the power of the air, causes it (Ephesians 2:2). Jesus said that satan is a thief and a liar and comes to steal, kill, and destroy. Jesus said He has come to give us life more abundantly

(John 10:10). We can see no abundant life coming forth from the world system.

The world has a spirit of debt and a spirit of death; there is killing, stealing, and destroying going on. If God were in control, another person, another baby, in a mother's womb would never be killed. If God were really in control, no stealing or destruction would go on. So it is silly and absurd to say that God is in control of this world. He might control you if you are submissive to Him, but you cannot get a whole nation to obey Him.

Even Israel fell in the desert. God could not get that nation of two and a half million to four million people on the same page as Him. The Israelites were destroyed in the desert except for Joshua and Caleb, who went into the promised land with the next generation (Numbers 14:28-30). Joshua and Caleb were the only two who were actually in agreement in that generation, yet they had to wait forty years to enter the promised land.

God decided that He would give man free will, and He told Jesus that man would fall because of the liability. Because of God's foreknowledge, He knew that Adam and Eve would choose not to follow Him. God gave us free will, which made us in His image. God can do what He wants, but He chooses to do good. When we fell, we couldn't choose good anymore because we were seduced. We were tempted to do evil because we now knew about it. We would never have known what evil was if we had not eaten the fruit; evil would not have been an option.

> *All who dwell on the earth will worship him, whose names have not been written in the Book of Life of the Lamb slain from the foundation of the world.*
>
> —Revelation 13:8

Before the worlds were created, Jesus agreed to come back and be man's Redeemer. Jesus was slain from the foundation of the world, meaning it was already known and planned. For a large part of my Christian life, I did not understand why God allowed us to fall, why satan was allowed to come in, and why the world was broken. Unfortunately, I had to go to Heaven to see these things and then be sent back.

God's will on this earth is not done most of the time because He must find someone to agree with Him and then work with that person on the earth. God found Abraham, but then He constantly struggled with Abraham's offspring, as you see God working with Isaac and Jacob, then Joseph, Saul, and David, and all the difficulties in the Bible. God is always looking for people to work with Him and to do His will on earth. God had different tasks for different people: David took out the giants, Samuel prophesied, and Samson delivered the people. At times, God needed a deliverer. God had Noah, then Moses, and then He had Jesus come.

> *God is looking for warriors like you who want to agree with God's Word and let God perform His power through you.*

Today, we have all these generals of the faith who have come and gone. Jesus found He could get these people to agree with Him on the earth, making history together. God is looking for warriors like you who want to agree with God's Word and let God perform His power through you. He wants you to go out and display His calling, fulfilling God's desire.

God put everything He has into us, then secured Jesus from the beginning to come to earth and purchase us back. As a born-again, Spirit-filled believer, the Holy Spirit is burning inside you and wants you to grasp that everything about this life and even history has been about us. Unfortunately, we were stolen from God; no one likes to be stolen from, so God bought back humanity.

God has already done everything He will do for us. He now waits for the church to rise up, take hold of the enemy, and subdue him on earth (Hebrews 10:12-13). God has put so much into you and has done so much for you. From the beginning, He gave you free will and wants to hear from you to affirm that you will be an ambassador for the kingdom of God and that you are on the same page as Him.

13

THE FATHER LIVING IN YOU

*Jesus replied, "Loving me empowers you to obey my
word. And my Father will love you so deeply that we will
come to you and make you our dwelling place."*
—John 14:23 TPT

God has allowed us in this generation to walk with Him. In the
forty years I have been with the Lord, I have seen a significant
shift from knowing about God to focusing on relationship with the
Father. There have been many different moves of God, such as the
charismatic movement, where we see the gifts of the Spirit in
operation; the Word of Faith movement, where we hear about

standing on the Word of God; the healing movement, and the prophetic movement.

The Vineyard movement focused on hanging out with Jesus, and different aspects circled the camp, but what about the Father? What about the One who did all this for us? These movements have all emphasized certain elements of truth, but we have never focused on the Father, the love of the Father, and having an intimate relationship with Him like we are seeing now.

In the desert, the children of Israel had their chance to go up and meet the Father on the mountain, and they would not do it (Exodus 19:9-25). They had an opportunity to meet the One who redeemed them, who had planned everything about their deliverance, but they would not go up to meet their God. God sent Joseph ahead to Egypt to become second in command to Pharaoh himself. God finally delivered the Israelites after four hundred years of captivity in Egypt and waited for them to come up and meet Him on Mount Sinai, but they did not want to come. God had fulfilled His covenant with them, but they wouldn't come, and God was very hurt. Several times, God has revealed that He can be hurt.

In recent times, we have emphasized healing, the gifts of the Spirit, faith, worship, and more. Yet there, the Father sits on His throne, waiting for us to interact with Him. Jesus purchased that relationship for us, but the fivefold ministry of the church has not built us up with the understanding of this teaching into maturity, as Paul talks about in the following passage in Ephesians.

> *Now these are the gifts Christ gave to the church: the apostles, the prophets, the evangelists, and the pastors and teachers. Their responsibility is to equip God's people to do his work and build up the church, the body of Christ. This will continue until we all come to such unity in our faith and knowledge of God's Son that we will be mature in the Lord, measuring up to the full and complete standard of Christ.*
>
> —Ephesians 4:11-13 NLT

Paul is saying here in Ephesians that the fivefold ministry of the church is to build up the body of Christ in the maturity and unity of the faith. If unity of the faith and maturity has not occurred, it is due to a failure of the fivefold ministry, based on what Paul said. As individuals, we must also consider that we may be lukewarm because of the failure of the fivefold ministry or because we decided not to listen to the fivefold ministry of the church. It all comes back to these questions: Do we understand why we were bought, what we were restored from, and in whose image we were originally made?

The enemy, helel (satan), was originally created perfect, yet he became corrupted and is now the god of this world. We must realize how much more we, who were created in the image of God, are made perfect in the Spirit through the blood of Jesus. What if we need to go to the next level in understanding in this last day to know who we truly are and who we are to our Heavenly Father?

> *And in that day you will ask Me nothing. Most assuredly, I say to you, whatever you ask the Father in My name He will give you.*
>
> —John 16:23

Jesus said a day was coming when you would not have to ask Him anything anymore because you could go directly to the Father yourself. What an amazing revelation; however, it does not take root in people's lives. So many profound truths regarding our relationship with the Father are revealed as you read what Jesus prayed in John 17. If you understand this chapter, it will change your Christian walk forever. You will realize who you are and become outwardly productive, which is what you want.

We want the harvest to come in, but the harvest comes in through us. As you grasp this, you can go out with confidence, flowing with the Holy Spirit inside you to perform the works of God through you. It's all about yielding so that people will see that God is working through you and that you manifest His love.

> *Jesus replied, "Loving me empowers you to obey my word. And my Father will love you so deeply that we will come to you and make you our dwelling place."*
> —John 14:23 TPT

Jesus is saying that loving Him empowers you to obey His Word. Then He expresses that His Father will love you so deeply that He will come with Jesus and make you their dwelling place. Now you have the Father and the Son dwelling within you, making you their living quarters. What does that look like? We have seen it through Jesus Himself, and we have seen that at times on earth through heroes of the faith, e.g., Smith Wigglesworth and John G. Lake.

Think about the Father and the Son living in you, and of course, the Holy Spirit is with you already. Jesus said He would give you another Helper, the Holy Spirit of truth, who will live with you forever and not leave you as an orphan (John 14:16-18). The Holy Spirit creates the fruit inside us and is the giver of the gifts of the

Spirit, so we should let Him have His way. If we did that, how would that look?

For example, if you had the revelation of what we are reading about in John 14, you would become one of those heroes of the faith. But what if twenty thousand other warriors for Christ got this revelation too? Then we would have that many heroes in this generation instead of just a couple. Who else was there when Smith Wigglesworth was living? We can name John G. Lake and a couple of others. But how about twenty thousand of you all getting this, having the Trinity living in you, operating freely through you, and doing what they want? What would that look like?

BECOMING THE SECRET PLACE

But we all, with unveiled face, beholding as in a mirror the glory of the Lord, are being transformed into the same image from glory to glory, just as by the Spirit of the Lord.

—2 Corinthians 3:18

What if you are a different person tomorrow morning when you wake up? This happens all the time to people because they go from glory to glory. The problem is that satan comes in and tries to stop us from notching up and keeps us from going to different levels. Jesus said they would come to you and make you their dwelling place; it would be a habitation, and you would become the secret place.

That may be hard to understand because we always consider the secret place somewhere we must go, like a most holy place. People say they must go to Jerusalem, up to the Mount of Transfiguration, to this church or concert, or see this man or woman of God to get touched or changed. However, the truth is what Paul said to the Corinthians when he said that your body is the temple of the Holy Spirit (1 Corinthians 6:19). Paul said if you join yourself to the Lord, you become one with Him in Spirit (1 Corinthians 6:17).

> *You have become one with the Spirit of God. It has already happened in your spirit, but the next step is to let the environment of Heaven invade your soul all the time.*

When you become born again, you become a new creation in Christ, the old things have passed away, and everything is new (2 Corinthians 5:17). You have become one with the Spirit of God. It has already happened in your spirit, but the next step is to let the environment of Heaven invade your soul all the time. You must saturate yourself in that heavenly environment to mature and grow in your soul, and then you can discipline your body. You must make your body do what it is supposed to do.

God has a process and wants us to go on to maturity. The born-again experience is significant, but the soul part of you is one of the biggest challenges. The soul of a human being—the mind, will, and emotions—must be involved, and only then will we agree with God. I have studied many people who have done things for God and found that they allowed God to win them over in their souls. Although this was not described as a great spiritual experience, they were obedient and did everything God wanted them to do. It was a gradual, continual transformation in their souls. When their mind, will, and emotions were affected, they handed their free will back to God and agreed only to do what He wanted them to do.

The Father, Son, and Holy Spirit are being released inside you; They are there, but your mind, will, and emotions need to be altered. When your spirit and soul align with your body, your body is made to be the sacred temple of the Holy Spirit. John G. Lake changed history by operating this way, but so should many more. I want to see a generation take back what satan has stolen from humanity.

> *You can experience habitation not just in your spirit but also in your soul, so you become the secret place for God.*

The church should be the most influential organization on earth. The body of Christ should be in unity and take back territory. If God is in you and is communicating with your spirit, you need to frame your mind so an expansion happens from your spiritual life into your soul life. You can experience habitation not just in your spirit but also in your soul, so you become the secret place for God. God is in you, and you are in God. You do not have to go to the secret place because the secret place has come to you. You just need to pray.

Jesus is the vine, and you are the branches (John 15:5). You are in the vine and receive your life flow from Him. Then you can ask what you will, as Jesus said in John 16:23. Jesus essentially says that you are in the image of God, and God is inside you, and from the inside out, you will be walking with God. This does not have to be a physical location because God sits on a much bigger throne than you can imagine. The throne room I saw in Heaven is so big that I don't think you could cover that area in a day. According to John 14:23, the Father loves you so deeply that He will come and live in you when you obey Him. When you think of the dimensions of God, we are much more expansive on the inside than we think.

When I go to the secret place, I get still and block out the influences of this realm, then I sit and wait in His presence and meditate on Him. Suddenly, I enter a whole other world within, and I don't have to go to Heaven to encounter God. God has come to me, and this is part of being in His image. In the secret place, you get still, and this physical realm fades away. Your reality and focus are on God; you realize that He is inside you, and you cannot fathom the dimensions of your intellect.

God wants to give you what you will ask of Him because it is a local call, and He is right there within you. He already knows everything you need and want. When you ask, ask from your heart and believe that what you say with your mouth will happen. It goes from within you out into this physical realm once you speak it, and it will happen, and it is all for your benefit.

FILL THE EARTH AND SUBDUE IT

In Genesis 1:28, God blessed Adam and Eve and said to them, "Be fruitful and multiply; fill the earth and subdue it." Not only was mankind supposed to fill the whole earth, but they were to subdue it. *Subdue* is a forceful word that has to do with dominion, authority, and aggressiveness.[14] God said they would have dominion over everything. Adam named the ocean, the air, and the land, representing three different levels: under the water, on the land, and in the air, which covered everything.

As I mentioned earlier after man fell in the garden, they eventually interbred, and God had to destroy the earth, saving Noah and his family on the ark (Genesis 6). God renewed that original covenant with Noah and his family when the flood receded, the same covenant God had made with Adam and Eve and all mankind before that. When God destroyed the earth, He started over with Noah, reestablishing the same covenant. We are still under those generations that came from Noah and that command.

When Jesus came back, He talked about authority and about having faith. Faith is understanding authority. Jesus commended a Roman centurion who was not Jewish for having the greatest faith that Jesus had encountered in all of Israel (Matthew 8:5–13). The centurion was commended because he did not need Jesus to go to his house and lay hands on his servant.

---

[14] "Lexicon :: Strong's H3533 - kābaš."

The centurion answered and said, "Lord, I am not worthy that You should come under my roof. But only speak a word, and my servant will be healed. For I also am a man under authority, having soldiers under me. And I say to this one 'Go,' and he goes; and to another, 'Come,' and he comes; and to my servant, 'Do this,' and he does it."

—Matthew 8:8-9

The centurion understood authority and knew Jesus's word was all he needed. Jesus marveled at that man's great faith and attributed the understanding of authority to great faith. However, this secret has never been taught. God has given man great authority over the garden and the whole earth. That is the way we were created and the mindset we should have.

Yet we are constantly being manipulated and controlled because of the fallen system on earth. In this world, we discussed how we are under a debt system where we appear to be enslaved and servants to the system, but we must realize we are not of this world. We are of the kingdom of God if we are born again, but there is a fight. By continually transforming and renewing our minds, we do not get caught up in the corrupt system, which is a constant struggle for us if we let it be. Remember, the devil has lost because Jesus has already defeated him, but we must enforce that in our lives.

The garden of Eden's borders are listed in Genesis (Genesis 2:7-14). As I mentioned earlier, the borders of the land God gave Abraham and Joshua to enforce are fifteen hundred square miles (Genesis 15:18-21, Joshua 1:1-5). If you look at these borders, they are the size of the heavenly Jerusalem that comes down from Heaven (Revelation 21:21). Those are the true borders of Israel that cover most of the Middle East. Israel would have had all the oil there if they had been obedient.

Israel would have been fifteen hundred square miles, owning all the oil and that whole fertile area to this day. The garden of Eden was there before the flood, where all the foliage accumulated and settled after the flood. All that decaying foliage and sediment produces oil. Oil is formed when foliage is trapped between layers of sediment and ferments there.

The Middle East is like a war zone because it is the disputed territory of lucifer with God. God gave Abraham the nation of Israel to be a blessing to the world, but now it has been whittled down to a small country the size of the state of New Jersey. Even past presidents wanted to make it smaller to negotiate peace, but they failed to realize that God said this was His territory. God gave us authority over the whole earth, yet now His country, Israel, is as small as one of the smaller states in the United States. The enemy, satan, is trying to whittle down what God has said to stop God's will from being done.

We are starting to realize that we are called to the Father to honor, worship, and walk with Him. This last great movement of God on the earth is the intentional revelation of the Father God. We are not victims or orphans. We are accepted and beloved; we are ambassadors of the kingdom of God on earth. The great revelation coming forth is that we are sons and daughters of the living God.

14

THE RULER OF THIS WORLD

*Casting down arguments and every high thing that
exalts itself against the knowledge of God, bringing
every thought into captivity to the obedience of Christ.*
—2 Corinthians 10:5

Adam and Eve were so close to God that they did not need
anyone else because they had God Himself. Interestingly, of
all the animals in the garden, helel was allowed somehow to enter
the serpent. In Hebrew, the word for "serpent" or "copper" is

nahas.[15] As previously mentioned, the Hebrew name helel[16] means "bright and shining one", so there is a correlation. I do not know how helel did it, but he managed to deceive Eve so that she questioned what God had said. At that time, God was already coming down and talking to Adam and Eve daily. They didn't need to speak to the serpent about anything as they could converse directly with God, and I want to emphasize that. If you understand this, you will avoid many problems in your life.

CAST DOWN WHAT EXALTS ITSELF
AGAINST THE KNOWLEDGE OF GOD

We often discuss topics with people or battle demon spirits with no business being involved in our relationship with God. I do not accept anyone's opinion that doesn't match what God has spoken. In the Word of God, His will is revealed; the Word of God *is* His will. In spiritual warfare, we match what is said and done around us with what God has already said. If what is being said exalts itself above that knowledge, we must bring it down.

Casting down arguments and every high thing that exalts itself against the knowledge of God bringing

---

[15] H5175 - nāḥāš - Strong's Hebrew Lexicon (kjv)." Blue Letter Bible. Accessed 1 Feb, 2023. https://www.blueletterbible.org/lexicon/h5175/kjv/wlc/0-1/
16 "Lexicon :: Strong's H1966 – hêlēl."

every thought into captivity to the obedience of
Christ.

—2 Corinthians 10:5

Paul said we should pull down any thought that exalts itself above what God has already said. Adam and Eve should have done this because the serpent had no authority. They should have told the serpent, "No, we are not talking to you." When you encounter people, demonic spirits, or both, make sure you discern whether whatever is being said or done matches what God has already revealed. If it is exalting itself above the knowledge of God, you do not even have to answer or engage those people or beings.

But the natural man does not receive the things of the
Spirit of God, for they are foolishness to him; nor can
he know them, because they are spiritually
discerned. But he who is spiritual judges all things,
yet he himself is rightly judged by no one.

—1 Corinthians 2:14-15

A spiritual person makes judgments about all things, but they are not subject to any man's judgment, especially one who is either a carnal Christian or carnal in the sense that they are not redeemed. A carnal or unredeemed person cannot judge the things of God or a

Christian because they don't have the Holy Spirit, so they have no way of discerning spiritual matters.

God had already made Adam and Eve close to Him, not just in physical proximity but spiritually. They were made in God's image—spirit, soul, and body—so they were already like Him. They did not need any other input from any other being trying to give them answers, wisdom, or communication. Our struggle today is that we live in a fallen state.

We have been redeemed, but we misinterpret thoughts, events, and circumstances because we judge based on our fallen world and how we are treated. We have difficulties because it is a broken world, and we might get sick or hurt. Many automatically judge their relationship with God based on that discrepancy. But what if it wasn't God's fault at all?

What if you or God were stolen from? What if God had a specific intention that didn't happen? God is stolen from every day. In fact, every day, satan is trying to steal me away from God. I must constantly discern if something or someone is drawing my attention away from Him. Every day, I ask what is trying to draw me away, just like what happened to Adam and Eve in the garden of Eden.

THE EFFECTS OF A FALLEN WORLD

God wants to talk to you personally, so read His Word, pray in the Spirit, and have fellowship with Him. You do not have to go to Jerusalem or a holy place to encounter Him. The secret place has come to you and is inside you. If everything you do on this earth, you do for God, He will favor you, bless you, and reward you for diligently seeking Him (Hebrews 11:6). Everything you do for the Lord is recorded, such as paying your tithes, giving your income or time, or helping others who cannot pay you back. You have chosen to operate in the kingdom of God, not the world's system, yet you are still in this fallen world; you might still struggle even though you are doing everything right, and I have seen this.

Suppose you notice someone needs new tires but cannot afford to buy them. You then decide to buy them a brand-new set of tires, knowing they cannot pay you back. You proceed to the tire store, give them the information on the correct tire size, and prepay for their tires. You even tell the store that they will come in to pick up the tires and instruct them to charge it to you if there is anything extra. You know that our Heavenly Father does things like this for us, and you want to do the same by gifting them. Did you know that angels are recording what you are doing?

However, this system is so corrupt. You could pay for the tires, call your friend, and tell them to come down and have the tires put on, but then you have a flat tire when you go out to your car to leave. You could then say, "God, I just bought them a brand-new set of tires, and You let this happen. Why?" You could blame God, but God didn't cause that; it happened because of this fallen world.

> *You cannot judge your relationship with God, His love for you, or anything about Him, and you certainly cannot judge Him by what happens.*

On earth, we have the devil, demons, destruction, theft, and deterioration. You might have run over a nail the day before but only started to see its effects today, and it had nothing to do with what you just did. What you did was right. You cannot judge your relationship with God, His love for you, or anything about Him, and you certainly cannot judge Him by what happens.

The devil wants to discourage you from buying another set of tires for anyone, so he will slander God, and God will sometimes let bad things happen. As you mature and grow in your walk with God, you need to start to plead the blood of Jesus over everything. You can pray and get to where you begin to walk in the favor of God to the point where these things are not allowed to happen anymore, but it does not happen instantly.

It can take a long time for the favor of God to permeate a person's life. However, you can reach a point where you do not get sick anymore, and you are walking in divine health and will never have to ask for healing. You will have divine protection so that you do not experience many failures, which is part of walking with God.

Enoch was sixty-five years old when he started walking with God, and he walked with God for three hundred years. It took three hundred years until he pleased God so much that God just took him, and he did not die (Genesis 5:21-24). Notice that the same thing happened with Moses because it took a long time for Moses to get with it, but in the end, he was in perfect health at the age of 120. God had to tell him it was time for him to go; Moses went up to Mount Nebo to die even though nothing was wrong with him at his death (Deuteronomy 34:1-8).

On earth, we are in a broken system, but God wants to walk with us, so you can never judge God by what is happening here. God came down daily to converse with Adam and Eve, yet He let that serpent talk to them. Why? Because God had given them free will. We must reach a place where we are walking in the will of God because then our spirits will start to synchronize with Him. God's will becomes our will, and He will begin to favor us.

You will start to see blessings in your life over the coming months and years so that the evil in the world will not be able to penetrate and work as it did in the past. Never get upset if your prayers are not answered; instead, just double down. Say, "You know what, Lord? I am not letting go of this because I know that You hear me, and I know that You are willing. And Lord, You said I could ask whatever I desire, and it will be done" (John 15:7). I tell the Lord that I am not letting go of this, and I am not stopping.

> *We must reach a place where we are walking in the will of God because then our spirits will start to synchronize with Him. God's will becomes our will, and He will begin to favor us.*

When you think about the thief stealing from people, God had nothing to do with it. But if your prayers are not being answered or if satan's allowed to come in, then you just seal up any open doors and double down on your efforts. You say, "No, I know my rights and privileges, and I know my God, and He will not withhold any good thing from me" (Psalm 84:11). Persistently go after it; your prayers will be answered.

Never say bad things happen because of your past; if you are a Christian, your sins are forgiven and wiped clean. Now, you might have to deal with the consequences of what you did. For instance, you cannot undo that you may have had a child out of wedlock because it does not disappear. However, within the covenant of God, He makes it better than if it never happened. God is not punishing you for what you did in your past. There is forgiveness, and you go on, and there is favor, so you cannot judge.

You cannot stress out over what happens to you daily because you will find out when you get to Heaven that it has nothing to do with you. It had everything to do with the enemy that was against us. Living in a broken world, we will always have to fight evil while we are here. We will always have to fight the thief, sickness, deterioration, destruction, and all these problems because the world is broken and fallen. However, we are not fallen anymore because we have been redeemed.

OUR LAST ENEMY IS DEATH

Paul said that the last enemy that will be destroyed is death (1 Corinthians 15:26). We will still die at a certain age, even though we are born again. We don't live forever like Adam and Eve were supposed to or even live longer when we are born again. People live to a certain age, and it seems like it is getting shorter and shorter when it seems like it should be getting longer and longer. So the length of our life is not necessarily due to the born-again experience but because we live in a broken world.

> *But if the Spirit of Him who raised Jesus from the dead dwells in you, He who raised Christ from the dead will also give life to your mortal bodies through His Spirit who dwells in you.*
>
> —Romans 8:11

Paul said that the same power that rose Jesus from the dead dwells in you and will quicken your mortal body. The word *mortal* here means "death, the body of death."[17] When Paul was caught up, he saw the resurrection of the dead (2 Corinthians 12:2-4, 1 Corinthians 15:20-22). He saw the revelation of being in Christ and what Jesus did for us positionally. He also saw that the power of God within us could quicken or revive us (Romans 8:11 KJV).

---

[17] "G2349 - thnētos - Strong's Greek Lexicon (kjv)." Blue Letter Bible. Accessed 1 Feb, 2023. https://www.blueletterbible.org/lexicon/g2349/kjv/tr/0-1/

Even though Moses was under the old covenant, amazingly, he lived until he was 120 years old after being face-to-face with God on the mountain. Nothing was wrong with him at his death (Exodus 24:18). Joshua and Caleb lived longer than anyone in the Israelites' camp in the desert. So, God can do that.

When we start to realize what is inside of us as children of God, we can put God in a position to answer our prayer to live longer. We can say to God that He said that He would limit man to 120 years of age and that we want to live that long (Genesis 6:3). When you position yourself like that, God will start to speak to your heart about how you are to live.

What is in our environment can negatively affect our health. Things are happening that shouldn't be happening in our environment, but they are. So we must be wise and know which foods to eat and which ones to avoid. We need to avoid contaminants. By asking for the wisdom of God, we can take many proactive steps to live longer.

I will not let this broken world dictate what God has for me and will not interpret what happens to me every day as being from God or not of God. Since I walk with Him, I am confident He is a good Father and will never do terrible things to me. When something negative happens, I automatically know that it is because I am in a fallen world and that satan is the god of this world. Unless I have disobeyed God personally or done something to open the door to the enemy, I already know how this happened. I understand that I live in a fallen world with the devil in charge, and I must exercise authority over him.

My stance is that I demand that the devil pays back what he has stolen. I have to pray, knowing that my prayer will be answered. When something terrible happens, I do not blame myself or God. I automatically look at the fact that I am operating as a child of God in His kingdom, but I live in a broken, fallen world.

My body is fighting a disease at the time of this writing, just like yours may be; you constantly must overcome your thoughts and the weaknesses in your body and mind because you live in this world. Our enemy, satan, is a terrorist and is disrupting this physical environment so that man will not live long. He also corrupts people's minds through the media and constantly shows them false images. The devil does not want anyone to hear the gospel. The people who dedicate themselves to the devil often live long because he prospers them, yet he fights against people who believe God will prosper them, heal them, and answer their prayers. The devil will not favor Christians; he will only favor his own, explaining some of the trials you are going through.

Jesus answered them, "Most assuredly, I say to you, whoever commits sin is a slave of sin. And a slave does not abide in the house forever, but a son abides forever. Therefore if the Son makes you free, you shall be free indeed."

—John 8:34-36

Now the Lord is the Spirit; and where the Spirit of the Lord is, there is liberty.

—2 Corinthians 3:17

When lucifer took mankind away from God, lucifer enslaved them, but Jesus came and set us free. He gave us the Holy Spirit, and we now experience freedom in Him. So the Son sets you free, and the Spirit constantly enforces that freedom, which explains some of the warfare you are going through every day.

And you He made alive, who were dead in trespasses and sins, in which you once walked according to the course of this world, according to the prince of the power of the air, the spirit who now works in the sons of disobedience, among whom also we all once conducted ourselves in the lusts of our flesh,

fulfilling the desires of the flesh and of the mind, and
were by nature children of wrath, just as the others.

—Ephesians 2:13

During the day, when you encounter people, demons may be operating in them, including family members, coworkers, anyone you know, or even strangers. Certain people will predictably act up around you due to demonic spirits. Once you become aware of this, you can manage your day, knowing that you are praying for people, avoiding certain people, and only acting and speaking as God leads you. Remember, lucifer is in charge on earth, and if people do not withstand him, he will overrun them. Paul said that people of the world cannot resist the spirit of the world, the prince of the power of the air. He explained that we were all once there, and those desires drove us until we were born again, but then we were transferred to the kingdom of God (Colossians 1:13).

A person in the world will not be able to withstand an evil spirit coming to attack you through them. If an evil spirit wants to get to you and cannot get to you personally, they will find someone who will be a mouthpiece for them, becoming like a guided missile, such as that serpent in the garden that came to Adam and Eve. Manage your day by being aware of this and being wise to the enemy's schemes. Jesus did this daily and was always ready to answer anyone, including the Pharisees.

15

FREE FROM THE LAW OF
SIN AND DEATH

*For the law of the Spirit of life in Christ Jesus has made
me free from the law of sin and death.*
—Romans 8:2

Moses was born a deliverer, and satan tried to take him out at his birth, but God had another plan (Exodus 1:16). Moses had a lot to learn; his first forty years were spent training in Pharaoh's court (Exodus 2:1-10). Then, he spent another forty years in the middle of the desert as a sheepherder when God called him at the burning bush (Exodus 3). Moses trained for a total of eighty years. Interestingly, God knew that Moses needed to understand the courts of Pharaoh, and he also needed to understand the middle of the desert because that is where the children of Israel were taken.

SATAN'S WAR WITH DELIVERERS AND THE PROPHETIC

Even though Moses grew up in Pharaoh's court, he never accepted the witchcraft, sorcery, and everything opposed to God that was going on there. The magicians in the Egyptian court could change a staff into a serpent and reproduce some of the curses coming upon Israel. Yet Moses never accepted their ways.

After being in the desert for forty years, Moses encountered God at the burning bush, and God sent him back to Egypt (Exodus 3:1-17). Moses's staff turned into a serpent to show that God was the God of all the gods. When the court's magicians changed their staffs into serpents, Moses's staff turned into a serpent and swallowed up all the magician's serpents to show who was the one true God (Exodus 7:8-13). God had set it all up in Moses's favor.

We can be thankful that even though humanity was made in the image of God and fallen, now in the New Testament, through Christ, we have the born-again experience and are way ahead with that experience. It took eighty years of training to prepare Moses to take those millions of people out of Egypt into the desert and enter the promised land. As you know, Joshua led the Israelites into the promised land. God had a plan through all that happened with Moses and the Israelites, even though it should have taken only two weeks to get to the promised land instead of forty years of wandering in the desert. God wanted all His people to enter the promised land right away, but the Israelites operated in the sin of rebellion. First, Pharaoh and then the desert were part of Moses's training.

With the New Testament today, we have the Word of God written in its entirety. We have the gospels and all the letters written to the churches through the various apostles given to us by God. We have Timothy receiving instruction on being a pastor. We have the books of Titus and Jude and all the smaller books. We have Peter's writings, the numerous writings of Paul, the book of Acts, and the Gospel of Luke. We have all these different writings and the Spirit of God, and we do not have to take eighty years to prepare for what God has for us.

> *When you come into the land which the Lord your*
> *God is giving you, you shall not learn to follow the*
> *abominations of those nations. There shall not be*

found among you anyone who makes his son or his daughter pass through the fire, or one who practices witchcraft, or a soothsayer, or one who interprets omens, or a sorcerer, or one who conjures spells, or a medium, or a spiritist, or one who calls up the dead. For all who do these things are an abomination to the Lord, and because of these abominations the Lord your God drives them out from before you.

—Deuteronomy 18:9-12

The Old Testament says you are not to consult wizards, witches, warlocks, or mediums, which are an abomination to God. In Isaiah 47:13-15, you were forbidden to consult astrologers, stargazers, and monthly prognosticators. This is what happened in Nimrod's city of Babel and why it was destroyed (Genesis 10:8-10, 11:1-9). Nimrod was creating a system, a way to chart stars and to communicate using the heavens. Bible scholars have much conjecture about what was happening in Babel, and a door may have been opened to allow evil entities to manifest. However, God overthrew it all. God forbade them from inquiring into the evil teachings of that time.

We are forbidden from consulting entities or astrologers, such as in the Old Testament. In the New Testament, as believers, we have access through Jesus Christ, which is what it means to be in the image of God. We have been restored, and you and I are allowed to go in and inquire of the Lord and seek Him face-to-face to get our instructions and strategies from Him.

In the New Testament, we can see Herod talking to the Magi, who were following a star (Matthew 2:1-12). However, the magi knew a deliverer was about to be born. Records show that some of these magi were influenced by Daniel, who was in Babylon and taught them the ways of the Messiah. The angels of God gave Daniel a revelation, and he saw the end times (Daniel 12:1-13). I believe he was influential in training the magi.

> *We have been restored, and you and I are allowed to go in and inquire of the Lord and seek Him face-to-face to get our instructions and strategies from Him.*

The Lord has appeared to many people at different times, influencing history each time. Sometimes, it was through an angelic visitation, and other times, it was through people like Moses, who were born to impact their generation. We can see God intervening, talking to Cain, Moses, John the Baptist, and Mary, the mother of Jesus. In all these situations, we see God trying to help people.

God appeared to Cain and tried to influence him, but Cain didn't listen and still killed his brother Abel (Genesis 4:5-8). Abel was a deliverer, and God had a plan for him. God also had a plan for Moses, and satan tried to take him out but failed. Writings show that Noah was almost taken out at birth, but God had a plan for him and intervened. Another example was Samson. An angel appeared to Samson's mother and told her a deliverer was in her womb (Judges 13:1-24). God was looking for an opportunity to make war with the Philistines, which is why he was born. Throughout his whole life, Samson was constantly at war with the Philistines. The adversary tried to take Jesus, our Redeemer, and Deliverer, out by killing all the male children in and around Bethlehem (Matthew 2:16-18). We find this war against deliverers happening throughout history.

Today, because of abortion, a whole generation has been taken out of the womb. Satan could probably see that this Joshua generation in the womb was the forerunner of the second coming of the Lord. The enemy is trying to take out this prophetic generation in the womb through legalized abortion and anything else he could do to destroy them. There is still a great battle over the generation in the womb and their prophetic destiny.

God's original plan was that we would walk and live with Him forever. When we understand His original plan, we see what was given to us through Jesus Christ. If Jesus is the image of God and we originally were made in the image of God, then we need to know how that restoration will manifest. Unfortunately, death has not yet been defeated, so we will still die (1 Corinthians 15:26). We will not live forever in the flesh, but eternally, we will live forever. Paul tells us that everything else has been secured for us through Jesus Christ except that we will physically die (1 Corinthians 15:51-55). The solution for sin has been taken care of, but has not yet for physical life. Our goal for a long life should be 120 years because that is the restriction placed on man (Genesis 6:3).

THE HOLY SPIRIT GIVES LIFE TO OUR MORTAL BODIES

People will dispute you if you believe God to live to be 120 years old. If a pagan religion can claim that people live to be 174 years old, why can't Christians with eternal life and the power that raised Jesus from the dead living within them live to 120? Why couldn't that same power quicken our mortal bodies to live longer if we wanted to or at least live in health? (Romans 8:11 KJV). God has taken care of and given us a solution for sin through Jesus Christ, and the Bible teaches us how to live victoriously. If we adhere to the Word of God, we should start to see manifestations of differences from what the world would produce.

Why do evil people live to an old age? I could name some of these people, and you would know of them. They are wicked and possessed by the devil, but they don't get sick or die early. I consistently see this happen. These same people will say that you have to take this vaccination or medication, but they don't take it, which is a gross injustice. In this fallen world, satan favors his own, but not someone who has eternal life.

Why can't we allow the Holy Spirit to lead us so that we can usurp authority over that system? What would that mean? When we have eternal life, we are led by the Spirit of God, and if we yield to the Spirit, then we are sons of God (Romans 8:14). The Holy Spirit wants to lead us into truth (John 16:13). You may be unaware of something you are doing that hurts your chances of living to the age you would like. If the Holy Spirit were leading you into all truth, He would want to tell you what you could do to live a healthier and longer life. The Holy Spirit might ask you to stop doing something so that you live fifteen years longer than you would have otherwise. Your longevity could change because you were making certain decisions and consuming unknown contaminants, such as pesticides, chemicals in water, food additives, and other harmful products. What if the power of the Holy Spirit led you to stop using or consuming those products? Your physical body could live longer based on knowing that certain foods or products aren't good for you.

FREE FROM THE LAW OF SIN AND DEATH

The wisdom of the Holy Spirit also applies to your soul; certain activities might be permissible, but are they helping you? You would be better off if you made the right choices and did not feed your soul—your mind, will, and emotions—with certain things. Everything within your soul affects your body and your spiritual life. If you fill your mind with stress-producing thoughts, your body will deteriorate more quickly, shortening your life.

> *There is therefore now no condemnation to those who are in Christ Jesus, who do not walk according to the flesh, but according to the Spirit. For the law of the Spirit of life in Christ Jesus has made me free from the law of sin and death.*
>
> —Romans 8:1-2

Sin and the condition of your spiritual state have been resolved through the blood of Jesus on the cross; there is now no condemnation in Christ Jesus. The old has passed away, and there is no case against you. Accepting that you are forgiven is not just spiritual but psychological. When you know this, your soul is at peace; you should not worry about your past because it is resolved. Don't be worried about making mistakes, but you must get to the place where the favor of God is operating in your life. You must realize that it is rigged in your favor because the New Testament allows you to walk out this life victoriously.

Just like God had already set up Moses to be a deliverer, in the New Testament, we are all called to be ambassadors who walk with God in a very profound, supernatural way. The religious system did not like Jesus because He was supernatural, and they will not like you walking in the supernatural (John 15:18-27). Jesus was walking in the manifestation of the Holy Spirit, and when you start to walk in that same way, the religious system will come against you.

You will experience warfare with the religious system when you only want to do the works of your Father in Heaven. The religious system wars against healing, tongues, deliverance, and other supernatural manifestations. It hates these because the things of God are very powerful. It hates when people stand against the killing of babies in the womb, the enslavement of people in the debt system, and people on drugs due to the medical system. The body of Christ must courageously teach how to walk in freedom from all bondage.

Evil spirits will work through the religious system to enslave you, and you go from one program to another, never getting free. The ungodly system religion is described as having a form of godliness but denying its power according to 2 Timothy 3:5. Jesus once showed me that He had bought man back, yet so many choose to live on the fence, which grieves Jesus. When He showed me this, it changed my life. Jesus is against being lukewarm because He paid the price for us to be bought back into the image of God (Revelation 3:16). We should be living in a profound supernatural walk with God.

> *Jesus told me that He wanted us to be in the hottest spot in Heaven, where the holy fire comes up through the sapphire floor.*

Jesus had more encounters with the enemy through the religious system that was withstanding Him than anywhere else. The crowds who followed Jesus were sick, poor, demon-possessed, and like "sheep without a shepherd" (Matthew 9:36). Jesus was always ministering to them, but the Pharisees, the religious system, were constantly confronting Him, trying to stop Him. The Pharisees told Jesus and the disciples they could not heal on the Sabbath, but people go to church on the Sabbath to be healed and delivered. When we go to church, we want prayer and help, to be ministered to, and to minister to others.

Sitting on the fence is not an option; Jesus told me He didn't die on the cross so that people could be lukewarm. Jesus said He wanted us to be in the hottest spot in Heaven, where the holy fire comes up through the sapphire floor (Exodus 24:10).

> *Christ has redeemed us from the curse of the law, having become a curse for us (for it is written, "Cursed is everyone who hangs on a tree").*
>
> —Galatians 3:13

Jesus replaced us on the cross and took the law's curse upon Himself so that we would no longer bear that curse. We will live forever spiritually, but down here, we should take advantage of the covenant and encounter habitation in the secret place as much as possible, implementing what we receive from the Lord. The favor of God will then permeate your life so that even in famine, you sow and reap one hundredfold, just as Isaac did (Genesis 26:12).

Jesus always wanted people to overcome and do what He was doing. By always teaching His disciples, Jesus helped them walk on water, heal the sick, cast out devils, command the waves and the wind to obey, and make declarations. Jesus taught them that what they asked would come to pass if they believed in their heart and said it with their mouth (Mark 11:23-24). He wanted people to understand what

He was saying so they could do what He was doing. Jesus was equipping them to do the ministry that He was doing after He was gone.

All the difficulties you encounter on earth may try to box you in so that you live in a small place out of fear, doubt, or unbelief. Most importantly, you must not judge God by your circumstances but by what He has already said about Himself. Create an environment of Heaven in your life and find a place where you can be quiet for a while without interruptions, a place you can go in the Spirit and grow. Grasping the reality that you are made in the image of God, and God created you because He wants fellowship with you.

Jesus came and bought everything back except physical life. Your body will not live forever because physical death has not yet been defeated, but you have eternal life. So on earth, the limitations have been taken off except for your physical lifespan of 120 years.

The pure gospel is a good message, good information, and good news so that you are set free and no longer in bondage. The Holy Spirit wants to expand your borders so that you are much more than you are now. It is time for the image of God inside you, through the born-again experience, to be released into your soul and body. The holy fire exposes anything in you that is not of God and brings out the pure, which is the image of God in which you were made.

16

THE SHED BLOOD OF JESUS

And according to the law almost all things are purified with
blood, and without shedding of blood there is no remission.
—Hebrews 9:22

When Jesus came, He taught us how to operate in authority, the authority with which Adam and Eve operated. The enemy must submit to any Christian who uses the name of Jesus; satan knows that we have authority over him because of what Jesus did on the cross. However, he also knows that if he can keep this information from Christians, they will not operate in it because they won't understand it.

Adam and Eve never knew evil until they ate the fruit in the garden (Genesis 3:6-7). Once they knew good and evil, they could choose either, which became a problem because they became divided within themselves. Now they faced temptation, which they had to fight for the rest of their lives. Even today, we can be seduced and encounter fear, unbelief, and doubt. The only enemy that hasn't been taken care of on the cross is death, and we will all physically die, yet we can still be tempted. Adam and Eve were created to live forever, and even after they fell, they both lived over nine hundred years.

Besides physical death, on earth, we also encounter the confusion that results from the evil in this world system, and satan is the god over all those evil spirits. Those who do not obey God and have not been born again cannot resist the spirit of the power of the air (Ephesians 2:1-3). The unbelievers do not even know they are being controlled. When we encounter these things, we can resist and overcome them.

Adam and Eve lost their innocence, but we have regained that innocence through the blood of Jesus. However, we do not stop knowing the difference between good and evil. Instead, we now have the power to choose good, just as our Heavenly Father is good. When Adam and Eve sinned, their eyes were opened, and they lost their innocence as far as their sinlessness because they were corrupted. They had to cover themselves because they lost the covering God had given them. Although they previously had a robe of righteousness, they became uncovered because of disobedience.

On the other hand, Abraham obeyed God when He told him to leave his country and go to another country (Genesis 12:1-4). It was credited to Abraham as righteousness because he had faith and was obedient (Genesis 15:1-21). Abraham did not even know where he was going, but he was looking for a city whose builder and maker was God (Hebrews 11:8-10).

A FORM OF GODLINESS BUT DENYING THE POWER

When Adam and Eve fell, they lost their glory garment and were uncovered. The nearest thing to them was a fig tree, and when they saw the fig leaf, they grabbed it to cover themselves. The fruit they ate in the garden was probably figs, and the leaves were large enough to cover them.

In the New Testament, Jesus cursed the fig tree, not because He was having a bad day, didn't like figs, or was just mad at the fig tree. He remembered that Adam and Eve used the fig leaves to cover themselves and saw that the fig tree was not producing fruit, a characteristic of the religious system. The religious system of the day has a form of godliness but denies the power thereof (2 Timothy 3:5). They are like clouds without rain and proclaim that they have salvation, just like the Pharisees did, but they deny the power of God (Jude 1:12).

The religious system does not believe in miracles, the Holy Spirit, casting out devils, healing the sick, raising the dead, preaching the good news, or that God can prosper you. They deny all these things exist, not believing in any of them. Altogether forfeiting the gospel message, their message is that God is powerless and does not interact with humanity anymore. These people are called agnostics or Calvinists, a type of false doctrine. Be aware of people today who claim to be saved but do not adhere to the Bible. They say that all miracles have ceased, God does not speak to people anymore, He does not help people, His Spirit does not move, and the gifts no longer manifest. Paul said we should not have anything to do with these people because of their false doctrine. He said, "And from such people turn away!" (2 Timothy 3:5).

The solution to the problem was not the fig leaves because Jesus saw that the fig tree was not bearing fruit. The idea of the fig leaves covering them without addressing the root issue was like the religious system of the day, the Pharisees under the law. Before I was born again, I was in the Reformed Presbyterian Church. They were Calvinistic and wanted me to join the church and be water baptized with the sprinkling of water. They told me that if I behaved, the Lord might choose me to be in Heaven if that was His will from the beginning.

I was confused because Jesus said, "You must be born again of the Spirit" (John 3:5-6). Jesus said that if you believe in your heart and confess with your mouth that Jesus was raised from the dead and is Lord, then you will be saved (Romans 10:9-10). What I was being taught was contrary to what the Bible says. I began investigating and found they did not believe miracles were for today and did not believe in the born-again experience. I needed to leave that dead religion. After becoming born again and Spirit-filled, I realized that I had been covering my sin with a fig leaf, just like Adam and Eve did; I was doing good works in hopes that I would be saved. However, no one in the Bible ever preached this doctrine, not one person.

A BLOOD SACRIFICE

God gave Adam and Eve the solution to their sin when He gave them animal skins to cover themselves (Genesis 3:21). Since the animals had to provide their skins as a covering, they had to die. The animals lost their lives and shed their blood, and the idea of blood being shed to cover our sins started right from the beginning, which is very important. Adam and Eve taught their children about blood sacrifice because God showed them it was necessary and required blood.

Abel offered the proper sacrifice, his lamb (Genesis 4:1-16). God required a blood sacrifice, so blood needed to be shed, and the offering could not be from the fruit of the earth. Cain did not offer the sacrifice he was supposed to, even after God taught and coached him face-to-face that it was by blood. Afterward, Cain killed his brother Abel instead of doing what God had said. God said to Cain, "Where is your brother Abel? Listen! Your brother's blood cries out to Me from the ground" (Genesis 4:10). So blood was shed, and Abel's blood had a voice and was speaking and crying out for revenge.

All through the Bible, we see that life is in the blood, and the blood has a voice (Leviticus 17:11). In the book of Revelation, the saints who had been slain were crying out for their blood to be avenged, and their death would not be in vain (Revelation 6:10). Blood has a voice, and blood was the solution to the sin problem.

In the New Testament, when Jesus cursed the fig tree because He did not find fruit on it, that represented the religious system that did not bear fruit. John the Baptist said we must produce fruit in keeping with repentance (Luke 3:8). Jesus said that believers have fruit that lasts and that you will know people by their fruits (John 15:16, Matthew 7:16). These Scriptures are all about the life-giving Spirit inside you, not a religious system you obey.

Until I was born again at nineteen years of age, my experience growing up in that church was that they could not guarantee that you would get to Heaven. You were left hoping that God would be in a good mood that day or that you had done everything you were supposed to do. In the Calvinistic form of thinking, you were chosen to go to Heaven or hell before being born, which is called predestination. This doctrine is entirely contrary to the Word of God because even though God knows things ahead of time, He does not manipulate or control us; He gives us free will.

> *The Lord is not slack concerning His promise, as some count slackness, but is longsuffering toward us, not willing that any should perish but that all should come to repentance.*
>
> —2 Peter 3:9

God does not wish for anyone to perish but wants everyone to have eternal life. Jesus said hell was not made for human beings but for the devil and his angels (Matthew 25:41). We were made in the image of God, but we lost our innocence in the garden.

Jesus was hung on that tree, and the law says, "Cursed is everyone who hangeth on a tree" (Galatians 3:13). Why would the law say that? Why did Jesus tell the disciples, "If anyone desires to come after Me, let him deny himself, and take up his cross, and follow Me" (Matthew 16:24)? When Jesus said this, He had not even died on the cross. Jesus was talking about the crucified life before He was crucified. We are redeemed by what Jesus did on the cross, but we must acknowledge that we will live eternally with Him.

THE POWER OF AGREEMENT

The perfect will of God is very rarely done. The Lord doesn't want anyone to perish but wants everyone to have eternal life, and no one should go to hell (2 Peter 3:9). We should not have killing, stealing, and destroying, but we do. We have all kinds of situations that would not exist on earth if God were in control. If Christians implemented the kingdom in their lives, taught others, and built up the body, it would alleviate some of what happens.

When a group of people comes into agreement, the Lord will take sickness away from their midst, just like He did with Israel. Then

Jesus would have His way with those people. Then if we agreed as touching anything, it would be done for us (Matthew 18:19). Imagine what would happen if we could convince a group of people of this so that they understand what God is teaching us and do it.

If Christians agreed in their respective countries, many events would not happen, and the governments would be different. The officials elected to the government would be different because people would take authority and do everything necessary. Then you would have the right people in office, but if not, fraud and inconsistencies because of injustice and a corrupt system would be exposed. When a body of believers rises up, agrees, and legitimately produces fruit, evil cannot succeed. Then, the right officials and judges are elected to avoid fraud or inconsistency in what God wants.

> *When a body of believers rises up, agrees, and legitimately produces fruit, evil cannot succeed.*

So often, God's perfect will is not done, but in your lives as disciples, you must learn how to pray, disciple others, and get favor. Once many believers agree as touching one thing, then situations will start to shift and change. Suddenly, righteous officials will be elected to your government. Then honest judges will be elected, righteousness will prevail, and there will be peace with the people.

We can focus on individuals and the remnant, then on smaller groups of people, guaranteeing we won't see failure among us. God can handle you if you submit to Him, want to grow, and do not adhere to the religious system. If you adhere to the Spirit of God and the kingdom of God, you will start to see the overthrow of the enemy take place in your life. Then you need to teach others.

It is exciting because you will see the body of Christ grow in this knowledge over the next few years, and then you will see overthrow happen. Until then, we must get people out of the lukewarm status as God would call it; otherwise, we will hinder what God wants to do. You can do something about it by studying and allowing the Word of God to have preeminence in your life. Then you can take your authority, and God will favor you.

With God's favor, you will sow in famine, and even though the world is in famine, you will have a hundredfold return (Genesis 26:12). This kind of favor will be limited to people of the remnant who believe, follow God, submit to His authority, and obey Him. The image of God can be individual, but it can also be implemented in a group of people when we all agree on touching one thing, and then it will be done.

Jesus was the pure gospel, He represented the Father, and everything He did was pure and of the highest standard. During His three and a half years in ministry, look at everything that happened in the early church. The same things that happened with Jesus were happening with the disciples, which is what we want.

REPLICATING JESUS

We want to be Jesus's disciples and replicate Him so that the world sees us and says, "They've been with Jesus!" They will recognize us as the disciples of Jesus, and we will turn the world upside down. However, individually, we must fully grasp these lessons and teach them from that purest, highest standard, representing Jesus and what He did.

Jesus wanted Peter to come to Him on the water when they were out on the lake. Peter knew this was not impossible because he had been with Jesus; he learned it would be done if Jesus gave a command. Peter witnessed the miracles Jesus did, so he asked Jesus if it was Him, saying, "Lord, if it is You, command me to come to You on the water" (Matthew 14:22-33). When Jesus told Peter to come, Peter stepped out of the boat because he took Jesus at His word.

With the pure gospel, we can take Jesus at His word. Like Peter, we were made in the image of God, even though we are in a fallen state. Peter was born again, and when the day of Pentecost came, he received the Holy Spirit and became a leader in the church. He wasn't always confident and was like us in our weaknesses until then. All the disciples wavered at times and weren't always sure, but they were willing to die for what they believed by the end of their lives.

It was a risk for Peter to walk on water, but he knew it could be done if Jesus said to do it. The problem came when he looked down. You can imagine these waves were at least four to six feet tall. They would have to be that tall to come into the ship so it would sink. When we think of walking on water, we picture a nice, calm body of water and an easy walk across, but this was not the case. They had been toiling in strong winds and waves all night, and it was hard to imagine Peter walking to Jesus on those waves. Think about a six-foot difference from the bottom of a wave to the next wave's crest because Peter dealt with that.

As long as you keep your eyes on Jesus, you hear the One Who gave you the command to do it. However, once you look down and take your eyes off Him, things can quickly go wrong, which happened with Peter. In his spirit, Peter did right because he thought if he could hear Jesus's command, then everything would work out for him; that is how we need to walk with God.

We need to hear from God and then do what He says. Even if things do not go right, we cannot forget the word He gave us. Jesus was not working against Peter. Think about how Jesus did not stop the winds and the waves when Peter asked to come to Him; that is how it is with us. We want to get to Jesus in our storm, but He does not stop the storm. Sometimes He just says, "Come to Me," and we must learn to walk that walk of faith toward Him even during the storm. We need to hear from God, fortify our lives, and then obey and not judge our relationship with God by difficult circumstances.

> *And we know that all things work together for good to those who love God, to those who are the called according to His purpose.*
>
> —Romans 8:28

Peter obeyed from the beginning, and Jesus was right there for him and even grabbed him. One version of the incident says the boat immediately went to the shore, and another says the storm stopped immediately. Jesus had to step in and ask, "Why did you doubt?" (Matthew 14:31).

Jesus was correcting people all the time. Why? He kept the gospel's message to a certain standard and would not allow it to become compromised. Jesus wanted to keep it pure so that all the following generations would have that standard and not compromise or become lukewarm. People make decisions every day not to do the will of God. However, in the beginning, we were made in the image of God, not to go against the His will. You are fully human, but you are redeemed, and because of that, you have a supernatural side to you, and you are also a child of God. As a child of God, you can overcome because God is with you.

God would never let you pass away in a storm if He told you to go across that lake. He will not let you perish after telling you to act. There is always a way out, which you must see. That godly part of you, that divine nature inside you, is the part that won't give up and wants to adhere to God's words.

This charge I commit to you, son Timothy, according to the prophecies previously made concerning you, that by them you may wage the good warfare, having faith and a good conscience, which some having rejected, concerning the faith have suffered shipwreck.

—1 Timothy 1:18-19

You might have been stolen from or faced difficulties. God's perfect will is not always done. Yet you must still step in and side with God and then fight for that position in the covenant. In other words, you wage war with those prophecies that you received. Whether at the highest level of your country, government, or personally, you must take a stand and side with God because you have free will, which is part of being in the image of God.

Paul had a reconciliation ministry, which believed everyone was supposed to be saved and no one was chosen to go to hell. In 2 Corinthians 5, Paul's doctrine is that all believers have the ministry of reconciliation, and we need to tell people that the price has been paid. Everyone's debt for sin has been paid through Jesus Christ. People are already bought back, so no one needs to go to hell, which is the bottom line.

> *Remember, there is a place in everyone's heart that needs God, so it is not too late, no matter what people say or how they act.*

When you are out and about, remember people are going to hell; some already have one foot in and are working hard to get there. Some people you will talk to say they want to go to hell because they are so deceived. God's way of looking at people is that if they are still alive and breathing, He will send His ministers to talk to them. He will send His angels to help them and give them the gospel, the good news, and that is where we come in.

We must stay consistent with living in the image of God, knowing that God never planned for anyone to go to hell. Remember, there is a place in everyone's heart that needs God, so it is not too late, no matter what people say or how they act. If they are still alive, you only need to let the Lord lead you to reach their heart. They need to know that they are valued and safe in God and that He has a plan for their life.

Sometimes, the best way to witness to someone is to tell them that God has a plan for them, written in Heaven since before they were born. People need to hear the good news of the gospel and how religion does not fulfill God's righteous requirement—only the blood of Jesus does.

17

A LIVING SACRIFICE

I beseech you therefore, brethren, by the mercies of God,
that you present your bodies a living sacrifice, holy,
acceptable to God, which is your reasonable service.
—Romans 12:1

We always think about God in a certain way, based on what we know, but I want to expand your perception of Him. Not only is God big, but He is powerful and created the universe (Genesis 1:1). In the Spirit, I was shown a representation of God's desk in an office with a globe on it, like one that you might have on your desk. However, this globe was four or five inches in diameter and just sitting there. But it wasn't the earth but the whole known universe! God wanted me to see how massive He is. Even the known universe is a tiny model on His desk, and nothing compares to Him. I still find it hard to wrap my mind around some of what I was shown.

In the beginning, when God created the heavens and the earth, the Holy Spirit covered the earth (Genesis 1). That gives you an idea of His size. The Spirit of the Lord was hovering over the face of the waters. When the Father spoke light into existence and everything into being during all six days of creation, the Holy Spirit was there to manifest whatever God said. The Holy Spirit is very powerful. God created the heavens, the earth, and everything on it out of nothing. The Father released the powerful and amazing Word of God; through Jesus Christ, everything was created.

HE MAKES HIS MINISTERS A FLAME OF FIRE

We serve a God who made us in His image, yet the Holy Spirit is so huge that He can cover the whole earth. Yet He is small enough to come down to the world as a dove (Luke 3:22). The Holy Spirit came down upon Jesus, and He comes down upon us and lives within us. Ponder this—the Holy Spirit can descend on us like a dove and, at the same time, is large enough to cover the whole earth.

One of God's attributes is that He is omnipresent or everywhere. This concept is incredible, and it is difficult to wrap our minds around it. Yet God says He made us in His image and wants us to be partakers of the divine nature (2 Peter 1:3-4). Think about that. We know that the Holy Spirit is also described as fire, water, oil, a dove, and many different symbols.

When I saw myself on God's desk, I watched everything the Lord showed me in the vision. I saw myself standing there, and as I raised my hands over my head, I became like a candle with a flame. I burned brightly, and the Lord sat there and gazed at me. Why? Because He made me in His image and was just adoring me. He showed me that I was part of His display.

Through all the ages, every one of us has been created, and we are displayed as God's prized possessions. It was so wonderful. I wanted to share this with you because He makes His ministers, whether humans or angels, a flame of fire (Psalm 104:4). We are unique because we were the only ones made in the image of God, which is why God brags about us. God even bragged about Job (Job 1:8). God is so into His creation, which is why it hurt Him when man decided to do evil and go his own way.

In this time we live, we are supposed to be plucked out of the fire from the altar of God so that we can burn brightly in this generation and represent Jesus Christ and the Father on this earth. We should want to be on the hottest spot in Heaven, the sapphire platform in the throne room of God. In Exodus 24:10, God stood on that sapphire platform when He came down on Mount Sinai.

THE HIGHWAY OF HOLINESS

Encourage yourself: You were made in the image of God, and in these last days, you are supposed to shine. We are supposed to represent the sons and daughters of God, who are not diminishing but increasing. Jesus wants you to walk in holiness and the fire as one plucked from the altar to be a standard or the plumb line for this generation.

> *A highway shall be there, and a road, and it shall be called the Highway of Holiness. The unclean shall not pass over it, but it shall be for others. Whoever walks the road, although a fool, shall not go astray.*
> —Isaiah 35:8

Those who fear God and walk before Him in holiness represent the altar, the sapphire floor, and the highway of holiness. We are to walk with God and in the fear of Him as Enoch did so that we walk in power in a divine way that is evident in these last days.

In Heaven, Jesus showed me a white fence with many Christians standing there. Interestingly, it represented where the world ended, and Heaven began. In this place of division, Christians were asking where the fence or line was to have one foot in the world and one in Heaven. They wanted to enjoy the world but then have enough of themselves in Heaven to make it. They wanted to live in both worlds and just get by, which significantly hurt Jesus.

Jesus shared with me that He was hurt because He died for everyone to go to Heaven and walk on the highway of holiness in Isaiah 35. One of the biggest problems in the church is that people are not hot but lukewarm. The Father planned for us to be hot spiritually. Everything that Jesus did was with that goal in mind. He was sad and told me that He didn't die on a cross so that people could sit on the fence. He died for everyone to walk in the fear of the Lord and holiness.

Jesus shared this with me, and I am sharing it with you; we should start walking with God as they did in the garden. We should encounter God on such a spiritual level that we even change our physical appearance. After Moses's encounter with God on the mountain, his face shone. We are supposed to encounter an even greater glory in this new covenant.

When God wants to move, He will move through you. Then He will use you to move in your family, your job, and your neighborhood, city, state, and country. He may tell you to get involved with government and legislation to overturn evil so that righteousness reigns. And because you wanted to walk with God, a whole people and nation will no longer be robbed.

I know you are praying for God's will to be done. The next step is asking God what He is saying and doing right now. When you ask Him, you will discover that God's will is not being done on the earth as you thought. God will start moving in your life so that His will is done.

PRESENT YOURSELF APPROVED

You may have a wake-up call as God prepares you because you will find that He does not want you in poverty, sick, or being oppressed by devils anymore. God does not want you to be oppressed by unjust judges and rulers or in bondage to a financial, health, or medical system because they are all corrupt. He does not want you to be involved or in bondage to these things. That might be a necessary wake-up call because the Spirit of truth wants to show you these things.

> *Be diligent to present yourself approved to God, a worker who does not need to be ashamed, rightly dividing the word of truth.*
>
> —2 Timothy 2:15

After you shut down the devil in your life, you will help your friends because you will tell them what the Lord has been doing. You will begin proclaiming the gospel and shutting down the devil in other people's lives by coming against those evil spirits. You will start to affect the environment around you beyond your personal life. You must study to show yourself approved, but it will be a fight (2 Timothy 2:15).

The devil does not want to let go because he knows about momentum and what that means. The demons must give up and yield every foot to you. They know they may never get that ground back and will also lose others; they will lose the people they have entrapped because you will tell them, which is discipleship. The point of producing disciples and students is so that they can produce others. As these disciples become teachers like you, that rate multiplies and accelerates into a worldwide movement, which is happening right now.

PROCLAIM THE GOSPEL: DRIVING OUT SICKNESS, POVERTY, AND DEVILS

There is no shortage of the gospel message in Heaven, but we need people to speak it here on earth. We need to speak the good news that it is the Year of Jubilee, and your debts have been forgiven. That means that your sins are forgiven, but it also means that you will be freed from the debt system, so poverty is eradicated. You come against poverty because even the Old Testament says, "There should be no poor among you, for the Lord your God will greatly bless you in the land He is giving you as a special possession" (Deuteronomy 15:4 NLT).

> *There is no sickness in Heaven and no shortage of healing on the earth because the Holy Spirit is the Healer, and He wants to heal.*

Even in the Old Testament, God was against poverty. Suddenly, when poverty is exposed, you must justify that. There is no lack in Heaven; as believers, you are provided for in this earthly realm.

After you encounter God's provision, you will find out there is no shortage of money, and you need to tell others. There is plenty of money on earth, but it is in the wrong hands. There are plenty of provisions; it just needs to come to you.

> *Nevertheless I tell you the truth. It is to your advantage that I go away; for if I do not go away, the Helper will not come to you; but if I depart, I will send Him to you.*
>
> —John 16:7

You will see that health must come to you even if you often encounter sickness. There is no sickness in Heaven and no shortage of healing on earth because the Holy Spirit is the Healer and wants to heal. The Holy Spirit is doing the work of Jesus right now on earth because He was sent here in place of Jesus.

Jesus was always giving. He always had a flow and was always giving out. Jesus was not giving people sickness, poverty, or demons. He provided for the poor, gave health to the sick, and freed those in bondage. Jesus preached the good news of the gospel, which caused sickness, poverty, and devils to leave constantly. We receive everything we need supernaturally from Heaven.

As you walk out your life in Christ, you go from being a disciple to eventually becoming a teacher, if you are not already. As you minister to others, you are giving them the tools they need, but you are also proclaiming and driving out poverty, sickness, and devils. You are driving out the bad news and allowing the good news to enter.

We must always tell people that God is a good God, no matter what happens. God is not doing these terrible things; they happen because we live in a fallen world. When we give them the gospel, the good news, and the Word of God, signs will follow us because they always follow those who preach the good news. God works with us, confirming His Word with signs and wonders (Mark 16:20).

You must now accept what God has done for you through Jesus Christ. If you do that now, say, "Lord, from now on, I will do your perfect will. I was made in your image, and my nature wants to do your will." Then you ask the Lord for mercy to help you, and you will be put in situations where you begin walking out of all the terrible struggles in your life.

After you commit to Him, you will see that everything will begin working to take you out of the curse and into the blessing. It all stems from acts of obedience. The Lord will tell you what to do or where to get involved. He will ask you to give your time, money, or substance to help others, and when you obey Him, you are sowing into what God has for you. It is your way out, your way of escape.

The next step is to say, "Lord, I dedicate my friends to you. If you do not want these people in my life, help me walk out of this." Certain people will leave your life at that point, and new people will come in. However, you must be discerning to see if God is doing this or if evil, familiar spirits are bringing people into your life. You can be set up by satan to meet the wrong person for friendship or a given situation. God will now be your friend, and you will walk with Him and see favor.

DEDICATE YOURSELF TO GOD

I want to take a moment to explain the dynamics of what will happen when you dedicate yourself to the Lord. God's angels will come to help you, but evil spirits will also try to trip you up. When you dedicate yourself to the Lord and put yourself on the altar, you must be like Abraham when God made His covenant with him (Genesis 15). Abraham brought his offering as the Lord instructed, cutting the animal sacrifice in half and placing them opposite each other. But Abraham had to chase away the vultures until the sun went down, and then God came and walked between the sacrifice. And we must also chase away those evil spirits, those vultures that come in to try to desecrate our sacrifice.

The parable of the sower also touches on this idea of warfare when you dedicate yourself to the Lord (Matthew 13:1-9). Jesus said the sower sows seed, which is the Word, but some seed falls on the ground where the birds steal it. The enemy comes in immediately to steal the Word. That can happen when you more fully dedicate your life to the Lord.

Once you realize that you are in God's image and want to make this consecration, you must keep the altar clean and undefiled. You cannot let anything come in because you are vulnerable when you dedicate your life to the Lord in this manner. Now the Lord will start leading you. You are made in His image, and you want to be a partaker of the divine nature, and you begin to add virtues to your life (2 Peter 1:3-4).

> *But also for this very reason, giving all diligence, add to your faith virtue, to virtue knowledge, to knowledge self-control, to self-control perseverance, to perseverance godliness, to godliness brotherly kindness, and to brotherly kindness love. For if these things are yours and abound, you will be neither*

barren nor unfruitful in the knowledge of our Lord
Jesus Christ.

—2 Peter 1:5-8

As Peter says, you must add these virtues—knowledge, self-control, perseverance, godliness, brotherly kindness, and love—to your faith, with faith as the foundation. Peter says that if you do these things, you won't fail. The foundation is faith, and then you add all these other things. Quite a war will go on when you start, which many people are unprepared for and do not understand.

You may receive a lot of revelation and understanding as you study God's Word. Still, you must ensure that everything takes root and that the enemy does not come in and steal the Word because he immediately tries to do that. Every day, I receive the Word of God, but I must fight evil spirits that want to take that joy and that Word I received and try to negate it by stirring up controversy. You must be aware of that also.

The Lord will answer your prayers and will start to lead you. He might also tell you that you cannot do certain things anymore. He might tell you to let go of certain people because you have asked for a higher level in your walk with Him. You will have to pick and choose who you are around.

The Lord may be speaking to you about the job that you have. As you build yourself up in the Lord, He may use you in your situation, and then you can stay. However, if that job is contrary to what God has for you, He might want to move you. Are you ready for Him to speak? Sometimes, someone leaves your life, and another person comes in, and you think you have a friend. Then God says, "No, it is not right. It is the enemy." I have seen that happen.

Once you have dedicated yourself to this walk with God and have put yourself on the altar committing to walk as Jesus did, you must remember that Jesus only did what His Father said. You will have the strength to make the right decisions. The Lord wants to make you a plumb line for this generation, which means you will be wholly His.

I had to give up things that might not be wrong for you. I cannot sit and watch TV all day. I cannot even read other books because I am writing my own, and I must read God's Word daily and study. I am not supposed to be doing certain things anymore because the Lord has me on assignment. Some people think that the things I gave up are not wrong, but for me, they are wrong. I must stay on track with what the Lord wants for my life.

> *If you want to be God's friend and walk higher with Him as Enoch did, you must like what God likes and hate what He hates.*

If you want to walk in that supernatural life, you cannot participate in certain activities anymore, and the Holy Spirit wants to lead you and guide you in that. The Holy Spirit knows who you are inside and where you are going. If you want to be God's friend and walk higher with Him as Enoch did, you must like what God likes and hate what He hates. God does have preferences, and He does have things He likes.

Some people appear to be God's favorites because they have been obedient to consider Him above themselves. They know God does not like certain things, so they just quit doing them. The Lord knows when a person has made that sacrifice, but the public may never see the price paid by people who will do anything for God because they never talk about it. As you put yourself on the altar and become a friend of God, you will see amazing things in your life. You need to get on the highway of holiness, be separate, and let the Lord use you in a mighty way.

Father, I thank You so much for your power and this message. As the readers present their bodies as a living sacrifice, holy and acceptable to You on the altar right now, show them what the good, perfect, and acceptable will of Your heart is for them. I pray that their sacrifice will be fully accepted and that You will protect them. I thank You for giving them the strength to walk as Jesus did. Thank You, Lord, that they live the crucified life and walk in the Spirit of God as sons and daughters of God in Jesus's name. Amen.

Salvation Prayer

Lord God,
I confess that I am a sinner.
I confess that I need Your Son, Jesus.
Please forgive me in His name.
Lord Jesus, I believe You died for me and that
You are alive and listening to me now.
I now turn from my sins and welcome You into my heart.
Come and take control of my life.
Make me the kind of person You want me to be.
Now, fill me with Your Holy Spirit,
who will show me how to live for You.
I acknowledge You before men as my Savior and my Lord.
In Jesus's name. Amen.

If you prayed this prayer, please contact us at
info@kevinzadai.com for more information and materials.

We welcome you to join our network at Warriornotes.tv for access
to exclusive programming.

To enroll in our ministry school, go to:
www.Warriornotesschool.com.

**Visit www.KevinZadai.com for additional
ministry materials.**

About Dr. Kevin Zadai

Kevin Zadai, Th.D., was called to the ministry at the age of ten. He attended Central Bible College in Springfield, Missouri, where he received a Bachelor of Arts in theology. Later, he received training in missions at Rhema Bible College and a Th. D. at Primus University. Dr. Kevin L. Zadai is dedicated to training Christians to live and operate in two realms at once— the supernatural and the natural. At age 31, Kevin met Jesus, got a second chance at life, and received a revelation that he could not fail because it's all rigged in our favor! Kevin holds a commercial pilot license and is retired from Southwest Airlines after twenty-nine years as a flight attendant. Kevin is the founder and president of Warrior Notes School of Ministry. He and his lovely wife, Kathi, reside in New Orleans, Louisiana.

CHECK OUT OTHER WORKS ON THIS
SUBJECT BY DR. KEVIN ZADAI

 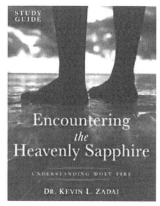 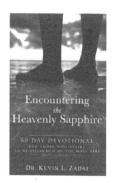

**Kevin has written over sixty books and study guides.
Please see our website for a complete list of materials!
www.Kevinzadai.com**

HOLY
FIRE

A Friend of God

BOOK TWO

HOLY FIRE

A Friend of God

DR. KEVIN L. ZADAI

Please note that Warrior Notes publishing style capitalizes certain pronouns in Scripture that refer to the Father, Son, and Holy Spirit, which may differ from some publishers' styles. Take note that the name "satan" and related names are not capitalized. We choose not to acknowledge him, even to the point of violating accepted grammatical rules. The author and Warrior Notes have made an intentional decision to italicize many Scriptures in block quotes. This is our own emphasis, not the publisher's.

Cover design: Virtually Possible Designs

Warrior Notes Publishing
P O Box 1288
Destrehan, LA 70047

For more information about our school, go to www.warriornotesschool.com. Reach us on the internet: www.Kevinzadai.com

ISBN 13 TP: 978-1-6631-0049-8

DEDICATION

I dedicate this book to the Lord Jesus Christ. When I died during surgery and met with Jesus on the other side, He insisted that I return to life on the earth and that I help people with their destinies. Because of Jesus's love and concern for people, the Lord has actually chosen to send a person back from death to help everyone who will receive that help so that his or her destiny and purpose are secure in Him.

I want You, Lord, to know that when You come to take me to be with You someday, I sincerely hope that people remember not me but the revelation of Jesus Christ that You have revealed through me. I want others to know that I am merely being obedient to Your heavenly calling and mission, which is to reveal Your plan for the fulfillment of the divine destiny for each of God's children.

ACKNOWLEDGMENTS

In addition to sharing my story with everyone through the book *Heavenly Visitation: A Guide to the Supernatural,* God has commissioned me to write over sixty books and study guides. Most recently, the Lord gave me the commission to produce the *Holy Fire* series. This book addresses some of the revelations concerning the areas that Jesus reviewed and revealed to me through the Word of God and by the Spirit of God during several visitations. I want to thank everyone who has encouraged me, assisted me, and prayed for me during the writing of this work. Special thanks to my wonderful wife, Kathi, for her love and dedication to the Lord and me. Thank you to a great staff for the wonderful job editing this book. Special thanks as well to all my friends who understand what it is to live in the *Holy Fire* of God and how to operate in this for the next move of God's Spirit.

Contents

INTRODUCTION

Jesus shared with His disciples that He no longer considered them servants but friends. Today, He longs for friends on the earth, friends with whom He can share intimate insights from the Father. The holy fire makes us His friends by separating us from the world and burning away everything that does not make us pure. To go to the next level, we must learn to place our lives on God's altar and turn ourselves over to Him.

Many believers lack this revelation: Our position through Jesus Christ has to do with intimacy with Him—it is not militaristic. Those who do not have that relationship often struggle when facing hardships, blaming God when life gets difficult. The body of Christ is the glorious church, the intimate bride of Christ, and we must preach the relational part of the gospel.

I pray that as you read this book, you experience the love of God, the freedom of the Holy Spirit, and intimate friendship with Jesus as you encounter His holy fire. May you shine brightly and hand the fire off to the next generation.

Blessings,
Dr. Kevin Zadai

1

A FRIEND OF GOD

*No longer do I call you servants, for a servant does not
know what his master is doing; but I have called you
friends, for all things that I heard from My Father I have
made known to you.*

—John 15:15

Many people in the Bible were used mightily of God and
encountered God in amazing ways; however, only a few
were called friends of God, such as Enoch, David, Abraham, and
Moses. I want to be a friend of God. Jesus wants to make us His
friends, which is what the holy fire does.

3

For no other foundation can anyone lay than that which is laid, which is Jesus Christ. Now if anyone builds on this foundation with gold, silver, precious stones, wood, hay, straw, each one's work will become clear; for the Day will declare it, because it will be revealed by fire; and the fire will test each one's work, of what sort it is. If anyone's work which he has built on it endures, he will receive a reward.

—1 Corinthians 3:11–14

The holy fire separates you, and when exposed to it, it will burn up everything that is not pure gold or silver. Anything that can be burned will be burned up, but whatever is left will be refined and imperishable.

Jesus explained to His disciples that He no longer considered them servants but friends because He took what He heard from the Father and made it known. An example of this would be when Jesus taught the parable of the sower to the multitudes in Matthew 13. After Jesus finished telling the parable, the disciples came to Him and told Him they did not understand what He was saying. I am glad they learned to ask because Jesus went through the whole parable and explained the meaning.

He answered and said to them, "Because it has been given to you to know the mysteries of the kingdom of heaven, but to them it has not been given."

—Matthew 13:11

Jesus told them that if they understood these parables, they would understand the deep mysteries of the kingdom and essentially understand everything. After they listened to Jesus explain every part of the parable, they wondered why He didn't tell the whole world. Jesus said these teachings weren't meant for the multitudes but only for them. As a disciple, they are also meant for you. When Jesus shared these mysteries with the disciples, they became His intimate friends.

I often share the importance of putting yourself on the altar of God and turning yourself in. If you want to go to the next level, you must let God dictate who your friends are and what you do with your time. Your life is not your own anymore. Many believers experience this all the time at different levels.

Unfortunately, some people have a choking point and do not want to go past a certain level. They count the cost, and sometimes it is too high for them, so they find themselves on the fence. At the end of their lives, they were not productive and did not give God a return for their talents (Matthew 25:24–27). I don't want people to find themselves in that situation.

When you are a friend of God, He entrusts you with secrets about Himself. He trusts that you will stay stable and faithful. As God sees that He can trust you, He gives you even more. If a person doesn't do anything with what they have been given, it is taken away and given to trustworthy people (Matthew 25:28–29).

The body of Christ, who is also the bride of Christ, must understand that we can walk individually with God. We are now considered friends of God because Jesus has given us intimate insights that He heard from His Father. The apostle Paul revealed the kingdom's mysteries and God's plan from when he was caught up and was essentially missing in action for a while (2 Corinthians 12:1–6). When Paul reappeared, he explained that he did not receive this revelation from people; it came directly from the Lord Jesus Christ (Galatians 1:12). Jesus taught him, but we don't know how long that lasted. We only have a record of his disappearance when he said he was caught up and was mentored by Jesus.

WHO WE ARE IN CHRIST

That He might sanctify and cleanse her with the washing of water by the word, that He might present

> *her to Himself a glorious church, not having spot or*
> *wrinkle or any such thing, but that she should be holy*
> *and without blemish.*
>
> —Ephesians 5:26–27

> *The body of Christ is the end-time glorious*
> *church, the bride of Christ, so we need to*
> *emphasize the relationship part of the gospel.*

In this dispensation, God is preparing the Church as the bride of Christ, which Paul introduces in Ephesians 5. Verses 26 and 27 speak of our position and identity in Christ. Through his letters, Paul essentially pulls back the veil, revealing what occurred behind the scenes when Jesus was seated at the right hand of God. We have been adopted as God's children and seated with Christ Jesus in the heavenly realms (Ephesians 1:5; 2:6). For those who believe, all of God's plans from before birth are being established (Psalm 139:16). On the other hand, if you do not believe, His plans are not implemented, so your position is significant. The emphasis here is who we are in Christ. Paul's letters, the epistles revealed to Him by Jesus, give us an understanding of our identity in Christ.

Believers need to understand the position given to them through Jesus Christ—however, it is not militaristic. In other words, you are not a soldier following orders without any interaction or relationship. Soldiers are punished or rewarded based on their actions, but God also has a relationship with us. Throughout the New Testament, Jesus and the apostle Paul reveal this truth.

The body of Christ is the end-time glorious church, the bride of Christ, so we need to emphasize the relationship part of the gospel. Intimacy needs to be a priority because we are in a relationship with God as His friend. If I cannot do what I am supposed to do in Christ, I need to turn myself over to Him, not as an officer, servant, or slave, but as a friend of God. This is true whether it is a physical, psychological, or spiritual problem. I must say, "Lord, I have reached my limit, and I can't go any further unless you intervene."

Your relationship with Christ needs to be based on intimacy, not just a position. You cannot think, *Oh, I was told to do this, and if I don't, I will get into trouble.* I see a lot of this in Christianity today. That attitude is not about a relationship; it is about your position. I see a military-style organization with the angels, but I do not see that with the saints. The saints are much higher than angels, so our interaction with God differs from that of the angels.

Angels are made to serve God, and they are servants. The angels love to harken to His voice (Psalm 103:20). They heed His voice, do exactly as they are told, and don't question it. Why? Because they were made to do that. They don't grumble or drag their feet because they love doing God's will. They serve God but do not have a relationship with Him like we do.

We were originally made higher than the angels, but then we fell. The angels seem greater than us because of their bodies and function, but they are not. They are not in a position greater than us; we are higher than them through Christ. A day will come when we are commanding the angels (1 Corinthians 6:3). The angels that work for us right now will work for us in eternity. Currently, they serve us, and we need their help, but a time will come when they will be assigned to us, and we will be over them (Hebrews 1:14). That will happen when this age ends, and we enter the next one.

FRIENDSHIP WITH GOD

I want to emphasize the friendship part of our relationship with God when God trusts us, and we can turn ourselves over to Him. We can say, "Lord, I need more strength and more intervention," or "I need to rest because I can't deal with this anymore." You turn yourself over to Him when you cannot deal with a particular person or face a situation you can no longer bear. You have a relationship with your Heavenly Father. So many Christians act as if they have a deadline they are expected to meet, and if it isn't completed, they won't be paid or will be punished. This attitude has permeated Christianity today.

In the body of Christ, you have the bride, who is essentially the wife of Jesus for whom He is coming back. This intimate relationship has nothing to do with all the demands of a worldly system or the military. It has to do with being friends, which is a big problem for many Christians. People who do not have that relationship do not know how to deal with hardship. They falsely believe God is mad at them when life gets difficult.

Situations pop up, and we judge our relationship with God by what happened; however, problems may have nothing to do with our relationship with Him. It might be because the devil is evil and loves to cause trouble. We might have to take a stand against this kind of situation instead of just accepting the idea that we did something wrong. We may not have done anything wrong. Often people who pray in the Spirit, read the Word of God, and love God with all their hearts encounter many of their troubles because of warfare, not because they are doing anything wrong.

But God, Who is rich in mercy, because of His great love with which He loved us, even when we were dead in trespasses, made us alive together with Christ (by grace you have been saved), and raised us up together, and made us sit together in the heavenly places in Christ Jesus, that in the ages to come He might show the exceeding riches of His grace in His kindness toward us in Christ Jesus.

—Ephesians 2:4–7

We know our position in our daily lives because we have Paul's revelation of who we are in Christ. We are seated with Him in heavenly places and have all the benefits of the new covenant. We would never know about this if it weren't for Paul's writing. However, when the holy fire comes in, it destroys the effects of sin in our souls and maybe even our bodies so that we feel free to have a relationship with God instead of just a position with Him.

If you are born again, your spirit is already perfected, but when the holy fire comes in, it ignites your spirit. It is like being baptized with the Holy Spirit. It is another experience in addition to being born again, and it happened in the Bible all the time (Matthew 3:11). People who didn't know about the Holy Spirit didn't automatically receive Him, even though they believed in Jesus and repented (Acts

19:1–7). They were born again, but that did not mean they were baptized in the Holy Spirit. It was a separate event. Other events can happen with sanctification because of your relationship with God, but your position does not change.

RELY ON YOUR RELATIONSHIP WITH GOD

The holy fire burns out wrong mindsets, affecting how you think, frame your world, and process your circumstances. This strengthens your relationship with God. I want you to be ablaze with the holy fire, not just because you are in Christ positionally, are going to Heaven, and have authority over the devil. I am talking about speaking to the Lord and saying, "Lord, I want you to talk to me and audit me. Communicate with me about why I feel this way. Why is this going on?" Interact with Him. He might tell you that you need to rest or give you specific instructions.

In some situations in the Bible, God shared His plans with His friends, such as Abraham and Moses. They responded with intercession, reminding the Lord that He made a covenant, so He could not carry out plans that would make Him look bad. God responded by granting their requests (Genesis 18:16–33; Exodus 32:9–14). Like Abraham and Moses, King David was known as a man after God's own heart (1 Samuel 13:14). David behaved in all kinds of wrong ways, yet his relationship with God went beyond his position; therefore, God gave him a good report at the end (2 Samuel 7:12–17).

Even Lot was commended for his righteousness (2 Peter 2:6–9). Yet Lot was in a city he wasn't supposed to be in, and Abraham had to come and rescue him. We don't know what would have happened to Lot if it weren't for Abraham. God came in and got Lot out, and then he was commended as a man of faith (Genesis 18:22–19:29). No matter what you are going through, remember to rely on your relationship with God, especially in these last days.

YOUR SINS ARE FORGOTTEN

"This is the covenant that I will make with them after those days, says the Lord: I will put My laws into their hearts, and in their minds I will write them," then He adds, *"Their sins and their lawless deeds I will remember no more."*

—Hebrews 10:16–17

When you were born again, you gave your life to the Lord and repented; therefore, your past sins were forgiven. It does not matter what you feel or think about your past sins from that day on. How often have you felt bad about what you did in the past? Were you reminded of your sins so much that you even hesitated for a few seconds? Unfortunately, that was wasted time because it was already finished. If you go to God and say, "I'm sorry for what I did thirty or forty years ago," He honestly does not know what you are talking about because it was wiped away, as stated in Hebrews 10:17. Your sins were not just covered, they were cleansed. In other words, your record was expunged, which means it does not exist anywhere anymore.

> *He has removed our sins as far from us as the east is from the west.*
>
> —Psalm 103:12 NLT

The Lord washed your sins away, removing them as far as the east is from the west. Well, how far is that? That eternal value goes on forever, meaning they are completely gone and will never return. It is wasted time to concentrate on something that no longer exists.

Your relationship with God is the same today. As God's friend, just turn whatever you are worried about over to Him today and say, "Lord, I don't know why I'm worried about this." Then pray it out in the Spirit, in tongues, which is what I do when I have a concern. I'll pray, "Lord, this situation is bothering me. I will dedicate the next ten minutes to praying it out in tongues, and I want to pray about this situation." At the end of that time, if the matter has not been resolved in my heart, I continue to pray in the Spirit. I will keep praying until I eventually reach the place where it is settled and finished. Sometimes I will even get something in English from the Lord, which seals the deal, and there will be a resolution. The Holy Spirit shifts our perspective so that we can see the way God sees. That is what you want and what being in a relationship is all about.

I am telling you by the Spirit of God that as you develop your friendship with God, you will continue to receive His resolution, and He will trust you with more and more. As He unfolds these intimate truths, you will be grateful to receive revelation from Him that you would have never known, which changes you immediately.

YOUR INTIMACY WITH GOD INFLUENCES YOU

Think about Peter, James, and John. They encountered Jesus in His pre-existent state on the Mount of Transfiguration (Matthew 17:1–9). Jesus allowed them to see Him transfigured as God in His glorified state from before time began. Later, Peter talked about this revelation in his letters because he never forgot it (2 Peter 1:16–18). It changed him forever. Those three disciples saw something the other nine did not.

At times, Peter, James, and John went with Jesus where the others were not meant to go. Jesus only took those three whom He favored. However, when you look at what Peter, James, and John did and how often they were mentioned in Scripture, you can see that these experiences influenced them, which is another example of how our intimate relationship with the Lord can influence us.

When Jesus took Peter, James, and John up on the Mount of Transfiguration to show them His pre-existent state, they saw Moses and Elijah talking to Jesus. As they came back down the mountain, a multitude was gathered at the foot of the mountain, arguing. When Jesus asked what they were arguing about, a man came forward and told Jesus that His disciples could not cast the devil out of his son and cure him. Jesus was upset and called them a faithless and perverse generation and asked why they doubted. Then He cast the demon out of the boy (Mark 9:2–20).

Surprisingly, Peter, James, and John, who had just had this incredible supernatural experience, didn't jump in and say anything as this situation was happening. The other nine disciples were embarrassed because they could not cast the demon out. After seeing Jesus in His pre-existing state, can you imagine the glory coming off Him as He stood there? After their experience on the mountain, those three should have stepped in and driven that devil out, but they did not act. Of course, the other nine had no idea how to drive the devil out, so Jesus had to do it.

ALL THINGS ARE POSSIBLE TO HIM WHO BELIEVES

When the disciples could not cast the demon out of the man's son, Jesus perceived that the man had lost faith and was defeated by everything that had happened. Look how Jesus responded to him.

> *Jesus said to him, "If you can believe, all things are possible to him who believes." Immediately the father of the child cried out and said with tears, "Lord, I believe; help my unbelief!"*
>
> —Mark 9:23–24

Interestingly, this is all in the same chapter. You have the three who were at a higher level of intimacy with Jesus than the other nine. Yet none of the disciples could do what Jesus was trying to teach them since He knew He was leaving.

The goal of anyone who desires to produce disciples to carry out the Lord's ministry—such as a pastor, apostle, Bible teacher, or mentor—is to teach and train others. Concerning the gospel message and other aspects of ministry, you do not want to pass away without handing it off to someone else. You want to produce disciples equipped to run the ministry, which is what we are doing at Warrior Notes. We will raise up thousands and thousands of people that can carry this work on, which will be much better than if I stayed and tried to do it by myself. It will always go on until Jesus comes back.

> *Concerning the gospel message and other aspects of ministry, you do not want to pass away without handing it off to someone else.*

All twelve disciples failed to do what they were supposed to in that situation after the Mount of Transfiguration. Then again, all twelve failed to speak to the winds and the waves when they crossed in the boat to the other side of the lake while Jesus slept (Luke 8:22–25). Only one walked on the water to Jesus (Matthew 14:22–33). None of them seemed to get it. The problem was their lack of understanding of relationship. They did not comprehend what Jesus was investing in their lives; He gave them everything He had.

> *I baptize with water those who repent of their sins and turn to God. But someone is coming soon who is greater than I am—so much greater that I'm not*

worthy even to be His slave and carry His sandals. He will baptize you with the Holy Spirit and with fire. He is ready to separate the chaff from the wheat with his winnowing fork. Then He will clean up the threshing area, gathering the wheat into his barn but burning the chaff with never-ending fire.

—Matthew 3:11–12 NLT

The baptism of water, an outward physical sign, was for repentance, but the baptism of the Holy Spirit was for power. When the Holy Spirit filled the disciples on the day of Pentecost, they were empowered to be witnesses, to testify of Jesus. John said that Jesus would baptize not only with the Holy Spirit but also with fire (Luke 3:16). You have the Holy Spirit with fire, but then you have the winnowing fork that Scripture says is throwing the chaff into that fire to be burned up.

Christians go through judgment, which is not a negative experience at all. With believers, the holy fire separates and discerns between what is of God and what is not. That is good. As a friend of God, you trust that He will prune you so that you are separated with only the good remaining (John 15:2). You want to trust God to remove the chaff.

John preached repentance and baptized people in water. Jesus also came preaching repentance and baptizing in water, but then expounded about ministry in the power of the Holy Spirit. Jesus said every believer would go out and do what He did. He prayed for those who would believe in the future, which was us (John 14:12; 17:20–23). Jesus wanted us to know that the same Father God that sent Him is also our Father. Jesus said that He treated them as friends, praying,

> *And the glory which You gave Me I have given them,*
> *that they may be one just as We are one: I in them,*
> *and You in Me; that they may be made perfect in one,*
> *and that the world may know that You have sent Me,*
> *and have loved them as You have loved Me.*
>
> —John 17:22–23

God is with you in a mighty way, but He is treating you as a friend. Out of intimacy, Jesus gives you information and revelation, yet He also expects you to manifest the same works He did.

2

HOLINESS IS YOUR PLATFORM

Because it is written,
"Be holy, for I am holy."
—1 Peter 1:16

When we encounter Jesus, we will experience a higher level, revealing how lukewarm we really are. You'll experience the heat of God's holiness when engaging the other supernatural realm. I felt that heat when He allowed me to walk on that holy sapphire floor in Heaven, which was way beyond anything I had ever experienced. After that, He took me into a room where I encountered the love of the Father as I had never had before. We can discover higher levels not only because God trusts us but also because He wants us to be transformed so that we may influence and help others.

When Jesus spoke, I was living far below what He had intended, yet when He explained the Scriptures, they became alive to me. I was in a deficit, even though I thought I was doing pretty well in this life. I was sent back with a new desire to walk closer to Him, and I knew I had to keep that level up. Well, how do you do that? You must expose yourself to more of what is true.

TRANSFORMATION IS UNCOMFORTABLE

It was no longer enough for me to pat people on the back, comfort them, and say they would make it so they would feel better. I did not want to minister to people's feelings. I would spend two hours talking and praying with someone, leave, and not even get home before they would call me for more prayer or want to come over. That is why I no longer minister in a private setting. They did not receive anything from what I was saying and doing. I could not effectively minister to people's souls.

People want to feel better, but sometimes, you don't feel better when you encounter the truth. Sometimes, you feel worse because you need correction so you can advance. The truth sets you free, but it does not always feel comfortable if you are in the wrong zone. Many psychological things relate to comfort, and it is not enough to comfort people where they are if you will not help them get to where they need to go. You have to tell them the truth, which means they might have to move and start to allow transformation, which is uncomfortable.

If you believe or are doing the wrong thing, it is very disappointing if you thought you were doing fine and weren't. Do you want to live the rest of your life feeling good but not encountering the truth? Or do you want to actually know the truth? I want to know the truth, even if it makes me uncomfortable. God gave me the revelation to change me, and then He sent me back, not for my benefit but to benefit others.

God wanted others to be influenced by the truth I had been shown. That was God's heart. It was not just about receiving revelation. Think about the apostle Paul. What if he decided not to write or talk about his revelations? I did that for many years. I held on to what happened to me for thirteen years. I didn't talk about it or write a book. I didn't do anything. I sat on it that long, and the Lord said, "You need to write about this and start talking about it." What if Paul had done the same thing? Eventually, I did write about it, and now I talk about it.

What if Paul had never written or shared? We would not have the revelation that he had, which really helps us. Ephesians, Colossians, and all the books Paul wrote have transformed me, and I know they have changed you. It is not enough to have the information. It has to transform you, and then you have to apply it to your words and deeds. It is all about you and how you affect your environment.

The devil is not afraid of someone who knows the truth because many people can spout off Scripture. However, do they apply it or understand what they are saying? Some Christians are like parrots repeating the Scriptures. A parrot doesn't know what he's saying or understand the language but just repeats what he hears as he is trained to do. It is entertaining but not effective. When you ask these believers how they are doing, they are doing terribly, yet the Scripture they just quoted is the answer to their problem. They never connect the truth to the reality of their everyday lives.

Christianity is about living where the rubber meets the road. I do not want to say or do anything if it does not help someone. If it adds to the problem, I don't want to say anything. I tried to help many people in my early days, but they did not apply what I said because they were in the soul realm. Jesus wants us to be transformed in our hearts, and He wants our souls to side with our hearts. The lack of application of truth is the problem.

When you get to Heaven, you will realize the value you had, but it will be too late to do anything about it down here. Your books will be sealed once you die, locked right then and there. When you leave your body, you cannot change anything. Whatever you did with what you were given, that's it. However, I did get another chance and was shown the right way to live. I got the inside scoop and was sent back to do it right. When I came back, I knew the truth, but I also knew I had to make a transition or transformation to be effective.

Every day since I came back to the earth has been an onslaught from the enemy to stop me from manifesting what I know to be true. Warfare is going on with all of us to prevent us from hearing and experiencing the truth. That is what I want for you—to hear and experience the truth. It is not enough to be a friend of God. Are you experiencing Him in reality every day? If you are not, I can help you, but that help will have to be a permanent transfer.

HOLINESS IS THE PLATFORM WHERE CONNECTION HAPPENS

You cannot keep hearing and hearing and then never understanding or doing anything. A time must come when you get it, and the light comes on. Warfare is a constant problem down here. Holiness is being separate and set apart; it is a platform, and you connect on that sapphire. In this world, satan is doing everything he can to convince, corrupt, and compromise people to be lukewarm so they can never experience this platform where the connection happens.

You are a friend of God because you are born again, but the yielding and the relationship part of it is up to you. When you reach the point of being done with the world, you will come out and be separate. However, you are supposed to have done that already. I want you to make that decision and allow experiential revelation to flow. It will not be a conscious thought process or repeating words like a parrot. I want you to encounter the heavenly sapphire.

> *The only way to relay the truth is to be set apart, encounter the holy sapphire, then speak from that platform to the people.*

You are valuable, and you do not have to go to Heaven to learn this because you might not be permitted to return. Many people have gone to Heaven, and they never wanted to return. Very few people get a chance to come back. I did get to come back, and the attack from the enemy has not been what you would think. The onslaught has been strongest against relaying the truth so that people get it.

The only way to relay the truth is to be set apart, encounter the holy sapphire, then speak from that platform to the people. It becomes permanent because that anointing and atmosphere come out of you when you speak from that place. It is eternal life. You move into a teaching gift when you speak from the Spirit. This proclamation from the prophetic means it is permanent in people that hear it.

DON'T LET THE DEVIL PULL YOU INTO HIS RING

Jesus is not just around you and sitting in Heaven—He is in you. He can be in multiple places at once and instantly travel. He is not restricted by distance, time, and space because it is all limitless in the Spirit. Jesus can speak to all of us so that we think we are the only ones and His most special people. Every one of us should feel that way.

> *You saw me before I was born. Every day of my life*
> *was recorded in Your book. Every moment was laid*
> *out before a single day had passed.*
> —Psalm 139:16 NLT

As this verse says, we all have a plan of God that has already been given to us and written down before we are born. Jesus will personalize that plan and work with us. He can do anything He wants in our lives in an instant. The fruit of what you see in this realm is based on our relationship and trust in Jesus. Those who want to go further and have set themselves apart will encounter that.

The trick of satan is to get people to come into his ring to start fighting him. He has the advantage in his environment and methods, so you cannot afford to be pulled into the soul realm or arguments. If people think badly of you, just let them believe that. Do not allow yourself to be drawn into that kind of fight. Do not defend yourself. The truth is the truth, and God will protect you.

If you let the devil pull you into his ring, he will beat you because he does not play by the rules or the standards of righteousness or justice. He will not come into the ring with you when you are in your environment of Heaven, in your calling, and on track. He won't touch you because you are in God's ring, and he can't win. He cannot beat you with God in there with you, so he tries to draw you away.

That is why the devil separated Eve in the garden, talked to her, pulling her into the deception first. Adam followed. You should learn a lesson from the devil's strategy and never allow yourself to be pulled out. God came and met with Adam and Eve and walked with them daily in the garden. Eve could have conversed with Him about all this. She should not have discussed these subjects with the devil and disobeyed God because someone else presented another view. This type of deception takes place every day; however, do not allow this to happen to you.

LIVE ACCORDING TO THE SPIRIT

When I was in Heaven, Jesus and the angels were with us, standing beside us. But I also noticed that Jesus is not just outside us but inside us. The Holy Spirit is not leading us by the arm, but He is literally inside us, talking to our spirit as our guidance system. Do not let satan, the flesh, or your attention draw you away. Always allow the Holy Spirit to have the top priority, and let His voice be the loudest. You get to know the Holy Spirit's voice by reading and constantly meditating on the Word of God. The Word has a voice, and the Word and the Spirit agree.

> *For if you live according to the flesh you will die; but if by the Spirit you put to death the deeds of the body, you will live. For as many as are led by the Spirit of God, these are the sons of God.*
>
> —Romans 8:13–14

If you live according to the Spirit, you will reap life and put to death the misdeeds of the body; however, you will reap death if you live according to the flesh. *You* must actively put anything contrary to the Spirit or the Word to death. *You* must put to death the misdeeds of the body by the Spirit. The Spirit tells you that you must put something to rest or eliminate it. The Spirit will tell you where you cannot go or what you cannot do; He is coaching you. Those who are led by the Spirit of God are the sons of God. Paul says that if you walk in the Spirit, you are a son of God. However, if you fulfill the lusts of the flesh, you will reap death (Galatians 6:8). Those who walk in the flesh cannot please God, which is pretty straightforward (Romans 8:8). If you want to please God, walk in the Spirit.

PULLING DOWN STRONGHOLDS

You have no reason to allow deception in your life any longer. I will not let deception come into my life nor allow people to pull me away. What is the Lord telling you right now? Is He speaking to you about all the great things He has for you? Or are you living in fear that something terrible will happen? I know how to combat satan and stand against fear. I do not allow satan to pull me into the realm or that ring of fear.

For the weapons of our warfare are not carnal but mighty in God for pulling down strongholds, casting down arguments and every high thing that exalts itself against the knowledge of God, bringing every thought into captivity to the obedience of Christ and being ready to punish all disobedience when your obedience is fulfilled.

—2 Corinthians 10:4–6

Paul teaches that the weapons of our warfare are not carnal but mighty in God to pull down strongholds. What could be a stronghold in your life? Could it be the unknown? Jesus said that the Spirit would tell you things to come (John 16:13). The Holy Spirit can give revelation concerning these strongholds. The weapons of your warfare are spiritual and come against anything that speaks louder in your life, like fear. God is love, and perfect love drives out fear (1 John 4:18). I will not allow satan to exalt himself by putting anxiety or fearful thoughts or feelings in my life. If my perspective is wrong, it needs to be confronted with God's perspective, which is where warfare happens.

Right now, allow the Holy Spirit to deal with you and get you to a place where you encounter the manifestation of the Spirit. If you know God's weapons are mightier, let Him have His way and remove fear. Bring into captivity any thought or anything against what you already know is God's will. Our flesh or analytical mind may be acting up, but we must never allow satan to question what God has already said or cause *us* to question what God has already said.

> *Now the serpent was more cunning than any beast of the field which the Lord God has made. And he said to the woman, "Has God indeed said, 'You shall not eat of every tree of the garden'?"*
>
> *And the woman said to the serpent, "We may eat the fruit of the trees of the garden; but of the fruit of the tree which is in the midst of the garden, God has said, 'You shall not eat it, nor shall you touch it, lest you die.'"*
>
> *Then the serpent said to the woman, "You will not surely die. For God knows that in the day you eat of it your eyes will be opened, and you will be like God, knowing good and evil."*
>
> —Genesis 3:1–5

You can see how satan planted deception by questioning Eve regarding what God actually said. After she engaged him, he lied, telling her that if she ate of the tree, her eyes would be opened, and she would become like God, knowing good and evil. But Adam and Eve were already like God.

> *But avoid foolish and ignorant disputes, knowing*
> *that they generate strife.*
>
> —2 Timothy 2:23

People will argue with you about the Bible but do not allow that to happen. If you win the argument, the person might not get saved. They might stay in deception and still go to hell. You have won an argument, but have you won them over? Arguing is often very unprofitable. You have to present the truth to a person, and then they must decide if they will follow it.

Christians need to be fully convinced of what they believe, and then, when they talk, they do not need to argue. They can just say, "This is what the Word of God says, and you need to decide whether to serve Jesus Christ. Do you want help from Heaven or not?" I put it right back on the person, but I don't argue with them because people will just think what they want. Do not get pulled into this deception. When satan conversed with Eve, he created a conspiracy or controversy that did not exist, which is where this type of dialogue eventually leads.

When I got saved, I gave my life to the Lord and was born again, and people criticized me. They said I needed to be rebaptized because I was sprinkled instead of immersed, so I was not saved. They argued with me against having to be born again to inherit the kingdom of God. The same thing happened with tongues, healing, and deliverance. People started arguing with me, and I needed to find the truth. I needed to stand on that holy sapphire, be set apart, and let the Holy Spirit burn impurities out of my life.

Jesus allowed me to have that experience with the holy sapphire so that I could bring it back and tell you. That is the kind of life you are supposed to live all the time. Even if you cannot look down at that floor and see the heavenly sapphire, it still exists. In the same way, the Holy Spirit is here right now, even if you don't see Him. You might not even feel Him, but it is not physical or emotional. The Holy Spirit is a Spirit, and He will influence you spiritually. If you feel emotion, that is just a bonus. You have to judge it by the Word of God. You cannot always go by your feelings.

PROCLAIM GOD'S WORD AND WILL

God created us as perfect at the inception of man. However, people are born into this broken and fallen world. They are born into sin, and they also learn how to sin. People can acquire it, which is why we cannot allow satan to influence our children or us. God never created man to be broken. We became broken, and this world is suffering because of it. There is so much harm that people need to be healed, delivered, and set free. They need salvation, the truth, and spiritual eyesight, which were all given to us through Jesus Christ. You must go out there and tell people about this gift, or they won't know.

> *It must get to the point where there is a manifestation—a tangible anointing and presence that permeates from my heart and affects the realm around me.*

We are encountering situations, and we have to live by faith. Every day, we must be on our game and pronounce God's will and His Word. Even if we do not see it happening, we must proclaim His Word because God will have His way with His people. What about the people that are going to hell? You have to tell them to make a decision. Are they going to live for God? Will they accept Jesus Christ, or will they go to hell? You have to tell them because they are deceived and don't know. They have to see something different about you.

I want to walk on the holy sapphire with God as a friend. It must get to the point where there is a manifestation—a tangible anointing and presence that permeates from my heart and affects the realm around me. I have seen the vilest evil people—hateful people who did terrible things and threatened to kill me. Yet after a while, they broke down because the power of God was stronger. I did not defend myself, and I did not get offended. I loved people and stayed at a distance, letting them decide. The love of God, His holiness, and the righteousness and justice of God became more tangible, and sometimes, it took years.

In some cases, I witnessed to people for years. One person took seven or eight years, and finally, one day, he broke. I prayed for him all the time, and I considered this person the most challenging case I ever had at my job at Southwest Airlines. Yet that person repented and gave his life to the Lord right there toward the end of my career. I had to fight that spirit constantly, but I would not compromise.

You need to put your foot down and tell the devil, "I am in authority here, and I have the name of Jesus, and I am trampling on serpents and scorpions and pushing you out. I am standing for God, and I will walk in holiness." Do not let satan make you compromise in any way. I have seen this happen in the body of Christ. The remnant needs to stand out and be separate. From there, you will have experiential knowledge, not just head knowledge.

3

BUILT UP INTO MATURITY

Greater love has no one than this, than to lay down
one's life for his friends.
—John 15:13

W e must experience the revelation in the Word of God because we need to understand and have this relationship with God as a friend. God has sown so much into the body, even in these days that we live. The body of Christ and the bride of Christ are evident in these New Testament times. From the time Jesus ascended on high and dispersed the gifts to all of us, the Holy Spirit and the baptism of fire are being poured out, and we are being built up into maturity. Paul talks about the fivefold ministry of the church equipping the body and building us up in unity and the maturity of the faith (Ephesians 4:11–16).

SOW THE WORD OF GOD INTO GOOD SOIL

But he who received seed on the good ground is he who hears the word and understands it, who indeed bears fruit and produces: some a hundredfold, some sixty, some thirty.

—Matthew 13:23

So much seed has been sown that I would have expected more of a harvest as we are coming to the end of the age. However, the Lord showed me that the parable of the sower only had a 25 percent return of the seed sown (Matthew 13:1–23). Only one field in four produced a crop, meaning only 25 percent was planted on good ground. Then out of that one field, some yielded thirtyfold, some sixtyfold, and some a hundredfold returns.

So shall My word be that goes forth from My mouth; It shall not return to Me void, But it shall accomplish what I please, And it shall prosper in the thing for which I sent it.

—Isaiah 55:11

When I am sowing the Word of God, it will never come back void. His word goes forth and returns with the intention that He had for it. The Word of God is incorruptible and produces fruit (1 Peter 1:23). As I sow the word to you, I am convinced I will get a hundredfold return. Not only will you have a crop, but it will be a hundredfold, and I believe that for your life.

More than two thousand years have passed since the time that Jesus taught that parable of the sower. Think about what should have come forth from all that seed. When you see what is happening in the world, you realize that we have to take care of the soil in people's hearts because the problem is with the condition of the soil.

When I pray with everything in my spirit, I believe I receive it, and when I don't see the answer, I am so surprised. When I see the corruption in the government, I am surprised after all the word that was sown and all the prayer that was prayed. I hoped to see more results from our prayers, but then I realized what happened. We must build up the body, which needs to agree that we may have a hundredfold return on the seed.

Jesus said that the soils represented men's hearts, and they must be receptive to the Word of God. Jesus talked about hindrances to receiving, so as a friend of God, you must allow God to show you any obstacles you may have. You might have hard ground, thorns, briers, or rocks in your heart. The soil might be shallow, and birds might come in and grab the seed before it takes root. Only one soil produced a crop from the seed. Jesus told me personally that if I help people's hearts by taking care of their hearts' problems, I could see increased reaping. If you sow the Word of God and it goes into good soil, you will get a harvest that could potentially be a hundredfold.

> *You need to develop good soil saturated with Heaven and the Word of God, creating an atmosphere where you grow.*

This parable and sowing seeds in nature directly correlate. Do you have the proper soil? Do you have the appropriate water, sunshine, and temperature? The environment must be correct to produce growth. Are you doing everything to create the proper atmosphere where you can grow? Are you doing what's necessary so your heart can be delivered of anything that is not helping? You need to develop good soil saturated with Heaven and the Word of God.

We could go beyond the limits in the parable of the sower because Jesus was talking about the soil condition, but He wasn't saying that condition was God's will. Imagine if everyone could apply this and ensure their soil was good and their heart was clear of anything that hindered their harvest. Imagine if everyone had the right temperature, sunshine, and the water of the Word being produced; what an excellent harvest we would have! I would be so happy because everyone would have a hundredfold return.

Then you could do the same for others; as a general rule, one person affects seven people. You can multiply each person you affect by seven. If I influence you, you influence seven people, and each of those seven influences seven more people, so that it increases exponentially. In that way, you have thirtyfold, sixtyfold, and a hundredfold. You replicate yourself multiple times, and if you do the calculations, you see what could happen. The potential is with one seed. If you keep planting it, it will only take about three years to have an incredible number of fields.

If you take a seed and plant it, producing wheat, then on each stalk, you have seven or eight heads with thirty-two seeds on each head. Then you take those seeds and keep planting them; by the third year, the harvest is astronomical. You have fields and fields and not just plants. The replication is truly exponential, and so it is with the Word of God. When God sowed Jesus, He got His whole creation back. He got human beings back, the entire family. He bought back all of humanity. However, how many really come into the kingdom of God? That has to do with this fallen world and the world's condition. Everyone should be saved, but they're not. Why? Because of free will.

BE COMMITTED TO GOD'S PLAN

> *Enter by the narrow gate; for wide is the gate and broad is the way that leads to destruction, and there are many who go in by it. Because narrow is the gate and difficult is the way which leads to life, and there are few who find it.*
>
> —Matthew 7:13–14

You enter the kingdom of God by the narrow way, but few find it, and they are the remnant. You want to be diligent and work with people, work with their soil and fertilize it, and do everything you can. God wants permanent disciples because He and Jesus are permanent. We are family to Him because we all came from Him. We cannot lose if we stay with Jesus, and as His friend, you are in it for the long run, committed forever. It's a covenant.

> *Then Jesus answered and said to them, "Most assuredly, I say to you, the Son can do nothing of Himself, but what He sees the Father do; for*

whatever He does, the Son also does in like manner."
—John 5:19

Jesus was committed to the Father because they were One in eternity. He came down to earth as the Son of Man and is committed to the plan for eternity. We see Jesus for a few years on earth as the Son of Man, but He was forever in existence long before that, so it is permanent. Jesus never did His own thing down here because He was committed to the plan. Jesus said that the Holy Spirit would not do what He wants but only do what the Father tells Him (John 16:13). The Holy Spirit does not speak on His own. Why? Because the Holy Spirit was sent as part of the plan too.

> *As a friend of God, you must establish your role in eternity in your heart, knowing that you are also part of His plan.*

Now we, as friends of God, are also committed to doing God's plan, which is eternal. However, many believers feel they have one hundred years, and it is so hard in this fallen world that they just want Jesus to come back. However, we are all part of a bigger plan, and God has already said that it will not be easy. Jesus said,

These things I have spoken to you that in Me you may
have peace. In the world you will have tribulation;
but be of good cheer, I have overcome the world.

—John 16:33

God wants to do His work through you with the Holy Spirit's help, just like He did through Jesus and the Holy Spirit. As a friend of God, you must establish your role in eternity in your heart, knowing that you are also part of His plan. You have to submit and only do what the Lord wants you to, just like everyone who came before you.

ALLOW GOD TO PREPARE YOU FOR THE GREATER WORKS

Grace and peace be multiplied to you in the
knowledge of God and of Jesus our Lord, as His
divine power has given to us all things that pertain
to life and godliness, through the knowledge of Him
Who called us by glory and virtue, by which have
been given to us exceedingly great and precious
promises, that through these you may be partakers of
the divine nature, having escaped the corruption that
is in the world through lust.

—2 Peter 1:2–4

Peter assures us we have been given these exceedingly great and precious promises. Through these, you can partake of the divine nature, having escaped the corruption in the world through lust. As friends, God will include you in secrets that He will not tell just anyone. Jesus said that a servant is not privy to the intimate details of their master's household and his dealings, but the children are (John 15:15). In other words, the children are included because they are part of the family.

We need to realize that we are in partnership with God and that He trusts us. As partners, we have no choice but to submit ourselves to the refining fire of the Holy Spirit. You must allow God to purge you and prepare you for the greater works (John 14:12). Even though we are born again, areas of our psychological and physical makeup need to be corrected, or the Holy Spirit will not have His way and will be grieved. You don't want that, and neither do I. Of course, God has already planned on taking care of that through the precious promises we have been given in which we can be partakers of the divine nature.

As believers, we have to study the Word of God and be disciplined to show ourselves approved, as Paul told Timothy (2 Timothy 2:15). Timothy was a disciple and instructed by Paul. God is guiding us Himself, helping us understand these matters.

In other words, Peter is saying that we need to understand certain matters and that we cannot fail if we apply them. He asked us to add to our faith all these other attributes so that through these qualities, we can be partakers of the divine nature, escaping the corruption in the world through lust (2 Peter 1:5–7).

GUARANTEED TO BE PRODUCTIVE

Jesus has sent the holy fire, and we can submit to that. We are supposed to judge ourselves so that we are not judged with the world (1 Corinthians 11:31). We are supposed to be separate from the world so that the world does not judge us because we have already judged ourselves. We must discern that God has called us to Himself and reject what the world offers.

Peter wanted us to understand how important it is to submit and allow these attributes of God the Father to be added to us so that we are godly. We are partakers of the divine nature and made in God's image as we allow Him to coach us into being friends. God includes us in this, but we must add certain things to our faith.

> *In view of all this, make every effort to respond to God's promises. Supplement your faith with a generous provision of moral excellence, and moral excellence with knowledge, and knowledge with self-*

control, and self-control with patient endurance, and patient endurance with godliness, and godliness with brotherly affection, and brotherly affection with love for everyone.

The more you grow like this, the more productive and useful you will be in your knowledge of our Lord Jesus Christ. But those who fail to develop in this way are shortsighted or blind, forgetting that they have been cleansed from their old sins.

So, dear brothers and sisters, work hard to prove that you really are among those God has called and chosen. Do these things, and you will never fall away. Then God will give you a grand entrance into the eternal Kingdom of our Lord and Savior Jesus Christ.

—2 Peter 1:5–11 NLT

The more you grow like this, the more productive and valuable you will be in the knowledge of our Lord Jesus Christ, and that is what we all want. Peter warns those who fail to develop in these ways that they will be shortsighted or blind. We know that we have been forgiven of our sins. We are not shortsighted or blind, but we need to make every effort to demonstrate that we really are in Jesus

Christ. God has called us and chosen us, but we need to make that call and election sure. We will never fall away if we do these things, which is a profound promise. In this way, we cannot fail and will always be productive.

Jesus gave us the Holy Spirit and the holy fire to bring us to a place where we are partakers of and then develop the divine nature. We add to our faith the attributes of the divine nature Peter listed for us. Remember that we will never be shortsighted because we do these things. We will not forget that we are forgiven of our past sins, will always be productive, and will not fail.

The key is personal development through cultivating the right environment for our soil to produce a hundred-fold crop of whatever was sown into us. You start by planting the Word of God into the soil of your heart; then, you constantly remind yourself that you are a partaker of the divine nature.

> *But you, beloved, building yourselves up on your most holy faith, praying in the Holy Spirit, keep yourselves in the love of God, looking for the mercy of our Lord Jesus Christ unto eternal life.*
>
> —Jude 1:20-21

Next, your top priority should be building yourself up in your most holy faith. Once you have faith, you should add these godly traits listed in 2 Peter 1:5–7, guaranteeing that you will be productive and not fail, which is what we want. In these last days, the Holy Spirit is leading us to receive instruction about the divine nature and being God's sons and daughters.

> *Not that I have already attained, or am already perfected; but I press on, that I may lay hold of that for which Christ Jesus has also laid hold of me. Brethren, I count not myself to have apprehended: but this one thing I do, forgetting those things which are behind, and reaching forward to those things which are ahead, I press toward the goal for the prize of the upward calling of God in Christ Jesus.*
> —Philippians 3:12–14

As Paul says, keep striving for the high calling in Christ Jesus. Take hold of that which Christ has already taken hold of for you. You must not let anything stop this endeavor and do not allow anyone or anything to ruin your momentum.

> *Assuredly, I say to you, among those born of women there has not risen one greater than John the Baptist;*

but he who is least in the kingdom of Heaven is greater than he.

—Matthew 11:11

Jesus said to the multitudes that everyone born until then was not as great as John the Baptist. What about Moses, Abraham, or Adam? John was greater in the kingdom than anyone else who had ever come. Then Jesus said that the least in the kingdom is greater than John. Why is that? In this day and age, Jesus made us sons and daughters of God, co-heirs with Him and heirs of God (Romans 8:17). This all started with Jesus; He accomplished it when He went to Heaven, then He sent the Holy Spirit to help us here on earth. The deal is sealed in Heaven, but God takes us through a process, exposing what hinders us. Our daily life becomes a journey of discovery.

I am always learning something about God and myself that I didn't know. I am constantly receiving and remain in discovery mode. I never know what my God will show me that I didn't see before, which has been happening for forty years. What do you think Enoch learned by to walking with God for three hundred years? Enoch was so advanced in the end that God just took him, and he never experienced death (Genesis 5:21–24). Enoch never experienced the sacrifice of Jesus or the gospel, yet he walked with God and pleased

God so much that he was taken. So how much more do we have access to in the New Testament? We don't have three hundred years, but we have a greater revelation than Enoch had because of the Holy Spirit and all the benefits of the new covenant. It took Enoch a while, but he still did it. We have the Holy Spirit, the actual Advocate, Comforter, and Counselor within us, and He wants us to walk in step with Him right now.

Walking with the Holy Spirit is easy, even though it can seem challenging. However, the Holy Spirit is not the one making it hard for us; the problem is that people are not submitting to the fire and are not allowing the chaff to be burned out of their lives. They are not going on to maturity but are still on milk instead of eating meat. God has given us the grace to reveal the goodness of God to people, which we need to show them so that they can repent. They need a revelation of how good God is, that He doesn't want us sick, poor, or in bondage. God wants us to be free. He has come to give us everything we need for life and godliness (2 Peter 1:3). He has given it to us through the gospel message, through Jesus Christ, and the blood. We need to preach that gospel message to all people. If they put their faith in Jesus, they will experience God's goodness, which will lead them to repentance (Romans 2:4). Paul said the goodness of God, not preaching the fear of hell and damnation, leads people to repentance. God wants to reveal Himself as a Father and Friend, which is what Jesus did. He redeemed us as children of God, not as slaves or servants.

4

HOLY FIRE IS YOUR FRIEND

O Lord, we have passed through Your fire; like precious
metal made pure, you've proved us, perfected us, and
made us holy.
—Psalm 66:10 TPT

We must understand that the holy fire is our friend and submit to it. I want you to get to where God has His way, and then you can teach this to other people. When you teach, you will have to help people apply what they hear because they need to walk in it. Jesus wants all of us to walk in the reality of being doers of the Word and not hearers only (James 1:22). We are not good hearers if we are not also doers of the Word.

Psalm 66:10 is packed with revelation, which is why we must read the Bible word for word. You cannot just skim over it quickly and then draw a conclusion. You must look at each word and ask why the psalmist or author used that word. Your judgment must be based on revelation and the fact that you read every word in context. Psalms is a very poetic book and was initially recited with music playing in the background. This verse is essential because of the secrets in it. Most people, when they read, will not grasp these concepts unless they carefully study them word for word as a student.

YOU MUST PASS THROUGH GOD'S FIRE
TO BE PERFECTED

The psalmist addresses Yahweh, the Lord God, saying, "We have passed through your fire." Remember that satan, your enemy, has fire as well, and he can curse, torment, and punish people. He comes to steal, kill, and destroy. Not all fire people go through is the fire of the Lord. I am not saying that God doesn't use difficulties, but your Heavenly Father, the Lord, will tell you not to touch something hot from the beginning. He doesn't wait for you to burn yourself and then tell you not to do that again. He knows your disobedience could result in getting burned or facing difficulties. God is not teaching you through killing, stealing, and destroying.

Whenever you see stealing, killing, and destroying in your life, in people's lives, your government, city, or nation, you already know that it is the enemy (John 10:10).

Jesus would tell you what you need to do as a friend because He cares about you and wants you to progress and mature. We sometimes learn by what we suffer, which can happen if we do not inquire of the Lord or submit to the fire. Sometimes we inquire of the Lord, but we do not obey Him.

When I am with someone who knows more than me, I don't talk, I listen. When I am being instructed, I ask questions because, in the past, I have walked away from people, realizing I didn't ask enough questions. I have met astronauts and test pilots and asked them questions about flight training that I might need to know at some point. But later, I thought about what else I should have asked them. After asking a question, I quietly listen and let them speak. When they stop talking, I ask another question, and then I stop talking and let them continue. I have sat and listened in some conversations for an hour straight, because I knew I was being instructed and taught.

Now if anyone builds on this foundation with gold,
silver, precious stones, wood, hay, straw, each one's
work will become clear; for the day will declare it,

because it will be revealed by fire; and the fire will
test each one's work, of what sort it is.

—1 Corinthians 3:12–13

Part of the purifying process is that the Lord will instruct you, but He will put you through His fire, which is your friend. The cleansing fire of the Holy Spirit, the baptism of fire, will eliminate and expose anything that is not pure gold, precious metals, or precious stones. The wood, hay, and stubble that Paul mentions will be burned up in the end. I asked for that to happen now in my life. Anything in me that is not right, I ask the Lord to expose it to the fire and submit to Him. I want to instruct you on this because Psalm 66:10 TPT says they had passed through *His fire.* There is a difference between refinement and the enemy coming in and killing, stealing, and destroying. Many people falsely attribute the enemy's works to God.

We must differentiate between the work of God versus the enemy, especially for today's unsaved people who think God is wreaking destruction on the earth, working through war, corruption, and injustice. Human behavior is corrupt; people with free will are siding with the enemy to steal, kill, and destroy. You cannot say that it is God. God doesn't need to kill, steal, and destroy to get what He wants, and He certainly does not have to do that with His children. He can talk to them. Remember, we are friends of God.

God places us in the purifying process of the Holy Spirit's fire; the Holy Spirit will expose and remove anything not of Him. The quicker you learn and submit to this, the faster you progress. You can take years to accomplish this if you want, but I would not recommend that. I recommend you submit to the fire, and you can get through the refining process in much less time. You can allow the Lord to start purifying you right away so that He can burn up what is not of Him. He will show you what you need to expose to the holy fire and let go of, which may not be for everyone.

What the Holy Spirit is showing you is personal because of your walk with Him. You are chosen, and He is preparing you. I can mentor you and speak into your life, but I cannot speak for you. I cannot assume that my process also applies to you because it may not. In general, I can say and teach what is in the Word of God.

Another aspect of the Lord's process is understanding that I will never do things others have been called to do because I have been chosen for a particular task. I am special forces and will do what God has asked me to do, which means I will be disciplined, walking a narrow way. In the same way, God's dealings will be geared toward you, your personality, your temperament, and what you are called to do.

I do not always speak against certain activities because some people might not be at that place yet. They don't want to be there, or God is not working with them yet. I respect people and their will. However, circumstances might be building up for war between nations because of all the current corruption in the world and what is happening in governments. The enemy, satan, has had his way for too long. I want the body of Christ to quickly mature in these last days so we can encounter the move of God that has already started on earth. As of this writing, in December 2022, His move has been going on for over a year.

At this point, I want everyone to submit to the holy fire, whatever that is for each believer. I long for this acceleration. Only precious purified metals like gold and silver will remain when you walk through the fire. Silver is symbolic of redemption, and gold is symbolic of the purest part of Heaven because it is clear. Gold is one of the most expensive precious metals on the earth. These days, other metals like platinum and titanium are more costly than gold because they are rare, but in the Bible, gold and silver are significant.

Psalm 66:10 says that only the precious metals will remain when we go through His fire because they are made pure through that heat. The process of purifying metal is first exposing it to very high heat. When heated, the impurities or dross separate, come to the surface, and can be scraped off, which leaves the pure metal. You can watch many videos that explain this process. The only thing left is pure metal because all the impurities have been taken out, and it is the same with us. We are put into a crucible with high heat, and God exposes all the impurities in us and removes them, leaving only pure, precious metal. Being approved or proven refers to going through the fire and leaving nothing but purity. That has to do with holiness and holy fire so that we are perfected.

That is what happens at the end of the age when we go to Mount Zion and see the spirits of righteous men made perfect (Hebrews 12:18–24). We are being tested in the crucible right now, and God is seeing who is really His. After we have gone through this test, perfection and purity come out on the other side, which is the process of being made holy. When you have been refined, God takes that pure metal of your life and puts it in His private stock, displaying you as His trophy.

Certain people have gone through the fire because you can see it in their faces and eyes. I met this type of person from time to time when I was first saved and throughout my college years. I have seen others at my meetings whom I have not met personally. There is a purity about them because they have gone through the crucible, and even though I have never met them, I can tell when a person has gone through the fire. They have brokenness and humility, and the beauty of the Lord shines through their faces, which is what I want. I know you want it too, and the Lord wants this for us also.

> *The preciousness of our faith tried in the fire shines like gold, like pure glistening gold, and shows up in the glory.*

You are just passing through the crucible and will not have to endure the intense heat forever. Once you have been tested, the experience seems to anchor in your soul. Many people tell me that they are never going back—one of the reasons is that they never want to go through that fire again. They have been proven, and they know the Lord is good. They know He is faithful, and they trust Him.

It is very counterproductive for the devil to push a person who has been through this crucible of fire. If he drives a person like this, they run into the fire, right into the glory, knowing that the recognition has to do with the fire. The fire seems to happen first, and then the glory comes. The preciousness of our faith tried in the fire shines like gold, like pure glistening gold, and shows up in the glory. The glory of God comes after the fire. You run to the glory when you need help and when you need to talk with your Father God. You run into the glory cloud with God when you need communion and fellowship, need to be strengthened, and need wisdom and knowledge. And because you have been purified, it won't harm you. Certain people cannot handle the strong presence or the glory of God. It is counterproductive for the enemy to pressure those who have been purified or do anything against them because they have learned they are not going back and will run immediately to God.

Every time King David sinned or faced a challenge, every time he had a victory, he always went in and met with God, no matter what. He always resolved issues with the Lord, making him a successful and popular king and a friend of God. These types of people are few and far between, and they have changed my life. I wish those people could live forever and be by my side in every part of my ministry. I always desire to have these types of people around me, and I believe God will send them to me. The devil leaves people alone who have been through the fire because they don't respond the way he wants them to, which is counterproductive for him.

KEEP GOD'S HOLY FIRE BURNING

When you are after God's heart, you feel a burning inside, a passion for living for God and doing what He wants, not what you want.

I want you to get to where you have been in the crucible and walked through the fire. You have come out purified on the other side, and the enemy does not want to deal with you anymore because whatever he does, you will just become like King David and run to God, seeking His heart. When you are after God's heart, you feel a burning inside, a passion for living for God and doing what He wants, not what you want.

Never restrain or put out the fire of the Holy Spirit.
—1 Thessalonians 5:19 TPT

Paul told the Thessalonians to keep that fire burning and not quench it. So how do we feed the fire? First, let the fire have its way but also enter the environment of fire: the throne room, the altar of God, and similar places. Picture the seraphim above God on His throne, pronouncing He is holy (Isaiah 6:1–4). Flames of fire are everywhere, and God loves the fire—that is where you have to make your home. Fire is your friend, and you do not have to fear it. You will have to get used to it anyway.

In Heaven, some people are not ready to go to the throne room immediately because of the intensity of what is happening there; you have to get used to the atmosphere. In different places in Heaven, you will experience the power of God as Isaiah did. You will experience God's presence and glory so that you will be undone as Isaiah was (Isaiah 6:1–8). He was a major prophet, and everything was fine with him until he saw the Lord high and lifted up and saw what was happening in God's throne room. He was undone and needed help immediately; this experience profoundly changed him. When Isaiah was sent back, he became one of the most fervent men of God and wrote sixty-six chapters in the Old Testament in his book, which was named after him.

You may want to be mentored but are limited because you need impartation, a touch from the other realm so that you change. As believers, we don't offer a religion to people. We offer a way of life where the breath of Heaven, the substance of Heaven, goes into a person's spirit, and they are born again. From there, a believer continues to grow and mature through the baptism of the Holy Spirit, the baptism of fire, the gifts of the Spirit, and the fruit of the Spirit. They receive ministry and speak forth the mysteries of God.

As you grow, it is as if you explode inside as you mature into what God has for you. If everyone would do this, even if only three hundred people expanded and allowed God to move them into maturity, those three hundred people could change the world. What if we had thirty million or three hundred million people like that? Before long, the whole world would listen to these messengers, and they would shake nations.

People must allow the holy fire to start to purify them. Unfortunately, that process usually takes a long time, but it shouldn't be that way. If everyone took a week off, closed themselves in, and saturated themselves with God's presence, they would see a tremendous change in their countenances and lives.

5

FAN THE FLAME

I am writing to encourage you to fan into a flame and
rekindle the fire of the spiritual gift God imparted to you
when I laid my hands upon you.
—2 Timothy 1:6 TPT

Paul mentored Timothy, encouraging him to rekindle the fire of the spiritual gift that God imparted to him. Paul released an impartation to Timothy, and he was saturated, so Paul told him to fan this into a flame and rekindle the fire. So, you need to saturate yourself by attending conferences, watching videos, taking courses, reading books, and listening to teachings. By doing this, you are fanning what has been imparted into a flame. It is already there, but

God knows that in this fallen world, in this state that we live in, we need to rekindle the fire and fan it into flame.

THE EFFECTS OF THE SPIRIT OF GOD

The Holy Spirit is an actual Person that we cannot see, but we can see His effects. Jesus was trying to explain this to Nicodemus when He said it wasn't necessary to go back to your mother's womb to be born again (John 3:1–8). The new birth happened in your spirit, and a person could be born again of the Spirit. Jesus explained it like this:

> *The wind blows where it wishes, and you hear the sound of it, but cannot tell where it comes from and where it goes. So is everyone who is born of the Spirit.*
>
> —John 3:8

The wind is invisible, but you can see its effects as it blows through the trees, making them sway. In the same way, you cannot see the Spirit of God, but when He is blowing and moving, you can see the effects. Remember, the Holy Spirit is an actual person.

Timothy was a young pastor, being prepared by Paul. Timothy had been given spiritual gifts when Paul laid hands on him. Paul reminded Timothy that he had a fire inside, which he needed to rekindle by fanning it into flame. Apparently, when Paul laid his hands on Timothy, fire fell, and in the books of 1 and 2 Timothy, Paul is writing to Timothy to encourage him. Paul wanted him to rekindle the fire by fanning it. When only coals are left in the fire, it is red hot, but there are no flames. You have to rekindle it by putting wood in it and blowing on it or fanning it back into flame to get oxygen to it. The air accelerates the flames so that they return. Paul said that Timothy only needed to fan the gift inside him back into flame, which pertains to all of us. It is time to fan the fire within us into flames.

All of us have the fire of God because we have the Holy Spirit inside us. We all have spiritual gifts because Paul said that the Spirit gives gifts severally as he wills to each individual (1 Corinthians 12:11). God has already chosen which of the nine gifts of the Spirit is assigned to each of us. Whatever you are supposed to do, through whatever gifts are inside you, you need to do with the faith given to you.

> *Having then gifts differing according to the grace that is given to us, let us use them: if prophecy, let us prophesy in proportion to our faith: or ministry, let us use it in our ministering; he who teaches, in teaching;*

he who exhorts, in exhortation; he who gives, with liberality; he who leads, with diligence; he who shows mercy, with cheerfulness.

—Romans 12:6–8

If you are supposed to prophesy, you need to prophesy the deep mysteries of the kingdom and speak God's heart. Prophecy is speaking God's heart and intention as you speak out what He is saying. It doesn't matter whether it looks like it will happen. You keep saying and reinforcing it as God calls those things that are not as though they were (Romans 4:17). A war is going on down here; if you do not actively engage the Holy Spirit and speak forth, they will not happen. God does not always get His way because a war is going on down here, and satan comes to kill, steal, and destroy. We need to reinforce God's will by speaking His heart and not allowing satan to rob from us.

And I will give you the keys of the kingdom of Heaven, and whatever you bind on earth will be bound in Heaven, and whatever you loose on earth will be loosed in Heaven.

—Matthew 16:19

Whatever we bind is bound; if we don't bind it, it will not be bound. Often corruption takes place, allowing satan gets away with many schemes in our lives and even in our governments because we do not actively stand up and speak in the power of the Holy Spirit to confront them. Many harmful circumstances happen because of the lukewarmness of the body of Christ that Jesus warned us about (Revelation 3:16). But they should not be permitted at all. We need to get hot again, and Paul told Timothy how to do that.

The apostle Paul was a mighty man of God, and God imparted these spiritual gifts to Timothy through his hands. Paul must have gotten an alert in his spirit that these gifts were not manifesting in Timothy as they should have. Timothy may have fallen back and gotten cool instead of remaining hot. Whatever the reason, Paul told Timothy that the fire would not be rekindled if he didn't fan the flames, which is not being taught today. I was never told this in any religious circles I was part of.

GOD IS WAITING FOR YOU TO MOVE

You could wait forever for God to move, and He might not because He is waiting for you. That is why Smith Wigglesworth said if God is not moving, he moves God. How did he do that? By his faith. People did that all the time in the Bible. At times, Jesus was not going to do anything, and then suddenly, He acted because of the person's faith. Jesus responded to their faith in situations where He would not have acted apart from it.

At times, people's faith surprised Jesus. On one occasion, in a multitude of people, someone touched Jesus, and virtue came out of Him (Luke 8:43–48). He looked around and asked, "Who touched Me?" The disciples observed the many people who were around Him, touching Him. Jesus told the disciples that someone had touched Him, and an impartation from Heaven came out from Him. Then they found the woman who believed that she would be healed if she only touched the hem of Jesus's garment. Her faith drew it out from Jesus.

If you do not respond to the Lord's instructions and put your faith into action, you will not see the results you want. For example, if you're going to get out of debt, you will have to attack it like you are coming at a monster because debt is an evil monster from the pit of hell. If you do not come at it with all you have, it will win against you because it's such a massive stronghold. It has to do with satan himself and his merchandising in this world. He has corrupted this world system, and if you do not come at him aggressively with faith and action, you will not see debt removed from your life.

> *Even if you have to prophesy to yourself, your family, or your house, you need to speak forth God's mysteries and intentions.*

To be on fire for God, you must recognize that God has given you precious promises and deposited gifts inside you through the power of the Holy Spirit. They are within you. However, you must act on those promises and gifts. I draw out of those wells and out of that river of life in me. I want everyone to experience that flow from Heaven, so I have to aggressively place a demand on that. At times, I have to be as tenacious as a bulldog because this world wants to put us all to sleep. It wants to get you nice and comfortable so that you lay back and let corruption rule and reign. It doesn't want you to say or do anything but just back off. However, that will not happen in this generation because everyone is called to the fire. Fan it into a flame so the Holy Spirit burns brightly, whatever God has placed inside you. I do not know your gifts, but the Holy Spirit does, and you must find out what they are. Let the Lord show you and then exercise them.

Even if you have to prophesy to yourself, your family, or your house, you need to speak forth God's mysteries and intentions. I spoke over my life, my house, my wife, and our debt for seven years, and nothing of consequence seemed to happen. Suddenly, everything started getting paid off at the end of those seven years, which was profound. Even when it looked like nothing was going to happen, yet it did happen. What would have happened if we hadn't been diligent and pressed through those walls? What if we hadn't spoken? It would have never happened, but it was God's will the whole time. We were being stolen from the entire time; sometimes, we did not even know it. What about you? What about *your* life and ministry? What if it is time to be tenacious and fan that into flame and call forth the gifts of God within you?

For years, I constantly called forth the gifts of God in me. I would prophesy to myself and call forth the gift of prophecy, the word of wisdom, the word of knowledge, and the gifts of healing. I would also speak against debt and anything else that was of the devil and hell. Yes, that is aggressive, but isn't God aggressive? Isn't fire aggressive? Scripture tells us that our God is a devouring fire (Hebrews 12:29). That sounds aggressive because fire is always looking for more fuel and constantly expanding outward, devouring anything in its path. God is like that and wants to consume us in His holiness. Why? Because then nothing will stand between Him and us.

HOLY FIRE SETS US APART

There has consistently been a problem with people who get firm about their position in Christ. They quote the Scriptures saying that Jesus Christ has done all these things for us—we are the righteousness of God in Him, and we are holy as He is holy. Yet these people deal with many issues; they fall into sin and have all this trouble. They constantly talk about their position in Christ but do not seem to have the victory.

> *Behold what manner of love the Father has bestowed on us, that we should be called children of God! Therefore the world does not know us because it did not know Him. Beloved, now we are children of God; and it has not yet been revealed what we shall be, but we know that when He is revealed, we shall be like Him, for we shall see Him as He is. And everyone who has this hope in Him purifies himself, just as He is pure.*
>
> —1 John 3:1–3

When I was in Heaven, I realized we were victorious because of our relationship with God. The relational part of holiness is that we separate ourselves from the world because we love God and know our value and purpose in Him. We have a revelation of His love for us, which is not a position but is about our relationship. I got to where I did not do certain things because I knew God didn't want me to do them. Your behavior is affected when you love God, but holiness is not behavior. Holiness is the fact that God bought us and owns us; because we are His children, He puts us on display in His house. Then the Father sits and stares at us and adores us because we are His, which is private because God wants us for His very own. He does not need to display us to the world, but He does.

I don't think of holiness as a position or behavior anymore; I think of holiness as ownership. God highly values each of us and wants us for His own, so He bought us. Then God cleans us up, purifies us, and sets us on display for Himself. God has something so valuable that He would not even let anyone touch it or have it, which is the highest value.

> *The world does not want us because it cannot handle us, but God can.*

Holy fire is essential for life because it keeps us in holiness, God's will, and love. We burn for Him and are set apart. The world does not want us because it cannot handle us, but God can. It is all about ownership, which is what the holy fire is. When you restrain holy fire, you are slowing down an inevitable process. I would rather you run into the fire, submit to it, and let it have its way because that's the goal anyway.

You do not want to be like the Israelites, who took forty years to cover a journey that could have taken two and a half weeks. The Israelites went through that season for forty years in the desert, which revealed what was in their hearts. They were judged and purified, and only two made it through the desert to lead the next generation into the promised land (Numbers 32:11–12). Due to that first generation's unbelief, all except Joshua and Caleb fell in the desert (Hebrews 3:17–19). God wants to mentor and coach us, but He does it as a loving Father who disciplines us.

You have free will, but consider the account of the Israelites in the desert and accelerate your destiny by taking the two-and-a-half-week journey into the promised land instead of their journey of forty years, which was unnecessary. Even though we gained revelation from their forty-year journey, it was not God's perfect will. In addition, consider that God wanted to be the king of Israel, but they did not want Him. Instead, they wanted a man, which hurt God (1 Samuel 8:4–22). Life can go wrong when we want our own way; for the Israelites, it did not work out, which history shows us.

A LIVING SACRIFICE

I beseech you therefore, brethren, by the mercies of God, that you present your bodies a living sacrifice, holy, acceptable to God, which is your reasonable service.

—Romans 12:1

In this verse, Paul talks about how we need to offer ourselves to God. God does not just come after you; He wants you to come to Him. Paul is talking about an altar here where you put your living body. You do not sacrifice yourself—it is a *living* sacrifice where you are on fire in everything you do. God provides that fire in everything about us and everywhere we walk as we present ourselves to Him through it all.

Many read Romans 12:1 and declare, "I am a sacrifice, and I put myself on the altar." However, we do not realize that our will is tested in many situations. We are tested anytime we are pushed to defend ourselves; instead, the Lord wants us to remain silent while He defends us. Or when He tells us He has a different plan for us, you have to deny yourself. At that point, you realize that you are a living sacrifice, which is holy and acceptable unto the Lord. Many times during the day, I want to do certain things, and the Lord will say, "No, you are not going to do that. I have a better way." So He shows me a better way. My will is breaking as I offer my body as a living sacrifice.

> *Your ears shall hear a word behind you, saying,*
> *"This is the way, walk in it," whenever you turn to*
> *the right hand or whenever you turn to the left.*
> —Isaiah 30:21

Jesus taught me how to submit to Him and remain on the altar, offering my body and soul, which is the secret of what He walked in. I would go in a specific direction and even tell other people what we were going to do, and then the Lord would say what He wanted me to do. Well, I would have to reroute myself and get everyone else to go in that new direction. Sometimes that would happen at the last minute, so I had to bend to what the Lord was saying. Until a certain point, we might be misinformed, or the Lord might not say anything until the last minute, causing us to shift. It wasn't that God changed; He illuminated your progressive revelation of that situation, and you understood something new.

The Lord will let you go a certain way for a certain amount of time, and then He will bring correction or give you truth or insight. So you have to be ready for that, which is the altar experience we are walking in all the time. It is unlike the altar in Heaven with the holy fire, the burning coals, and other holy items. An altar is always there wherever you go, and I always see this altar in my mind's eye. That altar is your will bending, presenting your body as a living sacrifice. You allow the Lord to change your walk, plans, schedule, or mode of operation, and you will do it. It is a bending of your will, and then your body and mind will follow what you know is right. You will not always know everything; however, when God leads you in a particular direction, keep moving and let Him guide and direct you. You will know God's holy and acceptable will by consistently putting yourself on the altar.

> *I have been crucified with Christ; it is no longer I who live, but Christ lives in me; and the life which I now live in the flesh I live by faith in the Son of God, who loved me and gave Himself for me.*
>
> —Galatians 2:20

Think about what Paul said here in Galatians. Jesus Christ is living in you and has taken over your life, so He is actually living His life through you. In that case, you yield to Him on the altar, and when Jesus wants to go in a specific direction or do a certain thing, then all you have to do is back off and let Him do it. That is placing yourself on the altar; you can experience this all the time.

You might be at the drive-thru window paying for your food, and the Lord tells you to ask the person at the window how much the bill is for the person behind you and then pay it. You have to be willing because you might be in a hurry or do not want to spend your money, but the Lord is telling you what to do. It might be a test to see if you will be obedient because He is about to do something for you, which is part of your entrance into that. There is a death to self, a death that comes when Jesus wants to minister to those people behind you. When you do what the Lord asks, the angels record it every time. The Lord remembers and rewards you at a later time. When a huge breakthrough comes, the Lord reminds me it was because of what I did that day at the drive-thru. The Lord remembers. That is part of the process of holy fire. You lay yourself on the altar and allow Jesus to live through you, which becomes an amazing time of sacrifice.

> *Then Jesus said to His disciples, "If anyone desires to come after Me, let him deny himself, and take up his cross, and follow Me. For whoever desires to save his life will lose it, but whoever loses his life for My sake will find it."*
>
> —Matthew 16:24–25

If you want to gain your life, you have to lose it, which means yielding to Jesus and allowing Him to live through you. Losing your life does not mean you die physically, but your will is bent toward

God, and He wins. It is part of the discipline of taking that yoke upon you and letting the Lord teach you.

6

SHIFT YOUR PERCEPTION

And you shall know the truth, and the truth
shall make you free.
—John 8:32

So many feel-good messages are out there, but they rarely teach about discipline and sacrifice. We are not hearing the holy fire preaching that causes people to change. The feel-good messages won't help us. I don't want people to feel good in their souls and then walk out of a meeting defeated because the spiritual part of them won't engage the enemy with tenacity and with holy fire. I want a bunch of seasoned warriors that are strengthened and moved in their spirit so that their soul surrenders and they have that satisfaction of living a crucified life in Christ. They heard truth and were transformed very deep within themselves. That transformation came into the soul. Jesus said many profound things, but they were hard.

> *Then Jesus said to them, "Most assuredly, I say to you, unless you eat the flesh of the Son of Man and drink His blood, you have no life in you."*
>
> —John 6:53

> *Jesus was saying that unless you take Him into yourself, count the cost, and discern what is happening here, you will not last.*

That day, many people stopped following Him. In fact, so many people left that Jesus stood there and asked His disciples if they were going to leave too (John 6:67). Jesus was saying that unless you take Him into yourself, count the cost, and discern what is happening here, you will not last. Jesus was preparing them for warfare. It is incredible how much is available to us and how people want everything but do not want to pay for it.

WALKING IN THE FIRE IS A COMMITMENT

When I was in Heaven, I saw the different levels of people that came in. They all had a story and a testimony, but there were different levels. Down here on earth, there are different levels of commitment and productivity. People have specific talents but steward them differently; therefore, there are all kinds of rewards, depending on the level. In Heaven, I saw that we were all supposed to be very hot and productive, and we were all supposed to encounter the holy fire. Our goal was to be in the hottest spot in Heaven and experience that holy fire while on earth.

Because people were not hot, many things were permitted on earth that were not supposed to happen. Many situations looked like God had failed, but it was not God's fault. The church and the people simply had not done their part. There was an authority on the earth, but it wasn't Jesus because He was in Heaven with the Father. The church was baptized in the Holy Spirit with power and was supposed to be binding and loosing (Matthew 18:18). Whatever they permitted was permitted, and whatever they forbid was forbidden.

The people who knew how to pray and did not take no for an answer always got their prayers answered, but only a few people were like that. Groups of people were here and there, but it was supposed to

> *The process of the holy fire gets people to the place where they yield in intercession, knowing that God wants to do it, so they don't let go; they keep going after it.*

be the whole church. Think about the narrow way and the remnant. Imagine if out of seven and a half billion people on the earth, just two hundred million were part of the remnant on the narrow path, praying in unity. If they were all praying and agreeing on earth that what is in Heaven is coming to earth, that agreement would be powerful enough to push back the enemy. All witchcraft, demons, the occult, and satanists would be forbidden to operate, no matter what. The church would be hot. If we could find even thirty people who could pray and get a hold of God and get everything they asked for, they would make a significant impact.

So I am searching for those types of people and training people to pray, people who don't take no for an answer. They will keep going after it until God manifests and they get what they asked. The process of the holy fire gets people to the place where they yield in intercession, knowing that God wants to do it, so they don't let go; they keep going after it.

> *For I received from the Lord that which I also delivered to you: that the Lord Jesus on the same night in which He was betrayed took bread; and when He had given thanks, He broke it and said, "Take, eat; this is My body which is broken for you; do this in remembrance of Me." In the same manner He also took the cup after supper, saying, "This cup is the new covenant in My blood. This do, as often as you drink it, in remembrance of Me."*
>
> —1 Corinthians 11:23–25

Jesus wanted that type of person, but look what happened when He announced that you have to eat His flesh and drink His blood, referring to the communion table. He was talking about taking in the bread of Heaven and that we needed His blood in our spiritual veins. We needed to eat the bread that came down from Heaven, His body. It was the Word of God, and Jesus is the Word. We drink of the Spirit and the life of God. Life is in the blood (Leviticus 17:14).

God wants us to partake of Jesus, the pure Word from Heaven, and His blood so we can become one with Him. The masses who followed Jesus were not that committed. They loved to be fed by Him and to see miracles. They wanted to be healed and delivered.

They sat and listened to Him all day, but they could not handle what He was saying regarding a commitment.

Walking in the fire and this intimacy are commitments. The kingdom of Heaven is not from this earth. A time will come when something from the other realm has to come into this realm, and it changes us; then, we are not from here anymore. Suddenly, we are just visiting here, we are strangers, and Heaven is our home. People don't get that and try to fit in, not understanding why they are being rejected. The whole idea of being a Christian is that we are from another kingdom and do not belong here. We are here to do the mission God has asked us to do.

> *Again, the kingdom of Heaven is like treasure hidden in a field, which a man found and hid; and for joy over it he goes and sells all that he has and buys that field. Again, the kingdom of Heaven is like a merchant seeking beautiful pearls, who, when he had found one pearl of great price, went and sold all that he had and bought it.*
>
> —Matthew 13:44–46

These parables in Matthew 13 support the idea of being a Christian, putting yourself on the altar, and always walking in the fire. It is about knowing that your life is not your own and that when you find Jesus, you see the truth and sell everything you have. You give up everything because you have discovered treasure that is not from this world. Jesus said that when a wise man found the pearl of great price, he sold everything he had to buy it. When you find Jesus, you leave everything to follow Him. You want and desire Him only.

> *Jesus answered them and said, "Most assuredly, I say to you, you seek Me, not because you saw the signs but because you ate of the loaves and were filled. Do not labor for the food which perishes, but for the food which endures to everlasting life, which the Son of Man will give you, because God the Father has set His seal on Him."*
>
> —John 6:26–27

Sometimes, your perception needs to shift. This happened when Jesus dropped these hard sayings on the people, knowing they had a choking point. He probably did it on purpose because many came only to see the miracles and be fed. They took advantage of Jesus for their physical needs and were not embracing Him. True believers, true disciples, dedicate their whole lives to following Jesus. They embrace Him and become sons and daughters of God.

Right now, we are in that narrow way where division and separation have already happened. Suddenly, people are starting to count the cost of what they thought Christianity was, realizing that it is not convenient anymore. For whatever reason, a shift occurred, and they decided they could not continue being Christians. They have reached a choking point because it is not convenient anymore and is not working for them. Christianity is a lifestyle; being a believer is who we are and what we do. We are believers, but that belief manifests in different ways. The gospel, the good news, is supposed to be preached; if people do not know that God is good, they cannot preach the good news. Many Christians seem to focus on the negative and the bad news.

Throughout the years, I have seen trends go in cycles. One example is people who wait around, expecting the antichrist to come with plagues, bowls of wrath, and seals to be broken (Revelation 16:1–17). Paul mentioned this trend in 2 Thessalonians 2:1–4. He had to tell the Thessalonians, who were quitting their jobs, what would have to happen before the antichrist appeared. Paul had to tell them that if they did not work, they would not eat. He encouraged them to return to work (2 Thessalonians 3:10).

Before Jesus returns, certain things have to happen first, and the son of perdition, the antichrist, will not be exposed until these particular things happen. Paul wrote to the Thessalonians between 60 and 80 AD. We are now in the year 2023, and it still has not happened. Back then, circumstances looked so hostile to the believers that they were quitting their jobs, expecting Jesus to return immediately. How many cycles of anticipating the end times have we gone through since then that have not brought forth the antichrist?

> *And this gospel of the kingdom will be preached in*
> *all the world as a witness to all the nations, and then*
> *the end will come.*
>
> —Matthew 24:14

The gospel must be preached in all the world, and *then* the end will come. Every generation wants to usher this in, yet the harvest must come in first. A certain number of souls must be alive and born into the kingdom. Throughout the ages, the destinies of people and nations must come at a specific time the Lord has already preordained. Certain people, ethnic groups, and countries have to be on the earth, and particular events must happen. It is not for us to know but only for our Heavenly Father to understand (Matthew 24:36).

Since Paul wrote to the Thessalonians, millions and millions of people have lived and died. I would rather we yield to the fire, let

God purify us, and find that narrow way. Even if we are a small group of people, we will not believe that the end is coming until we preach the gospel. When we tell people how good God is and preach the good news of the gospel and do what Jesus told us to do regarding the gospel's message, we will see the harvest and the fruit of that. I prefer to reveal the goodness of God, which leads people to repentance, then constantly teach about Revelation and all the terrible things that are coming on earth (Romans 2:4). I don't think a generation has lived when it did not look like the end was near.

Right now, Jesus is seated at the right hand of the Father. Paul said that when Jesus came, He destroyed the works of the devil and made a show of them openly, triumphing over them in it (1 John 3:8; Colossians 2:15). As believers, Jesus wants us to lay hands on the sick so that they will recover. He wants us to drive out demons, raise the dead, speak in tongues, and announce the year of Jubilee and that debts are forgiven (Mark 16:17–18; Luke 4:18–21). His will is that we tell people that their sins are forgiven, and they need to accept Jesus, the only way and the key to eternal life (John 14:6). Jesus has already paid for them to go to Heaven. If a person verbally accepts that and believes in their heart, they will be saved. We should be sharing this message.

However, some of us continually expect something terrible to happen, like an earthquake or disaster, and we only wait for the next person to prophesy it. And that will probably happen, but that does not mean the end is coming. Instead, we should be binding and loosing, forbidding injustice from ruling and reigning in our governments (Matthew 16:19). We need to take control and prophesy what God wants in our nation, in the world, over our church, and in our location. We need to be prophesying and saying what God wants, even if it looks like it will not happen, because you still have to say what God is saying.

As I mentioned before, amazingly, the Israelites took an extra forty years to get to the promised land when it was a two-and-a-half-week journey, which was not God's fault. Joshua and Caleb did everything right, but they had to suffer for forty years while all their friends and family died, but people sometimes suffer for the sins of others. It was not God's perfect will, but God used it, and it is the same with us now.

DENY YOURSELF, PICK UP YOUR CROSS, AND FOLLOW JESUS

What happens when you prophesy and the situation shifts? Because it will, but it will take the diligent people that partake of the body and the blood of Jesus, the ones committed to denying themselves and picking up their cross. These people will experience the fire, but they will also see prophecy fulfilled and God's heart done on the earth. It is one thing to know God's will and have it proclaimed. However, think about all the prophecies that have come forth that never came to pass because people did not repent. They didn't turn from sin or apply what they heard.

Think of Israel. Jesus prophesied and all the prophets prophesied over Israel but look at what has happened throughout history. They have been destroyed and slaughtered many times, but this was never God's will. A point will come when you listen to what God is saying, realizing He has plans for you to prosper and have an expected end, like Jeremiah prophesied to Israel (Jeremiah 29:11). Hundreds of years after Jeremiah prophesied that word of God, Jerusalem was destroyed in 70 AD, which was not God's will. God's will was that they would hear the word from His heart through His prophets, embrace it, and act on it. Jesus prayed over Jerusalem,

> *O Jerusalem, Jerusalem, the one who kills the prophets and stones those who are sent to her! How often I wanted to gather your children together, as a hen gathers her chicks under her wings, but you were not willing.*

> —Matthew 23:37

Jesus revealed God's heart and intention for Israel, but it didn't happen, and they killed Jesus. The Israelites rejected Him and did not discern who Jesus was, completely missing out. Now the Gentiles, all of us, get to partake of the heavenly gift, but Jesus was first sent to the lost sheep of Israel (Matthew 15:24).

> *But He answered and said, "It is not good to take the children's bread and throw it to the little dogs." And she said, "Yes, Lord, yet even the little dogs eat the crumbs which fall from their masters' table." Then Jesus answered and said to her, "O woman, great is your faith! Let it be to you as you desire." And her daughter was healed from that very hour.*
>
> —Matthew 15:26–28

This Gentile woman was a foreigner, yet Jesus gave her what she wanted because of her faith. So now, Gentiles are encountering Jesus and are the focus until this part of God's plan is over, and then it will turn back to the Jews (Romans 11:25).

YOUR AGREEMENT WITH GOD MUST BE HEARTFELT

When Paul told Timothy to fan the flame of the gift in him, there were two parts: It was already in him, but he needed to do something about it. It would not have happened if Timothy hadn't acted on it or if Paul hadn't reminded him to think about those two things. Being just like us, Timothy would have let it go and then, after a while, thought, *If God wants His way, He can have His way.* Christians do this all the time, and it has got to stop. We can mentally agree that God will take care of a problem or situation, but that is not enough. Your faith must be heartfelt, the type of agreement that wins battles and gets you through the war. Heartfelt agreement will cause you to triumph over your enemy. Your adversary is vicious, so you must be tenacious and speak from your spirit, saying, "Thus saith the Lord, I will take care of that. I will move." If you start to yield to the Spirit and what God is saying and speak that, it is entirely different from just mental agreement. You must know what God is saying and then speak it from your heart.

Many times, God's will is not done. I have been around groups of people and knew what God wanted, but it never happened because they were not all on the same page. Imagine what it's like to get a whole nation on the same page so that there's an overthrow of the enemy. It takes a lot of people getting together and agreeing, but it starts with just a few. God is moving upon people now, their perception is changing, and they are not focused on the end times. They are focused on the harvest, on "thus saith the Lord," and God has good plans for us to prosper and have an expected end.

Think about the financial struggle that many people are going through right now. You may be one of the many who needs help. Yet they are unsure if God wants to help them or prosper them. They are facing an internal battle causing them to believe lies such as, "God keeps me poor because it keeps me humble" and similar ideas. But Deuteronomy in the Old Testament says this:

> *Except when there may be no poor among you; for the Lord will greatly bless you in the land which the Lord your God is giving you to possess as an inheritance—only if you carefully obey the voice of the Lord your God, to observe with care all these commandments which I command you today. For the Lord your God will bless you just as He promised you; you shall lend to many nations, but you shall not borrow; you shall reign over many nations, but they shall not reign over you.*
>
> —Deuteronomy 15:4–6

We are questioning if God wants us to prosper us or if He wants to help us, but He doesn't even want any poor among us. It is not just you. How about everyone? God's will is that all Christians may prosper (3 John 1:2). God has blessed us. Right here and now, you must change your mind and your perception. Once you get a group of people like that, they can affect even more people. Holy fire exposes and overthrows lies in our own lives, and then it should spread to others.

7

CHANGE YOUR MENTALITY

Are you so foolish? Having begun in the Spirit, are you
now being made perfect by the flesh?
—Galatians 3:3

In the Old Testament, people commonly knew that if you made a covenant with God and loved and obeyed Him, He would take sickness and poverty away from your midst. In the old covenant, He said no poor would be among you (Deuteronomy 15:4–6). In the New Testament, Jesus gave us an even better covenant (Hebrews 8:6–8).

When Jesus was a child, He was taught the Old Testament and learned the Pentateuch, which are the first five books of the Bible. The fifth book of the Bible was Deuteronomy, so Jesus grew up believing these words. As a child, Jesus was taught truths, such as lending to many nations and not borrowing. In the New Testament, when Jesus came, He believed that there would be no sick, poor, or tormented Christians among them. He believed and declared that all the demons would have to leave and you would live a full life. Believers are not meant to borrow from anyone but should lend to many nations; everyone would fear the people of God, but they would not fear any nation.

JESUS GREW UP BELIEVING IN THE OLD COVENANT

Jesus became the executor or the overseer of a better covenant called the new covenant, and He *was* the new covenant. He became a better covenant, and satan knows this, which is why satan planned to flip the whole script and deceive people. The enemy convinced people that we could not prosper in the New Testament. He wants people to believe that if you get sick, God might heal you, but He might not. These thoughts are terrible and all wrong, and Jesus was not brought up to believe this way.

The apostle Paul didn't believe that you had to borrow from people. He knew that Israel was supposed to lend to many nations. So why should we be part of a fraudulent faith? Why should we believe that God must have changed His mind and backed off in the new covenant about some of these truths? No, Jesus went around doing good and healing everyone oppressed by the devil (Acts 10:38). He did not borrow from anyone or tell anyone to give to Him, yet money was always going out of the money bag. I don't see one place where the Bible says that money went into that bag. These Jews did not believe they had to borrow from anyone, being under the old covenant at the time.

We forget that Jesus was quoting Old Testament Scriptures because there was no New Testament yet, and it was the same with Paul. Paul was speaking from his revelation and writing the new covenant. If you look at everything Paul was saying, he was quoting the Old Testament and saying that the promises were now fulfilled. Jesus was the fulfillment of Deuteronomy. Deuteronomy 28 lists all the blessings and curses fulfilled in the new covenant.

I will eat from the same table as the Old Testament people ate from, but I have a better covenant with better promises. I will eat everything off the table without leaving anything behind and enjoy everything God has for me. If God can call you and me as warriors and soldiers in the body of Christ, then He can pay the bills. What soldier goes to war at his own expense (1 Corinthians 9:7)? The answer is none. The government that calls you to go to war pays for everything. In God's kingdom, you do not have to pay your own way, but satan tries to flip it and make you think you have to pay. The reality is that God will provide everything you need (Matthew 6:33).

God likes fire, and His fire will expose these false beliefs. You cannot put up with satan stealing from you. God is a good God, full of provisions, and He has everything you need. There is nothing He cannot do for you. God says nothing is impossible. Nothing. Jesus stated that if you believe, then all things are possible (Mark 9:23). Jesus would tell you that you will borrow from no one; you will lend to many, but *you will not borrow*. He would say you are going to have an abundance. He said God would put the fear of you in other nations, and the angel of the Lord will pursue your enemies and drive them out. Jesus said they will come at you in one direction but will flee from you in seven directions (Deuteronomy 28:7). This is Old Testament talk, and Jesus grew up hearing this. And He read the Old Testament in same Bible you have.

THE HOLY SPIRIT IS AS POWERFUL TODAY AS ON THE DAY OF PENTECOST

In the Old Testament, the prophet Joel wrote what he saw, prophesying the outpouring of the Holy Spirit (Joel 2:28–29). Then in Acts, this prophecy came to pass. Joel saw what would happen ahead of time, and then it happened. The characteristics they saw on the day of Pentecost were rushing wind, fire, utterance, and unity (Acts 2:1–21), and they seemed drunk to the multitude there. Peter stood up and said,

> *For these are not drunk, as you suppose, since it is only the third hour of the day. But this is what was spoken by the prophet Joel.*
>
> —Acts 2:15–16

In Acts 2, we see all this movement of the Holy Spirit and extraordinary events that God proclaimed long before. Think about how long it took from when the prophet Joel prophesied that until it happened. As a result of this supernatural event, the kingdom of God to come to earth to be in people. So it wasn't just Jesus, the 12, or the 70 operating anymore. Those 120 disciples in the upper room turned into 3000 disciples within days, then 5000 disciples (Acts 1:15). Today, millions of people on earth are believers, all because

101

God had His way. A holy fire came down from Heaven, and people spoke in tongues and prophesied. Other manifestations also happened in Acts 2, such as fire on their heads, a mighty rushing wind, and other wonders of the Holy Spirit.

Shouldn't the manifestation of the Holy Spirit be as powerful today as it was on that first day because He is still the same person? He hasn't changed a bit and hasn't lessened at all. But we can become lukewarm and mentally appease ourselves as we drift further and further away from the potency of what God has for us. That is why you must constantly allow the Holy Spirit to burn within you, keep you hot, and get rid of all the junk so it doesn't obscure your hearing and seeing in the Spirit.

Jesus walked on the earth performing miracles, then commissioned the 12 and the 70 to do the same thing, and they were surprised that it worked (Luke 10:17–20). I am sure the 120 were surprised on the day of Pentecost when what Jesus foretold happened. Today, we are surprised if we get an answer to prayer or if a person is healed or raised from the dead. However, we should not be, because Jesus transferred His powerful anointing to His disciples, and it was never meant to diminish. Today, we should have the same intensity as the 12 disciples. In fact, it should have increased since more than twenty-one hundred years have passed.

Think about what has happened over the last two millennia. The church expanded because of the intensity of the Spirit on the day of Pentecost. However, just because two thousand years have passed does not mean the intensity of the Holy Spirit should dwindle, especially if we are entering the last days and the harvest has to come in. Shouldn't Joel's prophecy still be true today? When we get together, shouldn't we experience great signs, such as a mighty rushing wind, flames of fire on our heads, and everyone speaking in tongues? We should also have a deluge of the Holy Spirit to the point where the new wine takes effect, and people think that we are actually drunk because that is what they thought on the day of Pentecost (Acts 2:13).

Others thought the disciples were drunk because they were speaking in tongues, but that could not have been the only reason. I hear people talking in different languages all the time, and I have never thought someone speaking in another language was drunk. I thought they were a foreigner. It wasn't the tongues, fire, or wind that caused others to believe the disciples were drunk. It was the fact they were so filled with the Spirit of God. They were probably so filled with the joy of the Lord that they could not even stand up and were falling over, as we see at some of the services today. On the day of Pentecost, these were the characteristics of the Holy Spirit moving.

> *Then, when the good news of the gospel is preached, demons will be expelled, the dead will be raised, and people will be healed and prosperous.*

Today, however, we need to get out of the mental agreement, thinking, *Yes, we agree*, but our heart isn't in it. That is why we are not experiencing the intensity we should, and it is not God's fault. Our mentality and perception must change, and everything we do must be born of the Spirit. Then, when the good news of the gospel is preached, demons will be expelled, the dead will be raised, and people will be healed and prosperous. All these have to do with the preaching of the gospel. In addition, when we are together and the Holy Spirit falls, we should also see manifestations as we did on the day of Pentecost.

DON'T FINISH IN THE FLESH WHAT YOU STARTED IN THE SPIRIT

In these last days, once again, we need to fan the gifts within us into flame, submit to holy fire, and allow the Lord to expose anything hindering us. I am sure you and everyone else are done with religion. Jesus appeared to me and explained that a big test was coming, and the church was not ready for it because they were lukewarm. He showed me that there would be a migration from the religious to the real Spirit of God moving. God was bringing people into the fold, where people were preaching the good news and getting together and loving on each other. He showed all this to me and told me that a separation was coming. Jesus went through this with His disciples on that day that He said they had to drink His blood and eat His flesh or have no part of Him (John 6:52–59).

> *Then Jesus said to His disciples, "If anyone desires*
> *to come after Me, let him deny himself, and take up*
> *his cross, and follow Me."*
>
> —Matthew 16:24

You must leave what you know, follow Jesus, and let Him give you His perspective. God wants to change your perspective in these last days. As you look at or listen to something, you might not see what you are supposed to see or hear everything you are supposed to hear. Because of what is happening on the earth now, I want you to hear and see clearly so that your perspective is shifted. God is saying some things right now that you might not know, and one of those things is that He wants to mend and heal your heart. He wants your heart to be more receptive to what He says.

So many times, Jesus told His disciples that He had so much more to share with them, but they were not ready. I heard this from people

I was sitting under who were mentoring me. They would say they had so much more to tell me, but they couldn't go on because the Lord told them I was not ready for it and that I hadn't even understood what I had already been taught. One person went on to Heaven without sharing everything he knew, which always bothered me. I was ready and willing to go on because I knew what he had taught up to that point, and I had taken it in and accepted it. He always taught from certain Scriptures because he said I hadn't gotten it yet. He would say I thought I had, but I had not. I used to think, *I got it*, but now, after thirty years, I look back at that and think, *I didn't get it* at the time. But now I see the truth and am ready to go on.

After you go through the fire, you learn to let go, which is the crucified life. If you want to go on with the things of God, to hear these deeper truths, these mysteries, then you have to allow the Spirit to take you into the holy fire and let everything be exposed, and part of that has to do with the crucified life (Galatians 2:20).

O foolish Galatians! Who has bewitched you that you should not obey the truth, before whose eyes Jesus Christ was clearly portrayed among you as crucified? This only I want to learn from you: Did you receive the Spirit by the works of the law, or by the hearing of faith? Are you so foolish? Having begun in the Spirit, are you now being made perfect by the flesh?

> *You can put an end to this trap by living the crucified life*

Paul was preaching to the Galatians when he asked them if they would finish in the flesh what they started in the Spirit. He essentially asked who stepped in, cut them off, and ruined their momentum. Who had bewitched them? Who had put a curse on them? Paul thought they were doing so well, but suddenly, they started to use their mental and fleshly capabilities to do something that was supposed to be spiritual. You can put an end to this trap by living the crucified life. You end it by recognizing that Jesus has to live through you. If you want to go on, you have to realize that you do not see everything you are supposed to see or hear everything you are supposed to hear. It took me thirty years to realize that I was not getting it, even though I thought I was.

ASK THE LORD TO INCREASE YOUR CAPACITY TO RECEIVE

This is the prayer that I used to pray:

Lord, increase my capacity to receive. Give me the grace to say yes when I cannot say yes, and give me the grace to grasp those things You are trying to teach me. Lord, I don't know everything, but I want to learn. Spirit of God, open my ears so that I hear my Father God's words and understand the kingdom's deep mysteries. I ask You, Father, to grant that my eyes be opened to the things of the Spirit, that I would have discernment beyond what is normal, and that I would see and understand. Thank You, Father, for touching me and opening my eyes to the deep things. Help me accept them. I submit to the holy fire and the crucified life. I know, Lord, that You want to walk with Me. Enlighten and illuminate my spirit and explode that with bright light within me. Get rid of all the chaff and everything that hinders me. I thank You, Father, in the name of Jesus. Amen.

8

CHOOSE THE SPIRIT

I have been crucified with Christ; it is no longer I who
live, but Christ lives in me; and the life which I now live
in the flesh I live by faith in the Son of God, Who loved
me and gave Himself for me.
—Galatians 2:20

Before Jesus ever revealed to His disciples that He would die on the cross, He told them if anyone desired to come after Him, they had to deny themselves, take up their cross, and follow Him (Matthew 16:24). The disciples had no idea how He would die. Yet Jesus was already talking about how they would also have to pick up their cross and follow Him. Paul said very clearly, "I have been crucified with Christ" (Galatians 2:20). That was the secret to his power, and it is the secret to your power. You and I will change the world because Jesus can live through us through the crucified life. That means that we deny the flesh and *our own will*. We have a choice, but we side with God in our will. We do not have our own ideas or way of doing life. We submit by putting ourselves on the altar as a living sacrifice so that we can know God's holy and acceptable will (Romans 12:1). That means that we will exactly do the perfect will of God in our lives.

JESUS WORKS IN US AND THEN THROUGH US

In Galatians 2:20, Paul expresses that we are crucified with Christ, which means we no longer walk by sight but now live by faith because Jesus is doing His work and will *in us* and *through us*. We look to Jesus, keeping our focus on Him, and allow Him to talk to us. Then we will enable Him to propel and empower us to act.

Everything we do, whether in word or deed, we are doing for the glory of God. Everything we do is as though we are working for God—not for our employer, not for our church. We are working for God, representing Him in everything we do. You can feel the power of Jesus living His life through you, and He will make good on His word. Jesus will speak to you, and it will come to pass, and then you will help others. You are going to see an overthrow in your life.

THE PERFECT WILL OF GOD COMES WHEN WE CONTINUOUSLY YIELD TO HIM

> *You might think you don't want something, but if God tells you that it is His desire for you, then it is the best thing you can do.*

We will see an overthrow in the world and the church. We will see governments and all kinds of leadership bow to the will of God. Many lives will be changed through the preaching of the gospel. The crucified life allows entrance from the spiritual realm into the physical realm, so many people misunderstand this. They think the crucified life means you will be sent to a country you do not want to go to or have to do something you don't want to do. That is just not the case. You might think you don't want something, but if God tells you that it is His desire for you, then it is the best thing you can do. Nothing else will satisfy you or work for you.

The perfect will of God comes when we continuously yield to Him. God's perfect will is a flow, not just a onetime event, like when God moves in a service or you see an answer to prayer and are excited because you know it was God's will. Being in God's perfect will is not living from one experience to another. As His children, we are in his perfect will, and that flow is constant. Pressure can move a heavy object like a car—not a little water fountain but a giant fire hose. The Spirit of God is the river, a mighty flow, coming out of your inner being. This same power rose Jesus from the dead, and this mighty river of God is a rushing flow of life (Romans 8:11).

A SPIRIT-FILLED CHRISTIAN SHOULD
LIVE A LONG LIFE

Think about the power available to Enoch when he walked with God and what he must have experienced. Enoch was sixty-five years old when he decided to walk with God. What do you think happened during his first sixty-five years? How many of us have wasted time not deciding what we would do? Enoch waited until he was sixty-five to decide what to do when he grew up, and then he walked with God for three hundred years. He must have done something right because you know what happened to him.

Enoch lived sixty-five years, and begot Methuselah. After he begot Methuselah, Enoch walked with God three hundred years, and had sons and daughters. So all the days of Enoch were three hundred and sixty-five. And Enoch walked with God; and he was not, for God took him.

—Genesis 5:21–24

Enoch denied himself and submitted to the holy fire, and when his will was completely gone, Jesus—the pre-existent Jesus, who was with the Father from the beginning—revealed Himself to Enoch. Enoch walked with God for three hundred years, then disappeared because he pleased God so much. What about us? We wouldn't live that long unless it were a total miracle. However, think about what we have today in the New Testament and even the manifestation that happened two thousand years ago on the day of Pentecost, so there is a possibility that we can live longer.

With the life of God, a Spirit-filled Christian who walks in the power of God and obedience should be able to live a long time. The key is what Paul told Timothy: Fan the gift of God into flame, that gift placed within him by the laying on of hands (2 Timothy 1:6). We are drawing from that life instead of believing that we will live only seventy or eighty years. The adversary, satan, targets Christians, which is why a war is going on. People in the world live longer because they are serving satan. We need to change our mindset. When we live the crucified life and eat the bread of life, which is the Word of God, we will live for Him, and there is life in us.

Moses lived to 120 years old and was not sick or old. God had to tell him it was time to die (Deuteronomy 34:4–7). I will believe and agree with the Spirit of God that if Moses in the old covenant could live to 120 and had to be told to die, in the New Testament, I can live at least that long. It is the same with Enoch and other individuals who lived that long. Why did they live longer than we do today? I want to look into that.

Enoch walked with God, and he is a type of the Church. In the New Testament, a time will come when, in the twinkling of an eye, we will be caught up to be with the Lord (1 Corinthians 15:52–54), which happened with Enoch (Genesis 5:24). He just walked right over, and this will happen with the bride of Christ in the end days.

ANGELS ARE SENT TO MINISTER TO US

Are they not all ministering spirits sent forth to minister for those who will inherit salvation?

—Hebrews 1:14

Did you know that angels are sent to minister to us? There are different types of angels, such as seraphim and cherubim, and all kinds of creatures in the throne room that I do not even know how to classify. There are the four living creatures, and I saw other beings I was told I would never be able to talk about (Revelation 4:6–8). I did not understand them, and they weren't angels. I saw people like the elders who were neither human beings nor angels. I saw beings that looked like Melchizedek, along with other rulers and people, in the throne room of God. I saw angels coming to help us, and I did not understand all of it, but I knew they were eternal. They were saturated with the life of God and were full of power.

Being around angels changes us physically and mentally. When I am around these kinds of beings, I feel as though I am suspended and not encountering this realm anymore, and my spirit is ignited. Even my flesh, mind, and emotions seem to be suspended, so I can no longer doubt or fear. I know the other realm can influence us because this has happened to me many times. Imagine Moses encountering God for forty days on Mount Sinai and what that must have done to his body and emotions, not just his spirit (Exodus 24:18; 34:28).

All these supernatural beings have the life of God in them, and they are sent to minister to us and help us. The Holy Spirit, Who is in us and upon us, is not the only one sent to us. Angels surround us, and all kinds of supernatural things are happening around us. We have stopped plans and events of the enemy because we prayed. You look at some of the negative situations that have occurred on earth and think, *Why did this happen,* or *Why was this stolen?* We never stop to think about all the things we prevented from happening and how God has a plan, even in the midst of disappointment.

> *And we know that all things work together for good to those who love God, to those who are the called according to His purpose.*
>
> —Romans 8:28

> *By faith Enoch was taken away so that he did not see death, and was not found, because God had taken him; for before he was taken he had this testimony, that he pleased God. But without faith it is impossible to please Him, for he who comes to God must believe that He is, and that He is a rewarder of those who diligently seek Him.*
>
> —Hebrews 11:5–6

If angels are coming to minister for us and to us, then I will pay the price, whatever it is, to be led into the next step God has for us. The doorway we go through into this power is very much like what happened with Enoch when he decided to walk with God at age sixty-five. The next three hundred years for Enoch were off the charts. Enoch is mentioned in the book of Hebrews as an example of one who pleased God.

> *Knowing that angels will work with us and help us is empowering, so give them permission to work.*

Without faith, it is impossible to please God. Enoch lived a crucified life where he denied himself. Knowing that angels will work with us and help us is empowering, so give them permission to work. Angels are part of this holy fire and the process of cleansing. If I walk away from what I want, I will walk into what God wants. I know you really want what God wants, just as I do, even though you might not feel it at the moment.

YOU MUST WORSHIP GOD IN SPIRIT AND TRUTH

> *God is Spirit, and those who worship Him must worship in spirit and truth.*
>
> —John 4:24

117

You cannot necessarily do physical works all the time to please God because God is a Spirit, and there has to be a Spirit-to-spirit response. If you worship Him in the Spirit from the spirit, then you might play a physical instrument, raise or wave your hands in the air, or read. Some like to worship with a flag, dance, or in other creative ways. These are physical manifestations, but if they are born of the Spirit, you are worshiping God in spirit and truth. It involves your physical body, but you must initially live that crucified life. You have to choose not to act in your flesh and choose to act in the Spirit.

Whatever you give up, you will find it will come back to you. Everything I have given up has returned to me, and I was surprised when it did. That will happen to you if you are willing to leave everything. If you abandon yourself and pursue God, He will reward you, and this is where the angels come in because they want you to worship God in spirit and truth and to walk as Enoch did. Every angel sent to help you do the Father's will desires that you fulfill your mission.

When I started moving in the Spirit by praying in tongues, I eventually began to say things in English as well. I felt I was starting to understand some things, but it was not in my mind; it was in my spirit. As I prayed in tongues, something in English would come out of my mouth, and then I would go back to tongues, and I realized that I was interpreting my tongues. As that gift developed over the years, what I was saying in English would come to pass. God was moving and getting me into the spirit realm.

God told me that He wanted me to get a group of people to move in that revelation so that they could start to see the manifestation of the Spirit and declare things and see them happen. Now we have gotten to where I believe we will influence nations. And even though it is a higher level of war to have a nation receive what God wants, we have to wage a good warfare by getting enough people to agree as touching what God wants (1 Timothy 1:18). We could see whatever God desires for a nation come to pass by our agreement (Matthew 18:19–20). However, we first have to start individually with ourselves.

We must allow the angels to visit us and let the Spirit of God encourage us to worship God and communicate with Him in the Spirit. We cannot think that we will initiate it by what we do in the flesh. It must be initiated in the Spirit first. Whatever you do, whether in word or deed, you do it unto God from your heart, and that heart experience, that flow will come out. That is when you can grab an instrument or however the Spirit leads you, and you can worship God and express yourself differently. However, it must be born of the Spirit. Remember, the angels will be there to help you so that you flow as the Spirit leads.

People will live longer, and we will see the manifestation of the Spirit in a greater way because of the angelic involvement. This all starts when you are a perfect sacrifice and say to yourself, *I will crucify my flesh and walk in the will of God.* God's angels love that and will work with you because you are humble and let the Spirit of God move. Think about someone who might need encouragement and start praying for them. Then, if God leads you, call and get in contact with them. That is what I used to do.

Before I went to church, I would pray in tongues and put fifteen dollars in my pocket. I would ask the Lord to show me who I was to speak to that day to give an encouraging word and to whom I should give the fifteen dollars. It was amazing because I didn't attend church to be ministered to anymore. I came to give. Since I surrendered to the Holy Spirit, I have never gone to a church or meeting expecting anyone to minister to me. I always think I am going to give and minister. I think about what I can do for someone else. When the crucified life kicks in, an overthrow of your will takes place.

Build up other people and pray that God teaches you and shows you what to do, then minister to someone. Let God show you and lead you into that. Whatever you are doing, even if you are going to work or at a restaurant, ask the Lord to help you say what you are supposed to say or do what you are supposed to do.

> *For the Lord God is a sun and shield; the Lord will give grace and glory; no good thing will He withhold from those who walk uprightly.*
>
> —Psalm 84:11

9

JUDGE YOURSELF

For if we would judge ourselves, we would
not be judged.
—1 Corinthians 11:31

When you crucify the flesh and walk in the Spirit as Enoch did, demons can be expelled and evicted from your life. I am not talking about being possessed because, as a Spirit-filled Christian, there is no way an evil spirit can be in your spirit. However, evil spirits can influence a person's soul—mind, will, and emotions—and body.

KNOW YOUR AUTHORITY IN CHRIST

For the weapons of our warfare are not carnal but mighty in God for pulling down strongholds, casting down arguments and every high thing that exalts itself against the knowledge of God, bringing every thought into captivity to the obedience of Christ.

—2 Corinthians 10:4–5

In this passage, Paul talks about the mental realm, the soulish realm, being brought into captivity to the obedience of Christ. As we walk in this crucified life as Enoch did, we will find that we please God, but it also stirs up the demonic evil spirits because the Lord has given us authority over them. As evil spirits are stirred up against Christians, many take it personally.

There are a couple of reasons for this. One is that people automatically think they have done something wrong. They deal with a sin consciousness that they should no longer struggle with as Christians. We automatically assume that we have done something wrong when we might have done everything right, which is why evil spirits are stirred up. Demonic spirits know you have the power and the authority to drive them out, so they try to deceive you to get you off track. They don't want you to walk confidently or have a fully convinced heart. Many times, Christians do not understand their authority in Christ. These believers automatically misinterpret and take it wrong when evil spirits are stirred up.

DRIVE OUT DEMONS

The Lord does not want us to withdraw or compromise in any way. We need to be bold, knowing that we can drive out demons. Evil spirits will try to prove you wrong by creating situations to make it look as if the Word of God is not valid or that what God is saying is not happening. We need to stand firm in what God has said in His Word. The demons will try to convince you that you are wrong to beat you down and continually come at you to wear you out and get you to back off.

If you don't back down, the demons won't know what to do with you. So many Christians have backed down over the years, and evil spirits have gotten used to Christians backing off. When a believer finally stands up to them, they don't know what to do with that person, and they will eventually leave you alone. The evil spirits do not want you to have the edge over them.

The demons believe they have the edge over you in several different areas. First, you cannot see them, so they think they have the advantage of being stealthy and sneaking around. You don't know when they have come or gone. However, as you develop in the spirit, walk in the Spirit, and allow the holy fire to cleanse and purify you, you will have the edge over them. You will start to see and discern in the Spirit when demonic activity is around you. You can feel it because the evil spirits shift the atmosphere and you sense the difference. They will no longer be able to deceive you.

If evil spirits are around, you must be on guard and take authority over them, especially when you sense their activity. Your adversary satan can only stop you or beat you if he gets you to go into his realm, into his ring, so to speak, to fight him there by his rules that he never follows anyway. His strategy is to get you into the flesh, into your emotions and reasoning capabilities, which happened with Adam and Eve. He talked to Eve through the serpent and convinced her to reason (Genesis 3:1–6). He got her to look at the fruit, which appealed to her. She acted on her emotions. The enemy pulled Eve out of the Spirit and the truth of God's words and into what she could see and feel. If you look carefully at what was being said and done there, you can see satan's mode of operation.

If you allow the Spirit of God to be your Advocate and Attorney, He will act so that you are not deceived (John 14:26). This deception should have been stopped in the garden immediately because Eve and Adam both knew better. They let this happen, but you cannot let it happen.

DON'T ALLOW THE DEVIL TO RILE UP YOUR EMOTIONS

Do not allow these evil spirits to pull you into the emotional or reasoning realm so that your will is influenced and you cannot withstand temptation. Put a stop to it, define your boundaries, and always give the Holy Spirit free rein and input in your life. If the Holy Spirit speaks to you and defines the boundaries, you must honor that. Do not allow the devil to rise up and rile up or energize your flesh or emotions so that they rule you. Sometimes, you just need to walk away or be silent. Sometimes it is better not to say anything and even better not to react at all.

> *It is better to draw your battle strategies and boundaries by the Holy Spirit, your Advocate and your Lawyer, before you go into battle.*

Do not allow something to manifest inside you that you know is a temptation or is wrong. Never let those thoughts become an action; it is better to walk away and give yourself space, preventing satan from pulling you into his realm. The Holy Spirit will define these boundaries for you. It is better to draw your battle strategies and boundaries by the Holy Spirit, your Advocate and your Lawyer, before you go into battle.

DEFINE YOUR BOUNDARIES

In planning, always define your boundaries in a peaceful place so that when you encounter problems, you can withstand them once you get into the battle. It is harder to draw boundaries when you are already in the midst of the fight. You must constantly remind yourself of the boundaries so they don't get fuzzy and blurry as they did with Eve. She started to waver and to reason what God actually said. I will stand firm in what God has said, I will not let go of it, and I will not let some demon spirit talk me out of it. You must be firm—that's the way you have to be.

The Holy Spirit is holy; therefore, the defining lines are pure and obvious. The devil creates a gray area in situations, so you waver and reason about what you will do. Then, before you know it, you are off doing something that you would never have done if you had drawn your boundaries beforehand and stuck to them. Do not allow satan to do this. The power of the Holy Spirit is so much stronger; however, demon spirits are packed in down here, and if we allow our emotions to be riled up, we will get into a difficult situation.

People who grasped God's goodness understood they were adopted, fully accepted, and completely valued. The goodness of God led them to repentance all the time, and they did not seem to be tempted like others were. In a time of weakness, these evil spirits will try to lure you in, deceive you, and seduce you.

GOD LOVES AND VALUES YOU

Grasp the goodness of your Father God: He loves you and is not leading you into temptation. He is not purposely seducing you or making you fall because He doesn't do that. He is not tempted by evil and does not tempt anyone with evil (James 1:13). Once you grasp that and your value and that you are loved, you see that you are a son or a daughter of God. Stick with that, and it will bring you strength. You will realize you do not need these activities that tempt you to feel valued. You don't need to be recognized by others or involve yourself in addictive behaviors or the things that fulfill the flesh and your emotions. You are at peace, and your peace and value are with God Who loves you.

It is harder to take a stand for something in this realm than when you are in the Spirit. If you would have an experience where you go to Heaven, everything is clear and defined. There are no problems because you don't deal with the flesh, fallen emotions, demons, or other distractions. Down here, you have got to be in the Spirit to discern and make judgments so that you don't get into the fleshly or carnal realm.

GOD'S HOLY FIRE DIVIDES LIKE A SWORD

Holy fire is introduced into this realm from the heavenly realm to put out ungodly passions and to stop seduction. The holy fire is from the personality of God Himself and is like a sword of the Spirit that divides. It exposes some matters so they become easily discerned, which you would not have discerned before. At times, I have had the holy fire ignite in me, and suddenly I was shaken, awakened, and made aware of what was happening. I did not know at the time that I was under attack, which happens all the time with Christians.

When you abide in the Spirit, the holy fire is always there. Righteousness, justice, faithfulness, and all the characteristics of God are always there. These characteristics are always evident and real in a place deep down inside us, but we often get pulled away. I want to encourage you to judge yourself. Always have the Word of God in front of you in some way, and always pray in the Spirit, building yourself up. Always think about the reality that you are a spiritual being in a body and have emotions and a soul.

IF WE JUDGE OURSELVES, WE WILL NOT BE JUDGED

For if we would judge ourselves, we would not be judged. But when we are judged, we are chastened by the Lord, that we may not be condemned with the world.

—1 Corinthians 11:31–32

This passage contains quite a bit of revelation. As children and ambassadors of God, you are all called to be mentored and live in the Spirit. You are learning how to walk in the Spirit, being built up and equipped to excel. It is better to discern and judge matters spiritually, separate yourself, and refuse to be pulled into worldliness; this will prevent you from being judged by God. In other words, Paul said to judge yourself so that you are not judged. Then he said that if we are judged or chastened by the Lord, correction and discipline come so that we are not condemned with the world.

You do not want to be like the person in the Corinthian church who Paul had to turn over to satan for the destruction of his flesh so that his spirit might be saved (1 Corinthians 5:4–5). Everything would have been fine if that man had judged himself and corrected his wrong behavior. But because he didn't, Paul had them turn him over to satan. He was not allowed back into the church until he was chastened. In 2 Corinthians, Paul said he could be brought back because he had repented (2 Corinthians 2:5–11).

> *People who judge themselves make sure only to speak where they are going because they know their words are steering their lives.*

A Christian who is commended in Heaven reads the Word of God, prays in the Spirit, and then makes judgments about all things (1 Corinthians 2:15). However, they are not subject to any man's judgment because they judge themselves (1 Corinthians 11:31). One of the characteristics of spiritual people is that they always watch what they say. Their words are few, and when they do say something, there is life in their words. They understand that the tongue is a rudder that steers our whole life (James 3:4–5).

People who judge themselves make sure only to speak where they are going because they know their words are steering their lives. And because they are doing it correctly, they are not judged the same way as others who have not judged themselves. You must watch your tongue, only speak where you are going, discern what the Lord is saying and doing in your life, and then act on that.

He asked His disciples, saying, "Who do men say that I, the Son of Man, am?"

So they said, "Some say John the Baptist, some Elijah, and others Jeremiah or one of the prophets."
He said to them, "But who do you say that I am?"
Simon Peter answered and said, "You are the Christ, the Son of the living God."

—Matthew 16:13–16

Peter had a revelation; however, the next day, Peter told Jesus that He would not go to Jerusalem and die. Jesus turned to Peter and said, "Get behind me, satan! You are an offense to Me, for you are not mindful of the things of God, but the things of men" (Matthew 16:21–23). Jesus called Peter satan, and Peter was rebuked and corrected. Jesus judged him as being one who spoke by satan, which, as Jesus said, were the thoughts of man, not the thoughts of God. There it is. Peter was speaking his ideas, which were the wrong thoughts, so he was disciplined and rebuked. He was rebuked as one who spoke for satan himself, even though the day before, he had spoken the truth by the Spirit of God. If Peter had judged his thoughts, he would have had revelation and known that what he was saying was incorrect. He would not have said it. If he had judged himself, he would not have been rebuked and corrected in front of everyone.

The overcoming power of the Holy Spirit and the fire of God will burn these things out so that you can discern. Think about all the times you have thought about what you should have done or said after it happened. After a while, if you allow the Holy Spirit to help you, you can learn how to judge rightly and immediately say and do the right thing. Part of maturing in Christ is our ability to be in season and instant, which comes by allowing the Holy Spirit to work on us (2 Timothy 4:2).

The Holy Spirit wants us to judge ourselves; He is right there to give us the game plan and remind us of what is right and the truth. We never have to be disciplined or corrected if we rely on Him. If we don't allow this process, we will be disciplined and corrected, and we may also get into trouble in certain situations because the Spirit of God is not leading us. Sometimes believers blame God for something that was their fault. Think about all the things people blame God or each other for that were their fault. The responsibility was not other people's nor God's; they made a poor decision. They get mad because God didn't do something they thought He should do. The problem is that God often doesn't get His way because people do not cooperate. God will still say what He will do, even if people don't work with Him. God still has to speak the right thing.

Often, God does not get what He desires, which will always be righteousness, truth, and life. God wants to give life and wants to heal and deliver people. God wants righteousness and justice to reign. If it does not happen, it's not God's fault. People do not discern their responsibility in the Spirit. They are supposed to be speaking life and standing for justice, righteousness, healing, and prosperity, and when it doesn't happen, they find someone to blame—God or other people.

Blame shifting causes people to have a victim mentality, questioning why God allowed this to happen to them. When you think about it, God allows a lot to happen. We have been given free will, so God does not force us to do the right thing, which concerns me enough to be diligent. I choose to be disciplined and put myself in a situation where I hear, discern, and make the right decisions. Then, when things go wrong, I don't blame God or others; I handle it myself. It is never too late if you know what God is saying. You must inquire of Him throughout the situation and make the right choices.

Peter learned a lesson there and, as you see, did improve and become a great apostle and leader in the church. He saw many miracles and wrote 1 and 2 Peter in the Bible, which are profound books with incredible revelation. Even though Peter made many mistakes, he did great works and was very active in the church. Peter learned from what Jesus taught him; eventually, all the corrections helped, and he repented. He came back as one of the strongest generals of the early church. If Peter can make it, we all can make it.

10

MAKE UP FOR LOST TIME

For in Him we live and move and have our being, as
also some of your own poets have said,
"For we are also His offspring."
—Acts 17:28

Paul, whose name was Saul before Jesus appeared to him, believed he was doing God's will by getting rid of all the Christians because they were a threat to the religion of the day (Acts 8:1–3). Saul and the rest of the religious rulers felt especially threatened by Jesus because the people liked everything about Him. They followed Him because of His words and the signs, wonders, and miracles He did. The Pharisees rejected Jesus and His message.

Jesus was very puzzling to them. They did not discern that Jesus was the fulfillment of all the prophets who had spoken about the coming Messiah.

After Jesus left, Saul and the Pharisees pushed for Christianity's extinction (Acts 9:1–2). Saul was doing what he thought was right by persecuting Christians and having them killed (Acts 22:3–4) in order to remove what he believed were false doctrines. Saul figured that Christians would eventually be eliminated, and he would be recognized as a very zealous leader in his religious sect and an enforcer of the doctrine of the religious leaders.

RELIGIOUS SPIRITS STILL OPERATE TODAY

Interestingly, that religious spirit still operates in churches and other circles. Some people in these religious circles think others who believe in the whole Bible, operate in the Holy Spirit and believe in speaking in tongues, healing, and in the fivefold ministry are wrong. That religious spirit labels the believers today the same way the Pharisees labeled them in Jesus' day. The goal of these people is to stop believers from speaking the truth. They feel that their assignment is from God; however, it is from the pit of hell. Saul thought the same way—that he was doing God a favor by getting rid of all the Christians (Acts 26:9–11).

As he journeyed he came near Damascus, and suddenly a light shone around him from Heaven. Then he fell to the ground, and heard a voice saying to him, "Saul, Saul, why are you persecuting Me?" And he said, "Who are You, Lord?" Then the Lord said, "I am Jesus, Whom you are persecuting. It is hard for you to kick against the goads."

—Acts 9:3–5

When Saul heard the voice asking why he was persecuting him, he was surprised and responded, "Who are You, Lord?" He may have wondered when he persecuted Jesus; however, Jesus taught that what you do to one of His brothers or sisters, you do to Him (Matthew 25:40). It was a brand-new concept to Saul, who was very sorry for what he did.

PAUL, AN APOSTLE FROM BIRTH

After his encounter, Saul changed his name to Paul and eventually was caught up to the third Heaven and received the gospel (2 Corinthians 12:2–5). He wrote about all the revelations he received from his experience with Jesus.

But I make known to you, brethren, that the gospel
which was preached by me is not according to man.
For I neither received it from man, nor was I taught
it, but it came through the revelation of Jesus Christ.

—Galatians 1:11–12

Paul said the gospel he preached was not from man, and he was to deliver this message. Paul told the churches that he had been called as an apostle of Jesus Christ since birth (Galatians 1:15). Think about how Paul, in the beginning, was killing Christians and trying to extinguish the religion, and then he was called to be an apostle for that very religion. So what happened?

Paul did not receive his information from the Holy Spirit until the second half of his life. For the first half of his life, he received it from evil spirits and was actually working against the Lord and his own calling, which God allowed. Paul approved and consented to Stephen's death (Acts 22:20). God's will was not done. Paul was supposed to be an apostle since birth but wasn't saved until his mid-twenties. Before his mid-twenties, Paul was attacking Christians, yet God did not stop him. However, God did stop him at a certain point, and he changed.

A bright light blinded Paul, and he saw Jesus (Acts 22:6–11). Then he was caught up with Jesus and disappeared for years. When Paul reappeared and started to teach, he was completely transformed, yet people still feared him. He wasted half of his life because he was called as an apostle since birth, according to his own words (Galatians 1:15). How do you explain this to Stephen, who died prematurely because Paul refused to follow Christ? How do you explain why God let that happen?

We are deceived if we don't receive revelation, operate in the Spirit, and powerfully encounter the Holy Spirit. Paul lived half his life before being arrested by the Holy Spirit, judged, and transformed. Jesus came to him and essentially said that enough was enough.

For the rest of his life, Paul said, "I have wronged no man" (2 Corinthians 7:2). Paul let go of his past and walked into his present and future; it was just as though he had not sinned at all. However, the fact is that he worked against God, and God did not stop him until a certain point. Many of us could choose this day not to sow into destruction or the flesh and to stop working against God.

> *So then, those who are in the flesh cannot please God.*
>
> —Romans 8:8

If you walk in the flesh, you cannot please God. You are an enemy of God because the flesh and the Spirit war against each other (Romans 8; Galatians 5:17). Paul became an apostle and an overseer in the body of Christ. He wrote to Titus and Timothy and to the Romans, Corinthians, Galatians, Ephesians, Colossians, Philippians, and all the different churches he was over. Paul was encouraging them and speaking life to them. He did not speak death over them but constantly told them not to be carnal, to judge themselves, and to stand out from the world around them. Paul told them not to finish in the flesh what they started in the Spirit (Galatians 3:3). He said that they are seated with Christ in the heavenly realms (Ephesians 2:6). He instructed the Colossians not to focus on earthly things but on heavenly things where Christ is seated at the right hand of God (Colossians 3:1).

HAVE YOU WASTED TIME?

Paul consistently showed them how to access power and life from the heavenly realm. God's heavenly kingdom is completely holy, righteous, and just. Everything about Heaven is perfect, and we don't have to waste our lives when we have Heaven in our hearts. If you feel like you have wasted time, now is the time to surrender and say, "Lord, make up for lost time. I'm ready to turn myself in, and I want You to make me productive. I don't want to work against You, and I don't want to be deceived. I am submitting to that holy fire and will be Your faithful witness and messenger."

Then watch what the Lord does because it will be amazing. Paul stated that it's in Jesus we live and move and have our being, which is how you operate in that environment (Acts 17:28). He also said, "For to me, to live is Christ, and to die is gain" (Philippians 1:21). Paul was changed, and then he changed a lot of people.

THE LORD COMES AS A REFINER'S FIRE TO PURIFY AND CLEAN

"Behold, I send My messenger, and he will prepare the way before Me. And the Lord, whom you seek, will suddenly come to His temple, even the Messenger of the covenant, in whom you delight. Behold, He is coming," says the Lord of hosts. "But who can endure the day of His coming? And who can stand when He appears? For He is like a refiner's fire and like launderers' soap. He will sit as a refiner and a purifier of silver; He will purify the sons of Levi, and purge them as gold and silver, that they may offer to the Lord an offering in righteousness.

Then the offering of Judah and Jerusalem will be pleasant to the Lord, as in the days of old, as in former years."

—Malachi 3:1–4

In these verses, Malachi is caught up and sees the Messiah, the Lord, appearing in the temple. However, Malachi does not see the Lord hugging people and patting them on the back. Instead, the Lord was coming as a refiner's fire and as a launderer's soap. The purpose of the Lord's coming was to purify and clean, not a social visit. Interestingly, Malachi said that He would purify the sons of Levi, the Levites, and purge them as gold and silver. The Messiah was coming to purge the ministry and those who ministered before the Lord.

Interestingly, Malachi 3:4 says, "Then the offering of Judah will be pleasant to the Lord as in the days of old, as in the former years." Malachi's book was written before Jesus came; he was one of the last Old Testament prophets. Then a period called "four hundred years of silence" followed this, which ended with the coming of John the Baptist. There was a famine of the Word of God, and then suddenly, Jesus appeared (Amos 8:11).

The Church is now going through a season where the separation is occurring again, not only in the body but also in the ministry. Ministry is changing back to the ways of old, the ancient paths, as it did here with Malachi—it is the refiner's fire. A time comes when we have to stand for what is right, and we cannot apologize anymore. You must take a stand and square off with the enemy when you face challenging circumstances. When he starts to work his counterfeit signs and wonders, we must be bold, stand up, and let God respond with His true signs and wonders. We cannot allow the enemy to rule and reign down here.

This test has come with a refining process for people who do stay. They will face pressure and persecution. The people who stand firm, even if it's only a few, are history-makers because they will not compromise. They won't allow the message to be compromised; it is like the plumb line that always tells the truth (Amos 7:7–8). Even if someone calls it crooked, the plumb line reveals what is true. It shows what is straight up and down. That was what Malachi said and what is happening to us. Peter and Paul, who was Saul, both went through this. Malachi prophesied this refinement, one of the last indications of what would happen before the New Testament. There would be a refiner and a refiner's fire that would purify the gold and the silver.

ALLOW GOD TIME TO SPEAK

I want to make the right decisions. I don't want to be judged; instead, I judge myself. The perfect will of God for your life is to judge yourself so that you are not judged. We don't know everything; sometimes, we come to a fork in the road and don't know which way to go. It is better to stop and say, "Lord, I don't know what I should do, but You do. I don't care how long it takes. I will wait for You and let You show me what to do." Just be humble about it. I have had this happen so many times. I have faced significant life decisions and needed discernment in those situations. The Lord always came through for me, and He will come through for you. There is nothing impossible, but we must allow God time to speak.

First, create an environment and then take the time to meditate on His Word and see what God is saying. You have to be fully convinced of what He is saying. If you are not there, you need to judge yourself and say, "I will create an environment where I can hear from God." It might not take very long, but you have to be willing to wait until you hear from Him.

THE LORD CHASTENS THOSE HE LOVES

God determines your borders. He decides who you are, your personality, and where you live. And because God determines your boundaries, He is supposed to make those decisions. However, God does not make you do anything, so we must realize that God disciplines and chastens those He loves (Hebrews 12:6). His perfect will is not for us to go through all this stuff because He would rather be able to talk to us. If we are willing and obedient, we will eat the good of the land (Isaiah 1:19).

We will certainly be purified, be friends of God, and experience the overflow. If not, we will have to go through some difficult times and learn the hard way. That happens because we haven't discerned what it's like to judge ourselves. If you judge yourself, life will always go better for you. That's why you should always read and think about God's Word. As you go about your day, you should always be praying in the Spirit and letting God in on every detail. Pray, "Lord, I don't know what to say or do in this situation, but You do—I need your help." Constantly turn yourself over to the Lord and yield to Him.

GOD CONFIRMS HIS WORD

I want to depend upon the Holy Spirit and the Word of God. I am a son of God, and you are a son or daughter of the living God and are led by the Spirit of God (Romans 8:14). You do not need someone to tell you what to do because you have your own relationship with

God. Let the Lord talk to you, then let someone else confirm it if God wills.

> *We are not led by prophets; we are led by the Spirit of God, which makes us sons and daughters of God.*

New Testament prophecy confirms what God has already spoken, affirming a person's relationship with the Lord. I do not want to say something new to someone regarding specific guidance from the Lord. The New Testament prophet should confirm what the person already knows from the Lord Himself. We are not led by prophets; we are led by the Spirit of God, which makes us sons and daughters of God.

GOD OPENS THE WINDOWS OF HEAVEN FOR US

Now to Him who is able to do exceedingly abundantly above all that we ask or think, according to the power that works in us.

—Ephesians 3:20

This verse in Ephesians speaks to us personally. We can exceed and surpass the boundaries we may have placed on ourselves once we submit and have judged ourselves. God then opens up the heavens and begins to make our borders fall in pleasant places (Malachi 3:10; Psalm 16:6). He does "exceedingly abundantly above what we could ask or think," according to His power that is working right inside of us (Ephesians 3:20). As we walk with God, we start to discover what is in us. After a while, boundaries expand, and limitations are removed.

I see this all the time, and we are supposed to live this way in the New Testament. When we go through that refining process, we can walk in the "exceedingly abundantly above what we could ever ask or think." This power then releases that which is already in us. If the Lord says, "What I have for you is more than you could ever think or even ask for," I will say, "I want that!" I don't try to think about it or figure it out. I just say, "Lord, I want what you want, and I know that it hasn't even entered my mind. I know I cannot ask for it in English, so I will pray and ask for it in the Spirit."

Jesus discerns when people don't know what to ask for and when they miss it. At times, I am sure that you have known that people were missing it. You knew when people wouldn't get what they were praying for because they were in unbelief, doubt, disobedience, pride, and without repentance. You can tell when people will not get what God wants because they haven't met the requirements. A person must get to that place where they can receive from God, and then it will happen. For a state or country to change, a group of people must come into agreement; the church must align with the will of God for that area. People must gain momentum in the Spirit by coming into unity and refusing to take no for an answer. It becomes a huge deal when it turns corporate.

WE MUST GO BEYOND OUR LIMITATIONS

Jesus discerned what was in people, and He knew what was in a man and their limitations. He would correct Peter and different people because He knew they were about to make a mistake or had reached their choking point. How many of you have reached your choking point and need the Lord to help you? We have to go beyond our limitations, and the Spirit of God wants to help us do that.

Jesus stretched the rich young ruler's limitations in Matthew 19:16–22. He discerned that there was something good about the rich man, but he was missing something. Jesus told him that if he wanted to be perfect, to sell what he had, give to the poor and follow Him (Matthew 19:21). This was one of those times when Jesus had to say something and judge him. The man would have been fine if he had judged himself, but he hadn't. Jesus loved this young man and told him he was missing out on this one thing. Jesus told him what he needed to do; however, the rich young ruler couldn't handle it because he would have to give up control, and he liked having control. Being rich to him meant that he could call the shots. If he sold everything and gave it to the poor, he would give up his ability to control his life. He could not do that because he was very wealthy, so he went away sorrowfully (Matthew 19:22).

> *The Lord wants to trust you with great riches, but He has to see if you can handle the small stuff first.*

The problem with rich men or women is that they can write a check for anything. They can resolve issues quickly by depending on their money. Often, the wealthy take God out of the equation. The Lord wants to trust you with great riches, but He has to see if you can handle the small stuff first. This rich man was already wealthy, which was a massive problem for him. Jesus went right to the root of the issue, but the young man could not receive it. The Lord knows exactly how far you can go, but He will still speak the truth so that you go through a purifying process if you choose to do so. If you would judge yourself, you would not even have to have this conversation with Jesus as the rich young man did.

11

THE COURAGE INSIDE YOU

And I will pray the Father, and He will give you another
Helper, that He may abide with you forever–
—John 14:16

Jesus said that He was sent to the Jews, the "lost sheep of the house of Israel" (Matthew 15:24). Yet amazingly, He marveled over the faith of a centurion who was a Roman soldier (Matthew 8:5–13). In Jesus's day, the Romans had just taken control of Jerusalem and Israel, God's city and country. Interestingly, this Roman soldier was discerning and understood these matters that a lost sheep of Israel or a Jew would have understood. None of the people in that city impressed Jesus as much as that Roman centurion did. When Jesus entered Capernaum, the centurion approached Jesus and pleaded with Him to heal his servant who was sick at home. Jesus told the centurion that He would come to his house and heal his servant.

> *The centurion answered and said, "Lord, I am not worthy that You should come under my roof. But only speak a word, and my servant will be healed. For I also am a man under authority, having soldiers under me. And I say to this one, 'Go,' and he goes; and to another, 'Come,' and he comes; and to my servant, 'Do this,' and he does it."*
>
> *When Jesus heard it, He marveled, and said to those who followed, "Assuredly, I say to you, I have not found such great faith, not even in Israel!"*
>
> —Matthew 8:8–10

The centurion understood authority and knew that Jesus was God and the Messiah. He knew that Jesus could say it, and it would be done. The Jews viewed this Roman soldier as an invader; however, Jesus marveled at his faith, stating that He had not found such great faith, even in Israel. Think about someone from another country coming in and taking over, yet this person placed his faith in who

Jesus was and said, "Only speak a word, and it will be done." That centurion judged Jesus correctly; because of that, he got what he asked for from Him.

> *Then Jesus said to the centurion, "Go your way; and as you have believed, so let it be done for you." And his servant was healed that same hour.*
>
> —Matthew 8:13

DISCERN THAT YOU ARE UNDER GOD AND HIS AUTHORITY

When you discern the authority of God and submit to Him, the demons listen to you because when you give a command, you are representing God.

Jesus never spoke against Rome. He spoke against the Pharisees and the religious system but not against Rome. The centurion got what he wanted and needed because he discerned Jesus's authority. That was an example of rightly dividing and discerning well. You must discern that you are under God and His authority in everything you do. You humble yourself under His mighty hand, and He lifts you in due season (1 Peter 5:6). When you discern the authority of God and submit to Him, the demons listen to you because when you give a command, you are representing God. You are an ambassador for the kingdom of God.

The religious system crucified Jesus. The Romans carried it out, but Pilate tried to get out of crucifying Jesus if you read what he said. He wanted to set Jesus free. The Pharisees were the ones who instigated the whole situation and handed Jesus over to be crucified; they did not judge themselves.

Jesus said the Pharisees put heavy yokes on people instead of taking them off (Matthew 23:1–36). We must never be like these religious leaders. Instead, we must be the remnant in the body of Christ and preach the good news of the gospel and see people set free instead of putting yokes on them, as the Pharisees did (Luke 11:39–52).

The centurion had great faith because he discerned authority, whereas the Pharisees had no authority; they did not discern who Jesus was (John 8:37–47). The Pharisees were corrupt and put heavy burdens on the people. We are not religious, and neither is Jesus. The Pharisees and the world system have a religious spirit.

SOME DENY THE POWER OF GOD

They will act religious, but they will reject the power
that could make them godly. Stay away from people
like that!

—2 Timothy 3:5 NLT

We call certain entities the church, but they are not. Some people
are clouds without rain because they claim to have a form of
godliness, but they deny the power (Jude 1:12–13; 2 Timothy 3:1–
7). On the surface, it looks godly, but they don't have any power.
They don't believe in the baptism of the Holy Spirit. They don't
believe in healing and the gifts of the Spirit. They don't believe in
the born-again experience. They practice a dead religion, just like
the Pharisees did.

AUTHORITY AND DISCERNMENT

The Spirit of God is our only hope; without Him, we cannot discern
and judge what is going on, right or wrong. Without Him, we cannot
have the holy fire because the Holy Spirit *is* the holy fire. He is holy,
and He is fire.

For the Lord is the Spirit, and wherever the Spirit of the Lord is, there is freedom.

—2 Corinthians 3:17 NLT

> *Wherever the Holy Spirit is, He will create freedom and an environment of authority and power.*

Everyone should be walking in freedom and in the Spirit so that we see the enemy overthrown. People should speak to their mountains and speak from the Spirit, not the flesh (Mark 11:23). All this should be happening throughout the body of Christ; it is not just for certain people. It is not only for the fivefold but for whoever is manifesting the power. Wherever the Holy Spirit is, He will create freedom and an environment of authority and power. What prevents us from walking in this freedom? It is the fact that we do not discern, and we do not yield. We must understand authority and discernment.

> *For if we live, we live to the Lord; and if we die, we die to the Lord. Therefore, whether we live or die, we are the Lord's.*

—Romans 14:8

This verse in Romans speaks of ownership, so I cannot live for myself anymore, but only for the Lord. People think they have a choice, but in reality, they do not. God gives all people free will, but you no longer have a choice as a Christian. People make their own choices anyway, which leads to problems. For this reason, the body of Christ has not risen up as a glorious church that the gates of hell cannot prevail against (Matthew 16:18–19). What we have is a weak group of people that are unbelieving believers. What is permitted happens, and God does not step in; we can see this throughout history.

When there was strength in the church and the Lord was allowed to move, we saw matters taken care of in the Spirit. When people prayed, we saw God move; He intervened, and prayers were answered. Then, when people relaxed and became lukewarm, evil was allowed to rule and reign, and corruption entered the picture. We must fully submit to the Spirit of the Lord and His authority, and then God will have full reign in our lives. Then we will triumph over our enemies (2 Corinthians 2:14). However, if we do not engage God and do not do what is right, then we will struggle and deal with the fallout of our wrong choices, which would be unfortunate.

We need to step back, consider where we are, and encourage others to be on fire and hot. Even if you are left out and feel alone and life is not turning out the way you want, it is time to get under God's authority. Submit to Him and let Him start to move in your life. You know you are going to heaven, so you can ask the Lord, "While I'm down here, can you make my life count? Can you show me what I need to do?" When you do that, He will answer you. Revelation is going to come, but the holy fire will also come. A purifying process will come to answer your prayer because some obstacles are in the way.

JESUS WAITED FOR PEOPLE TO ENGAGE HIM

Jesus wanted people to come to Him. People pulled on Him; He waited to see their response to Him and answered their faith. When Jesus saw faith in their words or actions, He responded to them and did whatever they asked. Jesus walked past others or did not act when people did not engage Him. Interestingly, Jesus was waiting for people to encounter Him and was listening to what they were saying.

JESUS WANTS PEOPLE SET FREE

Come to Me, all you who labor and are heavy laden, and I will give you rest. Take My yoke upon you and

*learn from Me, for I am gentle and lowly in heart,
and you will find rest for your souls. For My yoke is
easy and My burden is light.*

—Matthew 11:28–30

Jesus invited people to come to Him because the Pharisees were putting yokes on the people, which were too heavy to bear. Jesus gave the previous verse as an invitation because the religious system was burdening people and making it all about behavior, good works, and control. You can see this happening in today's religious systems, in the powerless churches. I am not talking about those churches that preach the gospel; I am talking about any time you feel controlled or manipulated, which is what satan does. The Pharisees also operated this way because they did not want people to be free; they felt like they would not be needed anymore if the people were free.

Jesus was always trying to work Himself out of a job. He wanted the disciples to do what He was doing. Jesus told them they would do even greater works, which was hard to fathom (John 14:12). He said that the Holy Spirit was coming to help us and instructed us to remain in the Spirit. Paul said that those who walk in the flesh cannot please God, and those who sow in the Spirit will reap everlasting life (Romans 8:8; Galatians 6:8). He also explained that those who are led by the Spirit of God are sons of God (Romans 8:14).

Jesus and the apostle Paul showed us how to live in the Spirit. So even though you might feel lonely, abandoned, or weak, the truth is that everything you need for life and godliness, as Peter said, is already in you by the power of God (2 Peter 1:2–4). All those precious promises, all that empowerment, is already within you. God has given us these things so we can be partakers of the divine nature, which is the truth. However, the fact is that you may feel lonely, discouraged, or disappointed. You might not understand some of what has happened and need closure. You need resolution on some matters. Maybe you just need to experience God personally on your own.

> *And I will ask the Father, and He will give you another Advocate, Who will never leave you.*
>
> —John 14:16 NLT

Even in difficult times, you must focus on the truth that the Holy Spirit will never leave you. Jesus said that when the Holy Spirit comes, He will be like Jesus. He will never leave you and will be with you until the end of the age and will not leave you as an orphan (Matthew 28:20; John 14:18). I have to believe Jesus in this situation, even if I feel something different.

As you come to this place in your life and let it be right now, you realize you are not alone, and you are not discouraged. You have courage because you have the third person of the Trinity, the Holy Spirit, inside you. As Peter said, you have everything you need inside you for life and godliness (2 Peter 1:3–4). You can be a partaker of the divine nature, having these godly qualities coming up through you and experiencing them in your own reality.

THE HOLY FIRE REMOVES BLOCKAGES

The holy fire is so crucial because blockages and other issues come up. Many people are wired a certain way and have a way of thinking through problems and processing them. Then they automatically function a certain way when life happens. It is almost as if they have been preprogrammed to respond and think a certain way, but their thinking is wrong. For example, you might have a specific flow at your job and a particular way of working as a professional. When someone new comes in, they might have done it differently at their old company. Different professionals have specific safety procedures, which is why the government sets a standard for the aviation industry to which all employees must adhere.

The Spirit of God is not just the facts; He is the truth. He says, "Here is what has to happen. You are processing it wrong; here is what you should be doing and how you do this." He may show you why you are hesitating or getting the wrong result by processing it wrong. That always happens; you must be corrected in God's ways, just like in your profession. If someone doesn't step in and correct that, you keep doing the same thing, and it won't end up right. However, there is a way of truth.

The Spirit of God knows everything about you and how you process life. When something happens and you find yourself responding a certain way, ask yourself, *Why did I process it that way? That is not even true or right.* I have asked myself this, and then I started to feel certain emotions and thoughts, which I realized were not the Spirit of God. The Lord was inside me and wanted to release the truth so I could process it correctly.

THE HOLY SPIRIT WANTS TO TOUCH YOUR LIFE AND CHANGE YOU

If you are discouraged, it is time to connect with the courage inside you. The Lord does not see you as a failure and wants to give you courage. The Lord wants to encourage you so that you do not feel that you are a disappointment, even if you feel like it. But that is not the truth. God has appointments for you and wants to bring you into this place where you achieve them all.

But we all, with unveiled face, beholding as in a mirror the glory of the Lord, are being transformed into the same image from glory to glory, just as by the Spirit of the Lord.

—2 Corinthians 3:18

The Lord does not want you to feel lonely because He is with you; the Holy Spirit is inside you and wants to talk to you right now. So if you feel lonely, it is only a feeling. Now I understand you want friends; you want to have input and to be able to communicate with people in your life. However, if that is not happening, take advantage of that season and reinforce your relationship with God. Let the Lord bring those people into your life.

Instead of manipulating and trying to control the situations that you are believing for, why don't you let the Lord start to help you with them? Give Him some time to work because He has to move situations around, and down here in this realm, it is a lot slower than there, so you might have to wait. We are tested because of the time discrepancy between the realms; we want things right away because, in the Spirit, we feel them instantly. But we have to wait for the manifestation. So walk it out with the Lord, and let the Holy Spirit be your friend. Let Him encourage and establish you in truth as you yield to Him. Do not yield to carnal and fleshly desires; do not yield to thoughts that you are alone because you are not. The Holy Spirit wants to influence you so you can impact your generation. He wants to touch your life and change you.

SEE THE END FROM THE BEGINNING

Now faith is the substance of things hoped for, the evidence of things not seen.

—Hebrews 11:1

You cannot please God if you walk in the flesh. You only please God when you walk in the Spirit and have faith. You have to look in your spirit and see the end. You make it through these situations, so take hold of that. I look back and see the end to everything and think, *Wow, I make it.* I go to the future, knowing I make it and everything will work out. I don't understand it all, but I know God, and He is faithful. He will see us through whatever we go through. Sometimes, I prayed and forgot what I was worried about and why I came to prayer. I started laughing because I could not remember why I was worried or concerned. Other times, I had questions, but when the Holy Spirit touched me, the fire of God burned out what was shorting me out inside, and I had no more questions. I could not think about what I wanted to ask. Interestingly, problems can seem so real, yet they are so far away. Sometimes, our thoughts and situations feel so real, but they are far from what God has for us. Then, the Holy Spirit suddenly comes in and burns out those things. He touches you, and all of a sudden, you cannot remember what was bothering you or the questions you had. That shows you that your emotions and your thoughts can be fickle. They can change even though they seem real, but then God could suddenly move, and those things are burned out in a flash. Right now, the Holy Spirit is removing anything shorting out your communication and whatever is hindering you, and I see that fire just burning it out. Submit to the holy fire and let the Holy Spirit be your friend so that you triumph in everything.

12

A HIGHWAY SHALL BE THERE

A highway shall be there, and a road, and it shall be called the Highway of Holiness. The unclean shall not pass over it, but it shall be for others. Whoever walks the road, although a fool, shall not go astray.
—Isaiah 35:8

Isaiah talks about a highway of holiness. If you do not understand a passage when you read it, do not let it go. When I read a section that's a little confusing, I will go to another translation and begin to investigate. You can get Strong's Exhaustive Concordance of the Bible and look up the words used in that Scripture. You will uncover some truths, and it will significantly help you.

Isaiah 35:8 holds quite a bit of revelation. As we near the end of this dispensation, we need the whole plan of God for this generation to be revived. We need to be heated up and to have another move of God, a revival. We use words such as "revival," but He never willed that we would need to be revived or heated up because we are lukewarm.

God is always moving, and He never meant for His church to stop moving with Him. God initiated the first outpouring of His Spirit, and He wanted it to continue. Certain principles are established in Heaven, and God's Word is not compromised. However, many things do not happen down here on earth because we don't side with the truth—we side with facts. A highway of holiness and a move of God was started long ago.

The day of Pentecost was an initiation of the last move of God (Acts 2:1–4). The church was formed when the Holy Spirit came into that upper room, and now we have the body of Christ. We have the church. We have believers individually, but corporately, we have a body. The Holy Spirit produces unity so that we can bind and loose because the keys of the kingdom have been given to the church (Matthew 16:18–19).

IF YOU DON'T BELIEVE IN THE THINGS OF GOD, IT DOESN'T MEAN THEY DON'T EXIST

Throughout history, God seems to use certain people to initiate what you would call a revival or a move of God. However, the whole body is supposed to be hot and in a move of God; it is never supposed to wane, slow down, or be compromised. We were never supposed to need another move or revival of holiness. A highway of holiness already exists even when we don't believe it. Whether or not you are on the highway of holiness, it is still there.

Just because people don't participate in something doesn't invalidate it. It does not go away because we say it's not there or don't believe it. If you don't believe in God, it doesn't make Him go away. Even if you don't believe in the Bible, it is still true. It is the same with healing, prosperity, deliverance, and preaching the gospel's good news. It is all true, whether or not you believe it.

Some people don't believe in hell, yet they end up in a place they don't think exists. Then they realize they should have believed in Jesus Christ. They believed in a lie, got trapped in it, and now they have to live in eternity in that lie. All those individuals down there will tell you they didn't believe in that place but ended up there.

Their unbelief did not make it go away or even diminish it. They thought that because they didn't believe in it, it wouldn't happen.

As Christians, we can learn from this. We will never need to redo or rebuild the highway of holiness or build another one. The highway of holiness is established. One translation even says that if a fool accidentally finds himself on it, he will stop being a fool, which is how powerful this highway is. This highway exists, yet how many people know about Isaiah 35:8? How many people on earth claim to be Christians but don't even know about the baptism of the Holy Spirit or don't believe in it? If you are a Christian, you must believe in the Holy Spirit. If you are a true believer and born again of the Spirit, you must believe in the Holy Spirit. You cannot have a born-again experience without the Spirit of God. You cannot be a believer if you don't have the Word of God to believe.

THE WORD OF GOD TRANSFORMS YOU BY RENEWING YOUR MIND

And do not be conformed to this world, but be transformed by the renewing of your mind, that you may prove what is that good and acceptable and perfect will of God.

—Romans 12:2

A lot of foolishness is going on, especially with the following words: revival, renewal, reformation, and the move of God. The Word of God transforms you by the renewing of your mind, so it changes your thinking and your life. Your spirit is reborn and is a new creation in Christ. That means that everything old (in your spirit) has passed away (2 Corinthians 5:17). Your mind, will, and emotions need to be transformed, and your body, according to Paul, needs to be disciplined (1 Corinthians 9:27). That is the truth.

When you are on the highway of holiness, your spirit is ignited because you are born again. Your soul is ignited and in agreement with your spirit because it is transformed and changed. Your body is also in agreement on the highway of holiness because it is being disciplined; therefore, you do not yield to the desires of the flesh. Paul said that the mindset of the Spirit is against that of the flesh, so they war against each other (Galatians 5:16–18).

ON THE HIGHWAY OF HOLINESS, YOU JUDGE YOURSELF AND LIVE IN REPENTANCE

This highway is unknown, but it is our pathway, and we pass over it throughout our life. Life is much easier when we are on the journey with other believers. I picture myself on this highway with many people around me, and I just want to be around those people.

Everywhere I go, I am looking for people who not only have faith in God and a sense of purity but also strong character. I am not looking for people that are upset because they got caught. I am looking for people that live in repentance and do not have anything to hide. They are on the highway of holiness, meaning they have judged themselves.

> *Or do you despise the riches of His goodness, forbearance, and longsuffering, not knowing that the goodness of God leads you to repentance?*
>
> —Romans 2:4

The revelation of the goodness of God causes you to repent. I did not repent because I was afraid of going to hell; I repented because I had a revelation of the goodness of God. Jesus wanted me to be born again, which I had never been told about before. God's goodness leads us to repentance; His goodness caused me to be born again, to receive Jesus.

> *In those days John the Baptist came preaching in the wilderness of Judea, and saying, "Repent, for the kingdom of heaven is at hand!"*
>
> —Matthew 3:1–2

He did not tell them to repent or they will go to hell. He said that the kingdom of Heaven is at hand, and that kingdom is everything that Jesus and the Holy Spirit represent. I see Jesus as a representation of the Father, and the Father is good. That means that Jesus would be good and that what He did was good.

> *How God anointed Jesus of Nazareth with the Holy Spirit and with power, who went about doing good and healing all who were oppressed by the devil, for God was with Him.*
>
> —Acts 10:38

Jesus did not go around doing wrong and making people sick; He went around reversing the curse and doing good, which is God's goodness that leads people to repent. When people were forgiven, healed, delivered, and raised from the dead, they gave their lives to the Lord.

> *Every day it is a process. I am producing fruit, but I am living a lifestyle of repentance; I chose this way when I elected to follow Jesus and get on that highway of holiness.*

Produce fruit in keeping with repentance.

—Matthew 3:8 NIV

The Holy Spirit is the third Person of the Trinity and is good. When He comes upon us and up from within us, He works out God's goodness in us, which is how we produce fruit in keeping with repentance. Every day it is a process. I am producing fruit, but I am living a lifestyle of repentance; I chose this way when I elected to follow Jesus and get on that highway of holiness. You do not get off the highway of holiness. As I said, the highway of holiness does not go away because you don't believe it.

GOD IS KING AND CALLS THE SHOTS

But I say to you that for every idle word men may speak, they will give account of it in the day of judgment.

—Matthew 12:36

Holiness does not go away because you don't believe it; you will still be held accountable. According to Jesus, you will be held accountable for every idle word that comes out of your mouth. This is what the Word says, and you can't do a thing about it. You will be held accountable even if you don't believe it. You can say what you want, but you will be reminded of what you said, and your life will end up the way you talked, which is the truth.

> *I can tell when a person is holy because I can see that God owns them, controls them, has their tongue, and speaks through them.*

God has spoken many things and never reneged on His Word. That is how He is, despite what you say, think, or believe. If the Lord says, "This is the way it is," He means it. He ignores the naysayers because He has already established His kingdom without them. God has invited you to be part of it, but it is under His domain and rule. He is the King, and He calls the shots. You do not tell the King what to do.

Holiness is really about ownership. I can tell when a person is holy because I can see that God owns them, controls them, has their tongue, and speaks through them. They understand their tongue is a rudder and hand it over to God (James 3:4–5). People end up right because they speak right. They are speaking from the other realm about what God is saying, which happens when God calls us friends. Ownership was when Jesus bought us with His holy blood. He set us apart and gave us back to the Father. Our lives are not our own; we have been bought with a price (1 Corinthians 6:19–20). If God chooses to use us or display us to the world, that is His choice.

We are the Lord's; we are holy because He owns us. Being owned by God releases you to walk on the highway of holiness, to walk in the fire, and let everything that is not of God be burned up because you do not own yourself anyway. I don't want anything that is not of God in my life. I am saved, safe, and valued in God's house. I'm part of His family. I have His name, I have been adopted, and it is ownership. He calls us sons and daughters (2 Corinthians 6:18) and friends (John 15:15).

> *The Spirit Himself bears witness with our spirit that we are children of God, and if children, then heirs— heirs of God and joint heirs with Christ, if indeed we suffer with Him, that we may also be glorified together.*
>
> —Romans 8:16–17

We are joint heirs with Jesus and heirs of God. God has given us an inheritance. He talks to us and reveals secrets, which happens on the highway of holiness. Jesus will tell us what the Father is saying and doing through the Holy Spirit. Jesus has promised that we will never be left alone and will always have the Holy Spirit with us to talk to us and be our advocate and counselor (John 14:26).

THE HOLY SPIRIT SHOWS US HOW TO HANDLE GOD'S GLORY

I want the process of how God deals with me to be in the correct order. I do not want to see the face of the Father because that would be the end of it. I would not be allowed back in my body, and I wouldn't be allowed to function in this fallen realm. My physical body could not handle that. I am careful to say, "Lord, show me your glory," because I know what that means. You saw what happened with Moses when he asked this of God (Exodus 33:18–23).

I asked God for the holy fire because it would prepare me. Holy fire includes being submissive, sanctified, set apart, and owned by God; it means allowing the Lord to teach me and dictate everything concerning me. I will be able to handle seeing His glory because of the holy fire, experiencing His presence, and then, one day, beholding the face of my Father. However, if I am not ready for it and cannot handle it, I am not asking for those privileges. There are different degrees in the Spirit. We have limitations, but we can yield ourselves to God and allow ourselves to be placed in the refiner's fire on the highway of holiness. Then the Holy Spirit can do His work in us so we can handle these heavier, weightier matters.

Every time I had an angel experience, it was so strong, and I seemed to be getting more used to their presence. However, it was so intense at times that I did not even want it to happen again because it changed everything about me. It shook me because it was more powerful than what I was encountering down here. I want to mature into this, and I desire boldness to increase. As part of the process, I want certain parts of me incrementally exposed to God's holiness and glory. I have found that praying to the Holy Spirit and allowing Him to coach you will bring you into this.

YOU CAN NOW ENTER THE HOLY OF HOLIES THROUGH THE BLOOD OF JESUS

Therefore, brethren, having boldness to enter the Holiest by the blood of Jesus, by a new and living way which He consecrated for us, through the veil, that is, His flesh.

—Hebrews 10:19–20

This new and living way opened to us is the Holy of Holies. Once a year, the high priest would be allowed to go into the Holy of Holies, and he could not go in unless blood was applied and he spoke the name of God. He only had access once a year (Hebrews 9:7). Now, a new and living way has been made for us personally. Under the old covenant, if that high priest did not apply the blood correctly, if he were not ritually clean or if he did anything improperly, he would die (Leviticus 10:1–3)., but now we, under the new covenant, are allowed to freely enter. Think about that. We can go in there and be exposed to God's holiness, and what could previously kill the high priest if he did anything wrong does not now kill us. We can all enter through the name of Jesus.

Moses could not see God's face, but now we walk with God and have the same Holy Spirit inside us that was in the Holy of Holies (Exodus 33:20).

> *Jesus answered and said to him, "If anyone loves Me, he will keep My word; and My Father will love him, and We will come to him and make Our home with him."*
> —John 14:23

That is amazing. Today, for most believers, the Holy Spirit is more powerful than most people ever felt in the Old Testament. Very few people in the Old Testament felt the strength of God that Moses encountered, but we have the potential to experience that because God is inside us.

GOD LAUGHS AT HIS ENEMIES

The wicked plots against the just, and gnashes at him
with his teeth. The Lord laughs at him, for He sees
that his day is coming.

—Psalm 37:12–13

We need to get into this place of overthrow of the enemy and overflow of joy, where we can see victory even in our hardship. God is in Heaven and laughs at His enemies. We are seated with Him in the heavenly realms and are heirs of God and joint heirs with Jesus (Ephesians 2:6; Romans 8:17). Essentially, the Lord's enemies are our enemies, and our enemies are His (Exodus 23:22). God sees everything as though we are part of Him. That should encourage you—if an enemy is tormenting you, you are in God's house, and that enemy will hear from God. The Lord laughs because He sees that His enemy's day is coming. You will be on the right side because of the separation that is coming and already taking place. Your enemies are in trouble because you have separated yourself and are on God's side.

But as He who called you is holy, you also be holy in
all your conduct, because it is written, "Be holy, for
I am holy."

—1 Peter 1:15–16

We separate ourselves and stand with God, and when God is laughing at His enemies, He is laughing at your enemies, too, because you sided with Him. You can quickly go through the holy fire if you submit. If you let the fire be your friend and consume what is not of God, the process will be even faster. The holy fire is greatly needed.

13

TRANSFORMATION IS PERMANENT

*Dear brothers and sisters, when I was with you I
couldn't talk to you as I would to spiritual people. I had
to talk as though you belonged to this world or as
though you were infants in Christ. I had to feed you with
milk, not with solid food, because you weren't ready for
anything stronger. And you still aren't ready, for you
are still controlled by your sinful nature.*

—1 Corinthians 3:1–3 NLT

Paul was talking to the people of Corinth about being separate.
He explained that he could not speak to them as spiritual
people but had to speak to them as carnal, because they were still

babes in Christ who could not receive it. That church faced all kinds of issues. Paul had to spell out how they were to behave when they gathered, each taking turns sharing songs, revelations, and teachings for edification (1 Corinthians 14:26). Paul told them that they were carnal, flesh-ruled babies that should be on meat.

SUBMIT TO THE HOLY FIRE AND LET YOUR CHARACTER MATURE

"Come out from among them and be separate," says the Lord. "Do not touch what is unclean, and I will receive you."

—2 Corinthians 6:17

Despite their carnality and immaturity, the Corinthians were being used in the gifts of the Spirit. Interestingly, even so, Paul rebuked and corrected them. They were on milk and in diapers like babies instead of eating meat and being adults. Paul wanted them to be mature and go on to the greater things. They did not submit to the holy fire and let their character mature.

If you investigated what happened to past moves of God and revivals and why they ended, you would discover that it was because of the flesh. People were carnal and did not yield to the Holy Spirit.

The focus of the minister and the services switched, and these different dynamics involved the will of man. They no longer operated with integrity, and their character was lacking. As in Corinth, the people were not mature. They grieved the Holy Spirit and did not accept correction. Many moves of God and revivals were stopped because of carnality and immaturity.

> *If you have a body of believers that operates at the highest level in the Holy of Holies, the secret place, those people will continually see God move.*

God wants to permanently transform you by the renewing of your mind (Romans 12:2). That move of God started when the Holy Spirit first came and is still going on today. That transformation is mind-changing and permanent. If you have a body of believers that operates at the highest level in the Holy of Holies, the secret place, those people will continually see God move. They keep themselves in repentance, which produces fruit (Matthew 3:8). They remain in the flow of the Spirit because they constantly repent and produce fruit that never ends, so they don't need a revival. They won't need another move of God because they have been permanently transformed, and God owns them.

The fivefold ministry should teach us that God owns us and is jealous for us; we are valued and safe with Him. We should be a permanent habitation instead of people going in and out, seeing moves of God end and new ones starting. The emphasis on these different moves was much needed, but God offers many benefits on His table. Paul was caught up, but he also obeyed God's will. He saw God's plan for the church, wrote to the different churches in his letters, and imparted truth to them. And even though he was saying all the right words, the churches faced a disconnect, didn't they?

YOU MUST CONTINUE TO PREACH THE GOOD NEWS

It is the same way today. Some people read parts of the Bible and think they know everything. After forty years of reading Ephesians and Colossians, I still see truth daily that changes me. I read those words and make corrections. I cannot believe I missed what was being said, but we understand by revelation. Even though they were carnal, Paul kept speaking to the Corinthians and teaching them. Even though they had problems and were still babies, Paul taught them anyway, which is how it is today.

We must continue to preach the good news, pronounce the truth, and live as fathers protecting and valuing people and ministering by the Spirit. Paul was jealous over people because as an apostle, he was protective—he was a father. Paul was just like our Father God. God is very protective and does not want anything evil to happen to us. We are upset when we go through difficulties, but we realize now that we are highly valued.

In this fallen world, we face hard times. If we put our foot down, we will see fewer attacks from the devil. We deal with more enemy attacks when we aren't proactive and don't put our foot down. I am waiting for people to wake up. You understand this, so you need to relay this information to others. We have to spread this good news of the gospel around the world. Jesus told us that the church had been given the keys to the kingdom and that whatever we bind is bound (Matthew 16:19).

Paul talked about our identity in Christ. He was caught up, and according to Galatians 2:1, he probably received revelation for fourteen years. For a time, no one even heard from him, and he did not share everything that happened. We see that in his writings that he had some amazing revelations. So can you imagine what he knew and didn't share? Paul once said he wanted to teach more, but they were not able to receive it (1 Corinthians 3:2). Jesus said,

> *I still have many things to say to you, but you cannot bear them now.*
>
> —John 16:12

AS YOU RECEIVE UNDERSTANDING, YOU CAN HELP OTHERS UNDERSTAND

The world does not define us, and we are not defined by the people that judge us; the Word of God defines us. The Lord Himself identifies with us because He became human (Philippians 2:7–8). We identify with Him because He redeemed us and then had us sit with Him in the heavenly realms (Ephesians 2:6). Paul had these revelations, which shifted him so that he saw that we were owned and could identify with Christ. Paul talked about this in all his letters, which shifts your reality when you read them. They have so much revelation that you can read them repeatedly and see something different every time. God talked to Paul, and Paul spoke to us; when we read his letters, we are blown away by some of the things he was shown.

What about us? What if *you* start to receive understanding, and then God wants you to teach and help people as well? What if you are supposed to father people in the Spirit? God gave that transference to Paul and all the apostles as fathers. The father transfers his anointing down so that we always have fathers. As a result, fathers share their knowledge with others in ongoing transformation. The move of God or revival does not have to skip a generation. After the transformation, we participate in it; we do the job of mentoring and fathering others, then hand it off. That was why Paul was investing in Timothy, and Timothy went on to do what Paul did. We have to stay in the same atmosphere those people walked in because they understood holiness and the power of God.

THE FEAR OF THE LORD IS THE BEGINNING OF WISDOM

The fear of the Lord is the beginning of wisdom, and the knowledge of the Holy One is understanding.
—Proverbs 9:10

Our country today lacks the fear of God, which has caused many problems. The church has not stood up or walked in righteousness, so evil was allowed to sneak into our government and get into the system. The gates of hell cannot overcome the church, but we have been weakened. All this has to do with not having the fear of God and not understanding that the fear of God is the beginning of wisdom.

We should always discern that He is God and reverently fear Him. We need to worship Him, honor Him, and allow wisdom to come in so we know how to manage our lives. It is not just about getting out of diapers, being mature, encountering the holy fire ourselves, and everything we already discussed. A point must come when we start to influence people around us and see the results of that holiness, maturity, and influence. As we transform, everyone around us also starts to be affected by that transformation.

A HEALTHY FEAR IS KNOWING GOD'S AUTHORITY AND SUBMITTING TO HIM

We will not be denied. The Spirit of God is holy, and we are to be holy as He is holy (1 Peter 1:15–16). Angels have been sent to minister to us who are holy (Hebrews 1:14). However, a holy fear also comes with that. The holy fear is reverence, knowing that we are not all-powerful, but God is and has the last word. So if God doesn't agree with me, I need to back off and agree with Him. God is not taking advice from us; we are receiving the truth from Him.

> *Then Jesus said to them, "Most assuredly, I say to you, unless you eat the flesh of the Son of Man and drink His blood, you have no life in you. Whoever eats My flesh and drinks My blood has eternal life, and I will raise him up at the last day. For My flesh is food indeed, and My blood is drink indeed. He who eats My flesh and drinks My blood abides in Me, and I in him."*
>
> —John 6:53–56

Many people walked away from Jesus the day He said this, but He was trying to show us that we can do nothing without Him. If we don't have Him as our source, we are nothing, despite everything we think is good about us and all we do to maintain or better our lives. Jesus was trying to tell them that they had to partake of Him, which was a more considerable commitment. It was not actually eating His flesh or drinking His blood; it was the symbolism of what we call communion.

> *We are to take communion, to remind ourselves that we are partakers of the divine nature, living in the supernatural life of God.*

At the communion table, Jesus's blood corrects the problems in our blood, and His flesh corrects the problems in our flesh. Jesus comes in and takes authority over our flesh and blood, and He becomes part of us, and we become part of Him. A sharing happens between both parties. We are to take communion, to remind ourselves that we are partakers of the divine nature, living in the supernatural life of God. Jesus said, if you do not do this, there is no life in you because "the life is in the blood," according to the law (Leviticus 17:11). The Israelites were not to drink the blood of animals because life was in the blood.

What was Jesus saying when He said we had to drink His blood? He expressed that His blood is where life is, which is a spiritual matter. His flesh is also spiritual because His body is bread from Heaven. Jesus was the bread that came down from Heaven (John 6:51). The living God manifested in the flesh, and we are to partake of that. We are supposed to become more like Jesus and disappear so He can become more evident and alive.

We sometimes back off due to the current deception, so we no longer have any fear of God. However, we need a healthy fear of Him. I am not talking about a phobia, a fear of the dark, ghosts, or the devil. I'm referring to a healthy fear of God where you know He is holy, the full authority in Heaven and earth. Whatever He says goes. You honor and respect Him, bow down and submit to Him. That is healthy fear. Jesus said,

> *And do not fear those who kill the body but cannot kill the soul. But rather fear Him who is able to destroy both soul and body in hell.*
>
> —Matthew 10:28

DON'T BE LIKE THAT FAITHLESS AND PERVERSE GENERATION

The highway of holiness influences us, just like when we partake of the Word of God and the Spirit of God and acknowledge Jesus's blood and flesh. We recognize that we are on the highway of holiness and enter the Holy of Holies. These atmospheres exist and are not just a nice bedtime story. We also do not take communion as make-believe; we take it seriously, and it affects us.

> *Then Jesus answered and said, "O faithless and perverse generation, how long shall I be with you? How long shall I bear with you?"*
>
> —Mathew 17:17

Jesus wondered why they doubted Him and had unbelief. You do not want to be like that faithless and perverse generation, which is what is happening in the world today. People are losing out because they are not discerning a highway of holiness and the Holy of Holies. As we take communion, we intimately fellowship with God at His holy table. There is a holy fire. We cannot replicate what God has and cannot do it on our own. He has to give it to us, and we must entirely rely on Him. The fear of God is missing and needs to come back, which is all part of holiness.

I have experienced holiness to the point where I had a fear and a reverence for God, which the Holy Spirit showed me. Many times in meetings, I and the whole congregation have experienced this holiness, and it was so strong that there was no way we could replicate it. This holy experience will happen even more because we need it. God introduced the fear of the Lord to us from the other realm. When it happens, it changes everyone, and everyone seems to respond. There is a trembling, a fear, and a reverence. People get very low to the ground and start to weep and shake. They feel the fire of God and are in awe of His holiness.

This has happened often in situations where you wouldn't think it would happen. This holy atmosphere transforms people, and at times, I still see people that were there who remember that time. We must return to times at the altar, times on our faces before God in deep worship. I am praying that the fear of God starts to come into the meetings so that God's reverence, repentance, and goodness are revealed, transforming people.

As Jesus taught and mentored the disciples, He gave them the authority to minister, so Jesus wasn't always performing the miracles. Sometimes we picture the disciples just sitting there listening to Jesus, but they were actually out in the crowd, praying for people, casting out devils, and laying hands on people. Jesus sometimes sent them out, but they weren't always successful. They didn't always get the desired results, which was a test for them. Then the disciples would try to figure out why.

Testing is happening right now in the United States, the Church, and worldwide. As we are being tested, a separation is taking place. The Church is plagued with unbelief; there is a lack of reverence, holiness, and the fear of the Lord. The disciples experienced this too.

DON'T GET OFF TRACK AND GO ASTRAY

Then the disciples came to Jesus privately and said, "Why could we not cast it out?" So Jesus said to them, "Because of your unbelief; for assuredly, I say to you, if you have faith as a mustard seed, you will say to this mountain, 'Move from here to there,' and it will move; and nothing will be impossible for you."
—Matthew 17:19–20

The disciples came to Jesus privately and asked why they couldn't cast out the evil spirit, and Jesus said it was because of their unbelief. They didn't want to hear that because it had been working, so what happened? They got cold and off track, and Jesus had to correct them. Jesus was saying they were in unbelief, and even if they had faith the size of a mustard seed, they could move mountains.

Be sober, be vigilant; because your adversary the devil walks about like a roaring lion, seeking whom he may devour.

—1 Peter 5:8

You might not know it, but you will sometimes go astray. At times, you will cool off because we are in a broken world. We can become worn down or deceived. You must watch your words and be sober-minded, alert, and diligent, knowing that the enemy prowls like a roaring lion seeking whom he may devour. If you live like that—if you learn to be disciplined and have good character, keep the fear of the Lord, and watch your words—these things will not happen. You will always be aware. However, as with the disciples, many people need to be encouraged and need these wake-up calls.

The disciples were told it was because of their unbelief. They thought they were looking to Jesus, and He gave them the word and authority to do that. Well, what happened? They switched from the spirit to the mind and lost the fear of the Lord. They lost the closeness of operating in what they were doing, that sacredness and holiness, which can also happen to us. Through building our character, we need to learn not to allow that to happen.

14

HOLY AND ACCEPTABLE TO GOD

I beseech you therefore, brethren, by the mercies of God,
that you present your bodies a living sacrifice, holy,
acceptable to God, which is your reasonable service.
—Romans 12:1

If you want to walk before the Lord, lay yourself down, and know the perfect will of God, you cannot do that without actually making sacrifices. In the Old Testament, an animal's life was offered as a sacrifice. In the New Testament, Jesus was sacrificed for us, and we became a living sacrifice. Today, our living sacrifice is that we die to our own will.

The high priests were all supposed to stay separate in the Old Testament because if the priest touched anything unclean, they became unclean. According to the Old Testament law, if a high priest became unclean, they were forbidden from entering the Holy of Holies and doing other works. In the New Testament, we have been made righteous and clean by the blood of Jesus.

HOLINESS IS NOT TRANSFERABLE

Thus says the Lord of hosts: "Now, ask the priests concerning the law, saying, 'If one carries holy meat in the fold of his garment, and with the edge he touched bread or stew, wine or oil, or any food, will it become holy?'"

Then the priests answered and said, "No."

And Haggai said, "If one who is unclean because of a dead body touches any of these, will it be unclean?"

So the priests answered and said, "It shall be unclean."
                                                        —Haggai 2:11–13

This passage talks about how the high priest could have corruption transferred to him from touching something unclean, but he could not transfer holiness to someone else. As I sought God, I saw that holiness could not be transferred. You cannot lay hands on someone and make them holy, but if the high priest touched someone unclean, the high priest became unholy. I found it interesting that uncleanness was transferrable, but holiness was not transferable from one person to another.

AT THE ALTAR, YOU SET YOURSELF APART AND DEDICATE YOURSELF TO GOD

We separate and set ourselves apart today by presenting ourselves to God at the altar. When you became born again, you gave yourself to the Lord and presented yourself to Him. I kneeled in my room and created an altar right there. Then I got up publicly in church and testified that I was saved and was baptized in water in front of everyone as another testimony. Baptism is an altar. Also, when you kneel and pray, you create an altar. And when you stand up and testify, that becomes an altar.

We must return to the secret place where we meet with God and dedicate ourselves to Him. Imagine a boardroom as the secret place where you can sit and receive counsel; you have fellowship with

God and are safe there. God wants you to meet with Him in that boardroom or place of fellowship. At this altar, in this place of communion, you set yourself apart and dedicate yourself to God, and it becomes a memorial. Paul talks about presenting yourself to the Lord as a living sacrifice, and this is your reasonable service or your worship, and this has to happen.

Sometimes, I must go to the altar and present myself to God. At other times, I can sit at a table or kneel and meet with God, and we interact in communion; I talk to the Lord, and He speaks back to me. Two different things are going on here. Sometimes, I present myself to the Lord throughout the day. I am not communing with Him intimately, like in the secret place, because I am at work or out and about, but I am presenting and dedicating myself to Him. I am telling the Lord that I am committed to whatever He wants me to do, whatever is on His heart. Both of these are very important.

WE MUST HAVE COMMUNION AND ALTAR TIME

When you take communion, you come to the Lord at a table, and you are communing with Him, but it is also a sacred, holy altar. I want you to encounter both communion and the altar because God never wants you to take yourself off the altar. The altar where people come, wanting to commune with God and interact with Him in the

> *A warrior submits himself on the altar to the authority of God to where there is such a fear and reverence for God that a brokenness takes place.*

secret place, is missing in many believers' lives. However, God still honors holy altars, and we should dedicate ourselves and set ourselves apart, which is part of what a warrior does. A warrior submits himself on the altar to the authority of God so that there is such a fear and reverence for God that a brokenness takes place. Repentance happens, and you are presenting more of yourself to God. That is what is missing from our church services and our Christian lives.

We need both communion time and altar time. We should have that communion time, praying in the Spirit, meditating on the Word of God, and communing with the Spirit of God and the Word of God. At times, we must lay before the Lord and be silent, giving ourselves over to Him and allowing brokenness.

When I studied different revivals and the past moves of God, there were altar times and times of repentance and laying before the Lord. Great movements of God started with deep repentance, intercession, and time spent in God's presence. I did not see times of communion and interaction when the Lord was speaking to people. The focus was on people repenting and waiting on God. They were trembling in His presence and were deeply convicted.

EVIL SPIRITS LOSE THEIR POWER WHEN YOU LAY IN REPENTANCE BEFORE THE LORD

When we lay in repentance before the Lord, evil spirits lose their power. That is what is coming in the days ahead. The evil spirits cannot do anything about a person who is repenting, laying before the Lord in brokenness and speaking out their dedication at a memorial or an altar. They can't do anything about that.

I have studied documentaries of places on earth where revival has occurred and a great deluge of the Holy Spirit is poured out on the people. It is so powerful, and so many people all start to feel the need to repent. It reaches the point where bars are shut down, and all kinds of unusual signs and wonders happen in towns and cities, and you can study this. One of the people you can research is the lawyer Charles Finney, who quit his law practice, became a preacher and had great signs follow him.

Charles Finney had an associate named Brother Nash who would take a train to a town the Lord had designated for them to target ahead of the outpouring. Once at the designated city, Brother Nash would check into a hotel or find a place to stay. He would start to pray and not stop until revival broke out. Then Finney would telegraph him and ask him if it was time to come and if Brother Nash said yes, Finney would come. And they would start church services there in the town.

Brother Nash knew it was time to alert Finney that revival had started when he could look out the window and see that people had stopped going in and out of the bars. Another sign he noted was when people walked by where he was staying, and if they would fall in the Spirit right there at his door, he knew that revival had started. People would start falling in the Spirit and piling up outside Brother Nash's room.

Brother Nash created an altar where he was praying, and the effects of that power and repentance started to affect the people. The people were not necessarily believers and had no idea what was happening on the other side of that wall. They were just walking past that building and were hit by the power of God.[1]

---

[1] Charles G. Finney, *Memoirs of Rev. Charles G. Finney* (Carlisle, Massachusetts: Applewood Books, 2009) 122.

Kathryn Kuhlman had similar experiences. When she was escorted from her car through the back of a hotel to an auditorium service, people would fall under the power of the Spirit as she walked by.[2] These signs have happened to people who have created altars, and the deep repentance and the strong presence of God affected the environment around them. The evil spirits there were so disarmed that they could not derail the situation.

> *The demons don't know what to do with a consistent person who will not stop and refuses to allow offense, doubt, fear, and unbelief to come in.*

Demonic spirits operate behind the scenes and try to trip people up and stop them by getting them into unbelief, fear, and offense. They are always trying to prevent people from assembling. Any place where believers get together and agree as touching any one thing binds demons, which they do not want. So they try very hard to stop believers from getting together. Demons want to separate believers and try to divide them with offense or fault-finding when they get together. However, if one believer starts a move of God by praying and creating an altar there, it spreads to others. Then that group turns

---

[2] Joan Gieson, *Healing in His Presence: The Untold Secrets of Kathryn Kuhlman's Healing Ministry and Relationship with Holy Spirit* (Shippensburg, Pennsylvania: Destiny Image, 2017).

into a whole church or a whole movement. Demons cannot work effectively because of that momentum or a revival.

The demons don't know what to do with a consistent person who will not stop and who refuses to allow offense, doubt, fear, and unbelief to enter. It is hard to divide believers if they stay together and are strong-willed. Every time satan hits you, you should go into intercession at the altar in prayer and repentance. Tell the Lord that you are not going to get knocked out. The demons eventually leave you alone because they see it is counterproductive for them to come at you. Then call your friends to pray with you so that a group is praying and interceding for your town, state, nation, or country. If the demons cannot stop that group of people, they won't know what to do because they rarely encounter such passionate Christians. I have found this is the breakthrough and the key to revival and the move of God.

BE A LIVING SACRIFICE

God never stops moving. We do not need to be revived if we are already alive. When we become lukewarm, we must expose ourselves to the holy fire. You will always stay hot when you consistently expose yourself to the holy fire. I am talking about putting yourself on an altar. The whole idea of an altar is a memorial, a place where you present yourself to God as a living sacrifice. When Paul speaks of putting yourself on an altar, he does not mean physically taking your life because it is a living sacrifice.

That altar where you put yourself, the living sacrifice, is the holy fire. You are submitting to the fire. If believers consistently do this, they will never get lukewarm. They won't need revival or another move of God, so to speak, because God is always moving. He needs His church down here on earth, individuals and groups, the body of Christ, to stay hot, move, and do whatever He asks them to do.

After a while, if you are not responding the way an evil spirit expects you to, it is counterproductive for him to continue to pester you. You need to run to God, to your altar, and go into repentance and intercession. The heat will intensify, getting hotter and hotter. If you involve other people, you will reach the point where evil spirits will figure out what is happening and not bother you anymore. They will see that they are pushing you further into the fire and the glory of God, and it is counterproductive for them.

DON'T DO WHAT YOU THINK IS BEST, DO WHAT GOD THINKS IS BEST

King David never ran away from God. *He ran to God.* Saul was a king but was always making the wrong choices. He did not wait for

Samuel the prophet when he should have; at one point; he even went to and consulted the witch of Endor (1 Samuel 13:8–14; 28:3–25). In contrast, David ran to God when he made wrong choices and dealt with them. David would go to the tabernacle and worship God, which is an example of what we should do.

Jesus does not want us to find ourselves on the wrong side of what He is doing, and He once expressed this to me in a supernatural way. He appeared to me and expressed His concern that if I did not stay humble and at the altar, presenting myself as a holy living sacrifice, I could find myself on the wrong side of what He was doing. In other words, I could be working against what Jesus was doing because I was acting on my own. I realized that this was the sin of Saul and that I could not do whatever I thought was best. I had to check in with God.

Culturally, some independent people have been doing what they think is best for years. However, it has crept into the church and believers' lifestyles. Some automatically assume they know what God wants and then do what they think would be appropriate. Then later, as Jesus told me, they may find themselves on the wrong side of what Jesus is doing.

Jesus explained that I had not checked in with Him about a particular situation, and I automatically assumed I was supposed to do it. I found out later that even though it was correct, the Lord didn't want me to start a bad habit of not checking in with Him and asking if He approved of that direction. Interestingly, we automatically think it's God when an opportunity comes up, and sometimes we find out later it is not. Even though it might feel or look good, it might not be what God wants. Not every opportunity that presents itself is what God wants. To know God's good, acceptable, and perfect will, we must go to the altar and present ourselves as a living sacrifice, which is our reasonable service and worship (Romans 12:1–2). We need to get back to doing this again.

If you want to see the power of God as you have never seen it before, then you need to spend time at the altar. Repent and turn yourself over to the will of God with physical actions—kneel or stand with your hands raised. Surrender and say, "I present myself to You, Lord." You can find this kind of dedication in Jewish culture. The Israelites had to come to Jerusalem at least once a year and present themselves to the Lord and offer a sacrifice. They had to give a lamb and different offerings according to the law. They would all converge on Jerusalem together to participate.

KNOW GOD'S WILL—DON'T ASSUME IT

I want my life to be sharp and accurate, and I want to know God's will. If you keep assuming the will of God, your life might seem okay at times, but a time will come when you find yourself far away from what God intended, and then you will have to wake up. I do not want you to have to go through that. The evil spirits want to trip you up and get you to side against God. They want to do it so that you think you are doing the right thing, which is what they did with Adam and Eve. They were trying to get Eve to misunderstand or doubt what God was saying and work against God, and you can see what happened. Look where we are now because of Adam and Eve's decision.

Evil spirits know how to make wrong situations look right. They know how to change people's perceptions and how they process thoughts. They work on a person's mindset. I started learning that if I turn myself over and present myself to the Lord on the altar, He will clear out the clutter in my life. If you neglect to submit yourself to Him, you will be surprised at how evil spirits are working on getting you to doubt, fear, or believe lies. They like to reinforce something that seems like a fact, and before you know it, you believe it, but it's not the truth at all.

> *I will no longer talk much with you, for the ruler of*
> *this world is coming, and he has nothing in Me.*
>
> —John 14:30

You should be presenting yourself at the altar all the time because it shakes those demons and their influence off you, and they can't do anything about it. Once you dedicate yourself to the Lord, it is called sanctification, and you have set yourself apart. You present yourself in the holy fire, and the demons can no longer operate. You do not have anything in you that they can hook onto because you are clean before the Lord, as Jesus was in John 14:30.

Jesus spoke to me, saying, "I am the door, and do not go anywhere on this earth unless it is through Me." At the time, I was going from place to place, accepting speaking engagements and ministry opportunities. I assumed the Lord wanted me to do it all, but I never checked with Him. Jesus appeared to me and ensured that I understood He was my continual access forever. He explained that even while I was on this earth, I should continuously check with Him. Many Christians I speak with tell me that they have automatically assumed what they were doing was right. They never thought about how they should have asked the Lord for direction regarding their actions.

When you get to Heaven, you will realize that some of the difficulties you went through were because you did not check with the Lord first. It might shock some people, but certain struggles could have been prevented if they had checked with the Lord. So many people wonder why the Lord let a particular event happen. However, they will find out later that they had a sign or a warning. So you need to check in at the altar all the time. We live in a critical time, and we must bring the altars back into our lives.

15

DIVISION OF THE SOUL AND SPIRIT

For the word of God is living and powerful, and sharper
than any two-edged sword, piercing even
to the division of soul and spirit.
—Hebrews 4:12

The Lord has a sword—the sword of the Spirit, which is the Word of God, as stated in the passage above. This two-edged sword cuts and divides between the soul and the spirit. We must understand this because many people do not. Two different words are used here: the word for spirit and the word for soul. People sometimes try to use them interchangeably, but they are not interchangeable.

DO NOT LET YOUR SOUL AND BODY RULE YOU

Your spirit is the real you and the person who will live forever and eternally. You are a spirit being that lives in a body. Your body is your earth suit, which you need to live down here. Your soul is the part of you that ties your spirit to your body. Your soul has three parts—mind, will, and emotions—and needs to be redeemed.

The renewing of your mind transforms your soul (Romans 12:2). The Word of God renews your mind so that your will and emotions also come into line. Your body is just a vehicle, a suit you wear down here. Your body deteriorates and dies at a certain age because it is fallen and unredeemed. Your body needs to be told what to do continually. You must take care of it, discipline it, and set boundaries.

Your mind, will, and emotions must be presented with what is good, righteous, and just; you must renew your mind to only think about those things (Philippians 4:8–9). If you do not, your mind, will, and emotions will take control and do what they want, which is how you acted before you were saved. Paul talks about this in Romans 7. Your spirit must rule and reign over your soul. You must tell your soul what it needs to believe and what it sees and hears.

The adversary, satan, goes after people with the media because he knows it can impress or change them. He can easily control people by what they see, hear, and feel. That is why Hollywood has released so many scary movies with terrible plots and events. You might think it is just entertainment, which is what they tell you, but you are being programmed, which is how your spirit is trapped and overpowered by your soul.

Most people you encounter, even Christians, are ruled by their soul and body, but they don't know it. They will not progress past a certain point in their relationship with God. Listen to what they are saying and doing when you talk to them; you can tell who is ruling and reigning in their lives. Even though they are Christians and claim to be believers, they seem trapped in their bodies and emotions. They do not understand that they are supposed to rule and reign down here.

THE SWORD OF THE SPIRIT DIVIDES
BETWEEN SOUL AND SPIRIT

To divide between the soul and spirit means you must do what the Spirit of God tells you to do. You can't do it if you don't know what God is saying. Then, if you do know and cannot control your body, emotions, and thoughts, you are trapped. That is why these altars are so important. The sword of the Spirit comes in and divides the soul and the spirit. That is the only weapon in the Bible that can separate soul and spirit; there is no other way except by the Word of God. It goes in, separates, shows you what is you and what is God, and divides between the two. Suddenly, you realize that what you thought was God is really your emotions and part of your soul being energized in a certain direction. However, we can thank God that Paul explained this in Romans 7 and 8.

DISCIPLINE YOURSELF AND WALK IN THE SPIRIT

For if you live according to the flesh you will die; but if by the Spirit you put to death the deeds of the body, you will live.

—Romans 8:13

Romans 8 talks about how we can yield to the Spirit and put the deeds of the body to death, and we will live. Your soul can be trained to side with your spirit. Then your soul and spirit side together and overcome the flesh. Your body must listen. Believers who yield to the Spirit, discipline themselves, and overcome the flesh are victorious in this life. I have a vision in these last days of a group of warriors who have learned to discipline themselves and walk in the Spirit. That is what every Christian should be doing anyway.

HOLINESS IS A WAY OF LIFE

*By which have been given to us exceedingly great and
precious promises, that through these you may be partakers
of the divine nature, having escaped the corruption that is in
the world through lust.*

—2 Peter 1:4

Jesus wanted me to revive some of these messages about holiness,
holy fire, the altar, and walking in the gospel. It is not merely a
message—it is a way of life. People either participate in the divine
nature and partake of it or do not. A person who has escaped the
corruption that is in the world will have joy. They are free. For years,
I have seen people preaching the good news, but they are unhappy
and not experiencing it themselves.

I would rather work in the marketplace and be a successful believer
in life and business than claim to be a minister and part of what we
see as ministry today. I would rather simply be a believer and
encounter the overflow in a secular world. I would go to work and
see a significant return on my giving. I would share the Lord with
people and see them saved and healed. I would prefer to do that than
some of what I see in ministry where people are not experiencing
what they are speaking.

A war is going on in ministry, but I want to be where the rubber meets the road. I desire that the ministry of the gospel works for everyone, not just a few. So as we are seeking a great harvest, we must be missing some things here, and I know what they are: the holy altar and holy fire. The combination of these two causes the sword of the Spirit to divide between what is of God and what is not, discerning what is happening in every situation.

At times, satan comes in, stealing, killing, and destroying, and we need to discern if that is what is going on (John 10:10). We need to distinguish between God's judgment and the destroyer coming in and doing the work of hell. If it is satan, then we need to take authority over it and come against it, both in an individual's life and in a corporate setting. We need a powerful corporate anointing to war against major spirits over territories and countries. It will take the body of Christ coming against these powers to see this move. It will take a considerable amount of momentum in the Spirit through a group of people to deal with corruption at a high level.

The fivefold ministry of the church builds up the body, as Paul said in Ephesians 4:11–16. Once the fivefold ministry of the church does that, the body will come into the unity of the faith and reach maturity. Mature believers produce fruit, which will be evident on the branches. However, this is not happening as it should. It will look like a move of God, a revival, but we don't need to be revived. If we need to be revived, we have become lukewarm. We are not dead, so we should not need to be revived.

> *When we speak the message of the gospel, it should be so powerful that people hear it and turn because of the dividing of the soul and the spirit.*

God is always moving and has never stopped—in this dispensation, He has moved from the day of Pentecost until now. The church age is still happening. People think that because they were not hot and stopped moving with the Spirit that He stopped moving. Then the sword of the Spirit comes in and starts judging, discerning, and dividing, and we can see what is of the soul and the spirit. As believers and ministers, you have to submit yourself to this process.

HOLY FIRE AND GOD ARE PART OF EACH OTHER

The holiness of God, the altar, holy fire, the Holy Spirit, and the Word of God all work the same way together. The holy fire and God are part of each other. When angels speak, they are speaking for God. You may hear an angel speaking to you, but when you listen to what they say, God's Word is coming through a messenger. Don't you think it should be the same with us? When we speak the message of the gospel, it should be so powerful that people hear it and turn because of the dividing of the soul and the spirit.

When an evangelist gives a message and an altar call, it divides the person's heart so they can see they need to repent. They can discern what is of them and what is of God and know that they are far from what God wants. Then they run to the altar and get saved or repent. These kinds of manifestations of the Spirit have to become more intense, which means that the messenger and the message have to be correct. A believer who is an actual partaker of the divine nature has escaped the corruption in the world caused by lust (2 Peter 1:4). If you have escaped that, you are set apart and separate.

NEW TESTAMENT PROPHETS CONFIRM GOD'S WORD TO YOU

If you would present yourself on an altar and give yourself over to God daily, you would submit yourself to that higher level of intensity in the Spirit. You could rightly divide the Word of truth because you would be rightly divided, know what is of you and what is of God, and be able to discern the will of God. Many people do not know the will of God because they do not submit themselves on the altar, as Paul said in Romans 12:1–3. If you do all this and hear from God, start to discern the will of God, or have an inclination of the direction you should go, then the fivefold ministry of the church can confirm that. You should already know in your spirit what God is saying to you because you are a believer. You are a child of your Father God in Heaven, and you have your own relationship with Him. A person or prophet should not speak a brand-new word to you in the name of God.

You should be able to hear from God for yourself and not have to go to a prophet or an apostle. You should have your own personal relationship with Him. Many have slipped into the mentality of going to people to find out what God is saying, which is not right. In the New Testament, asking others for a new word is not biblical. It is biblical for the body of Christ to come to you and confirm what God is already telling you. Jesus bought us so we could have our own relationship with Him. All the gifts of the Spirit, the ministry offices, and the fivefold ministry have been given to edify the body and confirm what God is doing.

God is already working in you, and He wants to confirm it so people can be moved by the Holy Spirit to minister to you and help you be confident of what God is saying. Many people have been misled by people telling them what they should do. Too often, the word wasn't accurate, but the person acted on it. However, they should have already known in their spirit that something wasn't right or it was not the direction to go.

I check in with the Lord thousands of times daily because I don't want to be misled. I know right away when someone says something to me that is not right. There are very few times when I do not understand what the Lord is saying. I don't know everything, but I can tell by the witness in my spirit, which is what I want for you. I want you to be built up to the point where the Spirit of God can divide, telling you what is of your soul and what is of the spirit. By presenting yourself as a living sacrifice, you will find yourself in this situation, which will develop and mature you. As a living sacrifice, you will not find yourself in situations where you are misled, deceived, or failing. All kinds of demonic activities take advantage of Christians these days only because they can. If you listen to what is taught in the Bible, you can seal this up so that you are no longer deceived.

> But also for this very reason, giving all diligence, add to your faith virtue, to virtue knowledge, to knowledge self-control, to self-control perseverance, to perseverance godliness, to godliness brotherly kindness and to brotherly kindness love. For if these things are yours and abound, you will be neither

barren nor unfruitful in the knowledge of our Lord
Jesus Christ.

—2 Peter 1:5–8

Peter said that if you are a partaker of the divine nature, you have escaped the corruption in the world caused by lust. Then Peter gives a handful of virtues or personality traits that we are to add to our faith. He guaranteed that you will never fail and will always be productive if you do this.

WAGE THE GOOD WARFARE
WITH YOUR PROPHECIES

This charge I commit to you, son Timothy, according
to the prophecies previously made concerning you,
that by them you may wage the good warfare, having
faith and a good conscience, which some having
rejected, concerning the faith have suffered
shipwreck.

—1 Timothy 1:18–19

In this verse, Paul refers to the fact that Timothy had received some prophecies, which means that people had prophesied over him, and Paul knew about them. Paul possibly even prophesied over

Timothy. However, Paul said that Timothy had to take those prophecies and wage a good warfare with them, having faith and a good conscience. He said that people who had rejected what concerned their faith had been shipwrecked. Many Christians do not understand that just because someone receives a prophecy does not mean the word will automatically happen.

Prophecy is God telling His intention. God will say, "This is what I want, and these are the plans I have for you." Still, God's plans do not always come to pass. Throughout the Bible, people walked in disobedience and unbelief, so the things of God were not done. Paul said if you wage war using those prophecies, reconfirming them, doing them, obeying them, and inserting your faith into them with a clear conscience, they will come to pass. Why? Because you have to believe.

Peter walked on the water because Jesus told him to come. Jesus was right there, but when Peter took his eyes off Jesus, he began to sink, and Jesus had to pull him out (Matthew 14:22–33). That was not the perfect will of God. What happened? Everything worked fine until Peter started to doubt and fear, which is what Jesus said.

And immediately Jesus stretched out His hand and caught him, and said to him, "O you of little faith, why did you doubt?"

—Matthew 14:31

Peter's reaction undid God's intention for him. God's will was not done perfectly, which often happens. Many people receive words from God, but they never come to pass.

> *God will say what He wants, but you must mix it with faith for it to happen.*

When you receive a word from God, you *must* mix it with faith. You have to engage in what Paul called "the good warfare." You wage war with those prophecies, and you reinforce them. You speak them out and go to prayer, coming against the evil that is working against it. So many times, I have seen evil come in and steal what God intends to do. It happened throughout the Bible because there is war down here, and many Christians do not understand this.

New Testament prophecy is conditional. God will say what He wants, but you must mix it with faith for it to happen. In the New Testament, we mix everything with faith. That means we must pray, repent, fast, and wage warfare against the devil who comes to steal, kill, and destroy that word. We can see this in the parable of the sower (Matthew 13). So it should be nothing new to people, but many do not understand the way God works.

If prophecies were written in stone, why would Paul tell us to wage war with them? Most people think, *Well, God said it, and that means He will do it.* When it doesn't happen, everyone thinks they missed God or that God changed His mind, but that is not true. They simply did not activate the word through faith into this realm. They did not actively wage war with those prophecies. So it is conditional—it is not automatic.

> *Therefore I remind you to stir up the gift of God which is in you through the laying on of my hands.*
> —2 Timothy 1:6

Paul reminded Timothy to fan the gift already in him into flame; in other words, it had gone out. So the gifts are not automatic either. If the gifts were automatic and written in stone, why would Paul have to tell Timothy to fan his gift into flame?

Revival and the moves of God are much the same. People become lukewarm and need God to move or revive them, but that should never be the case. God is constantly moving, and a live person does not need to be revived. They need to be heated up by the holy fire. We must fan into flame the gift within us, and we wage war with the prophecies we received. We are active warriors. We see the holy fire burn out the chaff as we submit to the fire. We are connected with God, Who is constantly moving, so we don't need to be revived. We see our prophecies fulfilled and the gifts of the Spirit moving and burning.

16

A HIGHER STANDARD

And raised us up together, and made us sit together in
the heavenly places in Christ Jesus.
—Ephesians 2:6

Jesus purchased us back, not just from the grave or hell; He placed us on the throne. We are seated with Him in the heavenly realms. We need to realize that from that point, we are in authority, we are seated with Him, and we are heirs of God and co-heirs with Jesus (Romans 8:17). God has placed certain things within us and spoken specific words over us. We need to enforce those things. God wants us to be with Him on the throne so that those plans are implemented.

Many prophecies in the Old Testament did not happen because people disobeyed. Many times, Israel did not receive the blessing of Deuteronomy 28. Other times, their enemies destroyed them, but it was never meant to be that way. The Lord gave them the conditions when He gave them the covenant. He said that if they wanted to be blessed, they should obey His instructions; if they wanted to be cursed, they should disobey what He said. God gave them a choice that day: blessings or cursings (Deuteronomy 30:19). The Israelites knew God would bless them with these great promises if they obeyed, but they still made the wrong choices.

Israel was initially supposed to be fifteen hundred square miles, according to the borders given to Abraham in the book of Genesis. Today, it is a tiny country in comparison to what God intended. When you think about how Islam and all the turmoil there have taken over the area around Israel, it is a strange situation, but it is all because of disobedience. They did not discern what was going on with the covenant or discern the Messiah when He came, and they had Jesus crucified.

THE BODY OF CHRIST HAS BECOME LUKEWARM AND NEEDS A NEW STANDARD

God will confirm His word with us with signs and wonders following (Mark 16:20). We speak His word when we declare the prophecies over ourselves that we have received. When we fan the spiritual gifts within us, we submit to the holy fire. We will see the manifestation when we allow the holy fire to take over and control our lives. If not, we will become lukewarm. Today, the body of Christ, generally speaking, does not seem to be aware of how far we are away from the holy fire controlling our lives. The body of Christ has become lukewarm, but most people don't see that.

The body of Christ must be exposed to a higher level of the standard in Heaven, which is why we must return to the altar. We must return to submitting to the holy fire. We should always live at this higher standard and be at God's beck and call, doing whatever He wants. We should live in an atmosphere like Heaven on earth, but how many people know that or speak it? It has to start with a group of believers that grows and becomes a movement with a new standard. However, it should never have diminished in the first place.

LIVE AND MOVE AND HAVE YOUR BEING IN HIM

For in Him we live and move and have our being, as also some of your own poets have said, "For we are also His offspring."

—Acts 17:28

Paul here speaks about who we are inside and the atmosphere we can create. You can create boundaries when you are alone with God or have an atmosphere with worship music and the spoken Word of God while you are studying. Then you expand from there. I recommend starting with ten minutes a day. Build from there and create that atmosphere.

Because of your schedule, commitments, and sometimes children, you might struggle to spend a certain amount of time in the Word. However, God can create a miracle in your schedule so that you can do that. As you discipline yourself to do the ten minutes daily, the Lord will expand you. You will get to where you are being influenced by the other realm, not just from this realm, and time will open up for you. God will make a way; I have seen this happen many times.

> *When you encounter the other realm, you realize there is a higher standard.*

I have been touched by the Holy Spirit at times, just as you have. I still cannot define what happened or what I felt in some of those situations. I only know that it was not from this realm; it was from Heaven. When God touches you, you see that the standard we live by down here is not always suitable or high enough. When you encounter the other realm, you realize there is a higher standard. I have experienced the holiness of God to the point where I wondered what had happened. God sometimes lets us go our own way; we stray and do not even know it. That is why teaching about holy fire and altars is vital.

THERE IS A HIGHER STANDARD TO ENCOUNTER

I expect God to show up, and when He does, I expect that the standard I am living by will also be changed and go up. Then, I will have to make some adjustments. That happened with Moses when he went up to the mountain with God. He must have thought what happened at the burning bush was holy when he had to take off his sandals. However, it did not compare to the level of holiness when Moses went up to the mountain to meet God. There was thunder and lightning, and the top of Mount Sinai was literally on fire and melting (Exodus 19:16–20).

Even today, if you look at the top of Mount Sinai in Saudi Arabia, called Jabal al-Lawz, you can see the whole top of that mountain is charcoal black. People have taken stones from the top of the mountain, cracked them open, and found they were the same color inside as the ordinary stones below the fire line. The rocks on the entire mountain are the same color, but only the top was burned, and the stones prove that. Mount Jabal al-Lawz is in Saudi Arabia, as Paul said (Galatians 1:17), and not in the Sinai Peninsula, as some have thought.

Moses encountered God in many situations, from the burning bush to this mountain on fire, but it was not over yet. God told Moses that He would show Moses His glory because he asked God for that (Exodus 33:17–23). On the mountain, God told Moses to hide in the cleft of the rock as God passed by. Suddenly, Moses experienced a whole other higher level. At that level, God explained to Moses that if he went any further, Moses would die because he could not see God's face and live.

Amazingly, when Moses came down from that encounter with God, he had to hide his face from the people because his face glowed, and the people were afraid of him (Exodus 34:29–35). Moses had to cover his face with a veil because he looked like God. If you do a word study here, Moses looked fearsome, and beams of light were coming from his face, which the people could not take. In their fallen state, Moses looked like a god to them.

Moses was 120 years old and in perfect health when God told him it was time for him to die (Deuteronomy 31:14). Moses would not have died if God had not told him. There was no reason for him to die because he had been given life after being up there with God Himself, and that life was keeping his body preserved, and he hadn't aged (Deuteronomy 34:7). This standard kept increasing in Moses's life.

In these days we live in, I want to give you hope that you have a higher standard and so much more to encounter. When you get to Heaven, you will see that we were living way below what we should have here on earth. It shocked me when I was with the Lord and found this out and was sent back. I want to bring back the standard of the Bible. We should speak what is in the other realm in the Word of God. We are supposed to be speaking over ourselves, our families, our churches, and our countries.

The Holy Spirit is calling us to repent and come up on the mountain with Him and encounter His holiness at a higher level. We are all waiting on God, yet we are not accomplishing what we need to, and we are constantly having items and qualities stolen from us. They are stolen from people because the body of Christ is supposed to be in authority, standing in agreement and preventing theft.

DO NOT BE LIKE THOSE WHO WERE IN REBELLION

Therefore, as the Holy Spirit says: "Today, if you will hear His voice, do not harden your hearts as in the rebellion, in the day of trial in the wilderness, where your fathers tested Me, tried Me, and saw My works forty years. Therefore I was angry with that generation, and said, 'They always go astray in their heart, and they have not known My ways.' So I swore in My wrath, 'They shall not enter My rest.' Beware, brethren, lest there be in any of you an evil heart of unbelief in departing from the living God; but exhort one another daily, while it is called 'Today,' lest any of you be hardened through the deceitfulness of sin."

—Hebrews 3:7–13

We must understand what is being said here. The writer of Hebrews in the New Testament is speaking to Christians. He is talking to believers and urging them not to be like people in the Old Testament. What happened to the Israelites in the desert? They died because they were in rebellion. The Lord talked to Moses and wanted to kill them all because they were stiff-necked, rebellious, and would not submit (Exodus 32:9–10). A stiff neck is a picture of resisting the yoke. Jesus said,

Take my yoke upon you and learn from Me, for I am gentle and lowly in heart, and you will find rest for your souls.

—Matthew 11:29

We are supposed to be submissive to the Lord, but the Israelites were rebellious. They were like oxen fighting against the yoke and were not doing the work. The author tells believers not to be like those in rebellion whose hearts were hardened. He says to hear His voice today. So believers can have hardened hearts and be in rebellion. The people were judged because they tested the Lord, and God was angry with that generation. Their hearts went astray, and they did not know God's ways. That is what happens when we need another move of God or revival, but it should not be this way because we should always be walking with God.

Remember the parable of the sower in Matthew 13? The condition of the soil represented men's hearts; there were four types of soils or hearts, but only one type produced fruit. One of the types was hardened soil (a hardened heart), which is one of the problems we have today. We do not understand God's ways or what He likes.

God has a personality, and if you sit and talk with Him, you will learn some things about Him after a while. When you sit with someone, listen to them, and interact with them, you will pick up on some of their personality traits. After a while, you will discover who that person is and what they like and don't like. You then make decisions based on that information. You decide if you want to be around that person again, if you want to pursue a relationship as a friend or a deeper level of intimacy. It is based on gathering information by spending time with them and interacting with them. You watch them and listen to them. When you observe God, speak to God, and listen to Him, you see His ways. These are His pathways, the way He walks, what He chooses to do, and what He likes. It is His personality.

If you really want to be someone's friend, you must know what they like and don't like. Then you have to decide whether you will pursue it further. Sometimes, when people are a certain way, you don't like it and don't want to be around them because they irritate you. You have the right to choose the level of friendship and what type of relationship you will have. When you work in professional relationships, you have to learn how to get along with people, but you don't have to agree with them on every subject. You just stay away from some people, for example, if they are irritating, or try to tolerate them and do your best to manage.

God was very frustrated and irritated with them and could not tolerate the Israelites anymore. God told Moses that He would go ahead and destroy them and make a great nation out of Moses (Exodus 32:9–14). Moses, however, talked God out of destroying them, and God said He would send His angel instead because He could not be among them. God told Moses to tell the people what He liked and required, but they would not adhere to that. Even though the angel of the Lord led the Israelites, an entire generation still died in the wilderness because of their rebellion and the hardness of their hearts (Exodus 14:19). Only the next generation went into the promised land.

BE DILIGENT TO ENTER THAT REST

> *There remains therefore a rest for the people of God. For he who has entered His rest has himself also ceased from his works as God did from His. Let us therefore be diligent to enter that rest, lest anyone fall according to the same example of disobedience.*
> —Hebrews 4:9–11

The Lord is saying through this author that you must know God's ways. His ways are that you must enter His rest and allow Him to bring you into the promised land. He said they did not enter the rest, so beware, lest you have an evil heart of unbelief, and that is the problem. Here, we see the unbelief of the children of Israel. We are warned not to be like them and have unbelief by departing from the living God. That is still happening today.

We should never need a revival but should always be hot. We should never get lukewarm but should exhort one another daily while it is still called today, lest any of you be hardened through the deceitfulness of sin (Hebrews 3:13). When our hearts are hardened due to sin, we become deceived. Peter says that being a partaker of the divine nature causes us to escape the corruption in the world (2 Peter 1:3–4). We do not encounter this deceitfulness of sin because we have escaped that corruption, which is supposed to be the story of our lives. You are experiencing this because you diligently make every effort to enter the rest. You have chosen not to be hard-hearted, and you have chosen to know the ways of God.

As believers, we must learn the ways of God. We do not have to be like those who fell in the desert—we can enter that rest. Remember that for the Israelites, it was a two-and-a-half-week journey from where they left Goshen to Canaan. It should not have taken forty years. Joshua had to take the next generation into the promised land because Moses allowed the Israelites to corrupt him. Out of anger in the desert, Moses struck the rock twice to get water instead of speaking to it, which was in direct disobedience to God's command (Numbers 20:11). Paul told the Corinthians that the rock that bore water followed the Israelites around in the desert. That rock was Christ (1 Corinthians 10:1–5). We cannot strike Christ twice. He cannot be crucified twice. Jesus was struck once, and now we speak to Him.

> *What is most important to God and us is that we know Him, know His ways, and implement those truths into our lives.*

Today, if we know the ways of God, we have a higher standard from Heaven that we can encounter, and we have to expose ourselves to that. What is most important to God and us is that we know Him, know His ways, and implement those truths into our lives. That keeps us at a higher level. The holy fire will always keep us hot so we do not become lukewarm. We don't need revival or another move of God. That higher level also keeps us from the deceitfulness of sin, which is the standard that God has chosen for us.

17

THE WORD OF GOD

If you seek her as silver, and search for her as for
hidden treasures; then you will understand the fear of
the Lord, and find the knowledge of God.
—Proverbs 2:4–5

We find ourselves in a place where we have to rely on Jesus and choose to trust Him in everything for our deliverance. If you remember, the angel of the Lord was sent to the Syrian army, who had arrayed themselves against Israel. The Lord sent an angel who, with a drawn sword, killed 185,000 Assyrian soldiers in one night (2 Kings 19:35). The angel's name was not even mentioned, and that was just one angel with a drawn sword who physically killed 185,000 fighting men. The Lord's angel had a flaming, spiritual sword, yet it killed flesh. If God could use an angel to do that, what would He do for us in the New Testament if we cooperate with Him? How could the Lord use the sword of the Spirit to discern what is us and what is of Him? I want us all to know the will of God, but I know that we will have to be exposed to something greater from the kingdom of God.

ALLOW YOURSELF TO BE CUT AND DIVIDED IN THE HOLY SPIRIT

The altars of God are so important; we must present ourselves on those altars, surrendering to the holy fire and the sword of the Spirit, which is the Word of God. We must allow ourselves to be cut and divided in the Spirit (Ephesians 6:17; Hebrews 4:12). If God can kill 185,000 of His enemies, He can certainly go inside of us by the sword of the Spirit to help us discern and know His ways. God's sword of the Spirit is a higher standard.

When I read about Isaiah encountering God's throne room and how he changed to the point where he became undone, I was reminded of my encounter with the Lord (Isaiah 6:1–8). I remember exactly where I was when I had this visitation and revelation of what Isaiah experienced. I had flown to Portland, Oregon, from Houston, Texas, for the night. I was touched by God there, and I was shown how Isaiah was changed and transformed by his encounter in God's throne room. When I encountered the throne room, I became undone trying to explain it. Isaiah had become undone and needed intervention because he suddenly realized he was unclean and was around a people of unclean lips (Isaiah 6:5). Isaiah did not seem to notice that until he encountered that higher level of Heaven.

Isaiah then pled with the Lord to help him, and an angel came and cleansed his lips (Isaiah 6:6–8). When he was sanctified, he asked the Lord to send him back, and he was sent back with that message. Isaiah went on to write sixty chapters of the book of Isaiah from a changed perspective. I want this to happen with the body of Christ.

The other realm has already touched us in so many ways in the new covenant, but God loves us so much and wants us to go to a higher level. We are not going toward Him, and I know why: We have not been exposed to that environment in Heaven. Every child of God should experience the throne room. I don't know how that will happen because we don't choose those encounters; however, it might be similar to what you feel in a church service. I have already seen it many times, and I want it to happen at every service, and I believe it will.

I have been in many different places in the world where the holiness from God's throne room entered the service. People fell everywhere, all over the floor, crying out to God and encountering His holiness. I saw how much God loves us and needs us to have an overwhelming dose of Him because our standard down here has been compromised. Isaiah was changed because he was introduced to much more than he would have received on his own. We need the same thing today. Our relationship with Heaven needs to go to another level, but unfortunately, we are unaware of this need. Many experience this ascension in our conferences. Once this happens, you will realize how far below you have been living from what God has for you and that is was always available.

> *We do not need to convince God to do what He already wants to do, but we need to position ourselves to receive from Him.*

Our relationship with God means we learn His personality and ways, then make adjustments. You must commit to pursuing this relationship with Him, knowing that you will have to change because God will not change who He is for you. He wants you to come to Him. Rebellion and hardening of the heart can come in because we do not always know or want His ways. However, once we encounter Him and soften and humble ourselves, God can bring that coal from the altar and cleanse and help us. This process is supposed to happen, both individually and with all believers.

Unfortunately, it does not always happen because, for whatever reason, people do not take the necessary steps. They might not know what to do or be lazy or undisciplined. I can fast and pray and ask the Lord to move and give you an impartation to understand; however, it should be happening all the time individually because you do not have to twist God's arm to get Him to do something He already wants to do.

LET THE HOLY SPIRIT CHANGE YOUR ENVIRONMENT

We do not need to convince God to do what He already wants to do, but we need to position ourselves to receive from Him. Fasting and praying will put me in that position where I already should have been. I needed to make that adjustment, which didn't change God at all. I am telling you the truth. I do not miss meals to convince God to act on my behalf because He already wants to do it. He wants to move among His people and visit them. Present yourself at the altar, and then allow the Holy Spirit to consume you. You meet Him there, but what you are meeting is His standard and personality. He is consuming you, but you are not being consumed. Only what needs to go will go.

The angels always see the face of God. They all go back and forth between the Father and earth to minister to people. They visit you, minister to you, and complete their assignments, but they always see the face of your Father in Heaven. These beings around us are fully convinced of things that we are not, which should not be. We need to let the Holy Spirit change our environment, and He wants to do that. We are not ready for some wars because we have not been strengthened, trained, or developed.

WALK IN THE SPIRIT, AND YOU WILL NOT FULFILL THE LUSTS OF THE FLESH

We must submit to the yoke of Jesus Christ that He offered to us to teach us (Matthew 11:28–30). Jesus wants to help and introduce us to His ways and realm so that we can operate in the Holy Spirit. We will still go to work and church, spend time with people, and be involved in our daily activities, but we will do these things from our hearts and encounter the other realm while we are doing them. We will have escaped the corruption that is in the world caused by lust and will experience Heaven on earth (2 Peter 1:4).

The angels operate at a higher level than we do because they are not limited by the flesh. However, according to Scripture, we are at a higher level than the angels because we are redeemed (1 Corinthians 6:3; Hebrews 1:14). This is not evident now on earth because of the fallen state of our bodies. We used to be able to see these realms, but now, there is a separation so that we do not see everything happening around us. We call these three realms the spiritual realm, the soul realm, and the physical realm.

In addition, there are many different types of light; some we see, and some we don't. Now you have to have special sensors to see some of these light spectrums on the earth, but we used to be able to see everything. It is the same with our hearing. Dogs and other animals should not be able to hear things we don't hear because we are higher than animals. We encounter the fallen world through our bodies, and our senses down here are dulled. However, God's will is that we walk in the Spirit so that we do not fulfill the lust of the flesh. We have eyes that see and ears that hear beyond our physical senses.

ALLOW GOD TO BRING YOU TO A HIGHER STANDARD

If you sit and talk to most people, they will admit there has to be another realm. Most unsaved people believe that the supernatural realm is real based on evidence, including science. The highest levels of government know much more than they want you to know. They know another realm exists, which contains other beings. They know all that, but they won't tell you about it. They have hidden some of the artifacts they discovered because that would prove that the Bible is true, which would mess up their agenda for the new world order and the one-world government. Major museums hide evidence from people because it would prove that the biblical record is accurate, and at the highest level, they are anti-God. Not everyone in these institutions is anti-God, but satan's agenda has gotten into these systems. Many discoveries in science and archeology support what the Bible says and God's existence. We are God's remnant on earth, and we should allow God to bring us to this higher standard.

> *Beloved, now we are children of God; and it has not yet been revealed what we shall be, but we know that when He is revealed, we shall be like Him, for we shall see Him as He is.*
>
> —1 John 3:2

Here, John is talking about the fact that we are children of God. We have heard the Gospel, believe, and know about the spiritual realm. But we also know that we are limited down here. We do not see or understand everything as children of God, the highest order of any living being. It has not been revealed what we shall be, even though we have been told. We have not encountered the freedom angels have as far as their bodies are concerned. They do not have the limitations we have because we have a physical body.

MADE IN THE IMAGE OF GOD

If you did not have your body, you would be spirit, and then you could go faster than the speed of light. Because we are in a fallen state, we do not see everything yet, but as John says, a time will come when He is revealed. When God reveals Himself and we see Him as He is, "we shall be like Him." So we will see Him as He is one day, but then we will realize that we are like Him, which is what happened to me. I was so surprised. I was sent back after everything I saw. I thought, *Everyone needs to know this. everyone needs to know that we were made in the image of God.*

Jesus was talking to me, and we were going different places. As I looked at Him, I thought, *Oh, my gosh, we look like Him!* We are more like Jesus than we want to admit, and I did not have the limitations of my body at the time. I could not doubt or fear. I was experiencing a higher standard when I was there and did not want to return. At that point, I realized that what happens on earth is deceiving, and we are often shut out. I must constantly dig deep within myself to remember some of what I saw and learned there because if I am not careful, I might forget.

YOU WILL BE SHOWN WHAT YOUR POTENTIAL WAS

I have to keep the reality of what I saw and heard in Heaven before me because this realm wants to shut you down, shut you out, and limit you. One day, we will be like the angels and be above them (1 Corinthians 6:3). However, I want to remind myself and you that right now, angels are worshiping God around His throne, and the saints that have already gone before us are all falling down and worshiping the Lord. So much activity is going on in Heaven; this earth is so minute and so insignificant in comparison that I did not want to return.

Honestly, I did get rewards for what I did down here, which I realized, but they were nothing compared to eternity. I could not remember anything about my life; it was as though it had never happened. It was as though the earth were so far away, and the only thing that mattered about my life was that I had made it. I had stayed diligent, and I had accomplished everything that I was supposed to do at that time. Then, when the Lord asked me to come back, I was so surprised because I thought, *Why would anybody want to do that?* It wasn't needed as far as I was concerned, but the Lord said, "No, I need you to go back to tell the other people what you have seen and heard so that they know and understand these things too."

> *One day, Jesus will reveal His standard, all He did for us, and what we were capable of.*

The Word of God and the Spirit of God are here with us, but you must be diligent so that the atmosphere will increase to the point where others can see a higher level. One day, Jesus will reveal His standard, all He did for us, and what we were capable of. At that point, you will be judged, but it won't be a judgment where you think, *I'm in trouble,* and you get nervous. Instead, you will be shown what your true potential was. God's plan and purpose for your life will instantly be laid out before you. In a flash, you will know everything that was available to you. It is like being a penny pincher all your life, eating only fast food, buying cheap stuff, and then finding out that you had millions of dollars in the bank in an account in your name. That was what it felt like to me. I was skimping and trying to save money, but I didn't have to. I lived way below what I had to on earth.

DIG DEEP INTO THE WORD OF GOD

When I realized what Jesus had done and what the plan of God was for my life, I thought, *Why don't people know? Why was I not told?* All these thoughts were going through my mind in a flash. But it was my responsibility, and Jesus showed me at that very moment that I was supposed to be a treasure hunter and diligently dig deep into the Word of God. If what happened to me had happened to you, you would be in the Bible all the time because you would have seen that there are hidden gems like diamonds in the Bible. You need to find all these hidden gems, and the Holy Spirit will help you, but you must be diligent. You have to have the Word of God open all the time. If you don't, it will not happen.

The situations that arise in your life will be milestones where God gives you another chance to be diligent and be a treasure hunter. However, when you get to Heaven in a flash, you will be shown what was done for you. Will it measure up to what you did with what you were given? You will instantly realize that you should have been more diligent and cannot blame it on other people. You will see that you had the ability to open the Bible and pray. You could have asked the Lord to visit you, and you had all these different ways to draw closer to the Lord and know His ways and plans for your life.

Bless the Lord, you His angels, who excel in strength, who do His word, heeding the voice of His word.

—Psalm 103:20

Angels want to do what God wants. They hear His voice, and they do it, and they can visit you. They can come and minister, stand beside you, and help you, but they are part of what God is doing. The Holy Spirit is also in you and can start to move upon you at any moment. Angels and the Spirit of God all have fire and *are* fire.

For He shall give His angels charge over you, to keep you in all your ways. In their hands they shall bear you up, lest you dash your foot against a stone.

—Psalm 91:11–12

The idea in this Psalm is that angels have special assignments to keep you in all your ways. So you will have visitations and angelic encounters.

When I was in Heaven, I saw that we were supposed to dig into the Word of God, and then the Holy Spirit would be activated at that very moment to show us the truth. I want to encourage you to dig deeply into the Word of God. Do not wait until that day when you turn yourself in and stand before the Lord, and He shows you, in a flash, what you did on earth. Again, it will not be a judgment like the world's but more like a personal accountability audit. Jesus will show you what He did for you and what you did with it. I don't want you to go through what I went through and then be unable to return. I was able to come back. Don't wait until you are before Jesus; you can encounter that audit right now and begin to change.

18

BE A FIRE STARTER

A fire shall always be burning on the altar;
it shall never go out.
—Leviticus 6:13

In all the revivals and moves of God, the wonderful people God used all understood repentance and the altars. They understood holy fire and the holiness of God. God has used people throughout the ages. However, as believers, we are not supposed to call out for another revival or move in this day. Instead, we are supposed to submit to the holy fire and the flames of fire. We are to be fire starters.

FINISHING YOUR RACE WITH JOY

But none of these things move me; nor do I count my
life dear to myself, so that I may finish my race with
joy, and the ministry which I received from the Lord
Jesus, to testify to the gospel of the grace of God.

—Acts 20:24

Paul was not moved by the things that seemed to have their way around him. He was not moved by adversity but wanted to finish his life with joy. No matter what happened, he could tell himself, *I will finish what God has for me and complete my race with joy.* Paul always talked this way in his letters, and you also have to say to yourself that nothing will move you. Tell yourself that you will finish your race with joy.

God wants you to encounter, have, and accomplish certain things in Heaven. But there is a great war for you to accomplish those things on earth. You must always consider that whatever seems impossible is probably what God wants to do for you because He wants to get credit for it. I don't get discouraged when things look impossible or go wrong. It is a divine setup because I know God does not fail. The only problem is that His people fail, and God does not always get what He wants when He wants it.

You must always consider that whatever seems impossible is probably what God wants to do for you because He wants to get credit for it.

And we know that all things work together for good to those who love God, to those who are the called according to His purpose.

—Romans 8:28

As we finish discussing the altar and presenting ourselves before the Lord, remember that anything we do for the Lord will be rewarded when it comes down to it. You will not be punished for what you could have done and did not do. Instead, you will be rewarded for what you did. Some people will turn in one talent, some two or three, and some ten on that day. They will give a return on what they were given and what they did with it. It is like an investment because some people will have a better return than others, which is what the parable of talents is about (Matthew 25:14–30). Those who were faithful with what they had been given were given more. The parable of the talents shows that the talent was taken from the person who did not properly manage what they were given. That talent was then given to those who had done something. This parable is about this life because you won't need talents in Heaven.

The secret that no one talks about in this life is how often you can go to the altar, turn yourself in, and reset. I have received talents that others were unfaithful with. I am not permitted to talk about the details, but the Lord gave them to me. He assigned me to accomplish specific tasks that were not being done. Some of these people have passed on, and others are still alive, but I have received their impartation; however, the secret is not about how often you do things right or wrong. It is about turning yourself in daily, going to the altar, and getting a reset. The reset is starting all over again. You are given more, and then you go out and do what you are called to do. The bottom line is that you should not wait until the day you stand before the Lord to be audited or receive what is due; you must go to the altar now because you have been given this opportunity.

Our enemy, satan, fights holy altars, the crucified life, repentance, holiness, and holy fire. He knows these practices keep a believer from having a hardened heart and falling into rebellion. The Hebrews did not enter the promised land and fell in the desert because of their unbelief. Hebrews talks about this when it warns born-again New Testament Christians not to find themselves in the same situation that the Hebrews did. (Hebrews 3:8–11).

GO TO THE ALTAR AND STAY THERE

The secret to the power of being a believer on the earth today is that you turn yourself in to the Lord. How many times can you repent? How many times can you reset? How many times can you go to the altar and stay there? Can you produce fruit in keeping with repentance? You should go to the altar all the time and never think you have arrived; you should never be so sure of yourself that you become deceived. Always allow yourself time, space, and room for the Lord to move and talk to you. You have to create that altar time and that atmosphere of Heaven.

I do not go to church to sit there and expect the minister to move me, minister to me, give me a word, tell me something new, or even encourage me. I go to church to minister, give, and bless someone. The Lord told me to feed myself. I went to many places where I did not receive from the ministry. They were giving out a cold snack instead of a hot meal. At times, I had to pray for four hours before going to church because so much warfare was going on there. I was assigned to intercede for that church, and we saw everything turn around so that the power of God was made manifest and the Word of God was coming forth. However, we were assigned there to intercede and pray.

FEED YOURSELF BY BEING IN THE WORD OF GOD

I had to learn how to feed myself by being in the Word of God and studying so that I did not solely rely on what others taught. Even at certain Bible schools I attended, I learned *about* the Bible but did not learn the Bible the way I thought I would. But the Holy Spirit was inside me and wanted me to meditate on the Word of God, and then He would reveal truth to me. You cannot expect other people to minister to you all the time. I will get my hot meal because I will open my Bible, pray in the Spirit, and read and meditate on the Word of God. I will study and do everything I am supposed to do. I learned how to do this, which was amazing. I did not get a hot meal and would have starved if I did not do that myself. I want you to do the same thing.

Our Warrior Notes courses and publications are based on the Word of God and the revelation of the Word of God, so you are getting a hot meal. However, you must also become a self-feeder. In other words, you can set your plate with the Word of God, and then I want you to teach. I want you to become a minister who ministers life to others and gives *them* a hot meal. By studying men and women of God through the ages, I found out that no one could give them what they needed except God, and they had to be diligent.

If you read about Smith Wigglesworth, John G. Lake, and many others, they had to place themselves in a position where they became available to God and received from the Holy Spirit and the Word of God. That was their ministry. After they received from the Lord, they gave to others. Some people had received a mantle from others, like when Elijah passed his ministry to Elisha, and there was a hand-off (2 Kings 2:1–18). However, you must develop your relationship with God and your own flavor and ministry.

ALLOW THE HOLY SPIRIT TO SET THE BAR FOR YOU

I went through a process as a standard from Heaven, as all believers are supposed to be. We should set the bar extremely high by allowing the Spirit of God to set it for us. We are supposed to be hot, and others will either like us or not as people who encounter the actual presence of God, the true glory and standard. When people meet someone on fire for God, if they also want to be hot, they are attracted to them and want to be around them. However, if people don't want that standard and want to be lukewarm, they will be separated, which is happening right now. You won't have the friends you thought you had because people are separated and becoming goats. They are becoming the tares and the unwise virgins right before our eyes because God is raising the temperature for us today. The standard is high.

Studying church history throughout the ages, you see the church cooled off in specific cycles. Then people cry out for change, and repentance occurs. People are raised up, starting another cycle, and there is revival and a move of God. We read about the people and what happened in that move, and another group of generals comes forward. You can read about these different dispensations or eras, these times of revival, and we have come to that cycle again.

THE WISE WILL SHINE LIKE THE BRIGHTNESS OF THE FIRMAMENT

Something new is emerging, but it should never have happened that way. We should have always been hot, but we are not because of our humanity. We are not disciplined and do not stay in the fire. We need to encounter this ourselves, all of us individually. This last move, this cycle that we find ourselves in, has to do with individual believers who have yielded to holy fire and allowed the Holy Spirit to teach them and bring them into this reality.

> *A group of fighting men and women, warriors of God worldwide, will not accept anything but all that God has for them.*

Now it was so, when Moses came down from Mount Sinai (and the two tablets of the Testimony were in Moses' hand when he came down from the mountain), that Moses did not know that the skin of his face shone while he talked with Him. So when Aaron and all the children of Israel saw Moses, behold, the skin of his face shone, and they were afraid to come near him.

—Exodus 34:29–30

A group of fighting men and women, warriors of God worldwide, will not accept anything but all that God has for them. That means they will all have to submit to this fire from the altar and the fire inside us. People will catch on fire in these last days, and their faces will change. They will be glowing like Moses was on Mount Sinai (Exodus 34:29–35). Daniel was told that the people in the last days, the wise ones, would shine. This is mentioned in several different places in Scripture.

Those who are wise shall shine like the brightness of the firmament, and those who turn many to righteousness like the stars forever and ever.

—Daniel 12:3

We are in the times Enoch was when he started to walk over to the other realm. I do not think it happened immediately; I believe Enoch was walking to and fro and back and forth from one realm to the other and was encountering all these things before he was taken. Some of his physical characteristics were changing, and he was being transformed from walking with God for three hundred years. I do not believe that we have to walk with God that long to be caught up and be with the Lord. Under the new covenant, with all we have been given, we can yield to the Holy Spirit and, if willing, be transformed.

I encourage you to be a self-feeder, diligently opening your Bible. I turn myself in to the altar every day. Then I take a verse or two from the Bible, write it on a three-by-five card, memorize it, and review it during the day, going over it in my heart. Every eight hours, I think about a particular passage of Scripture, and I am careful not to overwhelm myself with a paragraph, a chapter, or a book of the Bible. I only focus on the Scriptures that stand out to me.

> *Bless the Lord, ye his angels, that excel in strength, that do his commandments, hearkening unto the voice of his word.*
>
> —Psalm 103:20 KJV

I think about how the angels excel in strength and hearken unto the voice of the Lord. I think about how they are there and are becoming excellent and accelerating. They receive strength from the Lord, hear His voice, and do His bidding. They do His Word and whatever He says, and I think about their immediate obedience. I think about how strong they are, accelerating and excelling. I think about those truths all day, and before you know it, I know that verse and have revelation.

I think about the times when I feel the air change around me, the tingling of the air, and I realize an angel has come. Then I think he has heard from God and is excelling in strength and hearkening unto that voice and doing the Lord's work at that moment. He has come because the Lord has told him to do something, and my expectation rises.

BE THE FIRE THAT IS HANDED OFF TO THE NEXT GENERATION

The church of the living God is not just an event that happens on Sunday or at a Wednesday prayer meeting. It happens no matter where you are; you could be the catalyst for changes at work. You may turn to your coworker and say, "You know what? God really loves you, and Jesus is waiting for you to make a decision to accept

Him. You need to look into your relationship with God and know that Jesus died for your sins and has resolved your sin problem." You start to testify about Jesus.

You can take a Scripture verse and allow it to be the catalyst for your day. You can do this daily by going verse by verse through several books of the Bible, such as John, Romans, and Hebrews. It can take years to go, one verse at a time; however, over forty years, I have continually fed myself a hot meal in the Spirit.

You are called to be with Warrior Notes in this generation and involved in what God is doing for a reason. We are at the beginning of a cycle, a higher standard, where the voice of the Lord is being spoken through His mouthpieces. A higher standard is being set than what we have previously encountered. That is not to make people feel intimidated, left out, or insignificant. It is to show us where we are supposed to be. There will always be that torch, that fire handed off to the next generation. The fire never goes out, but the standard must be at the forefront, which is happening right now. People are hungry for God and hungry for a move of God. They are hungry for the supernatural but do not understand it or know how to enter it. At the beginning of this cycle, God has given a proclamation and instruction about the altars, repentance, agreement in the Spirit among believers, intercession, and most of all, self-feeding.

You cannot depend on a lukewarm church at this part of the cycle because it is not predictable. You have to feed yourself. When you go to church or gather together, you should have already received a word from the Lord that you want to give and minister to people. You do not go to church or come together expecting someone to feed you.

> *But you have an anointing from the Holy One, and you know all things. I have not written to you because you do not know the truth, but because you know it, and that no lie is of the truth.*
>
> —1 John 2:20–21

The church has a fivefold ministry, including the teaching gift. However, the Bible also says that you have an anointing from the Holy One and do not need anyone to teach you because you have the teacher within you. This verse talks about the fact that instruction was given and false teachers were teaching wrong things. You will know if a teaching is right or wrong. The idea here is that you should not depend on the church or the lack of a church. You may not have a church you can go to now, but you can open your Bible and let the Holy Spirit teach you.

I encourage you to read God's Word, study, meditate on it, and be fed. It's also important to study because you will have to develop your ministry, teaching, and do whatever God has called you to do. The secret is those two things: be a self-feeder and always put yourself on the altar every day so that reset happens. When you lay yourself on the altar, you will know the perfect will of God. Submit to the fire and feed on the Word of God yourself so you will always have a hot meal.

Thank you, Father, in the name of Jesus, for each reader. I thank you that the power of the Holy Spirit that You have sent to us, the fire from Heaven, will come and baptize us right now. I thank You that no evil will befall them, for they are protected. Father, make this permanent in their lives. Transform them, and I thank You for sealing it up. Lord, let them remember the altars You have provided and remind them that they can feed themselves on the Word of God. The Holy Spirit will teach them and give them an anointing. I thank You for that impartation to remember those things in the name of Jesus. Amen.

SALVATION PRAYER

Lord God,
I confess that I am a sinner.
I confess that I need Your Son, Jesus.
Please forgive me in His name.
Lord Jesus, I believe You died for me and that You
are alive and listening to me now.
I now turn from my sins and welcome
You into my heart. Come and take control of my life.
Make me the kind of person You want me to be.
Now, fill me with Your Holy Spirit,
who will show me how to live for You.
I acknowledge You before men as my Savior and my Lord.
In Jesus's name. Amen.

If you prayed this prayer, please contact us at
info@kevinzadai.com for more information and material.

We welcome you to join our network at www.Warriornotes.tv
for access to exclusive programming

To enroll in our ministry school, go to:
www.Warriornotesschool.com

Visit www.KevinZadai.com for additional ministry materials

About Dr. Kevin Zadai

Kevin Zadai, ThD, was called to the ministry at the age of ten. He attended Central Bible College in Springfield, Missouri, where he received a Bachelor of Arts in theology. Later, he received training in missions at Rhema Bible College and a ThD at Primus University.

Dr. Kevin L. Zadai is dedicated to training Christians to live and operate in two realms at once—the supernatural and the natural. At age thirty-one, Kevin met Jesus, got a second chance at life, and received a revelation that he could not fail because it's all rigged in our favor! Kevin holds a commercial pilot license and is retired from Southwest Airlines after twenty-nine years as a flight attendant. Kevin is the founder and president of Warrior Notes School of Ministry. He and his lovely wife, Kathi, reside in New Orleans, Louisiana.

CHECK OUT OTHER WORKS ON THIS
SUBJECT BY DR. KEVIN ZADAI

 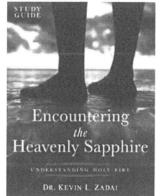 

Kevin has written over sixty books and study guides. Please see our website for a complete list of materials!
www.Kevinzadai.com

HOLY FIRE

The Kingdom of God

HOLY FIRE

The Kingdom of God

DR. KEVIN L. ZADAI

Unless otherwise indicated, Scripture quotations are taken from the New King James Version. Copyright © 1982 by Thomas Nelson, Inc. Used by permission. All rights reserved.

Scripture quotations marked (KJV) are taken from the King James Version. Public domain.

Scripture quotations marked (NLT) are taken from the Holy Bible, New Living Translation, copyright ©1996, 2004, 2015 by Tyndale House Foundation. Used by permission of Tyndale House Publishers, a Division of Tyndale House Ministries, Carol Stream, Illinois 60188. All rights reserved.

Scripture quotations marked (AMP) are taken from the Amplified Bible, Copyright © 1954, 1958, 1962, 1964, 1965, 1987 by The Lockman Foundation. Used by permission. www.Lockman.org

Scripture quotations marked (AMPC) are taken from the Amplified® Bible (AMPC), Copyright © 1954, 1958, 1962, 1964, 1965, 1987 by The Lockman Foundation Used by permission. www.Lockman.org

Scripture quotations marked (NIV) are taken from the Holy Bible, New International Version®, NIV®. Copyright © 1973, 1978, 1984, 2011 by Biblica, Inc.™ Used by permission of Zondervan. All rights reserved worldwide. www.zondervan.com The "NIV" and "New International Version" are trademarks registered in the United States Patent and Trademark Office by Biblica, Inc.™

Please note that Warrior Notes publishing style capitalizes certain pronouns in Scripture that refer to the Father, Son, and Holy Spirit, which may differ from some publishers' styles. Take note that the name "satan" and related names are not capitalized. We choose not to acknowledge him, even to the point of violating accepted grammatical rules. The author and Warrior Notes have made an intentional decision to italicize many Scriptures in block quotes. This is our own emphasis, not the publisher's.

Cover design: Virtually Possible Designs

Warrior Notes Publishing
P O Box 1288
Destrehan, LA 70047

For more information about our school, go to www.warriornotesschool.com. Reach us on the internet: www.Kevinzadai.com

ISBN 13 TP: 978-1-6631-0050-4

DEDICATION

I dedicate this book to the Lord Jesus Christ. When I died during surgery and met with Jesus on the other side, He insisted that I return to life on the earth and that I help people with their destinies. Because of Jesus's love and concern for people, the Lord has actually chosen to send a person back from death to help everyone who will receive that help so that his or her destiny and purpose are secure in Him.

I want You, Lord, to know that when You come to take me to be with You someday, I sincerely hope that people remember not me but the revelation of Jesus Christ that You have revealed through me. I want others to know that I am merely being obedient to Your Heavenly calling and mission, which is to reveal Your plan to fulfill the divine destiny for each of God's children.

ACKNOWLEDGMENTS

In addition to sharing my story with everyone through the book *Heavenly Visitation: A Guide to the Supernatural,* God has commissioned me to write over sixty books and study guides. Most recently, the Lord gave me the commission to produce the *Holy Fire* series. This book addresses some of the revelations concerning the areas that Jesus reviewed and revealed to me through the Word of God and by the Spirit of God during several visitations. I want to thank everyone who has encouraged me, assisted me, and prayed for me during the writing of this work. Special thanks to my wonderful wife, Kathi, for her love and dedication to the Lord and me. Thank you to a great staff for the wonderful job editing this book. Special thanks as well to all my friends who understand what it is to live in the holy fire of God and how to operate in this for the next move of God's Spirit.

CONTENTS

Salvation Prayer

INTRODUCTION

When Jesus visited me, He warned me that a season of testing was coming to earth and that many people were not ready due to their lukewarmness. Then I noticed that others were able to persevere in times of trouble and persecution. What was it that distinguished those who were prepared and those who were not? The answer is the baptism of the holy fire from the altar of God.

Jesus was the Son of Man, not just the Son of God, so His life, recorded in the Word of God, is an example to us. His life is written to help us to walk in the same fire of the Holy Spirit that He did. The baptism with holy fire paralyzes the devil and empowers you to function in your calling as a chosen one.

As you read this book, I pray that you will become more intimately acquainted with the Holy Spirit, who is a flame of fire, so that you may walk on the highway of holiness.

Blessings,
Dr. Kevin Zadai

1

TURN YOUR WEAKNESS INTO STRENGTH

And He said to me, "My grace is sufficient for you, for
My strength is made perfect in weakness."
—2 Corinthians 12:9

In the Old Testament, people were not led by the Holy Spirit like we are today because they did not have Him inside of them as we do. The Old Testament prophets and outward signs led them. The angel of the Lord led the Israelites in the desert, manifesting as a pillar of fire by night and a cloud by day (Exodus 13:21–22).

The Lord showed me that Joshua was constantly with Moses, and every time God had an opportunity to intervene, interject, or commune with Moses, Joshua was right there. When the tent of meeting was made and set up for all of Israel to seek the Lord, only Joshua and Moses entered and took advantage of it (Exodus 33:9–11). Joshua laid before the Lord continually, so can you guess who was chosen to take over for Moses—Joshua—and in his weakness, he became strong.

IN OUR WEAKNESS, THE SPIRIT OF GOD GIVES US POWER

Can you imagine spending time around Moses, witnessing everything happening with him, and thinking about the fact that the people did not want to engage with God? Moses was probably godly beyond what we could comprehend today, yet Joshua stayed there with him, and look what happened: Joshua became a mighty warrior.

As we see in the Bible, Joshua led Israel into the promised land, but he had to go and conquer all those cities first with the giants in them. In the cities of the land of Israel, like Jericho, vile, evil people had to be taken out. We often think of the weaknesses of an individual as a disadvantage. However, 2 Corinthians 12:9 teaches that in our weakness, the Spirit of God comes in and gives us strength.

Likewise the Spirit also helps in our weaknesses. For we do not know what we should pray for as we ought, but the Spirit Himself makes intercession for us with groanings which cannot be uttered.

—Romans 8:26

The apostle Paul was a strong and hard-headed man; before he was saved, he persecuted and killed Christians. I think about how strong and well-learned Paul was and how he was being trained as an orator. He studied under Gamaliel, the head Pharisee. From what the writings say, Paul, who at that time was named Saul, was being prepared to take over as the head Pharisee (Acts 22:3–5). He was persecuting Christians to impress those in leadership so they would see how zealous he was. Of course, God intervened, and Saul was converted and changed his name to Paul (Acts 22:6–16).

THE DEEP MYSTERIES OF GOD ARE GIVEN TO US BY THE HOLY SPIRIT

And I, brethren, when I came to you, did not come with excellence of speech or of wisdom declaring to you the testimony of God. For I determined not to know anything among you except Jesus Christ and Him crucified. I was with you in weakness, in fear, and in much trembling. And my speech and my preaching were not with persuasive words of human wisdom, but in demonstration of the Spirit and of power, that your faith should not be in the wisdom of men but in the power of God.

—1 Corinthians 2:1–5

After his conversion, Paul ministered in Corinth, a diverse and cultural city that was wise in the wisdom of man. In this letter he wrote to the Corinthians, Paul said he didn't come with enticing words of man's wisdom but in demonstration of the Spirit and of power (1 Corinthians 2:4). They might have thought that Paul would come and be an orator because he was well-learned and trained. Still, it says that Paul came with trembling. He was weak and only proclaimed the revelation that Jesus gave him. He talked about this wisdom given by God and how it is only spiritually discerned.

Paul told the people that "the Spirit searches all things, yes, the deep things of God" (1 Corinthians 2:10–16). The wisdom of the ages, the deep things of the Spirit, will be given to us by God, only from Spirit to spirit. Paul explained that the deep mysteries had been given to us through the Holy Spirit; the Spirit knows the mind of God and reveals it to us. Then he said, "But we have the mind of Christ" (1 Corinthians 2:16). Paul was no longer claiming to be strong in himself. What happened to change his personality? Paul realized that all that learning had not gotten him anywhere because he was on his way to hell.

The Pharisees were promoting a religion that put bondages on people. Jesus said that the Pharisees were supposed to be taking yokes off people, but instead, they were putting them on people (Matthew 23:4–5). Jesus strongly rebuked the Pharisees, calling them a brood of vipers (Matthew 3:7). Paul was humbled after he had a visitation from Jesus Himself, Who taught him about the gospel message that he would soon preach.

Amazingly, no man taught Paul the gospel. When you read his letters, Paul has extraordinary insight into what we have obtained through Jesus Christ, which was all received by revelation. In the books of Ephesians and Colossians, we see that we have been seated with Christ in the heavenly realms (Ephesians 2:6, Colossians 3:1). Throughout his writings, Paul explains that we have been given authority and the ability to understand the mystery of the ages about the church. He shares powerful insights about the body of Christ, the gifts of the Holy Spirit, and the fivefold ministry of the church. Paul revealed these secrets to the New Testament church and us.

Paul disappeared from the scene for several years, then reappeared with this gospel message. We have all this revelation from Paul, which he received in his deep, intimate time with the Lord. He was caught up in Heaven and was speaking from the heavenly realm. In the same way, Joshua was prepared by the Lord. We can see this when he encountered the angel of the Lord on the way up to Jericho (Joshua 5:13–15). He met the Commander of the Lord's army, and God showed him that an army of angels was working with him the whole time.

GOD'S STRENGTH IS SHOWN IN OUR WEAKNESS

And He said to me, "My grace is sufficient for you, for My strength is made perfect in weakness." Therefore most gladly I will rather boast in my infirmities, that the power of Christ may rest upon me. Therefore I take pleasure in infirmities, in reproaches, in needs, in persecutions, in distresses, for Christ's sake. For when I am weak, then I am strong.

2 Corinthians 12:9–10

Paul was very weak and humble, yet look at what he did. He told us that weakness was actually where God's strength was shown. He gloried in his weaknesses because that is where the power of God is revealed. You are being set up when your weaknesses are exposed because you still have to function in this realm. You will not cease to be who you are just because you fail, situations don't work out, or you sometimes feel like you cannot go on. The Spirit of God comes in at those times and wants to be a Comforter (John 14:26).

Even Joshua must have felt weak, always following Moses around. Moses was probably an intense person because of what he experienced on the mountain with God and with those angels around him. The first five books of the Bible were dictated to Moses. He wrote the Pentateuch, including Genesis, which was given to him verbatim—think about that. Moses was not even alive during Genesis, yet he wrote it. Now, how did he do that? The angels dictated to him.

Moses was given the law and all the instructions from God. He saw the glory of God and encountered that glory realm for days at a time. Joshua emerged from that environment as a leader. In Joshua's weakness, as he laid before the Lord, he was formed into who God called him to be.

> *But when God, Who had chosen me and set me apart*
> *before I was born, and called me through His grace,*
> *was pleased to reveal His Son in me so that I might*

preach Him among the Gentiles [as the good news—
the way of salvation], I did not immediately consult
with anyone [for guidance regarding God's call and
His revelation to me]. Nor did I [even] go up to
Jerusalem to those who were apostles before me; but
I went to Arabia and stayed awhile, and afterward
returned once more to Damascus.

—Galatians 1:15–17 AMP

Saul, who became Paul, was humbled and brought into the revelation of the gospel. Jesus caught him up to Heaven, and then he disappeared for years. During that time, Paul knew that God's strength was his friend. Paul said that when he was weak, he was made strong because the Lord revealed His strength through his weakness.

THE LORD STARTED YOUR FAITH, AND HE WILL FINISH IT

Therefore we also, since we are surrounded by so
great a cloud of witnesses, let us lay aside every
weight, and the sin which so easily ensnares us, and
let us run with endurance the race that is set before
us, looking unto Jesus, the author and finisher of our

faith, Who for the joy that was set before Him endured the cross, despising the shame, and has sat down at the right hand of the throne of God.

—Hebrews 12:1–2

Remember that whatever you are going through is a divine setup. You must look at it that way. I notice that when I start to feel weak in any way, I am about to take a step into the supernatural. The Lord is your Commander. He has begun your faith and will finish it; He knows how to set you up and make you strong. The Lord will reveal your weaknesses only to have you rely on Him, which is what took place in the lives of both Joshua and Paul.

> *I notice that when I start to feel weak in any way, I am about to take a step into the supernatural.*

When Joshua and Caleb came back from spying out the promised land, Caleb said, "Let us go up at once and take possession, for we are well able to overcome it" (Numbers 13:30). They were young, yet they had it within them to see God be faithful to their generation. They knew they could take the giants (Numbers 14:6–9). Unfortunately, the whole generation, except for them, doubted God and fell in the desert. They were all supposed to enter the promised land, but Joshua and Caleb had to wait forty years.

IT IS UP TO YOU TO KEEP YOURSELF
SPIRITUALLY HOT

Moses lived in the courts of Pharaoh until he was forty years old, then he had to flee and spend another forty years in the Midian Desert. Likewise, the children of Israel spent forty years in the desert, and then they all fell. The next generation entered the promised land. In our human frailty, we seem to become lukewarm.

We find ourselves in situations where we are promised so many blessings, and God is willing and ready, yet just a few people are prepared to go. The rest of the people seem to drag their feet. I am always amazed because I see this happen all the time. All of God's people suffer the consequences of lukewarmness, both those who are willing to do what God has for them, along with those who do not. Some churches resist the move of God, which you see throughout church history.

The demonic forces in the world want to wear you out, especially when you are willing and ready to go forth with God. You need to get other people on board with you. They need to learn spiritual warfare so that you all can bind and loose, waging good warfare in your territory (Matthew 16:19; 1 Timothy 1:18). Sometimes it is up to individuals to work with the Holy Spirit to bring about a move of God, even if it starts in a smaller group of people. In our weaknesses, God is revealed to be strong. Sometimes, regional breakthrough comes through small gatherings of people who meet; they become the remnant.

Sometimes you need to get away from a stiff-necked group, which is why people leave churches. People often want to go on with God, but their group does not, so they leave and join others who are hungry for God. Throughout history, God moved, and people moved with Him, causing His movement to grow. However, after a while, many seemed to grow cold. Then another group of people, a remnant, will emerge, and another movement will start. Throughout the years, I have studied church history and seen this cycle happen many times.

I formed Warrior Notes, the Warrior Fellowship Churches worldwide, the school, and everything we do at Warrior Notes for one reason: to stop the cycle of lukewarmness in the church. We see a remnant that wants to be hot again for the Lord, which is why we have the teaching on holy fire.

God wants us always to have that fire burning in our lives; that way, we will never grow cold. We should never have to have revival again because we are alive in Christ. We never have to have another move of God because God is constantly moving. We are called to remain hot, perpetually encountering the fire of God.

> *Having disarmed principalities and powers, He made a public spectacle of them, triumphing over them in it.*
>
> —Colossians 2:15

Paul made certain statements from his revelations that really should keep us hot. He was not a cold or lukewarm Christian and was adamant about what the Lord told him. One of the things he said that was very profound to me is in Colossians 2:15, which speaks of Jesus's triumph over the enemy. I have noticed in Christianity that groups of people and individuals are unaware or may have let it slip away from them. This truth may be mentioned, but it is not emphasized.

It is up to us to emphasize the truth and keep ourselves individually hot. Our spiritual temperature will cool down unless we each take action to keep it hot. Often, the church or ministry groups we are involved with are attacked by the enemy, their fire goes out, and they become lukewarm, so they no longer grow. Your spirit will no longer thrive in these groups. They do not get together to pray, intercede, or pull down strongholds. They do not proclaim what God has for the region and their nation.

NO MATTER WHAT DEMONIC ENTITY WE ENCOUNTER, JESUS HAS DISARMED THEM

Since we go through these cycles, we must understand and be reminded that Jesus already disarmed our enemy. If we feel weak and encounter demonic strongholds, we must remember that Jesus has disarmed them, no matter what demonic entity we face.

> *For we do not wrestle against flesh and blood, but against principalities, against powers, against the rulers of the darkness of this age, against spiritual hosts of wickedness in the heavenly places.*
>
> —Ephesians 6:12

Jesus has disarmed the principalities and powers, which are the four divisions of spiritual forces Paul lists in Ephesians. Paul mentions that Jesus made a public spectacle of them and triumphed over them, which means that He embarrassed them publicly (Colossians 2:15). What does that mean?

Think about where you are and where the church is. Then look at yourself in three periods: before you knew Christ, since you have known Christ, and in the future. What do you want to look like, and where are you going? Hopefully, you want to go into a fiery move of God.

If you want to dwell in a hot furnace with the flames of the Holy Spirit, you must understand some established truths that are not being emphasized at all. Jesus destroyed the works of the devil. He literally took their weapons away from them, which is what we should see when we encounter the enemy; they must lie down and listen to what we say. The enemy should be moving out of the way. If they are not, we may have to pray in groups of people or have the body of Christ as a whole address certain levels of demonic activity. Some things have to be done corporately.

> *You must remind the demons that they are defeated and drive them out because they hope you forget to enforce it.*

When dealing with a nation like the United States, you will need the corporate church to come in unity against certain territorial spirits, or the enemy will succeed in stealing, killing, and destroying. If we are not careful, the demonic spirits even try to use people above us in leadership positions. If the church is compromised, these demonic spirits also influence those people. Even though Christians cannot be demon-possessed, they can certainly be influenced by the spirit of the air. Peter was influenced in that way (Matthew 16:23).

If demons are attacking or influencing our lives, we must reinforce the victory of Jesus Christ, which has already been addressed in the Word of God. You must remind the demons that they are defeated and drive them out because they hope you forget to enforce it. The Bible has a lot of truth, but it is not being taught. As a result, we are seeing many people who are weak when they should be strong. If they knew some of these truths, they would manifest that strength.

JESUS WAS MANIFESTED TO DESTROY THE WORKS OF THE DEVIL

He who sins is of the devil, for the devil has sinned from the beginning. For this purpose the Son of God was manifested, that He might destroy the works of the devil.

—1 John 3:8

How God anointed Jesus of Nazareth with the Holy Spirit and with power, Who went about doing good and healing all who were oppressed by the devil, for God was with Him.

Here is another truth from the Word of God: The devil sins and has been sinning from the beginning; for this purpose, the Son of God, Jesus, was manifested that He might destroy the works of the devil. Jesus went around doing good and healing all who were oppressed by the devil. As He was manifested, He undid the works of the devil. He started to make people healthy again when they were sick. Jesus was doing good. So God is a good God Who sent Jesus to do good works. And these are all established truths.

The verses we just studied—Colossians 2:15; Ephesians 6:12; 1 John 3:8; and Acts 10:38—are essential to learn so you will not have a deficit. You must be able to deal with situations based on truth, but you can't do that if you are unaware of the truth. If you have heard these Scriptures before but don't keep them before you, you are not walking in that truth, which will hurt you. If someone knows the truth and walks in it, it is evident because there is fruit. If someone knows the truth but does not walk in it, it is just as bad as not understanding it. Either way, the result is the same. You have no fruit being manifested.

Jesus came to the world, was manifested, destroyed the works of the devil, and went around doing good and healing everyone. That is what we are called to do too. The devil has all these plans, yet Paul said that we are not ignorant of the enemy's battle strategies or his *devices,* which is what 2 Corinthians 2:11 says in the King James Version. Jesus undid and destroyed the plans and strategies of the enemy, which is essential information. If Paul said we are not ignorant of satan's devices, I would think *I need to know that.*

Years ago, when I didn't know satan's battle strategies, I asked the Lord for insight. Why is the devil allowed to work in a Christian's life if he has been disarmed? Why is he allowed to go around doing evil? Why aren't Christians going around doing good and healing everyone who is oppressed by the devil as Jesus did? I didn't know or understand these truths then and thought there was either a lack of knowledge or implementation, resulting in no manifestation.

The Lord revealed to me that in our weakness, He comes in His strength and girds us up so that we see His power in that weakness. As Christians, we must enforce our victory and forbid the devil to get away with his attacks. Christians are able to do what Jesus did. I want to see the manifestation of the power of God, which has to do with managing our weaknesses and allowing the Holy Spirit to come in and be our strength.

2

THE DEVIL CAN HAVE NOTHING
IN YOU

I will no longer talk much with you, for the ruler of this
world is coming, and he has nothing in Me.
—John 14:30

Many Christians exhibit weaknesses, but they are not experiencing the power or the strength of the Holy Spirit coming in. It is one thing to feel weak, but it is another to let the Holy Spirit come in and do a supernatural work in your life to strengthen you. I do not want religion to keep people weak, which the Pharisees did. They wanted people to stay in weakness and be enslaved in bondage. Jesus told the Pharisees that they were supposed to be taking yokes off people, which is what we want to do through Warrior Notes ministry. We train you to set people free.

When people think they are holy because they are suffering, poor, or sick, it can be a religious mentality, a victim mentality, or something similar. In contrast, the gospel is against all oppression and bondage; it is good news that brings healing, strength, deliverance, jubilee, debt cancellation, and forgiveness of sins. Not only does the gospel bring the good news of forgiveness of sin, but it also cleanses people from sin-consciousness. However, if you stay in a place of weakness and do not invite the Holy Spirit to strengthen you, you will remain weak, which is not pleasing to God.

EATING THE GOOD OF THE LAND

If you are willing and obedient, you shall eat the good of the land.

—Isaiah 1:19

Some people have this religious idea that God is making them sick because He wants to teach them something. Or they think that God wants them poor to humble them, but that is not how God works. God has already established His ways in the Word of God. God wants to prosper you because He said if you do all these things, you will have so much that you will lend to many, but you will not have to borrow, which sounds like prosperity to me (Deuteronomy 28:1–14). God promised He would take sickness from the midst of you, and you will not have to get sick anymore.

Do you remember how the Israelite's clothes and shoes never even wore out in the desert (Deuteronomy 29:5)? They were also supernaturally provided with manna and water and never got sick (Exodus 15:22–16:36). All these things were part of the covenant and promises of God. Although you cannot remain in your weakness, even so, weakness is your friend. Paul said that he gloried in his weaknesses because that was when the power of God was revealed (2 Corinthians 12:9). However, you have to go to that next step where God comes in and girds you up. That is when the Holy Spirit comforts you, brings resolution, and provides for you.

DO NOT LEAVE IT UP TO CHANCE

When you think about the world in its fallen state, it seems that if you let things go, they worsen; they do not fix themselves. We might straighten and clean up the house, but because of the fall, it gets dirty again; everything tends toward chaos. You organize your home, but everything seems to soon be in disarray again. Your house doesn't clean or straighten itself up or stay in order. If you let stuff go, it goes into chaos.

In the law of random chance with two choices, you have a fifty-fifty chance because there is only one answer or the other. If you leave it up to randomness, you should have a 50 percent chance of getting it right, so how could you fail 75 percent of the time? In this fallen world, when Christians rely on randomness, they allow evil spirits to come in, giving them a 100 percent chance of losing. Even though it would not be mathematically possible to lose that many times in a row, they do. If you flip a coin and say heads or tails, you have a fifty-fifty chance because there are only two choices, so if you do it four times in a row and miss it four times, at that point, something suspicious is happening. Evil spirits can supernaturally manipulate a Christian who lives by gambling or randomness, and you do not want to live like that.

LED BY THE HOLY SPIRIT

I will not be a slave to randomness because it is not in my favor. However, what *is* rigged in my favor is if I trust in God and the Holy Spirit leads me. The Holy Spirit can turn everything in my favor so that it is no longer random. That is better than fifty-fifty because you can win every time. If the Lord leads you, He will guide you into

His favor, not randomness; it is not like you are flipping a coin because the Spirit is leading you. The Holy Spirit is the Spirit of Truth, Who will lead you into all truth (John 16:13). That means you win, which is a higher law than randomness.

In the New Testament, when Judas hung himself, he was disqualified as one of the twelve and had to be replaced (Matthew 27:3–5). However, it does not say the Lord told them to choose another disciple or apostle. But they decided to follow an Old Testament practice and cast lots for who would replace Judas; they chose Mathias (Acts 1:26). In the New Testament, the Spirit of God is poured out. Now the Holy Spirit leads us. We are not led by prophets, the throwing of dice, or randomness—we are guided by the Spirit. The Holy Spirit inside each believer is doing away with chance and randomness.

The devil wants a Christian to operate in randomness or chance because he can get in there and cause trouble. However, the devil cannot manipulate the outcome if the Holy Spirit leads you. The Holy Spirit will always be correct and lead you to all truth. Now, the devil can steal that truth from you. The Holy Spirit could tell you the will of God, but it doesn't happen when evil spirits are allowed in to steal and take it away. That is what happened in the garden. God made the world and Adam and Eve perfect. Everything was fine, but the devil came in and stole people from God (Genesis 3). God permitted this to happen because we have free will. We see so many things like that happening today.

We do not want to be like the disciples who rolled the dice to choose the next person to replace Judas because God had already chosen each of them. In the Bible, Jesus did not roll dice to choose the disciples. He went up to the mountain and prayed all night, and God gave him the names of all His disciples in prayer (Luke 6:12–17). Jesus was led by the Spirit and chose the disciples.

So why were they rolling the dice and casting lots to select Judas's replacement? They ended up choosing Matthias, who is never heard of again in Scripture. It was never recorded that he did anything. That does not mean he didn't, but there is no record of him. However, there was a replacement for him—the one who announced that he was called to be an apostle from birth—Paul (Galatians 1:15–16). Paul was chosen to replace Judas, yet he came in another way. He became the apostle Paul, who did many great works for God and bore good fruit.

I do not make decisions by randomness or putting out fleeces as Gideon did (Judges 6:36–40). He put out a fleece, but that was in the Old Testament. Back then, they did not have the Holy Spirit inside them as we do. They did not have the gift of praying in tongues and all the resources we have today as believers. We have that intimate relationship with God. So in our weaknesses, we do not rely on astrology, tarot cards, or dice, and we do not get our income from gambling. We do not throw ourselves into situations with a fifty-fifty chance of winning. We do not do these random things because it is not of God. That is why we are forbidden to go to mediums, witches, or chart the stars.

> *There shall not be found among you anyone who makes his son or his daughter pass through the fire, or one who practices witchcraft, or a soothsayer, or one who interprets omens, or a sorcerer, or one who conjures spells, or a medium, or a spiritist, or one who calls up the dead. For all who do these things are an abomination to the Lord, and because of these abominations the Lord your God drives them out from before you.*
>
> —Deuteronomy 18:10–12

All these demonic activities listed in this passage are opposed to God's intimate relationship with us as believers. These practices are fueled by evil spirits, which is why you do not want to put out a fleece. You do not want to say, "If it is God's will, this or that will happen," because those evil spirits will hear what you say and go do it. Do not get into deception, be seduced, and drawn away by evil spirits by getting into wrong practices. Don't put yourself in a situation where the outcome is random.

You do not want to make decisions based on chance because it is not even a genuine chance—it is rigged. These evil spirits can rig situations against you, which you need to avoid. So do not involve yourself in those evil practices previously mentioned. Instead, place yourself in a situation where you seek God, petition the Lord in prayer, and have a 100 percent chance of getting your answer (Philippians 4:6–7). It is not random; it is *on purpose* because it is rigged in your favor by your Heavenly Father (Psalm 139:16).

RENEWED BY THE WORD OF GOD

I beseech you therefore, brethren, by the mercies of God, that you present your bodies a living sacrifice, holy, acceptable to God, which is your reasonable service. And do not be conformed to this world, but be transformed by the renewing of your mind, that you may prove what is that good and acceptable and perfect will of God.

—Romans 12:1–2

When you are born again, your spirit is redeemed, but your mind, will, and emotions are not. You must renew them by the Word of God. You must commit yourself to prayer, place your body on the altar as a living sacrifice, then deal with your soul and body individually as the Word of God says. You renew your mind, discipline your body, and build up your spirit by praying in the Holy Spirit and meditating on the Word of God (1 Corinthians 9:24–27; Romans 10:17; Jude 1:20).

God leads you in your spirit, not in your head or body. God took hold of your spirit when you were born again. He is not using outside forces to lead you because He can speak to your spirit. When the Holy Spirit baptized you, He got ahold of your tongue to control it. James said that if you have control over your tongue, you have control over your whole life (James 3:1–11). When the Holy Spirit controls your tongue, then when you pray in the Holy Spirit, you are led by the Holy Spirit.

THE SPIRIT PUTS TO DEATH THE MISDEEDS OF THE BODY

I love God's law with all my heart. But there is another power within me that is at war with my mind.

This power makes me a slave to the sin that is still within me.

—Romans 7:22–23 NLT

Here, Paul is talking about his struggle with being under the religious system. Paul says he knew and loved the law, but another power made him a slave to sin. He could not accomplish what he wanted to do and found himself doing the opposite—doing things he did not want to do. Paul was distraught in Romans 7 because of this, but at the end of the chapter going into chapter 8, he thanked God that the answer is Jesus Christ our Lord! Living in the power of the Holy Spirit puts to death the misdeeds of the body (Romans 8:13).

So now there is no condemnation for those who belong to Christ Jesus. And because you belong to him, the power of the life-giving Spirit has freed you from the power of sin that leads to death.

—Romans 8:1–2 NLT

In Romans 7 and 8, Paul shows us that we can now overcome our weakness through the Spirit's power, but we must engage actively. It is not enough to say, "Well, I'm going to struggle like Romans 7 talks about, and God is being glorified because I'm weak." When you do that, you are glorifying your weakness without any resolution. In Romans 8, we find out that we are supposed to be walking in the Spirit, which puts to death the misdeeds of the body.

> *I look within my heart as I pray in the Spirit, and I see that my spirit lights up inside me.*

As a born-again Christian, I resolved within myself that I have the power to put to death the misdeeds of the body. I also have the ability to correct my thinking and have the mind of the Spirit and not the mind of the flesh. I make that resolution within myself every day.

I look within my heart as I pray in the Spirit, and I see that my spirit lights up inside me. My mind is not fruitful when I pray in tongues, but the Holy Spirit is in operation. I cannot comprehend what I am saying because my spirit is talking to God, He speaks mysteries, and I yield to that (1 Corinthians 14:2). I can see that power within me, and then I know I can take that part of me and rule and reign in that place.

> *For though we walk in the flesh, we do not war according to the flesh. For the weapons of our*

31

warfare are not carnal but mighty in God for pulling down strongholds, casting down arguments and every high thing that exalts itself against the knowledge of God, bringing every thought into captivity to the obedience of Christ, and being ready to punish all disobedience when your obedience is fulfilled.

—2 Corinthians 10:3–6

I will not yield to the flesh and be called carnal as Paul described the Corinthians (1 Corinthians 3:1). I will cast down any thought or anything that exalts itself above the knowledge of God and bring it into captivity to the obedience of Christ. I will take it by force, arrest it, throw it down, handcuff it, and incarcerate it. I will not allow anything that exalts itself above the knowledge of God to rule and reign in my life.

In 2 Corinthians, Paul talks about the weapons of our warfare not being carnal but mighty through God, and he uses very strong language. I am taking my spiritual life to where the strength is. And even when I am experiencing weakness in my flesh and mind, I use my spirit to rule and reign. I am taking every thought captive to the obedience of Christ. I am causing my flesh to be put under submission because the Holy Spirit and the power of God ignite a stronger part of me.

THE WAR WITHIN

There are three parts to us—spirit, soul, and body—but only one part is redeemed: your spirit. Your soul is being renewed by the Word of God, so it is in the process of being saved, healed, and delivered. We go through a journey and a process in this life. As Christians start to understand this, they are healed and delivered, and you can see it happening.

Many Christians are wrestling with issues, but the problem is they are not wrestling with devils all the time—they are wrestling with problems within themselves. Sometimes they are torn between two opinions and oscillate back and forth. They have hurt, unforgiveness, and all these sins they are dealing with in their soul that Jesus said are bad for your soil (Matthew 13:1–23). Jesus noted how important it was to remove these hindrances or else you would not have a crop.

I always think about how I must deal with my soul and soil. One way is by asking myself, *Why am I responding this way? Why do I think this way?* Then I take what is in the Word of God with the power of the Holy Spirit, and I arrest these false ideas. I take them captive and incarcerate them so they can never exist again. I have to correct them, and then I put to death the misdeeds of the body.

> *To be good at spiritual warfare, you must start with the war within you.*

Whenever my body wants to act up, I say *no* from my spirit; as my mind starts to side with my spirit, I become stronger. As you practice this as Christians and warriors, you will begin to see this happen with yourself and others. You will start to excel to the place where you walk in dominion. That means you will have control from your spirit over your mind and body. As your mind is renewed and sides with your spirit, you will see yourself and others escape the corruption that is in the world because you have become partakers of the divine nature (2 Peter 1:4). The divine nature is inside your spirit. Still, your mind has to be renewed or else it will side with your flesh, which is where the battle is going on.

To be good at spiritual warfare, you must start with the war within you. Are you halting between two opinions? Are you oscillating? Are you struggling with unbelief, fear, doubt, and all these different areas that need healing due to traumatic events? Are you taken with the cares of this life? Or are you tempted by money so that you love and want to chase after wealth? Do you want recognition and have issues with pride? You need to deal with these struggles within you because Jesus said these problems in the soil would lead to no harvest whatsoever. The seed does not take root in three of the four soils Jesus mentioned in Matthew 13.

If your heart is hard, you need it softened, and if you need to be forgiven, you need to forgive. You must get the rocks and the thorns out of your soil, which needs to be soft and broken up. You need to be healed within you so that the battle is gone. Once you get all that out, you can discover how to engage in spiritual warfare with territories and all that entails.

> *I will not speak with you much longer, for the ruler of the world (satan) is coming. And he has no claim on Me [no power over Me nor anything that he can use against Me]; but so that the world may know [without any doubt] that I love the Father, I do exactly as the Father has commanded Me [and act in full agreement with Him].*
>
> —John 14:30–31 AMP

It comes down to this—when the devil comes, does he have something in you? In John 14:30–31, Jesus said that satan had no claim on Him; he had no power over Him or anything he could use against Him. Real warfare starts when the devil comes and tries to get you to fight yourself within yourself.

That happened to Peter. He was fine walking to Jesus on the water until he looked at his circumstances and started to waver (Matthew 14:22–33). He was dealing with issues going on within him that needed to be healed. Jesus told Peter that when he repented and turned, he would minister to the brethren (Luke 22:31–32). After the resurrection, Jesus met with Peter, and everything was restored, but this process must also happen with us (John 21:14–19).

We cannot stay in our weaknesses. Weakness is meant to reveal God's strength so we don't live there. We don't make a monument, a temple, or a denomination over it. We go on to resolve it in the power of God. The power of God must be revealed in our weakness, or we have not completed the whole process. Make sure you list what you are dealing with and need to take care of because I want you to be healed. You must eliminate the rocks, thorns, and hard soil within you so it can be perfect for producing a crop.

Prayer:

I ask You, Lord God, to remove those things from us, whatever is in our soil, in our souls, that is hindering us. Clean up our soil so that it is perfect, and we can produce a crop of thirtyfold, sixtyfold, and one hundredfold. In Jesus's name, Amen.

3

RESOLUTION AND PROVISION

Now faith is the substance of things hoped for, the
evidence of things not seen.
—Hebrews 11:1

There are works of the Spirit and works of the flesh. However, not everyone knows witchcraft is listed in Scripture as a work of the flesh. We seem to think that witchcraft is part of spiritual warfare. The demons are spirits, but they attach themselves to people in their souls, and they get witches and warlocks to side with them and use them. The demons hijack them to use them in the soul realm, then manifest through them in the flesh.

The demons want to express themselves in this realm because they are disembodied. They hijack people by intermixing themselves into their emotions and their wills. Then they can use people as guided missiles or puppets, which happened with Peter when Jesus rebuked him for speaking on satan's behalf. Jesus actually said to Peter, "Get behind Me, satan! You are an offense to Me, for you are not mindful of the things of God, but the things of men" (Matthew 16:23). Jesus talked to Peter as though he were satan himself. Peter was setting an example there to show that even believing Christians could be used to think and say the wrong thing.

> *Now the works of the flesh are manifest, which are these; adultery, fornication, uncleanness, lasciviousness, idolatry, witchcraft, hatred, variance, emulations, wrath, strife, seditions, heresies, envyings, murders, drunkenness, revellings, and such like: of the which I tell you before, as I have also told you in time past, that they which do such things shall not inherit the kingdom of God.*
>
> —Galatians 5:19–21 KJV

Galatians lists the works or the manifestations of the flesh, one of which is sorcery or witchcraft. You might think this is a spiritual problem, but here, Paul is talking about the manifestation of the spirit behind it. He says that the works of the flesh are evident. Paul is talking about evil spirits behind these works, manipulating people to manifest these sins. Paul said that you would not inherit the kingdom of God if you manifest these sins.

THE MANIFESTATIONS OF THE HOLY SPIRIT ARE THE FRUIT OF THE SPIRIT

So if you actively and consistently engage in these works of the flesh, you manifest the wrong spirit. You are manifesting the works of the devil through your own flesh. When you continually engage in these things, God cannot allow you into His kingdom. The manifestations of the Spirit are the fruit of the Spirit, which are all the opposite of what is being said here (Galatians 5:22–23).

Witchcraft is a work of the flesh, even though evil spirits have an influence. Paul said, "The weapons of our warfare are not carnal but mighty in God for pulling down strongholds, casting down arguments and every high thing that exalts itself against the knowledge of God, bringing every thought into captivity to the obedience of Christ" (2 Corinthians 10:4–5). This passage teaches about spiritual warfare on the highest level, yet it talks about dealing with thoughts in our minds, which is the psychological realm.

Paul says that we are dealing with manifestations of evil spirits in the flesh, and then he lists the works of the flesh. These works are essentially the evil spirits promoting their doctrine through a manifestation in people's flesh. I understand everything originates within the spirit realm because that was the first realm. Sometimes to explain a person's behavior, we say it is just how they are. However, if you looked into it, you would find that the root and origin of their behavior was sin. In the same way, the root and origin of the disease was sin, which had to do with the devil because he was sinning from the beginning (1 John 3:8).

THE DEVIL IS BEHIND SICKNESS, POVERTY, AND EVERY CURSE AND SIN

How God anointed Jesus of Nazareth with the Holy
Spirit and with power, Who went about doing good
and healing all who were oppressed by the devil, for
God was with Him.

—Acts 10:38

Jesus went around doing good and healing everyone oppressed by the devil. Right there, Acts 10:38 says that the sickness that Jesus was healing was from oppression by the devil. Everything has a spiritual origin. When you investigate someone, you find out it is not just about them; they somehow picked up that affliction from this fallen world. You will find the devil behind sickness, poverty, and every curse and sin. The devil is enforcing some traits and sins handed down through generations (Exodus 20:5). These evil spirits enforce the curse, and you will find those traits replicated in the next generation, and you wonder how that happened.

When someone dies, the evil spirits assigned to them don't die; they are just transferred. They live in a territory and follow family bloodlines. They stay in an area, enforcing what they are assigned to do. I have found that when you investigate why certain people are the way they are, the devil is somehow behind it, because he is enforcing the curse on this fallen world. In the same way, Heaven's angels are assigned to specific areas and individuals to implement their assignment. These angels provide security, but more than that, they enforce the blessing and the covenant and do God's bidding.

The devil wants to extinguish the human race and ensure that nobody goes to Heaven. He is so angry at God that he is not satisfied with the separation of people from God; he wants to destroy the human race. He wants to make it hard for us and torment us. Still, Jesus came back and destroyed the works of the devil (1 John 3:8). We cannot stay in our weakness very long because God's resurrection power has to come in, and the Holy Spirit wants to reaffirm that Jesus has conquered the devil and that He is healing.

When someone wants me to pray for them, I need to hear a brief explanation of what is going on. I want to know what I have to go after because I will take back what the devil stole from them. That is what Jesus did. He had compassion for people but wanted to correct what was wrong; He was restoring the kingdom for His Father. Jesus went around doing good and healing everyone. When ministering healing, you cannot glorify what the devil is doing. First, you must identify that it is the devil and what is happening. Then you connect with your Heavenly Father and transfer what God is doing by the laying on of hands. You pray and see God's will done.

> *For the word of God is living and powerful, and sharper than any two-edged sword, piercing even to the division of soul and spirit, and of joints and marrow, and is a discerner of the thoughts and intents of the heart.*
>
> —Hebrews 4:12

Hebrews 4:12 describes the Lord coming in with His word, discerning and separating, dividing the soul and spirit. At some point, God brings a resolution when He comes. You do not want to keep glorifying the devil and focusing on what he is doing. You want to discern what is of the devil and what is of God, and then you want to go right after what God is doing. God distinguishes between the soul and spirit not just to show you but because He wants resolution. At some point, you take care of what is of the soul; you cannot just stay stuck in your problem.

> *The Lord can define a situation through separation with the sword of the Spirit, but then you have to move forward into deliverance and healing.*

You must not continue sharing with people that you are sick, repeating all your symptoms and what you go through daily. The only way to take care of it would be to discern what is of the spirit, what is of the soul, and what is going on in your body. Then resolution must come, which is what ministry is all about; it is not focusing on the weakness. Ministry focuses on the solution or the strength of God. The Lord can define a situation through the separation with the sword of the Spirit, but then you have to move forward into deliverance and healing. There must be resolution and provision.

Ministry is not always about wrestling with demons. Sometimes, you are dealing with people's souls, which are just as real, even though they might not manifest demons. You can hear what they say or see how they act. A person does not have to be completely taken over to be influenced by a demon. You may realize that someone is deceived by listening to what they say, because what they say will reveal what is in their heart (Matthew 12:36).

In deliverance, people aren't generally thrown on the ground, spitting up, and speaking profanity, even though that sometimes happens. In most deliverances, people just feel something leave them. Often, they sense the demon leave that oppressed their mind, will, and emotions, or when they feel something leave their body, they have a manifestation of healing. Manifestations will differ because evil spirits have different degrees of how they influence people.

Not everyone is possessed. Christians cannot even be possessed because the blood of Jesus has purchased them, but they may need to be delivered in their soul (Galatians 3:13–15). An evil spirit may influence them, so they have problems in their minds, emotions, or wills. That is why I like to know what is happening with someone. Suppose someone has a characteristic or personal trait that does not align with being an imitator of God as a dearly beloved child

(Ephesians 5:1–2). In this case, they are not manifesting the fruit of the Spirit. That is how you know that there needs to be transformation and resolution.

First, people must understand that there is a problem and a discrepancy. Then you have to call their situation as it is. If a person's life doesn't align with the checklist of the fruit of the Spirit and if there are manifestations of lying, cheating, sorcery, adultery, or any work of the flesh, then you have to label that (Galatians 5:19–21). If you observe love, peace, joy, and the consideration of others more than the consideration of self, then you know that God's Spirit is manifesting in that person (Galatians 5:22–23).

For example, if someone is always late and cannot be on time, they are being inconsiderate of other people's schedules. It is chronic. A spirit is trying to cause others to see them in a bad light. If that person finds it hard to be on time, they must overcome this. I watched this happen with others and have seen many friends fired from our previous employment. Our job required us not only to be on time but to be ten minutes early. Even though it was one of the best-paying jobs you could have, people could not seem to overcome something that was constantly working against them. These evil spirits will try to trip you up and ruin your momentum so you cannot do what you want.

One area that demons use to trip up people involves keeping their word. In the past, many good Christian friends lost their jobs where I worked. They were solid people who were supposed to have those jobs but lost them because they could not show up when they were supposed to. Some people cannot receive certain truths from the Word of God. No matter what you say to them, they still cannot see it, no matter how hard you try to convince them.

RECEIVING, MANIFESTING, AND IMPLEMENTING THE WORD OF GOD

> *Your weakness is not an excuse for sin; you must come to a point where you take the grace of God and resolve the issue with His strength.*

If this truth is in the Word of God and is for us today, then you have to receive it. Once you receive it, it will manifest so that you can implement it in your life. When the truth does not manifest, it is not God working against you; someone else is stopping you, or something else is working in the situation. I tell you this because if there is resistance and something contrary to the fruit of the Spirit, you have to label it. You cannot put it off and say, "Oh, that's just them," or "That's just me." If these characteristics do not match up with a manifestation of the Spirit, they must be dealt with.

> *Now faith is the substance of things hoped for, the evidence of things not seen.*
>
> —Hebrews 11:1

Your weakness is not an excuse for sin; you must come to a point where you take the grace of God and resolve the issue with His strength. According to Hebrews 11:1, God asks us to have faith, which is "the substance of things hoped for, and the evidence of things not seen." This verse talks about resolution. If we are in a faith deficit, that is our weakness because we need something that we don't have. We must move toward resolution and cannot accept anything but what God has already shown us. That is what Hebrews 11:1 means.

Our attitude must be, "Well, then, I must receive this. I am going from deficit or weakness to strength or provision, a process of fulfillment." When you order something, it will be delivered to you, and eventually, you will receive it. I will not worry about things like losing my salvation or missing out on what God has for me because I understand those blessings. They are set because I have confessed Jesus as Lord, am saved, and am walking out my salvation in fear and trembling (Philippians 2:12).

I pray in the Spirit and am submissive to God, so I will not miss out on what God has for me. I walk in certain strengths now because God has already provided for me. I feel I am going somewhere in other areas, but I am not there yet. However, I do not focus on the weakness of not having what I want. I focus on the fact that I have the substance of things hoped for and the evidence in my hand. I believe that I receive what I have asked for; even though I do not have the manifestation yet. I know it in the Spirit. A transition, a process, is taking place.

If you are frustrated, want to see results in your life, or wish to get rid of certain bad habits, you have to turn your weaknesses over to God and let His fire burn them out. Let the fire of God, the resurrection power of the Holy Spirit, revive you and lift you up so that those strengths manifest. This provision is spiritual and will become physical. You do not want to get addicted to anything or rely on other crutches; you want to run to God, turn yourself in, and move from weakness to strength and provision. That is what Paul was talking about in Romans 8.

Joshua turned himself into God and went from weakness to strength. He was formed into a leader in his deficit as he waited on God and Moses, but Joshua was not recognized as a leader at that time. Afterward, Joshua ended up taking Moses's place. He was perfect for the job because he experienced everything Moses had experienced. Even though Joshua was not recognized at the time, he endured his process. Even though he appeared to be just a servant, Joshua ended up being a leader, which is what will happen with you.

Jesus wants us to identify with Him. He was a strength to many people when He was in this world. However, even though He was everyone's strength, He was hated and killed. Jesus was in the garden of Gethsemane praying and all His disciples fell asleep, and not even one person helped or supported Him in prayer (Matthew 26:36–46). Jesus asked them if they could not even stay awake an hour to pray with Him, but they fell asleep. As He is, so are we in this world (1 John 4:17). Jesus relied on God, the Father, in His weakness. The Bible says that Jesus learned obedience by what He suffered (Hebrews 5:8). We often find ourselves alone and weak, yet the Holy Spirit is with us, so we can find strength in Him.

No matter what we are going through, we must eventually go from weakness to strength. The books written in Heaven about you talk about how God, in your weakness, made you strong, so you will finish strong (Psalm 139:16). You will accomplish so much, but at times, you feel as if you are not going to make it another day. Remember, you are in transition because you are going from your deficit to your provision.

4

FROM GENERATION TO GENERATION

One generation shall praise Your works to another, and
shall declare Your mighty acts.
—Psalm 145:4

We have witnessed many events in this generation and should desire to be part of seeing God's faithfulness displayed. We should be moved to intercede, believe, and be part of what God is doing so that we can hand off what we have learned to the next generation. We should be able to report God's faithfulness to the next generation, which means we must break some curses off the bloodlines. Our responsibility in our generation is to prevent passing on the curses that may be in our bloodlines.

Believers must execute what God has already done; He already destroyed the works of the devil, but this needs to be enforced (1 John 3:8). If we do not do that, we are not fulfilling the purpose of the church of Jesus Christ on the earth. Instead, we are allowing evil spirits to come against that generation successfully. Evil spirits can enforce the curse when it should not even exist. The problems that we have today from the highest level down to the family level should not be happening.

STOPPING CURSES FROM TRANSFERRING TO THE NEXT GENERATION

Issues resulting from curses are not permitted in the lives of God's people, and yet they are happening because we have not been proactive. Most have not been educated to understand this. I will not allow certain matters to operate, which means that I will stop curses from being transferred to the next generation. I do this by educating and informing people. You can do this too. We must equip people to understand that when they address these evil spirits, they will not be allowed to work any longer and will not return.

For example, Joseph was sent to Egypt ahead of his family, even though his brothers tragically sold him into slavery (Genesis 37:18–36). Even though it was not God's will for all that to happen, God still used it and sent Joseph ahead. He interpreted the dreams of Pharaoh, the king of Egypt. There were to be seven years of plenty and seven years of famine. Joseph blessed Egypt, but he was really sent to help his family and the Israelites. As Joseph grew in favor, he eventually brought his father, brothers, and entire family from Israel to Egypt to survive the famine and be preserved (Genesis 47:1–17).

Unfortunately, the next Pharaoh did not remember Joseph (Exodus 1:1–8). So how did it happen that the Israelites then served four hundred years of slavery in Egypt (Genesis 15:13)? If Joseph was sent ahead of time to preserve his family line, genealogies, generations, and bloodline, how did slavery happen? It happened because their freedom was never enforced, and they became enslaved. Moses had to deliver the Israelites from Egypt, and he led them into the desert toward the promised land, and you know all the children of Israel went through the promised land in the desert.

If you remember, Joseph was sent to Egypt, and when his family came, they settled in Canaan, so they were *already in the promised land.*

> *Now the report of it was heard in Pharaoh's house, saying, "Joseph's brothers have come." So it pleased Pharaoh and his servants well. And Pharaoh*

said to Joseph, "Say to your brothers, 'Do this: Load
your animals and depart; go to the land of Canaan.
Bring your father and your households and come to
me; I will give you the best of the land of Egypt, and
you will eat the fat of the land.'"

—Genesis 45:16–18

They only moved down to Goshen in Egypt during the famine, and then they lived there for four hundred years before being led back to Canaan. It is written in history that God used Moses to deliver His people, but think about it: Joseph's family came out of Canaan hundreds of years earlier (Genesis 37:1–25). They were already in the promised land.

Generations and bloodlines are significant, but if we are not proactive, we will see sin patterns crop up again, repeating themselves. You can see this happening throughout the Bible and repeating in history, even in our nation, America. I see repeats of battles we have already won. Then we have to fight again for what we already fought for. Our privileges are taken away because we were not diligent in holding on to them. This happens when we are not mindful, but that is not how it should be.

God has a way of dealing with us and our bloodlines. You are not only dealing with these issues for yourself. You should tell yourself that *this will not be transferred to my children and will not go to the next generation.* You stop certain curses by finding how life should be in the Word and then enforcing that. Then you can go even further. You say to yourself, *I will now teach other families and my church, minister to people wherever God sends me, and stop this curse from working in their lives.* So you teach other people to take a stand so that history does not have to repeat itself. In other words, you should not have to fight for things twice.

JESUS MADE A SHOW OF THE DEVIL OPENLY

We have been talking about how Jesus made a show of the devil openly, defeated him, and went around doing good and healing everyone oppressed by the devil (Colossians 2:15; Acts 10:38). Yet believers sit around and argue about if healing is for today, if God wants us to be poor or rich, if He wants us to give or not give, if we should tithe or not, and other controversial matters. They argue about whether or not devils can even bother a Christian. We end up revisiting matters that were not questioned at the turn of the century or even when the church was formed. But now, these topics are questioned. We go through these cycles because we are not diligent in reinforcing what has already been given.

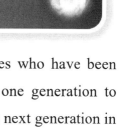

We should be passing on a legacy to the next generation in our family line and the body of Christ on the earth.

The bloodlines represent generations of families who have been given a heritage, an inheritance, passed from one generation to another. We should be passing on a legacy to the next generation in our family line and the body of Christ on the earth. We should be handing it over and giving them a greater legacy than we have encountered; we should be handing off a greater inheritance.

Jesus walked in the power of the Holy Spirit. He was crucified and went to the belly of the earth for three days, then He was raised from the dead. After His resurrection, He walked around for forty days in power (Acts 1:3; 1 Corinthians 15:4–6). However, the Holy Spirit Himself was the power that rose Jesus from the dead. So many times, we end up fighting battles for issues that should already be settled. The apostle Paul showed us that everything obtained through the finished work of the cross and the resurrection of Jesus is done; we do not need to revisit it or do it over again. As the saying goes, we should not reinvent the wheel. Certain truths in the Bible are indisputable, yet we sit around and argue about these matters.

THE SAME POWER THAT ROSE JESUS FROM THE DEAD LIVES IN YOU

But if the Spirit of Him who raised Jesus from the dead dwells in you, He who raised Christ from the dead will also give life to your mortal bodies through His Spirit Who dwells in you.

—Romans 8:11

The same power that rose Jesus from the dead now dwells in you. The Holy Spirit can quicken your mortal body, which means you could be healed and unable to explain it. You could suddenly have an answer when you didn't have that answer before. Suddenly, the Lord could show you, answer you, or deliver you, even though you did not know what was happening. Suddenly, an evil spirit that was bothering you could leave. You wouldn't know why or how; you would only know it was gone.

The Holy Spirit is on a much higher level than we are and has done more in the past than we even realize. God trusts us by putting His Spirit within us. The Holy Spirit is beyond our comprehension, yet He lives in us. Unfortunately, we do not seem to encounter Him in His fullness, but that is not His fault. That is our fault because we have not correctly handed the inheritance off to the next generation.

We need to have the pure teachings of Jesus and the disciples, and we should have the same experiences they had. We should be experiencing what happened on the day of Pentecost. We should have the manifestation of the Spirit that Paul talked about in Corinthians. This should be happening for us personally and in all our gatherings. It does not happen because we do not understand generations and family bloodlines. Most do not understand spiritual warfare regarding the bloodlines and what we are dealing with today.

WE HAVE BEEN GIVEN ALL THINGS THAT PERTAIN TO LIFE AND GODLINESS

> *As His divine power has given to us all things that pertain to life and godliness, through the knowledge of Him Who called us by glory and virtue, by which have been given to us exceedingly great and precious promises, that through these you may be partakers of the divine nature, having escaped the corruption that is in the world through lust.*
>
> —2 Peter 1:3–4

Everything we need for life and godliness has already been given to us through the power that dwells in us. We can see that God is a better Father than we know and has already provided all these things for us. They are already deposited within us. We have whatever we need to live out this life in full power and provision; we should partake of the divine nature and manifest it. Peter tells us that it has already been deposited in us through the divine power of the Holy Spirit. You should read this verse every day because it will put an end to the curses that transfer from one generation to the other.

> *Or what man is there among you who, if his son asks*
> *for bread, will give him a stone? Or if he asks for a*
> *fish, will he give him a serpent? If you then, being*
> *evil, know how to give good gifts to your children,*
> *how much more will your Father Who is in Heaven*
> *give good things to those who ask Him!*
>
> —Matthew 7:9–11

As Jesus said, our earthly fathers would not give us a stone if we asked for bread or a serpent if we asked for a fish, so how much more will our Heavenly Father give us when we ask Him? I do not doubt that our Father in Heaven desires to give us the kingdom. God is a good God Who is handing us what we need. I understand that I am under the blessing because God blesses His children. If God has a plan and it is His good pleasure to give us His kingdom, I will believe that my bloodline and my generation will prosper (Luke 12:32).

CURSE BREAKERS ENFORCE THE COVENANT

From now on, these evil spirits will no longer be able to operate in my bloodline. When I go to conferences, twelve hundred people may be there, with potentially almost that many family lines and bloodlines represented. If I release the Word of life there and break curses, those curses will not be passed on to the next generation. If you minister to people and tell them what we are talking about here, you can stop these curses from transferring to future bloodlines in other families and genealogies, which is what I want you to do. I want you to minister to people and stop this from continuing to happen.

Suddenly, when bloodline curses are broken, we will see people who walk on water, don't sink, and no longer doubt. We will see people who succeed in their generations, and their children will grow up to be miracle workers, gospel preachers, prophets, apostles, pastors, teachers, and evangelists. They will tell others of God's goodness, preaching to their generation and breaking curses. These curse breakers will enforce the covenant, talk about the goodness of God, and see people repent. An overthrow of the enemy and wrong mindsets will happen so that the next generation will not encounter those setbacks. People are already sprinkled throughout the world who are uprooting strongholds and putting demonic forces under their feet. This could happen so much more in this generation.

The uprooting of strongholds and spiritual revolution could happen in our generation; I believe this for all our Warrior Notes students. At this writing, we have between eighteen and nineteen thousand students. Can you imagine if every one of them continued to disperse the good news and cut off all these evil spirits from working in their bloodlines? If each of you spread this information to thousands of people in your lifetime, you would be affecting millions. We could see this turn in our generation by discerning what is said here and ending these demonic influences in our bloodlines.

> *Be encouraged that you are important in the day you live in; you have a message of deliverance and good news that people need to hear.*

And He has made from one blood every nation of men to dwell on all the face of the earth, and has

> *determined their preappointed times and the boundaries of their dwellings.*
>
> —Acts 17:26

The Lord has predetermined the times and seasons when people will be born, He has set their boundaries, and all truth has already been established. God has already done this as spoken in the book of Acts. Jesus told the disciples, "It is not for you to know times or seasons which the Father has put in His own authority" (Acts 1:7). God's times and seasons are not for us to know or understand; only the Father knows and predetermines them. God has established His plan for the nations and people living on the earth. Be encouraged that you are important in the day you live in; you have a message of deliverance and good news that people need to hear.

I deal with people's real problems by dealing with the root. I will tell them that bloodlines have been assigned familiar spirits, which are there to enforce a curse in a territory with family lines, and that we can break that. We can stop that from ever happening again. We can see that curse reversed, which is what I want you to do. I want you to be the true answer to people that want to know the truth. If people don't desire to know the truth, you don't have to talk to them.

Multitudes of people who wanted help followed Jesus around. Why? Because they were poor, sick, and demonized. Jesus said the gospel message was good news to heal the sick and bring deliverance from the devil. He proclaimed the year of Jubilee and debt cancellation; He broke yokes and raised people from the dead. The people who needed freedom followed Jesus because He had the answer. We are called to minister to people this same way; we have the answer and must tell people about it.

The demons will be terrified of you and will not want you to speak. They will not want you to show up because they know they will lose people. The demons cannot influence the people anymore because when they know the truth, the truth will set them free (John 8:31–32). God wants to sever the influence those demons have on you and your family, and then He wants to use you to sever and stop that influence in other people's lives.

God will prove you by bringing you into situations that cause you to grow. He will see how you respond to these situations and then mature you. As you gain knowledge, you will become trustworthy, and then you will be put into leadership. Once you overcome your domain and overthrow all the evil spirits assigned to your bloodline, God will send you to other people. Then you will see the overthrow in their lives. It is a step-by-step process, and God trusts you.

Remember that you are on an accelerated course in learning, and the whole goal is that you overcome because He overcame for you, and then you teach other people how to overcome.

Wherever you go and whatever you do, be mindful that these evil spirits do not want to let go of the people you encounter whether unsaved or saved. The demons influence people based on how much they hand themselves to them. Christians can allow evil spirits to control them if their wills have been given over to those evil spirits. They might have allowed evil spirits to influence their minds, wills, emotions, and bodies, but not in their spirits.

At the same time, satan used Peter because he had wrong thoughts, and he spoke them (Matthew 16:22–23). You must be faithful to let God train you as you put yourself in the position for the holy fire to burn out the chaff and teach you. You will then encounter deliverance, overthrow, and cleansing by the Holy Spirit and fire. As you grow spiritually and go into overthrow, you will then be able to minister this to others.

Why did Jesus have to go through what He went through? It says that "though He was a son, yet He learned obedience by the things which He suffered" (Hebrews 5:8). Even growing up, Jesus grew in the training and admonition of the Lord (Luke 2:40–51; Ephesians 6:4). Once He reached a certain age, He was launched into ministry.

Jesus, the Son of God, had to go through situations as a human being, just as we do. However, Jesus was known as the Son of Man because He submitted as a servant and did not consider equality with God as something to cling to (Philippians 2:5–11). We have to look at what Jesus did and what He went through. He was tempted in the desert and passed all His tests, just like you will pass all your tests.

You are the solution for your generation, family, and bloodline, but you are also the solution for the generations to come. We have the gospel message, deliverance, faith, and healing on our lips. We have that message on our lips and anointing in our hands.

5

WILLING AND OBEDIENT

If you are willing and obedient, You shall eat
The good of the land.
—Isaiah 1:19

The move of God has to manifest itself through willing people. God's angels are here, and we see this mighty move starting in the Spirit. Yet many manifestations in the flesh and the soul realm have hindered us. God has already planned for everything related to our genealogies and bloodlines. He gave us a resolution ahead of time. Yet evil spirits have plans to propagate their agenda and enforce curses, so you see characteristics transferred to the next generation.

It is no coincidence that people in the next generation struggle with the same sins the previous generation did. By tracing their sins, you can see that an evil spirit has been assigned to that bloodline, enforcing the curse, which needs to be overthrown. The problem is that people need to know the truth, but hearing it does not necessarily cause it to manifest. You can listen to the truth, but then you must receive it in your heart and understand it. How often have you been told something and then you forget it, or somebody tells you something, and you turn around and cannot repeat or do what they said?

HEARTFELT FAITH

For assuredly, I say to you, whoever says to this mountain, "Be removed and be cast into the sea," and does not doubt in his heart, but believes that those things he says will be done, he will have whatever he says.

—Mark 11:23

You must absorb the truth; Jesus explained that we must comprehend and understand it. It is heartfelt faith. You speak to your mountains from your heart; believe it and speak with your mouth. It is not mental agreement, which is limited to your thoughts. What Jesus tells you has to be received in your heart and become part of you. It is like bread from Heaven. You partake of Jesus by eating the Word of God. You take Him into you; He changes you by becoming a part of you.

The Word of God changes you. Then from that place of change, in that soil of your heart, you speak and produce a crop. You can move mountains with your words. In this generation, we have to be careful not to just mentally agree because we will not see the power of our faith. It has to be transferred into your heart and become part of your heart and spiritual being. Jesus explained that many people just mentally agree; however, it is not only what you hear because you can hear and not understand. So faith is about what you understand.

The disciples asked Jesus, "Why do You speak to them in parables?" He answered and said to them, 'Because it has been given to you to know the mysteries of the kingdom of heaven, but to them it has not been given'" (Matthew 13:10–11). Jesus would explain the deep mysteries of the kingdom to His disciples, but He would not mention them in a public setting, which is a mystery. If God has chosen you to understand things, it takes you far beyond those who only hear it.

YOU MUST TAKE WHAT YOU HEAR, THEN UNDERSTAND AND APPLY IT

Out of a whole class of students, only two will excel and reach the goal out of a large group of people. They are assigned the prize positions. They excel not by reciting the information but by comprehending and performing it. It is a matter of whether they can achieve it. In other words, can they apply what they heard and studied? That gets them promoted, and I have seen this many times.

> *Wisdom is the principal thing; therefore get wisdom.*
> *And in all your getting, get understanding.*
> —Proverbs 4:7

> *Happy (blessed, fortunate, enviable) is the man who*
> *finds skillful and godly Wisdom, and the man who*
> *gets understanding [drawing it forth from God's*
> *Word and life's experiences].*
> —Proverbs 3:13 AMPC

You can have a group of people who all want to be successful. They all study and sacrifice, but they fail when it comes to getting into that situation and performing. The people that are chosen for that job or position can perform what they have learned. It is the same with the gospel and what we deal with in this generation. Jesus told me that it is not just what you hear but what you understand. In everything you do, pursue wisdom and gain understanding. I can have the knowledge and spout it off, but do I understand what I just said? You may have a word of knowledge but cannot apply it if you don't have a word of wisdom.

> *In this generation, we are supposed to gain wisdom through experience. This is called experiential knowledge.*

At times, Jesus asked me if I understood what He was saying, and if I didn't, I let Him explain it to me. I have had to say things that God intends to happen, and even though I do not understand them, He tells me to say certain words. Other times, He gives me an understanding of it. The enemy does not understand everything. In this generation, we are supposed to gain wisdom through experience. This is called experiential knowledge. I can ask the Lord to unveil the truth, and He can do that, but I might not understand what I see or even know what it is. At that point, does it really help me?

However, if the Lord explains why something is happening, what is needed, and how to apply it, I gain a deeper understanding. Then you can teach people the dynamics of what the Lord is saying. It is not just hearing the Word of God—it is also understanding. Even though "faith comes by hearing and hearing by the word of God," you must reach the place where you have the wisdom to know how to apply it (Romans 10:17).

Jesus wants to take us further than we thought we could go, but it will take understanding. It will take seeing why we are the way we are and why things happen. I am not going to accept the fact that God has mysteries, and we might not ever know what just happened there. God wants to explain mysteries concerning the supernatural to us so that we can hear and understand them if we have ears to hear. I can get healed and not understand healing, but I am not talking about things like that. You do not even have to study healing to get healed. You could believe that the Lord will heal you, and He could heal you. He could touch you now, and you could be completely healed and not even understand what happened.

However, I am speaking of dealing with our generation and everything that happens within that generation. We are dealing with people's behaviors and personalities and their decisions for and against us. We must not deal with opinions but with established truths in Heaven, even when the truth is presented as opinions. Certain instructions from the Lord are presented to us as though we have a choice, but we do not, so this requires us to have a higher level of discernment. In this generation, God wants us to understand the warfare around us, which concerns the demonic enforcing curses.

Jesus wants us to understand how He operated. When we study Matthew 8:23–34, and Luke 8:22–39, we see that Jesus wanted to go to the other side of the lake with his disciples. While on the boat, they encountered a great storm, and Jesus was asleep. For fear of perishing, the disciples finally had to wake Him up. Jesus rebuked the wind, and they safely reached the other side. After arrival, Jesus dealt with a demoniac by casting the devil out, and then He got back in the boat and returned. Still, that only took several hours, and Jesus hardly had time to get out of the boat. We must understand why that storm came up because this story has a deeper meaning.

The Father told Jesus to go to the other side. So Jesus said, "Let us cross over to the other side of the lake," and they launched out, which meant they were going to make it (Luke 8:22). All the training that Jesus gave His disciples was so that every one of them could do the works that He did. He was training them to take over the ministry one day and do even greater works (John 14:12).

Jesus fell asleep because the Father had told them they were going to the other side. It did not matter what happened; Jesus did not doubt it. Instead of waking Jesus up, the disciples should have taken authority and spoken to the winds and the waves, commanding them to cease and be still, but they did not. It was the same in other matters: The disciples did not take authority when they should have.

Another time, they could not cast devils out when they were told they had authority over them (Matthew 17:14–19). We miss some of these insights, and we don't have the needed understanding and wisdom. When we get to the other side of the lake, we see a territorial demon with two thousand demons inside a demon-possessed man (Mark 5:1–20). Jesus confronted him, cast the demons out, and then got right back in the boat to go back and didn't even stay. The whole reason they went over to the other side was to take out that demon.

However, the disciples should have stopped the storm. That territorial spirit caused the storm in an attempt to take them all out before they even got there. We don't discern this was all warfare. Most who read this account do not notice that Jesus did not even stay for lunch; He didn't do anything except cast out those demons, then He got right back in the boat and went back to the other side. That was all Jesus was sent to do: deliver the area of the territorial unclean spirit.

The Holy Spirit wants us to glean from that experience and understand warfare. Through this passage of Scripture, we are taught to recognize the curse that was going on in that region. We must observe how Jesus destroyed the powers of the enemy.

Jesus was doing warfare, which we must discern. All the accounts of Jesus's life and ministry in the Bible and everything that Paul and the apostles taught are given to us for our generation. Even though a previous generation read the same verses, we need to have a revelation of them in this generation. We must understand what the Holy Spirit is saying in order to wage war properly. In this generation, we do not have to put up with what the previous generation had to because the Holy Spirit is working with us, giving us greater revelation. When Jesus returned to the boat, He had accomplished what He was supposed to do.

CENTURION FAITH

None of the disciples and the people that Jesus dealt with were commended for their faith like the Roman centurion was, and he was not even Jewish. Jesus was not sent to the Romans but to the Jews. Jesus selected twelve disciples, and the Roman centurion was not chosen as a disciple. Yet Jesus marveled and said, "I have not found such great faith, not even in Israel!" (Matthew 8:10). The

Roman centurion was not part of the covenant and had not followed Jesus. He had not heard Jesus's teachings and was not a chosen one, yet he got it. The centurion was commended for his faith and is mentioned in the Bible forever.

What did the centurion understand that the disciples missed, even though they were with Jesus for three-and-a-half years? I want to show you that you do not have to have all the things that you think you need to get it. God has given you the Holy Spirit, the Word of God, and you have the availability to excel. You do not have to have lived with Jesus for three-and-a-half years to do the works of Jesus.

> *The centurion answered and said, "Lord, I am not worthy that You should come under my roof. But only speak a word, and my servant will be healed. For I also am a man under authority, having soldiers under me. And I say to this one, 'Go,' and he goes; and to another, 'Come,' and he comes; and to my servant, 'Do this,' and he does it."*
>
> *—Matthew 8:8–9*

That centurion got it because he understood authority. He understood and discerned that Jesus was the Messiah. The centurion explained that his servants under him obey his commands, so he knew that if Jesus gave the word, it would be done. Jesus never even came to his house, but he got it!

In this generation, we will have centurion faith. In our school, conferences, and partners, I am instilling centurion faith in us to understand authority so that we reach a place where we can hear from God. We must say, "Lord, I know what Your will is. Just speak the word, and it will be done." Then we must refuse to accept anything else.

The Lord can command your bloodline, family, and generation right now. You commit to the Lord and say, "Lord, only speak a word, and it will be done," then wait on Him. Once the Lord speaks that word, you change your generation, family, and yourself because you now have God's word on it. When God speaks, He speaks a blessing over your family, and the devil's plans will not prevail. Evil will stop because you put a stop to it.

> *Do not wait for this to go to another generation; you need to put a stop to the enemy's plan right now.*

GOD WILL SHOW HIMSELF STRONG FOR THOSE WHOSE HEARTS ARE LOYAL TO HIM

I was sent back to tell people, "Listen, you need to be the one. Do not wait for someone else to do it." Do not wait for this to go to another generation; *you* need to put a stop to the enemy's plan right now. You can change and reroute history. You can change everything, and you do that through having centurion faith. You must understand authority and refuse to take no for an answer. You must understand God's will and not accept anything else; refuse to bend. I will see extraordinary things happen in this generation because I refuse to accept anything except what God wants.

The devil fears a person who is convinced of God's will. You are called to be an ambassador of Heaven (2 Corinthians 5:20). When you have faith like the centurion and understand authority, you become one who supports God's covenant in this generation. God can use a person like that.

I encourage you to have heartfelt faith; believe and say, "Lord, just speak. Tell me, and I will believe and do it." No matter what it looks like, this generation does not have to see the end concerning the antichrist and the evil that seems to surround us. This has happened many times before. We can stand against the enemy's plan and reap a massive harvest of souls. We do not have to allow this evil. It cycles through, and we can prevent it. We can stop it and see a harvest of souls come in.

> *For the eyes of the LORD run to and fro throughout the whole earth, to show Himself strong on behalf of those whose heart is loyal to Him. In this you have done foolishly; therefore from now on you shall have wars.*
>
> —2 Chronicles 16:9

In 2 Chronicles 16:9, the people did not discern the Lord, and God said they were foolish. Yet the eyes of the Lord are going back and forth today, looking for someone whose heart is loyal to Him—that is us in this generation. So we must raise our hands and say, "Lord, use me. I am loyal to You, and I will stop this. I will see Your heart's desire come to pass in this generation." Once this has happened to you and your family, you can help others by overthrowing evil. This is what I want to see. I encourage you to have centurion faith and say, "Lord, I agree with whatever is written about me in Heaven. Speak it over me, over my family, and over my generation."

Even if the majority are like the unbelieving children of Israel who did not enter the promised land, at least you can be like Joshua and

Caleb, like them, you can say, "We are well able to do this" (Numbers 13:30). Remember that if you are willing and obedient, you will eat the good of the land (Isaiah 1:19). Even if it is only us, just a small remnant, God will favor us. You do not have to be drawn in by the unbelief and doubt of a generation. You can eat of the good of the land. Let God use us in our generation and break those curses. Let us see this thing turned around for good. May God use us to change history.

6

REVELATION TO VISITATION

And God said, "Let us make man in our
image, after our likeness..."
—Genesis 1:26

The Lord wants everyone to have the revelation of Who He is. Once we realize who He is, we also realize who we are because we were created in His image. In the beginning, God made us in His image, which is important to understand. The church and those coming into the kingdom must know how much God cares for and values people. God is looking for people who are dedicated to Him and whose heart is loyal to Him; God will strengthen and help them. However, in 2 Chronicles 16:9, the children of Israel had chosen to do foolishly, so they encountered war.

Once we know Who God is, our value is known in Heaven; we realize He is loyal to us because we are loyal to Him. There is an exchange between God and man, which is when you become a friend of God. This occurs when you have fully allowed the holy fire and sanctification process, the purging and the purifying process, to manifest in your life. As you begin to mature, God will trust you more. In these last days, a remnant is giving themselves fully over to God.

THE REMNANT CHOOSES THE NARROW WAY

Enter by the narrow gate; for wide is the gate and broad is the way that leads to destruction, and there are many who go in by it. Because narrow is the gate and difficult is the way which leads to life, and there are few who find it.

—Matthew 7:13–14

This remnant is a group of people choosing the narrow way; they are people in churches all over the world. Many people are in churches and religious organizations that have grown cold. Today, many situations mirror what happened in the first several chapters of the book of Revelation with the seven churches. As a result, some believers are hungry for more of God. They want to be loyal to God and have a relationship with Him; they want more than what they experience at their organization. They are willing to meet with people in small groups for prayer, Bible study, and fellowship.

Since the world system is corrupt, the remnant desires to take care of each other. They also advocate for homeschooling, which is what we are doing at Warrior Notes. We are going with the flow of what is happening as people migrate out of the established churches and want to form Bible study groups and get educated outside the world system. Homeschooling is government-approved, but it is Bible-based. Different denominations were formed in moves of God throughout history, which developed into organizations. But these grew cold as they got bigger.

In past cycles, we have needed revival or a movement to take people out of ungodly situations in schools. These cycles keep going on and on, which you can see throughout history. God's will is not for us to grow cold or become so big that we don't meet people's needs and cannot function anymore. The kingdom of God on earth should keep growing and growing until Jesus comes back, but that is not how it works down here in this fallen world.

The fivefold ministry of the church seems to have gotten away from talking about our heavenly value. Most are not discussing Who God is or the holy fire and holiness. In my book *The Mystery of the Power*

Words, I explain why certain subjects are not spoken about anymore. When you see this happening, you can see why believers must migrate and find the right track where the full gospel is being preached again. God is searching throughout the whole earth to build up the remnant and strengthen those whose hearts are loyal to Him.

JESUS, THE NAME ABOVE ALL NAMES

> *Therefore God also has highly exalted Him and given Him the name which is above every name, that at the name of Jesus every knee should bow, of those in Heaven, and of those on earth, and of those under the earth, and that every tongue should confess that Jesus Christ is Lord, to the glory of God the Father.*
>
> —Philippians 2:9–11

When God moves, we need to stay with the pure message of the gospel and enforce what He is really saying. I often listen to sermons from different people and organizations and check the temperature with them to see what's popular. I see what most people watch and then look at the offered content. I have been shocked that hundreds of thousands of people are watching certain people that never mention the name of Jesus. Jesus's name is never in any of their titles, comments, or quotes. The word "God" is used but not "Jesus."

The demons are afraid of the name of Jesus because His name invokes full authority, and He has the name above all names.

> *The name of Jesus is so powerful that it paralyzes the demonic and sets people free at the mention of it.*

Did you know that when you go on a secular TV show, you are not allowed to mention the name of Jesus? (I can name the shows.) You can mention the name of God, but you cannot say the name of Jesus. I wondered about that because individuals would tell me they were on this or that show and were not allowed to say Jesus's name. If they did say it, it was bleeped out. When I attended different secular productions, I was told that also, and I realized what it was. The name of Jesus is so powerful that it paralyzes the demonic and sets people free at the mention of it. I was thinking, *Why would people fear the name of Jesus on secular TV?* Then I realized those demons don't want Jesus's name over the airwaves.

When I listened to different ministers and noticed they were not using the name of Jesus at all, I realized that the prince of the power of the air was starting to infiltrate and influence those ministers. I do not know if they were aware or did it on purpose. In my book

The Mystery of the Power Words, the Lord gave me those words; some are actually phrases and subjects. It is called *The Mystery of the Power Words* because satan does not want us to use certain very powerful words, subjects, and phrases anymore. If you take that list and listen to Christian ministers, you can check off every time these words are mentioned. Sometimes, none of these words will be mentioned in an hour-long sermon.

THE HOLY SPIRIT GIVES YOU THE BOLDNESS TO PROPHESY AND WITNESS

I first realized this probably twenty years ago, so I started to keep track, noticing how certain words and subjects were missing from the teachings. Recently, I checked again, and it is still happening. Throughout cycles of church history, the system would become ineffective and no longer meet the needs of the people. People who are hungry and seeking God migrate out; if you talk to them, they are looking for the fire of God. They are looking for a move of God and the Word of God that is preached with fire. They are looking for a hot meal, spiritually speaking, and want to encounter the presence and power of God. They want to encounter the Holy Spirit, Who gives them boldness at work to prophesy and witness.

I know your works, that you are neither cold nor hot.
I could wish you were cold or hot. So then, because

you are lukewarm, and neither cold nor hot, I will
vomit you out of My mouth.

—Revelation 3:15–16

I have often studied history, and I have seen these trends before. I know how the church goes through cycles, which is very predictable. In some cycles, the temperature changes overall, which is consistent with the content that is preached. If certain truths, words, and concepts from the Word of God are removed, the message isn't as hot, so the people aren't as hot. Their spiritual diet is not producing the characteristics of a hot church that Jesus wanted. In the book of Revelation, Jesus wanted them to decide if they were hot or cold, but He never wanted them to be lukewarm. Of course, Jesus wanted them to be hot but encouraged them to decide.

In 1 and 2 Corinthians, Paul wrote to the church of Corinth, and you realize that much of what is going on today was happening to the Corinthians at that time. Paul addressed carnality and people who thought they were spiritual because they were being used in the gifts, yet the flesh ruled them. When you read Romans 7 and 8, then Corinthians, you can see the contrast between how Paul addressed the people in Rome and those in Corinth.

And I, brethren, could not speak to you as to spiritual people but as to carnal, as to babes in Christ. I fed you with milk and not with solid food; for until now you were not able to receive it, and even now you are still not able; for you are still carnal. For where there are envy, strife, and divisions among you, are you not carnal and behaving like mere men?

—1 Corinthians 3:1–3

Paul wanted the Corinthians to stop drinking baby milk, grow out of diapers, and get on the meat of the word. It was time for them to change their diet and mature into adults. Paul wanted to address the Corinthians as mature adults but said he could not because they were carnal. Paul wanted to take them on to deeper things, but he couldn't because the Corinthians were immature.

That happened at a Bible college I attended. The president of the college, who was also a teacher, said the Lord would not let him go on to teach the deeper things that he knew. The Lord had shown him so much, but he was not allowed to teach it yet. The Lord told him that the people had not gotten the basics of what they were already taught. They had just not received it, and he was constantly repeating himself and going over the same teachings again and again. The president had to explain to those frustrated with the repetitive teaching that he was doing it on purpose because the Lord told him they hadn't gotten it yet. He told us that we would hear the same teaching every year until we went on with the Lord. It really shocked me because I knew he was right.

I was a younger student at the time, and I thought, *I'm ready*. We always think we are ready for something until it happens. Then we realize we are not prepared, and reality sets in. However, this is where God has you today. He was looking throughout the earth, and He found you, and He highly esteems and values you because you highly esteem and value Him, and you want to go on with Him. You might not be able to find a church or gathering that meets up to the standard or the fire you have been exposed to already through Warrior Notes or another organization.

You may be looking for groups of people who have a passion for seeking God, want the narrow way, want to walk in holiness, and be on fire for God, which is why we formed Warrior Notes Fellowships and Warrior Notes Churches. We already have different apps, such as Warrior Notes TV and the Warrior Notes Chat, and we will soon have Warrior Notes Health. We are planning many different programs for children and parents because we want groups of people with a passion for God to get together.

If the eyes of the Lord are running throughout the earth and He has found you, then He will provide a way for you to fellowship with people of like passion, which is what Warrior Notes is all about. We are connecting people worldwide, and then we will form an army ready to evangelize. We will teach, preach, and get people on the same page with God to see this end-time harvest come in.

REVELATION, VISITATION, AND HABITATION: THE STAGES OF YOUR RELATIONSHIP WITH GOD

[For I always pray to] the God of our Lord Jesus Christ, the Father of glory, that He may grant you a spirit of wisdom and revelation [of insight into mysteries and secrets] in the [deep and intimate] knowledge of Him, By having the eyes of your heart flooded with light, so that you can know and understand the hope to which He has called you, and how rich is His glorious inheritance in the saints (His set-apart ones), And [so that you can know and understand] what is the immeasurable and unlimited and surpassing greatness of His power in and for us who believe, as demonstrated in the working of His mighty strength. Which He exerted in Christ when

He raised Him from the dead and seated Him at His
[own] right hand in the heavenly [places].

—Ephesians 1:17–20 AMPC

When God favors you, knows who you are, and sees that you highly esteem Him, He will want to help you. He does that by getting closer to you in proximity. There are stages of your relationship with God. First, the Holy Spirit comes and gives you revelation of the Word of God. So the first stage you can expect is revelation. In other words, the Holy Spirit, according to Ephesians 1:17–19, will come in, and He will open the eyes of your heart. The Holy Spirit will actually flood you with light, which will expose the truth so that it rises to the surface.

As soon as you see that, you will be astounded, and as Paul says, you will know the hope to which you have been called because of the transformative power of truth. Suddenly, you will realize the truth about God and what He is doing for you. You will see that God gives you hope because you have been called to do specific tasks and given certain gifts.

Next, Paul prays that we would know the glorious inheritance in the saints. A table with a delicious meal has been set for us as God's holy people. We can partake of all these wonderful promises and benefits, the divine nature and fellowship with God, and the revelation that comes to us. With this revelation, you understand that the power that rose Jesus from the dead dwells within you. The power of the Holy Spirit is not only dynamite power but also authoritative power.

There are two Greek words, *exousia,* which is the power of authority, and an explosive *dunamis* power, and both are translated in the Bible as power.[1] For example, a law enforcement official has power, which is authority, whereas a soldier is strong and trained for war with brute force. There is the power of authority, and then there is explosive power, and the Holy Spirit gives these to us and reveals the truth about them.

We go through a revelation phase, which is part of our initiation. So phase one is receiving revelation from the Holy Spirit.

As we continue to pray and are exposed to the light, glory, and holy fire, that transformation causes us to be even more curious and want more. At that point, we may start to have visitations and sense the movement of the Holy Spirit, angels, and all kinds of supernatural events around us. Revelation floods our spirits, but we can also have visitations of the Lord's appearance. Some have seen angels or had

---

[1] "Lexicon :: Strong's G1849 – *exousia*," Blue Letter Bible, accessed May 23, 2023, https://www.blueletterbible.org/lexicon/g1849/kjv/tr/0-1/; "Lexicon :: Strong's G1411 – *dynamis*," Blue Letter Bible, accessed May 23, 2023, https://www.blueletterbible.org/lexicon/g1411/kjv/tr/0-1/.

supernatural events happening around them, and they can sense and feel the war between the demonic and the angels. Visitation is when God decides that He is going to come and start to interact with you.

We will have various experiences when God visits us. You can lift your hands even now and start worshiping God, and you will have a visitation because the Holy Spirit will come upon you and wrap you up to help you worship. When you pray, the Holy Spirit will well up within you and help you pray. This process is all part of phase two, visitation. Visitation is when the Lord comes upon you and comes up within you, flowing from the river of life inside you. However, for visitation to happen, you must first be flooded with light, which is phase one, revelation (Ephesians 1:17–23).

The Lord starts this process with you. Once you have revelation, you need to go immediately and sit and worship God, and He will visit you. While you are worshiping Him, quoting the Word of God, speaking to your mountains, praying, and interceding, suddenly, the fire will burn up these barriers inside you. You go to another level where you can handle interaction with the Holy Spirit, angels, and Jesus, and suddenly, another world opens up to you. These interactions should be common occurrences. Every time I raise my hands to worship God, pray, meditate, or study, I expect visitation. Visitation is a constant thing, but it is phase two.

> *Habitation comes when you have entered God's rest, you have entered the promised land, and the holy fire has had its way with you.*

When the Lord notices you because you are seeking Him and want to be loyal to Him, He will separate you, and the fire will come. Then revelation and visitation will come, and the third step is habitation. You will reach a place where the Holy Father has had His way, the fire has had its way, and the Lord has gotten you to a place where you are trustworthy. I never thought I could handle what I can handle now, and I never thought I could do what I am doing now. The boundaries I had set for my life were low, but they seemed very high when I set them, and I have already exceeded those.

Habitation comes when you have entered God's rest, you have entered the promised land, and the holy fire has had its way with you. Then all the barriers, all these things that have hindered you because of traumatic events, are removed. The barriers of hurt, such as being a victim and having a victim spirit or being an orphan with an orphan spirit, are removed. The barriers of feeling abandoned and hurt, always suffering, leave. When the fire of God wins out, displacing these barriers, you go from revelation and visitation to habitation.

7

HABITATION

And My Father will love you so deeply that We will come to
you and make you Our dwelling place.
—John 14:23 TPT

Habitation is when the holy fire has its way and exposes what needs to be removed, starting to burn out all the chaff in us. Once those areas are exposed, they can be destroyed. We are very complicated, intricate, and delicate beings. During this process, you must be patient with the Lord and yourself. If you are going through many hurts and related struggles in your heart and mind, you must understand that you were never made to function in a broken world. You were created to operate at a higher level.

We are dealing with discrepancies, disappointments, and discouragements that should not even exist. We are dealing with problems down here that God never designed us to deal with, and the bottom line is that we go through stress. You must let the Holy Spirit have His way with you to get you to habitation as soon as possible. However, remember it is a process; you cannot hurry it. The healing oil of the Holy Spirit must be applied because hurts must be dealt with and exposed, and deliverance must occur.

HABITATION IS ENTERING THE REST

So when that day comes, you will know that I am living in the Father and that you are one with Me, for I will be living in you. Those who truly love Me are those who obey My commands. Whoever passionately loves Me will be passionately loved by My Father. And I will passionately love you in return and will manifest My life within you . . . Jesus replied, "Loving Me empowers you to obey My word. And My Father will love you so deeply that We will come to you and make you Our dwelling place."

—John 14:20–21, 23 TPT

You may be dealing with real feelings, thoughts, and perceptions, but they are not the truth. The truth is that God highly values you. He has noticed you, you are favored, and He comes in to live with you. As Jesus explained, if you love God, are obedient, and passionately seek Him, He and the Father will come and live with you. That is why I use the word "habitation." As the remnant and the church, we will be purified through the fire, and then we will enter into rest: That is habitation. It is like when Joshua finally took the people to the promised land, and they entered after a trip that should have taken eleven days but instead lasted forty years. (See Deuteronomy 1:2 AMP.)

When you enter that rest and are confident in your habitation, God dwells with you, and you are not afraid that He will leave you. You do not think about losing your salvation or about being abandoned. You do not think of yourself as a victim. You do not doubt that God will answer your prayers; you *know* He will answer. You do not even question if He will listen to you; you know He will hear you. You have entered a place with God that did not seem possible in the past, but you are there. Now, you have to yield to this process. So let the holy fire burn, set yourself apart, and then encounter these three phases: revelation, visitation, and habitation.

YOU ARE BEING PREPARED TO BE A SENT ONE

When the Lord notices you and you start to feel Him drawing you, you will feel as if a change is coming. You are being prepared so that God can send you somewhere; no matter what, you will be effective. Even if people do not respond and you do not see changes, you need to understand that you are on assignment; you must stay on course when you are sent. God is your source, you are giving out, and God takes care of you. You do not need to depend on people's responses; you are sent to them because you are on assignment, so it's a different approach. God is supporting you in every way. Even when it gets hard, you must stay in there because you are a faithful soldier.

THE UNITY OF THE FAITH

Till we all come to the unity of the faith and of the knowledge of the Son of God, to a perfect man, to the measure of the stature of the fullness of Christ.

—Ephesians 4:13

You want to get to the place where God can use you, but He must win you over first. This happens as you migrate into places where you meet the people you need to connect with. You will grow and develop there because it is all about maturity and getting into the unity of the faith. That is the goal the Lord has for the body of Christ. That is why He sent the fivefold ministry to the church so that we would mature and be in the unity of the faith. If the fivefold is not developing you and bringing you into the unity of the faith, they are not doing what they are supposed to, and the body suffers. Each individual that does not do what they are supposed to do affects the rest of the body.

The Holy Spirit in these days wants you to be around people of like faith. The fruit of the Spirit, the gifts of the Spirit, the fellowship and communion in the Spirit, taking communion together, and teaching will begin to operate when you do so. Being around people who value each other and feel safe and comfortable together is part of the *koinonia*[2] or the fellowship God wants for His people.

> *Therefore "'Come out from among them and be separate,' says the Lord. 'Do not touch what is unclean, and I will receive you.'"*
>
> —2 Corinthians 6:17

---

[2] "Lexicon :: Strong's G2842 – *koinonia*," Blue Letter Bible, accessed May 23, 2023, https://www.blueletterbible.org/lexicon/g2842/kjv/tr/0-1/.

In the cycles of the church, excitement cools down, and people get off track, but a remnant wants revival, a move of God. They want us to return to the original message of holiness, repentance, and the crucified life. All the great movements of God and the heroes that came out of them were marked by intense hunger for God. They wanted to be intimate with God, our Creator, in a hot spiritual atmosphere when it was cold all around them. Paul told the Corinthians to come out from among them and be separate. We already have this Scripture and the doctrine taught by the apostles that we are supposed to be following.

THE END-TIME CHURCH IS SUPPOSED TO BE HOT

That you may walk worthy of the Lord, fully pleasing Him, being fruitful in every good work and increasing in the knowledge of God; strengthened with all might, according to His glorious power, for all patience and longsuffering with joy.

—Colossians 1:10–11

The established church goes through these phases because we are in a fallen world, and those strong power words—words like the crucified life, repentance, holy fire, the blood of Jesus, and the name of Jesus—that the Lord gives us in Scripture are not emphasized. You will notice that the fivefold ministry no longer mentions certain truths, which is a telltale sign that we are under attack in the church. The end-time church is supposed to be hot. Unfortunately, persecution usually has to come in so that people decide whether it is worth it to follow God. The people who are dedicated and loyal to God cry out for Him to catch them on fire because they want to be hot and want more. These are the remnant.

We are going through that phase again, and as that remnant goes out, it grows because people start to do what they should have done all along. The telltale sign is that the church cools off, and attacks begin to increase. It starts with an onslaught of persecution, and rights are taken away. There may be a disease or war; something occurs so that people realize their peace has been affected. People then have to decide how they will respond. Will they ask God for help, or will they blame Him? Some people actually blame God when evil happens because they never mature into adults who can stand against evil. The church is supposed to take authority and prevent corruption. God never wanted or sanctioned some of what is happening in the world, which is the church's fault.

When you see this happen, there will be a revelation phase where the Lord notices the people who have separated themselves unto

Him and strengthens them (Colossians 1:11). These people will receive revelation. They will see the truth in the Bible, all these power words, and start using them again. Then these believers will only want to be in services where they talk about Jesus all the time. They will speak of and pray in the name of Jesus; they will proclaim the blood of Jesus, the holy fire, the power of God, resurrection, raising the dead, healing the sick, and casting out devils.

You will see these small groups or pockets of people begin to form and grow because they have migrated out of the cold, ineffective church where they have stopped using the Word of God and the power words. Believers will want to leave that cold atmosphere and go to a hot church.

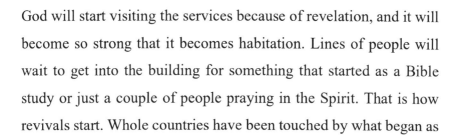

Whole countries have been touched by what began as a few people with a revelation that God had more for them than what they were experiencing.

God will start visiting the services because of revelation, and it will become so strong that it becomes habitation. Lines of people will wait to get into the building for something that started as a Bible study or just a couple of people praying in the Spirit. That is how revivals start. Whole countries have been touched by what began as a few people with a revelation that God had more for them than what they were experiencing (Zechariah 4:9–10).

When it gets hot, you get healed and develop into a habitation of God. You get rid of trauma, discouragement, an orphan spirit, and a victim's spirit, and the demons start to leave because it's getting hot. As you increase in fellowship with these people, you will see that the holy fire is beginning to burn in the group instead of just one person.

The holy fire brings healing, and the demons start leaving because they have nothing to hold on to inside a group of people on fire. As soon as a person is healed, the demons lose their grip and leave. If the demons try to return, they find that person occupied by the Holy Spirit and healed. Since they dealt with their issues, the demons no longer have a hook within them (John 14:30). They cannot stay because the person matured from revelation into visitation into habitation, and there is no room for them anymore. That is where we are going with Warrior Notes and with Warrior Churches. We are developing a place where on-fire people gather together from all over the world.

WE ARE CALLED WITH A HOLY CALLING

People will receive supernatural healing because of the power in these meetings, which has already started happening. The power is so strong. When the demons are expelled, people's minds change, and they can no longer doubt or fear because the power and presence of God are with them. They are built up, having fellowship with one another and hearing the Word of God. They are strong, bold, and have friends who believe as they do. They feel comfortable, accepted, and valued, which is all part of the process.

As healings occur, the public shows an interest, and unsaved people begin to come. At first, these people are driven by curiosity; however, just like in the Book of Acts, the church will start to grow exponentially when they get saved, healed, and delivered. A repeat of the cycle happens every so often, and we are in it now. Many people realize they are in an ineffective, powerless, cold religion and probably don't understand what has happened.

> *And as you go, preach, saying, 'The kingdom of Heaven is at hand.' Heal the sick, cleanse the lepers, raise the dead, cast out demons. Freely you have received, freely give.*
>
> —Matthew 10:7–8

The Spirit of the Lord is upon Me, because He has anointed Me to preach the gospel to the poor; He has sent Me to heal the brokenhearted, to proclaim liberty to the captives and recovery of sight to the blind, to set at liberty those who are oppressed; to proclaim the acceptable year of the Lord.

—Luke 4:18–19

Many Christians are good people who have allowed the enemy to wear them down and out, shifting their focus from the message. The pure message of the gospel is that you heal the sick, raise the dead, drive out devils, and preach the year of Jubilee. The acceptable year of the Lord, Jubilee, is complete forgiveness of debt and sin.

Therefore if the Son makes you free, you shall be free indeed.

—John 8:36

As you preach the good news, you break the yokes off people, and the Spirit of the Lord gives freedom. As Christians, this is what we are called to do. But unfortunately, we go through cycles of becoming cold, then hot, and so forth. As believers, we should not go through cycles because we should always be hot, but it's a war down here.

Who has saved us and called us with a holy calling, not according to our works, but according to His own purpose and grace which was given to us in Christ Jesus before time began.

—2 Timothy 1:9

Think about what Paul told Timothy here and how everything was planned. Everything about the holy calling of God was completed according to His purpose and grace, given to us through Jesus Christ before time began. It was already planned. All the missing endowments we should have right now have already been predetermined in Christ. Before this world was ever formed, God, in His infinite knowledge, had already provided and planned all this.

I do not want you as a believer to go through the rest of your life not receiving what you have coming to you. Unfortunately, because of false and wrong teachings, people do not understand that it does not just come to you automatically. There is a process, and you must be tenacious and pursue God. God notices those who passionately pursue Him and rewards them for diligently seeking Him (Hebrews 11:6). However, if you do not diligently seek Him, He does not reward you.

> *We must remember that Jesus looked for people who were hungry and were pulling on Him.*

Jesus did not just pursue people. He answered them when they sought Him, then made Himself available to them, but He did not go out looking for people to minister to. We must remember that Jesus looked for people who were hungry and were pulling on Him.

Many Scriptures support the idea that we must actively and aggressively seek Jesus and move toward Him (Jeremiah 29:12–13; Matthew 6:33; Luke 11:9–13; Hebrews 11:6; James 4:8). God favors those who are diligently seeking Him and favor Him. They catch God's eye, and He wants to strengthen them (2 Chronicles 16:9). When I studied church history through the ages and from my vantage point after visiting Jesus in Heaven, I can tell you that God does not do this for everyone, only for those who pursue Him.

God wants to favor and strengthen every person and make these blessings available to all but not everyone takes Him up on it. No one should go to hell, but people are dying and going to hell every second. It is unnecessary because Jesus died for them and has an amazing plan, yet people perish, but it is not God's perfect will. I do not want you to finish your life without knowing what is available; I want you to understand and participate in His revealed will. God has many wonderful things for those who love Him and are called according to His purpose (Romans 8:28).

WATCH AND PRAY YOU WILL NOT FALL INTO TEMPTATION

Keep actively watching and praying that you may not come into temptation; the spirit is willing, but the body is weak.

—Matthew 26:41 AMP

If everything was automatically given to you, why would Jesus say this? Why would He tell the disciples to keep watching and praying so they do not fall into temptation? From this, we can see that you can fall into temptation, and if you don't do anything, you *will* fall into temptation. You have to be actively watching and praying. The critical point that many miss is that the Spirit is willing, which is why they become lukewarm. The Holy Spirit in your spirit is on fire, and He is always ready.

When your spirit is born again, it is a new creation in Christ (2 Corinthians 5:17). The old is gone, and your spirit is ready and willing. You are as prepared as you are ever going to be in your spirit, and the Holy Spirit is in there with you, and He is willing. However, the flesh is unredeemed, weak, and struggling, fighting against God and you—this is happening to many now.

The faith in people's hearts is not strong enough to overcome the mind and the flesh, and because people are not being fed spiritually in churches, the flesh becomes stronger. In order to appease people and keep them, many churches appeal to their souls and emotions. In these churches, you will hear what we call feel-good messages. They will talk about sports and entertainment, sprinkled with all these stories about fun things that appeal to your flesh and emotions. Unfortunately, those ministers rob the people and God because they are responsible for feeding a person's spirit, lighting them up for God, and fanning the fire within them.

Revelation, visitation, and habitation will first bring the holy fire and then the harvest. People need to be delivered. You cannot feed your flesh and soul and think that demons will be expelled or people will be healed. You must increase the atmosphere of Heaven, which means you will have to feed your spirit.

We must allow the Holy Spirit to speak through us. The gospel is a message of the good news; as Jesus said, it is raising the dead, preaching Jubilee (debt cancellation) and the resurrection power of

Jesus, expelling demons, and healing the sick. We must preach the good news that God is good and Jesus is coming back again.

8

BE SPIRIT-RULED

Who will also confirm you to the end, that you may be
blameless in the day of our Lord Jesus Christ.
—1 Corinthians 1:8

Jesus explained that we need to be led by the Holy Spirit, Who will lead us into all truth (John 16:13). Be sure to be led by the Spirit; if you want the truth, then the Spirit is truth. If you want to be on fire, the Holy Spirit is fire. It is all about the Spirit of God. The Spirit will give you gifts from God and implement them in your life. Everything else will go well because the Lord will manage your life physically and mentally if *you* diligently tend to your spiritual life (Matthew 6:33).

I encourage you to ask the Holy Spirit to reveal Himself to you, ask Him to visit you, then ask Him to inhabit you. This process will expel the demonic that is coming against you. It will heal you from traumatic events and hurts that happened when you were younger, which you do not understand. God wants to heal you of all those traumas and rid you of any place where a devil can abide in your emotions or thoughts; He wants to deliver you.

REFUSE EVERY FORM OF EVIL

Abstain from every form of evil. Now may the God of peace Himself sanctify you completely; and may your whole spirit, soul, and body be preserved blameless at the coming of our Lord Jesus Christ.
—1 Thessalonians 5:22–23

Paul explained to the church at Thessalonica how God created them with three parts, which will help you to understand yourself. Many people do not know why they oppose themselves within themselves, and it is because we are made up of these three different areas. We were created in a very complex manner because we were supposed to operate at a higher level and a higher realm, but because we fell, we are in this broken world. It is challenging to function here because we were not made to deal with all this stress, disappointment, and discouragement. We were not created to have a separation of the physical, mental, and spiritual realms.

Paul tells us to abstain from every form of evil, so we are supposed to put a stop to evil and evil spirits. Then Paul asks that the God of peace sanctify you completely, and that word *sanctify*[3] means "to set apart." Then he asks that your whole spirit, soul, and body—those three different parts—be preserved blameless at the coming of our Lord Jesus Christ. So it is possible for us to be blameless. Three different words are used here in the original language. The soul is not the same as the spirit; people will try to combine or interchange these words, but they are different parts of us.

GETTING YOUR SOUL TO AGREE WITH YOUR SPIRIT

Your spirit is the real you that will live eternally, which can be born again by the Holy Spirit. Then you have your soul, which includes your mind, will, and emotions, which has to be renewed (Ephesians 4:23–24). Your mind must be transformed and renewed by the Word of God (Romans 12:2). So your soul must be corrected. It must be given the correct information so you can manage your thoughts and

---

[3] "Lexicon :: Strong's G37 – *hagiazō* ," Blue Letter Bible, accessed May 23, 2023, https://www.blueletterbible.org/lexicon/g37/kjv/tr/0-1/.

emotions based on the Word of God. Finally, your *body* needs to be disciplined. Paul said that after he preached Christ, he would be disqualified from his race if he did not discipline his body (1 Corinthians 9:27).

Paul said his body, if left undisciplined, could cause him to get off track and lose out (1 Corinthians 9:27). Your body will do what it wants if you let it, and your soul, which is your mind, will, and emotions, can also derail you. However, when your spirit is born again, it becomes a new creation (2 Corinthians 5:17). Your spirit is where you rule and reign. From your spirit, you can tell your soul what to think and feel and your body what to do. This truth is evident in Scripture, especially in chapter 8 of Romans.

It is possible to be spirit-ruled instead of body-ruled. It is also possible to be spirit-ruled rather than governed by your thoughts and emotions, which may be right or wrong. Your body, mind, will, and emotions are inconsistent in their behavior; however, your born-again heart, your spirit that is ruling and reigning inside you, is steadfast. If you are not born again, you are in trouble because you are powerless to say no to ungodliness. You have no power to say no to the prince of the power of the air and have no resistance to him whatsoever (Ephesians 2:1–3). As a believer, you must get people born again.

You need to pray in the Holy Spirit, building yourself up in your most holy faith in your spirit as a spiritual exercise (Jude 1:20). You must renew your mind by the Word of God and discipline your body, telling it what it can and cannot do. You will constantly have to do this during your journey on earth.

> *So that you come short in no gift, eagerly waiting for the revelation of our Lord Jesus Christ, Who will also confirm you to the end, that you may be blameless in the day of our Lord Jesus Christ.*
>
> —1 Corinthians 1:7–8

Once again, Paul is telling the Corinthians, who were carnal, that they can be blameless because God wants to establish them to the end. God wants to continually interact with you and confirm you, which is what having a relationship with Him is all about. This is the kind of relationship we are supposed to have with the Lord, where we allow Him to come in and influence us.

PUTTING THE WORD OF GOD BEFORE YOUR EYES, EARS, AND MOUTH

As you think, work through, and manage yourself in all these situations, you are essentially building up your spirit. You renew your mind by studying the Word of God and build yourself up in your spirit by praying in tongues (Romans 12:2; Jude 1:20). As you meditate on the Word of God, your mind, will, and emotions change into a framework that represents what the Word of God says. Essentially, you are getting your soul to agree with your spirit, which takes the surrender of your entire life.

> *I know the only way I will be effective is if my life is wholly saturated with God's presence.*

You can accelerate this process if you are totally immersed in an environment where you hear, see, and say the Lord's will for your life. That is why we have all the media available at Warrior Notes. Then, we have the conferences so that you get together with other people under a corporate anointing where you are saturated and completely immersed in God's presence. In my personal life, I do this all the time, not just at conferences. I not only want to walk in overthrow, but I also want to live in it. I know the only way I will be effective is if my life is wholly saturated with God's presence.

> *And all of us, as with unveiled face, [because we]*
> *continued to behold [in the Word of God] as in a*

mirror the glory of the Lord, are constantly being transfigured into His very own image in ever increasing splendor and from one degree of glory to another; [for this comes] from the Lord [Who is] the Spirit.

—2 Corinthians 3:18 AMPC

You need to put the Word of God before your eyes, ears, and mouth, and then you hit the devil in all those different areas. When that happens, your mind changes, which is what repentance is. You may experience a sudden breakthrough; however, remember that your soul is being saved continually (Philippians 2:12). You go from glory to glory as your soul is being saved, whereas your spirit is already saved. Your soul is being saved because it is being renewed. The change is coming because your perceptions are changing, causing you to ascend to a higher vantage point.

DISCIPLINING YOUR BODY

Your body just needs to get used to discipline. For example, if you exercise every day at a specific time, it becomes routine. I used to run every day at a certain time. It was amazing because ten minutes before running, I would start feeling my blood flowing with adrenaline and energy, and I would start to feel my circulation and energy increase. When I looked at the clock, I realized I was due to go on my run. My body had gotten used to going for that four or sometimes eight-mile run. My body was subconsciously tuned into that run every day to where everything my body needed for that run was already being pumped into my bloodstream beforehand. This took no conscious effort on my part; it was happening because I had disciplined my body to exercise at a specific time every day for years.

It was the same when I attended college for four years. After class, I rested and had dinner, and then I disciplined my body to study all night to ensure I could pass the coming tests. This way of life became commonplace and was not something I had to try to do. I just disciplined myself. It was not fun when I first started, but it got to where it was just part of my daily routine, and this is how it should be with us as Christians. It should be natural to speak to God when you wake up in the morning. Proclaim the Word of God, pray in the Spirit, and then go about your day, doing whatever you are supposed to do.

When you get used to doing things a certain way, it becomes a part of you and is automatic. As a student of the Lord, you take all these courses and are studying, being diligent, and understanding different subjects. Then when you are talking to people, you might automatically say, "Well, it says here in Romans chapter twelve that we are supposed to present our bodies as a living sacrifice, and this will help us know the perfect will of God." You will start to flow naturally with the things of God. All your studying, taking courses, and daily routine with the Lord will pay off because it becomes part of you and flows out of you.

Isn't it amazing how people have certain skills? Though very talented, professional athletes and musicians still have to practice constantly. You think, *Oh, my gosh, how could I ever do that?* But those professionals thought the same thing at one time. They just started to do it all the time. Studies have been done on specific sports that found that if you do them twice a week, you will only maintain the level you have already reached. However, if you go to that third time, that third day, that third practice, you will start to excel.

I applied to be a flight instructor at an airport school during my off time. They said they would hire me, but I needed to consider a particular detail. They knew I had been working with an airline I loved for over a year, and I was often on trips. They said they needed me to commit to their students flying with me at least twice a week and possibly three times because of that study. They knew that a student was required to practice two or three times a week to improve, so they wanted me to be available. I only worked three days a week at my job because I worked twelve-hour days. I could work a whole week in three days, so I was also available to take their flight instructor job.

My point with those examples is that it is the same with God's Word and your walk with Him. If you make prayer and studying His Word part of your daily routine, it becomes part of you. You do not even have to think about it anymore. When people desired to advance in any profession and started practicing for five and six days a week, they excelled exponentially and passed everyone. They went far beyond people who practiced only two or three times a week.

EXCEL IN THE THINGS OF GOD

Be encouraged that God will present you blameless to Him, but the process of how you excel and the level you reach is really up to you, and there is no limit. I know this to be true. Yes, you will go to Heaven because you have accepted Jesus. And yes, God will use you because you are studying and diligent. But how far you go and how much you are allowed to know is more up to you than you might like to admit. In other words, if you submit yourself to the Holy Spirit every day and ask Him to teach you, that will take you further and probably faster than someone who sits and reads their Bible once a week and then goes to church and listens to a sermon.

> *In this life, there are no limits, but it is up to you. You have to choose to saturate yourself in God.*

If you go and listen to a sermon, that helps. If you open your Bible once a week, that helps, and if you pray a prayer before you eat, that helps. What about waking up and praying for an hour, reading your Bible, then praying and reading your Bible at night before you go to bed? Then during the day, pray in the Spirit quietly to yourself, even while you are at work or out doing errands. Then have a Scripture card, which is one verse you chose for that day, and keep reviewing that during the day. I have done this over the years, which has helped me grow personally, and I will not hide or keep that secret from you.

In this life, there are no limits, but it is up to you. You have to choose to saturate yourself in God. If everyone else is doing ten minutes of spiritual activity a day, like reading the Bible or praying, and you were to do that twice a day, essentially, you would be doing double what they are doing. If you extend that to ten minutes every two hours and add to that praying silently in the Spirit while you are at work, can you imagine exponentially what that will do for your spiritual life? Imagine how you will develop spiritually over the years. You will be a spiritual giant and be able to weather anything, no matter what.

Right now, I see so many hungry people who want the supernatural. They want to be hot. They want to be in the holy fire constantly. They want to be able to handle not just revelation and visitation but habitation. They want to see the harvest come in. They want to create an atmosphere where people are saved, healed, and delivered, where it is not just casual. If you want that, it will take a commitment from you of more than just ten minutes a day; you will have to take time throughout your day to find a way to look at your Scripture card and pray silently in the Spirit. You can find a way to work this into your schedule and make it part of your life.

I am firmly convinced that I do not want to be labeled as just a Christian. I want to be a believer. You know a believer by their actions. Others do not have to tell you that person is a believer. I can feel faith around people when they have faith and holy fire when they have it. I can tell, but it is not from what they tell me—I can sense it and see it. It is a reality. It is an environment. The Holy Spirit is very willing right now to take you into this, but it must be a lifestyle.

Some people will come against believers with high standards. I guess people feel they can come against people enforcing a higher standard because if they get rid of that standard, they can live with lower standards and do not feel convicted. Unfortunately, this happens when believers take a stand for righteousness and justice; people want to get rid of them. People will try to chip away at you and say you are extreme, but we need hot people. We need people in the holy fire, set apart and saturated with God, because we need healing, deliverance, debt cancellation, and the harvest to come in. These will not come from lukewarm Christians but from white-hot, Spirit-filled believers that have saturated themselves with the environment of Heaven.

I will not hold back from you, and I am telling you all the secrets I know because I believe you want to know them. I have done these things for the last forty years and have invested in my spiritual life constantly. Even if it is in secret, you have to do it. People had no idea what I was doing all those years I was at work. They did not understand, even though it was happening the whole time. The Lord was preparing me over those thirty years at my job. The entire time I was there, my spiritual life was developing, even though I was working and doing what I needed for my company. In reality, I was preparing for what we are doing now.

I believe that God has put us all together and that we will excel in the things God has for us. It is never too late to grasp what you are supposed to be doing. You can go way beyond the norm others have settled for and start right now. I want you to excel in the things of God.

9

DESTROYING BARRIERS

Now when they saw the boldness of Peter and John, and
perceived that they were uneducated
and untrained men, they marveled. And they realized
that they had been with Jesus.

—Acts 4:13

A time must come when you face the issues in your life and allow God to heal you. It's time to flip the tables on the enemy. God did not do the hurtful things that happened to you because that is not His nature. Many people secretly blame God for allowing them to get hurt, but we are in a fallen world and have free will. The church is not teaching this, so there is confusion. Many people do not understand that God is not always going to step in and stop sin.

I have stopped people from dying on their deathbeds because I refused to let them die. It was not because I cried; I did not shed one tear, and it had nothing to do with my emotions. I did not even physically do anything except say, "No, no, it is not their time." I found people who would agree with me, and we saw a huge turnaround; I have seen it happen many times. However, you cannot think a breakthrough is based on your emotions or the tears you shed and believe God will respond to that; He responds to faith. You also cannot think that whatever happens is God's will, and then when something terrible happens, you blame God. That thinking goes against the fact that God is a good God; He doesn't kill, steal, or destroy.

THE DEVIL COMES TO STEAL, KILL, AND DESTROY

> *The thief does not come except to steal, and to kill, and to destroy. I have come that they may have life, and that they may have it more abundantly.*
>
> —John 10:10

If you are experiencing theft or destruction, the devil is doing that. Jesus went around doing good and healing everyone who was oppressed by the devil. God is good, and so He does good. Jesus said that the thief steals, kills, and destroys; Jesus gives life more abundantly. I judge if God is working by asking if this is abundant life. If there is abundant life, then that is Jesus. If stealing, killing, and destroying happen, I know exactly where that is coming from— the devil.

Look what happened in the book of Job as soon as the devil was permitted to attack Job (Job 1:6–12). All the evil that came against him had to do with the enemy armies operating through the weather, disease, killing, stealing, and destroying. Job's family and livestock were killed. You can see all the avenues that satan used against Job as soon as satan was told he could do it. The enemy even influenced his wife, who said to Job, "Curse God and die" (Job 2:9). The devil spoke through her. Even his neighbors came against him. Knowing this helps us understand how satan operates against us.

BUILT UP IN THE SPIRIT AND HAVING A COMMAND ABOUT YOU

Overthrow comes when you settle in, and all that chaff has been burned out of your life. All the barriers caused by blaming God for what has happened are gone. You have stopped asking yourself things like, *Why did God let that happen? I asked God to help me, and He didn't. I asked God to heal me. Why didn't He?* Did you ever think you had to drive devils out by being diligent and putting your foot down? You needed to say, "No, I am going to live and not die and declare the works of the Lord. I will be in the land of the living. I am going to prosper. I will not be in debt anymore" (Psalm 118:17).

My wife and I spent seven years speaking, standing, and fighting against debt before we got out of debt. It wasn't because I was crying, and it wasn't because I was trying. It wasn't because I was casually coming at it either. No. My wife and I aggressively came against debt for seven years. Nothing happened in the first three years we went after it, but we stayed aggressive, and then the overthrow happened. You must understand that you cannot appeal to God in your emotions or throw out a half-hearted prayer now and then, like you pray before you eat. There are different types of prayer.

If the issue is life and death and it has to do with demonic spirits, you must be diligent and aggressive; you must have a command about yourself. You also have to be built up in the Spirit. As soon as God reveals something to you, every single time, every demon in hell will come against you to steal that very revelation that has been given to you. As soon as you get an idea from God, as soon as you are shown God's intention, satan will try to ensure that it doesn't happen. The enemy will try to make you look like a fool; satan will try to make everything about your dream from God and what He said to you look as if it will never happen. The enemy will start to kill, steal, and destroy to get rid of that vision, that seed that God planted in you.

Why does the enemy take so much effort to come against God's will for you? If God brings Heaven to earth, it will not just change you; it will change other people because you will not keep quiet about it. You will tell everyone that you believed in God, and He came through. Once you get a bunch of people together believing, it creates momentum. Then satan will start losing people, and you know he does not want to lose anyone he has entrapped. Think about all the multitudes that went to hear Jesus as He ministered. Those people were not going to the synagogues or the temple, so you can imagine what the Pharisees thought. No one was coming to ask them questions or coming to the temple to worship anymore.

Multitudes went out to listen to this Jesus talk. The Bible tells us what the people were saying about Him. "No man has ever spoken like this Man" (John 7:46). Others observed that He spoke with such authority, unlike the Pharisees (Mark 1:22). You can see that people had turned and were no longer listening to the religious system. The Pharisees and religious leaders, who were under the influence of demonic spirits, came at Jesus because those spirits were keeping people in bondage through the religious system.

> *For men will be lovers of themselves, lovers of money, boasters, proud, blasphemers, disobedient to parents, unthankful, unholy, unloving, unforgiving, slanderers, without self-control, brutal, despisers of good, traitors, headstrong, haughty, lovers of pleasure rather than lovers of God, having a form of godliness but denying its power. And from such people turn away!*
>
> —2 Timothy 3:2–5

Today, many religious churches and people have a form of godliness but deny the power thereof. What if the devil is using religion to keep people lukewarm, in bondage, and spiritually starving? What if these dead, dry churches are causing people to question, "Is this all there is?" These are the same churches that are not mentioning the subjects that make devils tremble. They do not talk about anything that will turn on the holy fire in your life or even tell you that you need to be separate from the world.

> *When the church becomes lukewarm, people decide we need to return to the subjects that can destroy hell so that people are saved, healed, and delivered again.*

The Pharisees came after Jesus. Every demon in hell will come after you if you stand for the truth and speak that truth to others because of the momentum that it creates. At the end of three-and-a-half years, they killed Jesus because He had such a huge following. Thousands of people were following Him, which started a whole movement. They began to call them Christians because the believers acted like Jesus Christ, and they noted that those people had been with Jesus (Acts 4:13). They turned the world upside down. The church was birthed in the book of Acts and grew until we have this body of believers today.

When the church becomes lukewarm, people decide we need to return to the subjects that can destroy hell so that people are saved, healed, and delivered again. That religious cycle is essentially the lukewarm church, and people started coming out of it. Denominations are formed from moves of God, and they eventually become cold; then, movements come out of the denominations. This cycle seems to repeat itself every hundred years or so.

Jesus came speaking the truth, and they killed Him for it. He had such a following that even when they killed Him, it caused an increase, and then the Holy Spirit came (Acts 2). Now God gives you vision as He speaks to you and starts to heal you. You finally realize God didn't do those terrible things to you. He wasn't even permitting them; He was just not invited into your life and those situations. In Heaven, I saw many things I had allowed to happen in my past, whether through negligence or ignorance. It didn't matter. God only comes into situations when He is invited.

When Jesus was invited into situations, He helped; however, He did not go out looking for people to heal. Instead, people came to Him. Jesus ministered to people because they were lost sheep and knew they needed a shepherd. He did not go out looking for disciples. He had twelve chosen disciples and sent out seventy-two others (Luke 10:1–2). Jesus went places, and people came and sat and listened to Him talk, and then they were healed and delivered. It is like this today; Jesus waits for us to invite Him in.

AUTHORITY TO BECOME CHILDREN OF GOD

Jesus could not heal anyone in His hometown because people were not asking for help. They saw Jesus as the carpenter's son and failed to see Him as the Messiah (Mark 6:1–6). Jesus said He could not heal in His hometown due to their unbelief. Religious organizations have grown cold today and do not discern the Lord for who He is. As we read in 2 Chronicles 16:9, the Lord is looking to and fro for anyone who has passionately grabbed onto Him and honors Him, and He will strengthen those people. The Lord wants to dwell with those who have a contrite and humble spirit (Isaiah 57:15).

> *But those who embraced Him and took hold of His name He gave authority to become the children of God!*
>
> —John 1:12 TPT

Many people do not understand this about God, but they need to; He wants to be invited into situations.

Jesus gave authority to those who actively reached out and embraced Him, and they became children of God. It was the same way with the parables. When the disciples came to Jesus and said they did not understand the parable, Jesus would sit with them and explain it. They could not understand why He did not explain it to everyone. Jesus answered and said to them, "Because it has been given to you to know the mysteries of the kingdom of heaven, but to them, it has not been given" (Matthew 13:11). Jesus would not tell the public but shared with the disciples; that is how it is with God. Many people do not understand this about God, but they need to; He wants to be invited into situations.

Corrupt governments are all over the world because the people and the church have not invited God in. An overthrow needs to happen in the spirit realm, but the people don't ask for it. God said He would not destroy Sodom and Gomorrah if He found ten righteous people (Genesis 18:32). A big enough group of righteous people needs to talk to God, negotiate, and say, "Lord, this is not like You to do this, and we need you to work with us." Moses, Abraham, and David were all able to talk to God, and they came to an agreement with Him. They covenanted together with Him because they invited Him into their situation, which is what we need to do. You must actively reach out and ask God to help you.

THE TENACITY TO ENFORCE OVERTHROW

Most people today are hurt and mad at God because they think He let certain situations happen to them when they were a child. They feel that they asked God, and He did not do anything about it, but God will not necessarily answer an emotional prayer. The Father wants you to operate in sonship and as His friend. When you are not born again or not developed in maturity, you do not know how to pray or even know the different types of prayers to pray. Still, no matter what level you are operating on, God will help you the best that He can in that situation.

I had the revelation that we can permit things to happen. It might be that we did nothing about it, and that was enough for the devil to come in. That is what I saw, and I am telling you the truth. I don't know how else to tell people this, but we are supposed to take certain actions, or nothing will be done. History will show that many interventions should have taken place, but never happened. Wickedness is supposed to be overturned and blocked through us, but this will not be done if we do not do something about it.

You may pray for something to be done, and then God will elect *you* to do it. However, if you disobey or say you will do it and don't follow through, it will not be done. Those who prayed could say that they prayed and it did not happen, but God answered their prayer by telling someone (maybe them) to do it. If a person does not obey God, it will not be done. In some situations, God went through many people before He found one willing to do it. Think about that. How many people do you think God had to go through before He found a Kathryn Kuhlman or a Smith Wigglesworth? What about something you asked four years ago that still hasn't happened? Yet God might have asked eight people, and none would do it.

A point has to come in your life where you resolve the lie that God caused or allowed hurtful situations in your past. Some circumstances happened because you did not understand and were not actively pursuing God, asking Him to come into the situation. As we grow up, we must let go of those lies and realize that the devil is mean and we are in a fallen world. The devil is the god of this world, and often, God does not have His way. However, God can now have His way because you invite Him in and have become mature enough to take a stand.

I want you to get into the place where you have the tenacity to enforce overthrow. You ask, and you know that you receive; you seek, and you know you will find; you knock, and you know the door will be opened to you (Matthew 7:7). When Jesus spoke those instructions, He approached them differently than most of us have understood. It was as though He were saying, "You know you will receive when you ask, you know the door will be opened when you knock, and you know that you will find if you seek. Period."

> *Therefore I say to you, whatever things you ask when you pray, believe that you receive them, and you will have them.*
>
> —Mark 11:24

Jesus said that if you pray, believing that you receive it, you *will* have it. You must understand you already got it before you even ask, that is getting into overthrow. A sign of maturity, a sign that you are receiving and operating as a son or daughter of God, is that you don't hesitate. It's the same as when you train your body; you reach a point where it becomes a lifestyle without hesitation. Athletes make sports look so easy, but it is because they have done it for years, and it just looks seamless. That is how it is even in your spiritual life. When you encounter the devil, you should be so quick to respond and react that you even surprise the devil by taking care of it immediately.

Did you know that you can surprise the devil? The devil and his demons flip out over people in overthrow. They flip out because they see you have no hesitation or fear. God wants to mature you because today, we need warriors, people well-trained in spiritual matters to bring in the harvest and build up the body of Christ. When overthrow happens, it is because you have been delivered and healed inside your heart.

The traumatic events that happened to you were valid; you trusted people and were a victim. You now know these events occurred because we are in an imperfect, fallen world. However, you are no longer where you were and now understand truth you did not understand before. You are now in a new place spiritually; you are growing every day, and the devils know it. The devil and his demons know they can no longer operate against you, so they will try to stop your momentum. You will understand how to eliminate the ability of the evil spirits to get to you; the Holy Spirit will show you how to do it and seal it up for you.

10

ENFORCING OVERTHROW

Moreover whom He predestined, these He also called;
whom He called, these He also justified; and whom He
justified, these He also glorified.
—Romans 8:30

As we discussed, many things happened to you when you were younger because you were not where you are now and did not understand everything you do now. However, you cannot blame God, and you cannot blame others. You must forgive. Forgiveness releases you from the responsibility of dealing with those matters yourself. Forgiveness is a legal case turned over to God; when you forgive, you are, in reality, handing the whole matter over to Him so He can take care of it. Some people think that if you forgive someone, that exonerates them; no, it releases *you*. You do it for your own spiritual well-being, so release everything. People do not get away with sin just because you forgive them. God will handle it.

GOD WILL DIRECT YOUR PATHS

I do not blame God nor do I blame anything on anyone. I take full responsibility for where I am today, understanding that I can experience a reset and go on to be very productive for the rest of my life. So I will not blame people, circumstances, or God. If you meet Jesus, it will take you forever to get up enough guts even to say something to Him. Never mind telling Him that He was wrong or confronting Him by saying, "Why did this happen?" You will never say that, and you will never be able to blame Him because He is not at fault. Jesus is not wrong, has never been wrong, and will never apologize.

Jesus has given us everything we need for life and godliness, as Peter said (2 Peter 1:3). Jesus has done everything He is going to do about the devil and everything He is going to do about healing. He has already suffered and died, made a show of the devil openly, and provided for us (Colossians 2:15). You will find that out when you get to Heaven. When people pursue God and acknowledge Him in all their ways, He directs their paths because they engage God and include Him (Proverbs 3:6).

YOU SHOULD ALREADY KNOW WHAT GOD LIKES AND DISLIKES

Will a man rob God? Yet you have robbed Me! But you say, 'In what way have we robbed You?' In tithes and offerings.

—Malachi 3:8

During Malachi's day, God asked, "Will a man rob God?" The people neglected what they had already been told because they were supposed to be tithing. As a result, God let them face problems until they finally asked the Lord what was happening, and Malachi prophesied that God said they were robbing Him. When they asked God how they were robbing Him, He told them, "In tithes and offerings," and then they repented. It is sad because people who follow God should already know what God likes and does not like.

These six things the Lord hates, yes, seven are an abomination to Him: a proud look, a lying tongue, hands that shed innocent blood, a heart that devises wicked plans, feet that are swift in running to evil, a false witness who speaks lies, and one who sows discord among brethren.

—Proverbs 6:16–19

In the Bible, God says there are seven things He hates; if He hates them, you should hate them too. If God likes certain things, you should like them. Unfortunately, these truths slip away from us. When you reach Heaven, you will realize that you should have known and practiced all these, which I found out. I discovered they were all true even when I didn't think about or understand them. Even if I had known and ignored these, I still would have robbed myself and others because I could have been more productive. I will never find myself in that situation again. I will be fruitful for the rest of my life because I know I cannot lose.

WE ARE THE GLORIOUS CHURCH

I realize I could stop ministering right now and be fine; however, I choose not to because I know too much. It is all rigged in my favor if I obey the Lord; God has already provided all that I need and defeated the devil, having made a show of him openly. So it does not matter if it looks like the enemy is taking over the earth. God has us, His glorious church, on the earth, and the gates of hell cannot prevail against us (Matthew 16:18). We must stay in there and remember what God has already said.

> *You will realize that you cannot fail and are not a victim; then, you can turn and start to help others, which is the fulfillment of the body.*

Once you are delivered, you will realize all that Jesus has done and become comfortable with that. You will realize that you cannot fail and are not a victim; then, you can turn and start to help others, which is the fulfillment of the body. We should be ministering to each other, not just ourselves. Ministering only to yourself is the mentality of a victim and a sign you are in survival mode and want to self-preserve. The rich young ruler was operating in self-preservation, and Jesus was trying to get him out of that mode. Jesus told him to sell everything he had and give it to the poor, and he would have treasure in Heaven. Then, Jesus said to come and follow Him (Matthew 19:21).

The rich young ruler could not obey and follow Jesus because he was a victim, an orphan, in survival mode. Unfortunately, we meet wonderful people all the time with a victim mentality or who are just surviving, trying to preserve themselves. It is almost like they are in a chess game and trying to position themselves so they come out ahead. They are always strategizing, which is not how we should be as believers.

BELIEVERS IN OVERTHROW SHOCK DEMONS

A believer is supposed to turn everything over to God. You are not a victim, not an orphan, not abandoned, and not rejected. Let God accept you, love on you, prosper you, and bless you with good health (3 John 1:2). Build yourself up and get to the place where you are in overthrow so you can see the devil chased out of town. The demons are shocked when a person is in overthrow because they do not see that many people reach the point of walking in who they are in Christ.

When you realize who you are, you know it is not about pushing your position; you are who you are and do not have to defend yourself. You never have to prove yourself to anyone or apologize for who you are. You are who you are because God is who He is. You identify with Him, He identifies with you, and you walk in a close relationship with Him.

Believers in overthrow shock demons, who operate throughout the earth to keep people in a victim or rejection mode. The demons do not know what to do with someone not in victim, orphan, or rejection mode because none of their schemes work on them. You will see demons pushing and pressuring these people, but it is counterproductive because all they do is run to God, get into the glory, and get ignited. When the demons see that their plan isn't working and the opposite is happening, they back off and leave these people alone. They do not know what to do with a person who is thoroughly convinced of their God and who is not responding out of their emotions or mind but out of their spirit. You become like a fine-tuned machine because you have allowed the Holy Spirit to develop you.

SAVED BY FAITH, NOT BY WORKS

For by grace you have been saved through faith, and that not of yourselves; it is the gift of God, not of works, lest anyone should boast.

—Ephesians 2:8–9

The religious system is like a crutch because it teaches you to rely on man, programs, formulas, etc. They tell you that this or that will happen if you say specific prayers or commit to certain church doctrines. I was told I would go to Heaven if I joined the church, was baptized, and behaved for the rest of my life. I thought, *Okay, I have to join the church, be sprinkled with water, and be a good person for the rest of my life. Then God will decide if I make it into Heaven.* I had no assurance I would go to Heaven even if I did what the church told me to do. Then I discovered that I was saved not by works but by faith and that I needed to be born again.

My former pastor never mentioned the born-again experience and Jesus's name. He mentioned God but never Jesus, and I do not remember him talking about anything spiritual. When I asked him questions, he did not even know the answer. When I became born again, I was very upset because I felt the religious system kept me out instead of bringing me in. Since I was born again at nineteen, I have spent my whole life on this journey of discovery and learning the truth that the Bible teaches.

> *However, when He, the Spirit of truth, has come, He will guide you into all truth; for He will not speak on His own authority, but whatever He hears He will speak; and He will tell you things to come. He will glorify Me, for He will take of what is Mine and declare it to you.*
>
> —John 16:13–14

I found that the Holy Spirit was given to reveal the truth, which I was never taught. I was never told that the Holy Spirit is a Person Who is inside you and is teaching, leading, and guiding you; He is our friend. I was not taught that He is with us now or how to pray properly. I had a victim mentality and felt rejected and orphaned even when I was around people and in church two or three times a week. I was tithing, doing good works, and doing my best, but it did not help me overcome the evil that was working. Spiritual warfare was going on, and I knew it, but I could not do anything about it.

When I was born again, I was ignited and activated and started gaining awareness that I needed more understanding. I learned more about the Bible by spending time with people who believed in being born again, yet they did not understand warfare or what to do about the devil. They did not teach the in-Him doctrine that Paul taught in Ephesians 2:4–9, which is about being in Christ, the benefits of being in Jesus, and being seated with Him in the heavenly places. None of that was taught. I had to move out of that place and go where they were always teaching about being in Christ.

FINDING THE HOLY FIRE AND WHERE
GOD IS MOVING

As I searched for where God was moving, each step I took worked for a while, but then I noticed that people around me started growing cold, and the message started to change. At first, the leaders seemed to be doing the same godly works, but the results were not the same. I realized it was not heartfelt anymore, then I had to move again. I had to go out and find where God was moving and where the fire was. It forced me into this place of holy fire where I had to let the Lord work on me. I was called to be a standard-bearer, a leader who would operate in faith, calling things that were not as they were (Romans 4:17).

> *Yet in all these things we are more than conquerors through Him who loved us.*
>
> —Romans 8:37

> I realized my future was secure; all I had to do was be diligent down here and stay hot.

I got to where I knew the end was secure because when I died, I saw the end, and then I was sent back. I realized my future was secure; all I had to do was be diligent down here and stay hot. I was called to remain on fire and enforce the victory already given to me when I saw into the future. When I came back, I saw that I was more than a conqueror and that I was in overthrow. That was because I already saw I had made it to the end. I saw all the saints in Heaven that were ever going to live, every one of them that was ever born, and probably some that are not in existence yet.

In Heaven, I saw the end, which has not even happened yet on earth, but has already happened there. Then I was sent back. God told me, "Here is where you are going, and now I want you to be part of this." So here I am, and with everything we are doing, I essentially enforce victory and overthrow. It has already happened, yet I watch it unfold in this realm. It is slower, and in some cases, it has not happened yet, but I know it will. I am enforcing what God showed me about the future. I am not concerned about what people are worried about because I know it is already taken care of.

JESUS IS SEATED IN HEAVEN, WAITING FOR HIS ENEMIES TO BECOME HIS FOOTSTOOL

And we know that all things work together for good to those who love God, to those who are the called according to His purpose. For whom He foreknew,

He also predestined to be conformed to the image of His Son, that He might be the firstborn among many brethren. Moreover whom He predestined, these He also called; whom He called, these He also justified; and whom He justified, these He also glorified.

—Romans 8:28–30

In the book of Romans, Paul shares many insights and gives us extensive revelation. After His ascension, we know that Jesus Christ went to and remains in the timeless realm, our future; He is now seated at the right hand of God (Hebrews 12:2). Jesus is seated because He has accomplished everything He is going to perform and is now waiting for His enemies to become His footstool through the church (Hebrews 10:12–13). Jesus took captivity captive, ascended on high, and distributed gifts to everyone (Ephesians 4:7–10). Jesus took what He had won, distributed it among the body, and sat down. Now Jesus waits, but it is not *waiting* like we think because there is no time.

Time does not pass in Heaven like it does down here. There is no calendar. It is not like we have tomorrow, then we have off, or we have the weekend. It's not like vacation is coming next month. It is not like that with God. He is the I Am, and nothing bothers Him. There is no time in Heaven, so for God, it is already done, and waiting is nothing to Him. It could be a thousand years down here, which is a day up there (2 Peter 3:8). Time passes down here, yet nothing has happened on His timetable, because He is waiting for His enemies to become His footstool through the church.

So satan throws out these ideas to the body and the world that we are waiting on God. However, that is false. The world says that if God wants to do it, He will do it because He is in control. People say that all the time in the world and even in the church. However, it is an insult and an embarrassment to say God is in control of this world because it is a mess.

You can go to the drive-thru right now and order a meal, and you have a fifty-fifty chance that they even get it right. You are already on the road before you know they messed up. That is because it is a broken world. If God were in control, He would not mess up your order. Your food would not be cold; it would stay hot. You can apply this idea to everything down here.

Over the years at my job, I found discrepancies in my paycheck almost every month. A coworker figured it out and saw that the company had made mistakes in our paychecks for six years. I got back pay for six years of mistakes I did not know about, and it became a class-action lawsuit because someone else noticed it. God is not in control of that because He does not make mistakes. How can you pay your bills, and then have that company call you and say, "Hey, you need to pay your bills?" Now you have to prove you paid those bills by finding receipts. There are plenty of discrepancies, disappointments, and discouragements down here. However, God is not in control of those types of situations.

Now, God might be in control of your life because you invited Him in and included Him. However, God does not get involved if you do not go to the altar and dedicate your life and every part of your business, family, relationships, and everything about you. You must consciously and actively dedicate those things to God for Him to get involved, and this is the absolute truth.

GOD IS WAITING ON US— WE ARE NOT WAITING ON HIM

We think we are waiting on God down here, yet He is waiting on us. People think God is in control, and He is not because they have not asked Him into their lives. The world has chased God out of our schools and government and said they don't want Him there. Our schools and government all started to deteriorate at an alarming rate, then corruption and every evil came in. Suddenly we woke up, but it was almost too late because the manipulation and control were already there, and it would almost take a war to reverse the situation. God is not in control of this and is waiting on us. We are not waiting on Him.

When you get to Heaven, you will see that everything was established long ago. God revealed Himself and actively involved Himself; now He waits for us to respond to Him. We might be waiting on the Holy Spirit, but He has already been given, and God is waiting on us to invite Him in. The wake-up call comes when we get into overthrow. It is open season now, and we can do whatever we have in our hearts and spirit because that is where the Lord dwells and directs us. The demons do not know how to deal with a group of people like that. We are a serious threat to them.

The move of God has started. People are beginning to realize that God is waiting on them; He is not in control down here but wants to be in control through the church—through the believer. People are starting to realize that is their job. When people are accountable, knowing they will have to do something about it or it will not happen, this is when you get into overthrow. We see people praying, talking, and living that way more and more. These are leaders and history-makers who are no longer just surviving as victims. That is who you are, and it is all because of revelation, visitation, and habitation. You have been delivered, set free, and are now a leader.

You call the shots because God trusts you, just like He trusted Abraham, Moses, and David. They all did many exploits for God because God let them be who He made them to be.

11

THE KINGDOM OF GOD IS AT HAND

The time is fulfilled, and the kingdom of God is at hand.
Repent, and believe in the gospel.
—Mark 1:15

Jesus often talked about the kingdom of God. Interestingly, after He was raised from the dead, He was seen walking around the city, on the roads, and in many different places. Jesus appeared to many, and Acts 1:1–3 talks about how He taught about the kingdom of God for forty days after His resurrection. I am sure that the news of His crucifixion quickly spread around the city because He was so loved and hated by many people. You can imagine many people saw the crucifixion because Jesus was well-known and visible.

PREACHING THE GOSPEL OF THE
KINGDOM OF GOD

The former account I made, O Theophilus, of all that Jesus began both to do and teach, until the day in which He was taken up, after He through the Holy Spirit had given commandments to the apostles whom He had chosen, to whom He also presented Himself alive after His suffering by many infallible proofs, being seen by them during forty days and speaking of the things pertaining to the kingdom of God.

—Acts 1:1–3

If Jesus appeared to people for forty days after the crucifixion, how long do you think it took for that news to get around? The disciples and everyone must have been talking about it. Jesus chose to speak about and teach about the kingdom of God for forty days. The kingdom was the most important subject to Him and what the Father led Him to teach. Think about how Herod, Pilot, and all the Roman soldiers probably got wind of what happened. Who knows? Maybe some of them even saw Jesus. One of those centurion soldiers might have even seen Him talking to people during those forty days.

> *And this gospel of the kingdom will be preached in*
> *all the world as a witness to all the nations, and then*
> *the end will come.*
>
> —Matthew 24:14

Since Jesus said that the gospel of the kingdom must be preached in all the world, we need to think and be preaching it all the time. If Jesus picked this subject above all others to teach on for forty extra days after His death, burial, and resurrection, it should also be our priority. So what does that mean to us? And what does that have to do with holy fire and holiness? Once we have gone through this journey and yielded to the fire, we are ready to minister and preach to others. When we have allowed God to work with us and help us, we are prepared to release this message about the kingdom and Jesus.

REPENT AND BELIEVE IN THE GOSPEL

> *Jesus came to Galilee, preaching the gospel of the*
> *kingdom of God, and saying, "The time is fulfilled,*
> *and the kingdom of God is at hand. Repent, and*
> *believe in the gospel."*
>
> —Mark 1:14–15

Jesus came to Galilee and preached the gospel of the kingdom of God; this is what He said, and it is all recorded. I crave every word that comes from the mouth of God. Jesus said that people should not live by bread alone, but by every word that proceeds from the mouth of God (Matthew 4:4). I want to see everything I am supposed to see and hear everything I am supposed to hear. I desire to preach the kingdom and the gospel with accuracy and excellence.

I want to preach the gospel of God's kingdom according to the standard of Heaven. To do that, I must study and make myself available by the Spirit of God for the power of the resurrection to manifest. I will have to make myself available to be used in the gifts of the Spirit, prophetic utterances that God would need me to speak, and be ready to raise the dead and drive out demons. I will need to be prepared to do all this, as will you. However, what is crucial along with the kingdom's message is that we call people to repentance. We must share the gospel, announce the good news, and then call people to repentance. After they hear the good news, they have to turn to God; we have to bring people to that place of decision.

It is not enough to have a great message on Sunday in church or hear it on TV, YouTube, or whatever media you watch or read. That message has got to get you to a place where you turn, make a decision, and become accountable for what you just heard. We have discussed the message and its potency. We talked about how we must teach people about the fear of the Lord, brokenness, repentance, holy fire, holiness, sanctification, and all these different subjects. However, we must give people a chance to turn, repent, and acknowledge they fell short; then, we must provide them with the opportunity to make that decision to change. It is also good to do that publicly.

> *We need to not only preach the good news but also allow people to repent at the altar, turn to God, and get right with Him.*

We need to not only preach the good news but also allow people to repent at the altar, turn to God, and get right with Him. That is not happening today. Churches might have a great message, but it does not convince them to turn. And they are not given an opportunity to make a decision, which is most important. When Jesus presented His message, He taught repentance. If we are truly in Christ and genuinely moving by the Spirit, a point will come when the Holy Spirit, through us, allows people to make a decision and openly acknowledge it.

In Acts 17:28, Paul states that it is in Christ that we live, move, and have our being. This verse includes a resolution or a closure. Without a solution, I would not want to present a problem or dilemma to someone. Instead, when I share an issue, I want all parties involved able to walk away with a resolution. It is not enough to present a problem because people need closure. That closure is where people must be accountable and agree on a final resolution. That way, it never needs to be revisited once they walk away from it. They have agreed to a solution, which will happen. The involved parties trust each other to accomplish their part.

In the same way, the message of the kingdom of God must be presented with the opportunity for people to have a resolution. God has His desires, and then He makes them known. We hear them, but then we have to do something about it. Once we hear God's message, we must decide if we will believe it, agree with it, and abide by it. God gives His desires and tells us what He wants, and then He needs us to come into agreement with Him, which is a covenant. Through our accountability, we find closure. We know that if we meet all of God's desires and demands and He meets all of ours, He will seal this agreement. Then we can walk away knowing that it is all settled and resolved.

When you preach, share, and testify about Jesus, believe that God will confirm the word you preach with signs and wonders (Mark 16:20). When you do your part, God does His part. Jesus was doing what His Father wanted Him to do, but what the word was saying had to manifest. As a result of that preaching, people heard the word, mixed it with faith, and received it. Many people were delivered, healed, and raised from the dead. They were changed by what they heard and put their trust in Jesus. People must be given the same opportunity today.

THE KINGDOM OF GOD IS ADVANCING

Enter by the narrow gate; for wide is the gate and broad is the way that leads to destruction, and there are many who go in by it. Because narrow is the gate and difficult is the way which leads to life, and there are few who find it.

—Matthew 7:13–14

As we preach the kingdom of God, we must realize it is a real, literal place, a domain with a King ruling and reigning over it. God's kingdom realm has permeated this earthly realm through preaching and teaching the gospel and the demonstration of the power of the Spirit. As people receive the message of the kingdom, we have a harvest; they become subjects in the kingdom and part of the family of God because they hear the Word of God being preached. As the people grasp and take hold of that, the message must be preached about the holy fire, the advancing of the kingdom of God, and the entrance into that kingdom through the narrow way.

> *Let us be glad and rejoice and give Him glory, for the marriage of the Lamb has come, and His wife has made herself ready. And to her it was granted to be arrayed in fine linen, clean and bright, for the fine linen is the righteous acts of the saints. Then he said to me, "Write: 'Blessed are those who are called to the marriage supper of the Lamb!'" And he said to me, "These are the true sayings of God."*
>
> —Revelation 19:7–9

We enter the narrow way by separating ourselves from the world and subjecting ourselves to the Holy Spirit's work. As a result, we are disciplined and go through pruning, refinement by fire, and a cutting away as we are being purified. We are being readied for the marriage supper of the Lamb as the Lord's church, His body, His perfect bride without spot or wrinkle (Ephesians 5:26–27). The goal of the Holy Spirit is to get us ready so that we live and move in Him without any hindrance. The Holy Spirit is working and wants to present us perfect and above reproach to the Bridegroom, Jesus Christ. This is happening right now.

Not only will we get married to Jesus and sit at the marriage supper of the Lamb, but we will be given our next assignment. We are being readied for whatever we are promoted to by what we go through down here. You do not want to hide in your house, and you do not want to sit and wait for Jesus to come back; you want to make sure you are doing everything you can to be ready for the coming of the Lord. After that, everything that you encounter down here, all that you are being trained in, goes toward your next life, in the next job assignment that you will have.

PREPARING FOR ETERNITY

You are currently being readied for the job assignment you will be doing in eternity. You are an ambassador of Heaven and will represent God in other countries. Did you know there are other universes and not just our universe? God will put us in different places, and we will rule and reign with Him throughout eternity. It is so big, and we cannot comprehend it all now, but it is true anyway.

I want to give the Holy Spirit preeminence in my life right now, not just to prepare me for the marriage supper. It is beyond that. When

I was with Jesus, I was shown that I was being prepared for eternity as a representative of God and as someone in His household. I will be ministering for a long time, and so will you; we are all being made ready. You can be an example and an amazing minister down here, and it will continue forever. Be encouraged, and do not allow discouragement to come in because nothing is wasted at all. Everything you go through and learn will be used, and you will always remember how faithful God was to you down here.

INCREASING YOUR DISCERNMENT

You must allow to Lord to sharpen your discernment when you are going out and preaching the kingdom. You are part of the kingdom's expansion. Increasing your discernment is part of being a good warrior as you are being developed through holy fire. God wants you to have keen insight so you can see any situation, separate what is happening, and understand it.

Some people can look at something, like a camera or a table, and they can dissect it. They can see how it's built and discern situations you would not even begin to understand. Other people can look at a scenario or a problem and tell what is going on behind the scenes because they have the discernment to know how it functions. As born-again believers, we should be discerning in the Spirit and understand what is going on. We don't know everything, but it can be shown in the Spirit, whether good or evil. Our discernment in these last days needs to go to a higher level, and we need to know what God is saying and doing in situations.

At the end of the age, we will need to be wiser than ever. I see greater discernment coming to God's people. The holy fire will sharpen your discernment so that you will know right from wrong and be able to discern what is happening behind the scenes. You will even know what kind of spirits are operating, which happens with the gift of discerning of spirits, one of the gifts of the Spirit (1 Corinthians 12:1–11). However, we should all operate with simple discernment, which is a spiritual sensitivity to know what is happening around us.

BUILDING MOMENTUM

We also need to build momentum, which means you start to move in a specific direction and build up strength and power as you go. Think about how heavy a car is; it takes time to accelerate and gain momentum. But once you are traveling at a steady speed, you do not really notice the car's weight. The only time that you notice the car's weight is when you start and slow down. Braking and trying to slow down takes time because of the car's momentum and weight.

In the Spirit, momentum is when God sets you in a direction, and you start to build yourself up, becoming bold, strong, and established in what God has for you. You do not feel the weight once you get up to speed, but satan wants to slow you down and destroy that momentum. You are much weightier in the Spirit than you realize because you have accelerated and are either maintaining a certain speed or still accelerating. You can feel it when that is happening. Now, if someone wanted to slow you down, they would try to step in and distract you. If that happened, you could see and feel yourself decelerating.

You do not want satan to come in and hinder your momentum, which happens in different ways. One of the ways the devil does this is by drawing your attention away from God or creating situations so that you start to question Him. God is never working against you; He is accelerating and teaching you. Jesus wants to encourage you to discern between good and evil and everything that is going on around you in the spirit realm.

Jesus wants you to maintain momentum because a lot is invested in you. You have the Holy Spirit and the Word of God working inside you. You have the river of life and angels around you going back and forth from Heaven. You have ministry gifts inside you and the anointings of God upon you, and you have momentum. When you get groups of people together in agreement, even greater authority and momentum are established. The devil wants to slow down or destroy all this. Do not let anything get in your way to slow you down. Do not let it bother you when you face problems. Keep on going; continue thanking God and rejoicing. Do not let these evil spirits get in the way. The kingdom is full of discernment and momentum.

YOU HAVE BEEN GIVEN AUTHORITY

Assuredly, I say to you, whatever you bind on earth will be bound in Heaven, and whatever you loose on earth will be loosed in Heaven.

—Matthew 18:18

Another kingdom characteristic is that Jesus has a commanding air about Him. This idea of having a commanding air about you means that you are established in authority and sent like an ambassador. You have been given the authority to speak on behalf of someone in charge. You have been sent as a covenant keeper and representative of the kingdom. You represent the kingdom of God, and what you say goes. Jesus is giving you this ability.

I let the Word of God ignite in me. I allow that fire of the Holy Spirit to burn, and I feed the flame with the Word of God. Then I am ignited and speak from that place inside me; I speak from the fire. As Jesus has a commanding air about him, I want you to start to identify with Him and see He is the Commander. Yet that commanding air and authority have been given to you too. You must see yourself being ignited, meditating on the commands of the Lord in the Word of God. Then see that ignition happen so that you explode from within and walk with a commanding air about you.

I worked for an airline for many years, and I could tell a person of authority even when they were in plain clothes. When I checked on it, it was amazing because even though they did not have a uniform, I would find out they were high-ranking military, a police officer, or law enforcement. You could feel it because they had a commanding air about them, yet they did not have a visible badge or uniform. Despite dressing in street clothes, you could feel their authority, which is what I want for you. I want you to see that you are ignited with the Word of God and the fire of God and that you have a commanding air about you.

12

A STANDARD FOR OUR GENERATION

*So shall My word be that goes forth from My mouth; It
shall not return to Me void, but it shall accomplish
what I please, and it shall prosper in the thing
for which I sent it.*
—Isaiah 55:11

I often start to see and think about where God is. I picture what
happened when Isaiah saw the Lord high and lifted up and saw
all the activities taking place in the throne room. He was undone. I
often think about how incredible it was for a human body to be taken
to see the Lord and witness how majestic and full of authority He is.
I think of what it is like to see the white-hot fire in the throne room,
all the living creatures there, and the holiness that fills it. The

experience was so amazing and powerful that Isaiah says he was undone.

> *In the year that King Uzziah died, I saw the Lord sitting on a throne, high and lifted up, and the train of His robe filled the temple. Above it stood seraphim; each one had six wings: with two he covered his face, with two he covered his feet, and with two he flew. And one cried to another and said: "Holy, holy, holy is the Lord of hosts; The whole earth is full of His glory!" And the posts of the door were shaken by the voice of him who cried out, and the house was filled with smoke. So I said: "Woe is me, for I am undone! Because I am a man of unclean lips, And I dwell in the midst of a people of unclean lips; For my eyes have seen the King, the Lord of hosts."*
>
> —Isaiah 6:1–5

GOD IS IN COMMAND AND HAS FULL AUTHORITY

As we discussed, the Lord wants us to walk in an air of command, having full authority. God wants us to remember where He sits and that He is the great I Am in Heaven, the Creator of everything. We do not see Him in control, ruling and reigning here on earth, but He certainly rules and reigns in Heaven in full authority. God is in control of Heaven, and He deals with this earthly realm through us, the church, through the believers. We need to be good ambassadors and be on fire from the fire at the altar of the throne of God. The seraphim there are on fire, and we can see the full authority, the beauty, and the fear of the Lord. The holiness of the Lord is so evident there with a crisp holy presence where God is in command.

Everything God says is essential, and our response to Him should be one of awe. God speaks from His throne, giving out the commands for what He wants to accomplish. Everything God says goes forth and does not return empty because it accomplishes what He intends. We can think about how powerful God is, yet even though He is the King of the kingdom and His domain, He is also our Father, and we are His children. We are so privileged to be part of His family. We have free access to the Father, not just as servants, slaves, or subjects of the kingdom but as children of a loving Heavenly Father. We can approach and encounter God with a child's heart. We have free access to the throne without even being invited.

The Spirit Himself bears witness with our spirit that
we are children of God, and if children, then heirs—

heirs of God and joint heirs with Christ, if indeed we suffer with Him, that we may also be glorified together.

—Romans 8:16–17

Part of what we do and preach in the kingdom down here is that we must remember where our authority is: in the throne room, where the fire from the throne is, especially since we have a Heavenly Father who loves us. The Father has made us part of his family— we are heirs of God and co-heirs with Jesus. So we need to hear what our Father is speaking and then repeat it. We need to operate in that authority from the throne and speak what He says.

YOUR HOME IS IN HEAVEN

The Lord is not slack concerning His promise, as some count slackness, but is longsuffering toward us, not willing that any should perish but that all should come to repentance.

—2 Peter 3:9

Remember that God loves people and does not want anyone to perish; He desires that everyone has everlasting life. We love people because God loves people. We are part of His family and want other people to become part of that family as well. The kingdom of God is expanding and not just as a king with people under him but as a Heavenly Father that loves us and loves people; He wants them to come in and inherit this kingdom. Always remember that this is your origin and where you belong. You will return there one day and discover Heaven was always your home.

When I was there with Jesus, I was home and realized that anything I do for Him is out of my love for Him. I am just here visiting and am not part of this world system. When you are in the throne room where you belong, you understand that Heaven clearly was and is your home. Everything about Heaven is who you are. Down here on earth, you will feel uncomfortable. You will not feel accepted or fit in, which is common for all believers.

You must remind yourself that you are just visiting down here and are actually living your life out of love for God. That makes it a little easier to deal with life down here. I always longed to go back there and be part of what God is doing in Heaven because that is where my heart is, and it never leaves there. That is the way it is with you too. I have free access to go there in the Spirit at all times, but I also know Heaven will be my permanent dwelling place someday.

LEARN TO FEED YOURSELF THE WORD OF GOD

As a minister of the kingdom, you will be ministering the Word of God, and while you are down here, you will have to feed yourself in the Spirit. You will find that as you grow in the Lord and are filled with the holy fire, you are way beyond what you encounter around you. You will get to where you will find that only certain people or organizations feed you, and you will often have to feed yourself. That is why I allow myself time to study the Word of God daily and meditate on it, knowing that it might be the only hot meal I get for the day or the week. You must learn to feed yourself a hot meal in the Spirit because you might not get it from someone else.

As you submit yourself to the holy fire, your standard is of the highest level, and the holy fire will reveal all the things that need to go. Once you allow that to happen, you will only want the highest level and might not find that everywhere. If you are going to be a minister of the kingdom, you will have to learn to feed yourself with fiery messages that you receive yourself from the Word of God. I prepare meals for myself by studying the Word of God, meditating, and praying. I attach myself to the Word of God.

I want and need to hear from my Heavenly Father, so I attach myself to His words and latch myself onto the truth. I then pray in the Spirit often, which is my lifeline. Besides feeding myself a hot meal, I latch myself onto the Father and whatever He might say to me. Then I also pray in the Spirit as much as possible because that is the breath that keeps me going. I literally feel like I am attached to the Father, and He is the only One that keeps me going.

At some points in life, you might have no one else to help you as God Himself can. We still need the body of Christ; however, you must learn to feed yourself, attach yourself to your Father, and pray in the Spirit as though it is the very breath you need.

PRAYING IN TONGUES WITH THE UNDERSTANDING

Therefore let him who speaks in a tongue pray that he may interpret. For if I pray in a tongue, my spirit prays, but my understanding is unfruitful.
—1 Corinthians 14:13-14

I wish you all spoke with tongues, but even more that you prophesied; for he who prophesies is greater than he who speaks with tongues, unless indeed he interprets, that the church may receive edification.
—1 Corinthians 14:5

I speak in tongues a great deal and pray in the Spirit as much as possible. I pray silently in public and do it out loud in private. Then I pray that God would help me interpret or understand what is being said, even if it is just a word or two or a little glimpse of understanding. It is vital to gain some understanding because the Holy Spirit wants to take you in a direction, and your mind is not always fruitful. Sometimes, signposts along the way will let you know what is happening.

Paul said that we should pray that we can interpret, so I encourage you to pray that the Lord allows you to interpret your tongues and gain some understanding. He said, if you prophesy, you understand what you are saying because it is in your own language. I want to encourage you with that as well.

MOVING WHEN GOD MOVES

Then Jesus said to His disciples, "If anyone desires to come after Me, let him deny himself, and take up his cross, and follow Me."

—Matthew 16:24

At times, you will have to deny yourself and your flesh. Temptations come up, and you will have to say no to your flesh and mind, which is part of how the kingdom operates. At times, God will have priorities and will want you to do some things for Him that may involve changing your schedule and your own plans. If you really want to move with God in the kingdom and accomplish His heart's desire, you must be willing to move when He moves.

> *If you really want to move with God in the kingdom and accomplish His heart's desire, you must be willing to move when He moves.*

At times, I am sure Jesus wanted to rest and sleep, yet He was often interrupted. I don't know how much He even slept in His three-and-a-half years on earth. Many supernatural miracles happened during the day, but He would go into the mountains at night to pray. You might find yourself not sleeping at times because you have to pray, and then, during the day, you are ministering. Sometimes you will have to let your schedule be interrupted to fulfill what God has for you, which is also denying yourself.

Denying yourself is not just about trying to overcome temptation and sin. A time comes when you rest and walk with God. But God may also move you in a direction so that you deny yourself more than seems possible. Everyone deserves to rest, sleep, and have time for themselves. However, the Lord may have you do some things at times that are very important to Him, which is all part of life in the kingdom, walking in the supernatural, and denying yourself.

You must keep your edge about you in the Spirit, which is not easy. Even though you may think it's easy, you struggle because this is a fallen world. You can fall into chaos if you do not maintain your fire for the Lord. Notice that possessions break and don't fix themselves. They get dirty and don't clean themselves. They don't put themselves together. We see our stuff go from order to chaos all the time because of this fallen world, and it deteriorates and falls apart. You must maintain your walk with the Lord as you do with your natural possessions.

YOU ARE REWARDED FOR EVERYTHING
YOU DO FOR GOD

But without faith it is impossible to please Him, for he who comes to God must believe that He is, and that He is a rewarder of those who diligently seek Him.

—Hebrews 11:6

Hebrews says it is impossible to please God without faith, so you must have faith. It continues by saying that he who comes to God must believe He is. That is easy because you know that God exists.

It's harder to believe that God is a rewarder of those who diligently seek Him because you have to get rid of that rejection mentality that tells you that God won't reward you. Yet you will get a reward for everything you do for God. Recording angels are constantly taking notes and reporting on you, writing a book of remembrance.

> *Then those who feared the Lord spoke to one another, and the Lord listened and heard them; So a book of remembrance was written before Him for those who fear the Lord and who meditate on His name. "They shall be Mine," says the Lord of hosts, "On the day that I make them My jewels. And I will spare them as a man spares his own son who serves him." Then you shall again discern between the righteous and the wicked, between one who serves God and one who does not serve Him.*
>
> —Malachi 3:16–18

This verse in Malachi shows that books of remembrance are written for those who do right and honor the Lord. You have to believe that God exists, but you also have to believe that He is a rewarder of those who *diligently* seek Him. You have got to seek God, and the word there is *diligently*, which means you throw everything else aside and count the cost. The parable of the pearl of great price essentially instructs us to just go for it, giving all that we have in exchange for all He has for us (Matthew 13:45–46).

DILIGENTLY SEEKING GOD IN FAITH

As the deer pants for the water brooks, so pants my soul for You, O God.

—Psalm 42:1

I always pray, "Lord, make me willing to be willing. I give You permission to overcome my will. Overcome me, Lord, overwhelm me, convince me, win me over, work on me. I permit you to work me over." I have prayed that prayer for forty years since I was first saved. I want to know Him, and I must be convinced that He rewards me because I am diligently, aggressively, and outwardly seeking Him.

Diligently seeking God is not a religious exercise or mental agreement but a heartfelt drawing toward God. I desire Him, just like David expressed in Psalm 42:1. Like a thirsty deer desires water, this is how we should be with God. That was how David was—he was a seeker of God. I want to be like a child and discover the Lord as a treasure. I want to seek God and find Him. I want to find that treasure, the mysteries of God; I long to know the deep secrets of the kingdom. Now is the time to seek the Lord and get oil in your lamps. It is time to discover what God is doing and saying in the Spirit.

In the world right now, we have a lot of rebellious, strong-willed people that are opinionated and violent. We have all kinds of corruption at the highest levels. We have stealing, fraud, and evil happening around us. Yet with all that around us, we can diligently seek God, and He will take us into the land of Goshen, just like in Egypt. The Israelites were in Goshen and did not encounter all the plagues in Egypt (Exodus 9:13–35).

What pleases God? It is when we seek Him diligently and have faith. Faith pleases God, and He rewards us (Hebrews 11:6). Part of faith is diligently seeking Him so I will see the fruit of my labor. I will see that my diligence pays off. I have committed to building my faith, staying there, submitting myself to the holy fire, and seeing a whole generation change. I will see a deluge of God's power in this day we live and see people's lives change. We will see the harvest come in and see people set free; it will be the longest and greatest move of God we have ever seen. It will be a continual move that will usher Jesus into this generation. We can see that happen.

Sadly, we must have another move of God because we have slowed down our momentum and cooled off our fire for the Lord, making that move necessary. As warriors, as students of the Word of God, we must yield and let God use us to bring this move upon the earth. However, you will have to be really hot, very persistent, and fully convinced because it will be an aggressive move with the power of God. People in certain denominations will criticize it because they are not part of it. The move of God is happening outside denominations that did not want to be part of it.

For example, when you vote God out of schools and the government, suddenly, they are left to themselves, and then the system becomes corrupt. That is why we have the corruption that we have now. That is why people think they have to steal to win. They believe they must take from people because they cannot just get it honestly. That is what the enemy is doing all the time: stealing, killing, and destroying, but Jesus is blessing people because Jesus gives us life (John 10:10). He wants to teach us how to live, receiving from Heaven and giving life out—that interaction from the realm of Heaven to earth.

Certain people in history that I studied were rejected by the established religion of their day, yet they were heroes of faith. They are celebrated now but were not accepted when they were alive. It is interesting how that has happened throughout history. Jesus addressed the Pharisees, saying He had sent them many prophets, but they killed them all. Later, they celebrated those same prophets as their heroes (Matthew 23:29–37). Then He told them that they would do the same to Him: They would kill Him.

All the people we celebrate in history were not liked when they were alive. At the time, they were needed, but they were not popular. Think about some of the things people have stood up for and how we are free now because of it. Think about how women were not allowed to vote. It was ridiculous that they were considered less than others and could not vote, but the government still taxed them for working.

We go through all these struggles; some seem so ridiculous that it's hard to believe they were ever an issue. However, people had to stand up for women's rights and against racism at that time. Today we think, *How did we even have to struggle with that? It is all about revelation.* People God used in their generation had to stand up for the standard God put inside them. It was difficult then, but now we enjoy those freedoms because of the stand they took. In the same way, Jesus paid the price for us; now, we are all called to bear a standard for our generation.

13

KEEP MOVING INTO THE FIRE

Rejoice and be exceedingly glad, for great is your
reward in Heaven, for so they persecuted the
prophets who were before you.
—Matthew 5:12

A ll of us know people who go from church to church and even from denomination to denomination. Some of these people are simply church hopping. But others are looking for strong movements of God. These holy-fire, Holy Spirit–led groups of people at some point became denominations and were very popular and very large in their day. If I named them, you would know who they were and are today. Why do people leave one denomination for another? Well, when God was moving, they loved the church and were deeply involved. But the leaders of the denominations eventually stopped the move of God, so people left and looked for another church where God kept moving.

People want to keep moving with God. If a denomination stops moving, they will leave and go where the fire is. As we have been discussing, we must stay diligent and on fire in our humanness and this fallen world.

DON'T LET YOUR MOMENTUM SLIP FROM YOU

It is imperative that we keep moving and be more sober-minded and aggressive because these truths can slip from us. As I said, order goes to chaos; chaos does not go to order. In other words, your house, car, room, and bedroom do not clean or fix themselves. Our possessions break, get dirty, and get out of order, but you never see it in reverse. Your car doesn't fix itself, your bed doesn't make itself, and your house doesn't clean itself.

This broken world goes from order to chaos. You can make your bed and clean your house, but you will have to do it again in a couple of weeks. You might not be able to explain why that happens, but it does, and that is how it is. You must always be diligent, stay on fire, and keep reminding yourself that you are led by the Spirit and not by the flesh.

EVIL SPIRITS TRAP PEOPLE IN BONDAGE WITH FEAR AND CONTROL

As you discover the history of a denomination, you may think, *Oh, I want to be a part of this.* After being part of that denomination for a while, you might notice the leaders are controlling and manipulative. The same thing can happen with relationships. At first, everything seems great, and suddenly, instead of letting you make decisions and being free to be you, you start to feel controlled and manipulated. That is also what happens with big government.

In essence, you hire the government. You pay your taxes so they can protect and serve you. The government is supposed to take care of what you don't have time to do, and you pay taxes for them to do that. Suddenly, the government is telling you what you should believe and what you can and cannot do, which is manipulation and control. It eventually becomes a dictatorship, which is the antichrist spirit in operation.

> *And you He made alive, who were dead in trespasses*
> *and sins, in which you once walked according to the*

course of this world, according to the prince of the power of the air, the spirit who now works in the sons of disobedience, among whom also we all once conducted ourselves in the lusts of our flesh, fulfilling the desires of the flesh and of the mind, and were by nature children of wrath, just as the others.

—Ephesians 2:1–3

When religion and relationships become manipulative, the powers of the spirit of the air, which are under lucifer (satan), are in operation. These evil spirits entrap people in bondage through control and fear. If you do not allow the Holy Spirit to keep you free and moving, you may get into a group where you find yourself being controlled. Instead of walking in freedom, you will learn how to manipulate and control people. Operating in that wicked spirit is wrong, but it is part of religion.

For they bind heavy burdens, hard to bear, and lay them on men's shoulders; but they themselves will not move them with one of their fingers.

—Matthew 23:4

In Matthew 23:4, Jesus rebuked the Pharisees because they manipulated and controlled the people, putting heavy yokes on them. Jesus told the Pharisees they were supposed to take the heavy burdens off people instead of enslaving them. Jesus came to remove the yokes. Be aware of this deception happening in the world today. Jesus hates religion, corrupt government, and control.

IF YOU LOVE GOD, KEEP HIS COMMANDMENTS

> *If you love Me, keep My commandments.*
>
> —John 14:15

God, Who has given us free will, invites us to come to Him. However, God tells us what He likes and lets us know that if we want to know and serve Him, we must do what He commands as John 14:15 says. If we say we want God yet don't do what He commands, we cannot expect His benefits.

> *If you abide in Me, and My words abide in you, you*
> *will ask what you desire, and it shall be done for you.*
>
> —John 15:7

People say they prayed but did not get what they prayed for. Well, is His Word abiding in you, and are you abiding in Him? I often find Christians are putting stipulations on God, and they are not in a position to do that, but they do not seem to know it. They say, "I don't believe in healing because I'm not healed." Or "I don't believe in prosperity because I'm broke." The real problem is that they do not want to come under the authority of the Lord and abide in Him. They only want the benefits of knowing Him. Jesus hates that attitude because He wants to build up people, and He wants people to come to Him willingly.

DO NOT GIVE OUT OF COMPULSION OR MANIPULATION

But this I say: He who sows sparingly will also reap sparingly, and he who sows bountifully will also reap bountifully. So let each one give as he purposes in his heart, not grudgingly or of necessity; for God loves a cheerful giver. And God is able to make all grace abound toward you, that you, always having all sufficiency in all things, may have an abundance for every good work.

—2 Corinthians 9:6–8

Paul said, "God loves a cheerful giver." You should not give out of compulsion or for your own benefit. When you give, God can bless you, and you can have abundance not only for your own needs but then have extra to give to others. The whole idea here is that you should not give out of compulsion. You should not give because people manipulate your emotions and tell you how much they need the money. Paul told the Corinthians that he wanted them to take the offering before he even came to speak to them. He did not want them to feel compelled, manipulated, or pressured into giving (1 Corinthians 16:1–2).

We should give because we love God, and He loves a cheerful giver. In other words, I give to God because I love Him, which is part of my worship. When you give of your finances, it is in response to God's goodness; you love Him and want to give, not out of compulsion. When you give, you sow into God and reap the benefits of sowing into Him. When you partner with people, you love what God is doing and want to be part of that. So you should never do anything out of compulsion because Jesus hates manipulation and control.

> *Exposing yourself to the holy fire, being humble, and staying hot prevent you from succumbing to the spirit of the world.*

Our enemy, satan, is a dictator and a terrorist. He makes people afraid and enslaves them. He raises nations, governments, and dictators that manipulate and victimize their people with too much power. They are supposed to be serving their people and not controlling them. In this day that we live in, we must be careful that the spirit of the world does not get into the church. Exposing yourself to the holy fire, being humble, and staying hot prevent you from succumbing to the spirit of the world. Even though you are fighting this law of going from order to chaos and its pull on you, you can walk free of that pull. However, even though that pull does not affect you, you must always be mindful.

TAKE TIME TO EXAMINE YOURSELF

We should take communion because we must take time to examine ourselves and remember what Jesus did for us. I am finding that people who have problems with sin consciousness and do not feel forgiven have a deeply rooted mindset. We must remind ourselves what Jesus did for us by taking communion. We are connected and accountable to the body of Christ and everyone around us, because if one hurts, the body hurts.

> *Therefore whoever eats this bread or drinks this cup*
> *of the Lord in an unworthy manner will be guilty of*
> *the body and blood of the Lord. But let a man*
> *examine himself, and so let him eat of the bread and*

drink of the cup. For he who eats and drinks in an unworthy manner eats and drinks judgment to himself, not discerning the Lord's body. For this reason many are weak and sick among you, and many sleep. For if we would judge ourselves, we would not be judged. But when we are judged, we are chastened by the Lord, that we may not be condemned with the world.

—1 Corinthians 11:27–32

> *I would like you to take communion and think about what the Lord has done for you. Consider your responsibility to the body.*

In these verses, I want to emphasize that we need to discern the body of the Lord and know what the Lord did for us with His blood and body. We must understand that we are forgiven and that we forgive others. We also do not want to shorten our lives by not discerning the Lord's body. Paul said that many people who don't discern fall asleep, which refers to people who die early. Falling asleep is about death; we do not want to shorten our lives.

We do not want to miss out on what God has for us. We do not want to be lukewarm, fall asleep, and die early, so we must discern what Jesus has done for us. I would like you to take communion and think about what the Lord has done for you. Consider your responsibility to the body. Falling asleep early is not about taking a nap; it is literally premature death because a person failed to discern the body and the blood of Jesus. When you sit at the table and take communion, you must discern what that means and take it as a holy and sacred act. You set yourself apart for the Lord.

> *It is actually reported that there is sexual immorality among you, and such sexual immorality as is not even named among the Gentiles—that a man has his father's wife! And you are puffed up, and have not rather mourned, that he who has done this deed might be taken away from among you. For I indeed, as absent in body but present in spirit, have already judged (as though I were present) him who has so done this deed. In the name of our Lord Jesus Christ, when you are gathered together, along with my spirit, with the power of our Lord Jesus Christ, deliver such a one to satan for the destruction of the flesh, that his spirit may be saved in the day of the Lord Jesus. Your glorying is not good. Do you not know that a little leaven leavens the whole lump?*

Therefore purge out the old leaven, that you may be a new lump, since you truly are unleavened. For indeed Christ, our Passover, was sacrificed for us.

—1 Corinthians 5:1–7

In these verses in this letter, Paul addresses the sexual immorality in the Corinthian church. He told them that such abominations were going on there that he had not even heard of in the world. Paul said to them that when they were gathered together and the Spirit of the Lord was there, his spirit would be there also; they were to turn that sexually immoral person over to satan. Paul was not physically there, but he said even though he was absent in the body, he was present in the spirit. He said when they gathered together, the presence and power of God were there with them.

GOD'S JUDGMENT IN THE LAST DAYS

In 1 Corinthians 5:1–7, Paul described being absent in the body but present in the spirit, which is a step beyond most people's understanding; it has to do with apostolic authority. These types of judgments will happen again in these last days. We will also see situations like what happened with Ananias and Sapphira, who were slain for lying to the Holy Spirit (Acts 5:1–11). Paul instructed the Corinthian church to deliver the man practicing sexual sin to satan for the destruction of the flesh, that his spirit may be saved in the day of the Lord Jesus.

Paul wanted to set an example for the whole church so that they would not permit wickedness. If Paul let this situation continue without addressing it and let that person have his father's wife, it would condone those kinds of behaviors in Corinth. So Paul needed to set that example. He claimed he would be there with them in spirit, even though he was not there in the body, and this is amazing. When it comes to outward sin that the world and the church see, discipline must be established so that it does not spread into other areas.

After they put that man out, he was not allowed to return to the church and fellowship with them because he chose to sin and be part of the world. He was sent out, and because of that, we have this record, and that man repented in the end. He felt sorrowful and decided that what he did was not worth losing out on the Lord and fellowship. As the man repented and was grieving, Paul, in his second letter, told the Corinthians that it had been enough.

Paul instructed the Corinthians to bring the man who had been with his father's wife back after he repented so satan would not win him over with overwhelming grief (2 Corinthians 2:6–11). The destruction of that man's flesh so that his soul might be saved was accelerated so that it fixed the problem. Paul told them they should bring that man back into fellowship so that satan did not outfox them. This account has to do with apostolic authority, but it also has to do with the fact that the world and people in the church are watching, so we need to enforce holiness and correct behavior. It is okay to make decisions about the behavior of brothers and sisters in the body.

> *Arise, shine; for your light has come! And the glory of the Lord is risen upon you. For behold, the darkness shall cover the earth, and deep darkness the people; but the Lord will arise over you, and His glory will be seen upon you. The Gentiles shall come to your light, and kings to the brightness of your rising.*
>
> —Isaiah 60:1–3

In the last days, with the intensity of the Spirit of God coming upon the earth, the move of God, and the harvest, we will see more manifestations than ever before. In his vision, Daniel saw that people moving in the Spirit were wise and bright with their faces shining; Isaiah saw this as well (Daniel 12:1–4; Isaiah 9:2). In the last days, we will also see apostolic authority dealing with sin, like with Paul in Corinth. We could see God's judgment manifest as it did with Ananias and Sapphira. Jude 1:14–15 mentions Enoch's prophecy concerning the coming judgment against wickedness.

DEMONS FEEL THE HEAT OF THE HOLY FIRE IN YOU

Those who are wise shall shine like the brightness of the firmament, and those who turn many to righteousness like the stars forever and ever.

—Daniel 12:3

God's people will be the bright and shining ones in the last days. The intensity of the Spirit will reach the point where we will see instant judgment or things happening immediately that would not normally occur. When you start moving in the Spirit, you become hotter and hotter and start moving into the spiritual realm. The demons around you or people you are affiliated with this whole time are fine until you start moving into that realm. Suddenly, those demons will feel the heat turned up and start acting up; you may wonder what is happening. The temperature in you will be raised to the point where the demons will be uncomfortable, whereas before, they were not bothered.

When the move of the Holy Spirit intensifies in churches, the demons start acting up because people are getting hot. At that point, the people that do not want to go on with God begin having issues with the move of God, and they complain. Then satan will use some of those people, especially those who have a lot of money and can influence the church, to pressure the pastor and discourage the people who are on fire. We are legitimately supposed to be operating at that level with the holy fire, but unfortunately, the people that don't want that might influence the pastor. I want you to be ready in case this happens.

God may give you a dream or a visitation, He might have you praying in tongues more, or He might have you missing meals. However, I promise that once you start fasting, praying, and pursuing the Lord and holy fire, the demons will suddenly feel uncomfortable. When you enter the fire, you get hotter, and wherever you go, what used to be okay is not okay anymore. Problems will start to stir up, and people will shift and change, and then you will see that those demons were there the whole time, but they were not bothered like they are now.

As you start moving in the kingdom, preaching the kingdom, getting hotter, and not putting up with lukewarmness, the demons entrenched in the people around you will begin to act up; you must be ready for this. You will have dreams, visions, and experiences with the Lord that will bring you higher, but those around you who do not go up with you will have a problem. People will act up, scream, and say things they shouldn't. You will face resistance, manipulation, and control. You may think, *If I had not prayed or fasted as much and had just stayed the same, everyone would still like me as they did back then.* The problem is they liked you back then because you were not making a difference.

> *Rejoice and be exceedingly glad, for great is your reward in Heaven, for so they persecuted the prophets who were before you.*
>
> —Matthew 5:12

If you want to make a difference, you will inherit what Jesus inherited. Everywhere Jesus went, He was doing the Father's will, and devils were being driven out. The Pharisees flipped out because they had controlling spirits and did not like Jesus. I want to prepare you so that you will be ready for this kind of resistance when you face it. When it does happen, remember what Jesus said in Matthew 5:12. You will be rewarded in Heaven for your stand, but you will be persecuted down here for it.

14

SAVED, HEALED, AND DELIVERED

And this gospel of the kingdom will be preached in all
the world as a witness to all the nations,
and then the end will come.
—Matthew 24:14

The move of God has already started, and the Lord will bring in a future harvest of people. You have to realize that God wants to populate Heaven; however, we have to pray for this to happen and participate in it. A time is coming when people will be healed every time they get together with believers. When people are brought in to hear the gospel, there will be healings, deliverances, and manifestations of the gifts of the Spirit (1 Corinthians 12:7–11). There will be words of knowledge, words of wisdom, and all kinds of miracles. People will be full of joy, laughing, and having breakthroughs. All their yokes will be broken off, and their heavy burdens and bondages will leave.

THE HOLY FIRE IS GETTING YOU READY FOR THE MOVE OF GOD

Expect the angels to bring people to you. They will bring the unsaved in to be saved, the sick to be healed, and the demon-possessed to be delivered. God wants to give words to you by the Holy Spirit so that you can minister to people with words of knowledge and words of wisdom. I want you to be ready for this move of God, and the holy fire is preparing you for that.

We must submit to this fire. When the angels come, they ignite you with fire because they are flames of fire. The Spirit of the Lord is always willing; He brings freedom wherever He is welcome. Be expecting miracles of healing and deliverance, and they will come. I meditate on all this and anticipate how this move of God is coming.

For as many as are led by the Spirit of God, these
are sons of God. For you did not receive the spirit of

bondage again to fear, but you received the Spirit of adoption by whom we cry out, "Abba, Father."

—Romans 8:14–15

Romans 8:14–15 is an important verse to understand. The Spirit of adoption is the Spirit of full acceptance, and the Holy Spirit confirms that acceptance, crying out, "Abba, Father." He calls out "Father, Father," because we are His children, accepted and written into the will of God. We are heirs of God and co-heirs with Jesus (Romans 8:17).

And I will ask the Father, and He will give you another Helper (Comforter, Advocate, Intercessor— Counselor, Strengthener, Standby), to be with you forever—the Spirit of Truth, whom the world cannot receive [and take to its heart] because it does not see Him or know Him, but you know Him because He (the Holy Spirit) remains with you continually and will be in you. "I will not leave you as orphans [comfortless, bereaved, and helpless]; I will come [back] to you. After a little while the world will no longer see Me, but you will see Me; because I live, you will live also. On that day [when that time comes] you will know for yourselves that I am in My Father, and you are in Me, and I am in you."

—John 14:16–20 AMP

In this passage, Jesus describes the Holy Spirit as an enforcer of the blessing and a very aggressive advocate or lawyer. Jesus gives us all these names or different characteristics of the Holy Spirit in the Amplified Version—Helper, Comforter, Advocate, Intercessor, Counselor, Strengthener, Standby, and Spirit of Truth; He enforces the covenant and the blessing. He will not only present you blameless to the Lord on that day, but He is perfecting you now in preparation for the move of God and the harvest of souls (Jude 1:24). Then you will be ready for your job in the next life to come as well.

MANY WILL NOT TOLERATE SOUND DOCTRINE AND WILL TURN AWAY FROM THE TRUTH

For the time will come when they will not endure sound doctrine, but according to their own desires, because they have itching ears, they will heap up for themselves teachers; and they will turn their ears away from the truth, and be turned aside to fables.

—2 Timothy 4:3–4

In these last days, controversy will arise concerning doctrine and people's behavior, which is already happening and will continue to increase. People will turn away from the truth and turn to fables, so the Lord wants us to be ready for that. We will preach the pure gospel, the pure message of the kingdom, and then the end will come (Matthew 24:14). The Lord tells us to preach an aggressive message, this gospel of deliverance, healing, and debt cancellation. God confirms this message with signs and wonders, such as setting people free and raising the dead. He is a good God, who is not hurting people or causing problems, but that does not go over well with religious folks.

Often, religious people think God is making them sick and poor, causing all the trouble and destruction we see. These people just give up and say, "Well, you know, that must be what God wants." They do not know the Bible because God clearly says He is a good God, and it is the thief who hurts people. Jesus came to give us life and life more abundantly (John 10:10).

OUR GOD IS GOOD

Jesus said to him, "Have I been with you so long, and yet you have not known Me, Philip? He who has

> *seen Me has seen the Father; so how can you say,*
> *'Show us the Father?'"*
>
> —John 14:9

I trust in Jesus because He was the express image of the Father, sent to be our example (Hebrews 1:3). I will believe in God's blessings, which the Holy Spirit continuously enforces. The Holy Spirit reminds us of what Jesus said and will show us the future (John 14:26; 16:13). We must tell people that God is a good God (Jeremiah 29:11).

When Jesus appeared to me, He told me about the testing coming upon the church and the earth. He gave this warning because we were lukewarm. He explained that satan—not He and His Father— was causing these calamities. It is very interesting how religious people will side with the devil as to what is happening on the earth and think it's God. They say things like, "We're getting what we deserve." I am shocked at the religious people's responses and mentalities, but we were warned about them. As Paul said, the time will come when they will not tolerate sound doctrine.

The Lord wants to bless people in these last days with good health. He wants to bless them with freedom in their minds and to set them free from demonic spirits (Luke 4:18–19). God wants people to be financially blessed and prosperous in everything they do so that all their needs are met; then, they will have extra to help others. This is God's desire and what He is speaking to everyone. To share the message of the gospel is to preach jubilee, which was debt cancellation; to break bondages, not put them on; to heal the sick, not put sickness onto them; to deliver people from the demonic; and to raise the dead.

When the gospel is demonstrated, people are not dying; they are being raised from the dead. They are being healed and delivered, they are prospering, their sins are forgiven, and they are full of joy. Jesus preached the gospel, expressing how much His Father loves you. You can go to the Father on your own, using Jesus's name (John 16:23–28). Jesus said that if you love, embrace, and obey His Father, They will come to live with you (John 14:20–23). Jesus said that you could ask whatever you desire—not what you need, but what you desire—and it shall be done for you (John 15:7–11). He said this would be done to give glory to the Father and that your joy may be complete (John 16:24). That is in the Scripture. I do not see any scholar trying to discredit or fight over this passage.

THE UNFORGIVABLE SIN

Yet some people do not believe that God is a good God and that He answers every prayer. As Paul said to Timothy, people in the last days will not put up with sound doctrine. The holy fire and the move of God are increasing; the spiritual temperature is rising. In these times of lukewarmness, when people are falling away, it is dangerous to attribute the works of the devil to God. It is also very dangerous to say that the devil is working when it is God, for example, to say that speaking in tongues is of the devil. If you attribute the works of the Holy Spirit to the works of the devil, according to what Jesus said, that is not forgivable (Mark 3:28–29).

> *Therefore I say to you, every sin and blasphemy will be forgiven men, but the blasphemy against the Spirit will not be forgiven men. Anyone who speaks a word against the Son of Man, it will be forgiven him; but whoever speaks against the Holy Spirit, it will not be forgiven him, either in this age or in the age to come.*
> —Matthew12:31–32

If you speak against the Spirit of God, Jesus said it is not forgivable in this life or the next. He said you could speak against the Father and the Son, but you cannot speak against the Holy Spirit. I do not understand everything that entails, but I am smart enough to know not to do that. In these last days, when I listen to people mock Christians that believe in the Holy Spirit, miracles, and speaking in tongues, I cringe; it is unpardonable to attribute that to the enemy. Jesus said that is unforgivable.

ALLOW THE FIRE OF GOD TO CONSUME YOU

In the future, people will oppose the work of God and His move. They are on dangerous ground when they come against healing, deliverance, debt cancellation, speaking in tongues, and walking in the Spirit—as mentioned, this is unforgivable. The last days are upon us, and if we are going to serve the Lord and go the whole way with Him, we need to be hot and allow the fire to consume us. If we don't, people could fall away very quickly. You must either be hot or cold; lukewarm people won't last because of the spiritual environment that we are in.

> *Share all the good things the gospel brings: healing, the forgiveness of sin, debt cancellation, and God's supernatural financial provision.*

I call all the people associated with me to turn and repent and get hot. Allow the Word of God to ignite within you and give the Spirit of God free rein. Talk all the time about how good God is; speak about deliverance and freedom. Share all the good things the gospel brings: healing, the forgiveness of sin, debt cancellation, and God's supernatural financial provision. Discuss the ministry of angels. As you do this, you build each other up in faith, and then the kingdom of God advances. If people in the world don't want to hear about the kingdom, we can still encourage each other. We can always call friends, build them up, and preach to them. I am sure you can find someone who would want to listen to your preaching.

In these last days, give your finances to the Lord. With holy fire, God needs to know that you can be trusted, so you must pass your money test; you have to be able to give *and* receive freely. Be encouraged and allow the Holy Spirit to move in your finances so that you can be set free. God wants to get you out of debt, which is a miracle when He does.

When we were young, I could not see how God would get us out of debt because it seemed impossible, but He did it. We worked extra hard, cut out expensive extras, and took many steps on our own, and God came through with miracle after miracle. I believe that and am asking God to do that for you. Give God your finances and allow Him to advance the kingdom through your finances.

Give God your body and allow Him to heal it. It does not matter how impossible it looks or if your situation is stubborn and won't change. It does not matter that you are on medication. Continue to take it, but pray and ask God to show you what you can do and what He wants you to do and believe for supernatural healing in your body. God wants to touch your body and wants you to be pain-free; He wants you to move into supernatural healing. So let God influence you; I don't care how long it takes.

YOUR JOURNEY WITH GOD IS UNVEILED MORE AND MORE EVERY DAY

Let God talk to you. Feed on the Word of God for health in your body and believe that God will supernaturally deliver you from sickness and disease. Feed on the Word of God not only for healing but for finances as well. God can do it and can supernaturally keep you. God wants you to be healthy and pain-free; the Spirit of God is more than willing to do that.

With deliverance, in some situations, people do not understand or know why they are going through certain experiences. Evil spirits are in operation. They are being handed down and assigned through the bloodline. People inherit these and do not understand what has happened. These evil spirits are very tenacious and stubborn. You need to turn yourself over to the Lord in the holy fire and separate yourself so you can discern the workings of these familiar spirits.

You need to be the one that overthrows them and stops this from continuing in your family.

> *You can address these issues and break their power, and if you get pushback, you know you are making progress.*

I want to encourage you to turn your spiritual life over to the Lord so that you can get hot enough to know and discern what may be working against you. It is not your fault because these problems are common worldwide among people. But you have to take a stand against them even if you cannot see or understand what is happening. You can address these issues and break their power, and if you get pushback, you know you are making progress. You must also feed yourself on the Word of God, pray, and get hot enough so that you expose these demons.

You need to hand yourself over to God in the following areas: finances, health, regarding the demonic, and familiar spirits enforcing curses on generations through your bloodline. You hand your life over so that you can be strengthened to the point where you can come and stand against these powers working against you (Ephesians 6:12). When you turn yourself over to God in every area of your life, you will start to be delivered and healed and see the manifestation of the kingdom of God. I know this for a fact.

So many people do not understand why they are struggling. Then they hear the Word of God and experience some catalyst that causes them to act. Sometimes it is an encounter at a conference, reading a book, or praying and fasting. This catalyst causes them to see and take action, and then deliverance starts to break forth. The devil will begin to unravel, and he will no longer have a stronghold in that area of finances, healing, or deliverance. You start to encounter freedom. As you gain leverage, you can enforce that blessing instead of perpetuating the curse. Their ability to hold you diminishes.

The power of God rests in the name of Jesus. These demons shake and lose their control when confronted with the full authority in His name. Mention the name of Jesus in any area of your life where you want to see a breakthrough; invoke His name and authority daily. If any demonic spirits are involved in these areas, you will start to see a change in your finances, body, and spiritual life. You will start to see your finances break open. Your body will begin to heal, and you will see the bondages from these familiar spirits diminish. Invoke the name of Jesus, and pray in the Spirit. You are not perfect, but you are being transformed into what you are supposed to be. This journey is unveiled more and more every day.

> *Brethren, I do not count myself to have apprehended;*
> *but one thing I do, forgetting those things which are*
> *behind and reaching forward to those things which*
> *are ahead, I press toward the goal for the prize of the*
> *upward call of God in Christ Jesus. Therefore let us,*
> *as many as are mature, have this mind; and if in*
> *anything you think otherwise, God will reveal even*
> *this to you.*
>
> —Philippians 3:13–15

You are not striving to be perfect—it is God who is perfecting you. Paul said he did not claim to have arrived, but he pressed on toward the mark of that high calling, that perfection, even if he hadn't obtained it. Paul was always pressing on to the goal, which is what we are to do. I desire to see you get to the place where you do not fail, and you are not unproductive. Peter said that we are partakers of the divine nature, and if you add your faith to all these virtues—self-control, brotherly love, and kindness—and if you do all these things, they will help you be productive and never fail (2 Peter 1:4–8).

15

CHARACTER, PERSONALITY, AND ACCOUNTABILITY

Therefore, brethren, be even more diligent to make your
call and election sure, for if you do these things you will
never stumble.

—2 Peter 1:10

We think of faith as so important because, without faith, we cannot please God (Hebrews 11:6). Much emphasis was placed on the gifts of the Spirit during the charismatic movement and then on faith in the Word of Faith movement. However, until now, in the body of Christ, we have not yet placed much emphasis on character, personality, and accountability; a focus on these qualities will increase in these last days.

But also for this very reason, giving all diligence, add to your faith virtue, to virtue knowledge, to knowledge self-control, to self-control perseverance, to perseverance godliness, to godliness brotherly kindness, and to brotherly kindness love. For if these things are yours and abound, you will be neither barren nor unfruitful in the knowledge of our Lord Jesus Christ. For he who lacks these things is shortsighted, even to blindness, and has forgotten that he was cleansed from his old sins. Therefore, brethren, be even more diligent to make your call and election sure, for if you do these things you will never stumble.

—2 Peter 1:5–10

GOD'S PERSONALITY MUST BECOME
OUR PERSONALITY

Peter says he wants you to add these things to your faith. Previous to this, Peter said that we are partakers of the divine nature because of the promises given to us (2 Peter 1:4). As a result of these promises, we are partakers of or partners with the divine nature. To be like God is profound to me. Ephesians says, "Therefore be imitators of God as dear children" (Ephesians 5:1). These virtues that we are supposed to add to our faith are a group of characteristics that are God's personality but become our personality.

One of the virtues that you are to add to your faith is knowledge. You may think, *I have great faith*, but Peter is saying add knowledge to that faith, so I will add some knowledge to my faith. Then he instructed us to add self-control, perseverance, godliness, brotherly kindness, and love. Peter explains that if you possess these characteristics, you will never be barren but fruitful in the knowledge of our Lord Jesus Christ. On the other hand, if you lack these virtues, you are short-sighted and even blind, forgetting that you have been cleansed from your past sins. So 2 Peter 1:10 admonishes us to be diligent to make our call and election sure. You will never fail if you heed this very important instruction.

> *I pray that you always feel the supernatural need for knowledge and continually seek and want to know more.*

It is so crucial in these last days to focus on character. We think of faith that can move mountains, but you have nothing if you do not have love (1 Corinthians 13:1–13). Peter begins with your faith and adds all these different steps, and the very last virtue he mentions is love. Another one of the steps he mentions is knowledge, and you can never know enough.

KNOWLEDGE

After I went through different colleges, courses, and training for various professions, I thought, *I don't know if I can handle any more*. I studied to be a commercial pilot, and after I took the tests, which lasted two days, I got my commercial pilot license. Afterward, I was so exhausted that I slept for thirty-two hours. After that, I didn't think I could learn anything else. That was years ago, in 1989, and now we are in 2023. I am learning more about jet airplanes now than ever, and I still don't feel like I know anything.

We will never know everything. People often do not even see the need for knowledge. Sometimes we need it, but we don't see it until, suddenly, a circumstance arises that exposes that need for understanding knowledge. Then we get it. We will always need to add knowledge to our faith. I pray that you always feel the supernatural need for knowledge and continually seek and want to know more. After you have knowledge and develop and mature, Peter says to add self-control to that.

SELF CONTROL

As you know more, experience more, and do more, you will have to have self-control. For me, it is about knowing when to step in and when not to; when to say something, and when not to. It is managing your words, thoughts, and actions. As you develop, get smarter, and are full of knowledge, you must have wisdom because you have to be able to control yourself and know when to speak and when to be quiet. You could offer someone advice when they are not asking for it, and they will not want it. You can see that person will get hurt and want to help them, but you can't help them. You have to know when to hold back and when to speak, which is all part of self-control.

PERSEVERANCE

To self-control, you must add perseverance; in other words, you must stay in there. Peter was saying that he wants you to always be in gear, never go into neutral, and never get lukewarm in the days we live. You must persevere and keep going, and you have to tell yourself that. Perseverance is constantly engaging God and being led by the Spirit. Then to that perseverance, you must add godliness.

GODLINESS

We are to be imitators of God as dearly loved children and be godly (Ephesians 5:1). We are like God because we are imitators of Him, and we are always to be thinking about that. What is godly? What would God do? What would Jesus do if He were here? Think about being in a certain situation and what you would say or do. I mostly think about what Jesus would do in that situation; I think about Scripture and start implementing and applying it.

> *You temper your actions by imitating what God, your Father, would do.*

After you have learned to persevere, then you add godliness to that. So you temper everything with this thought: *This is how I will act because it is appropriate and godly to act this way. I will not say this, and I will not do that.* You temper your actions by imitating what God, your Father, would do. You act like your Heavenly Father and imitate Him.

BROTHERLY KINDNESS

Peter says that to godliness, we are to add brotherly kindness. Even after you feel like you are getting closer to God and becoming more like Him, you must seek to be kind to people. You must be tolerant in the sense that you understand people's weaknesses. However, I am not saying that you excuse people's sins, but you are kind about it. You must be understanding of what they are going through. Put yourself in their situation and try to outwardly grace your words and actions with kindness. After brotherly kindness, Peter advises us to add love.

LOVE

Love is patient, love is kind. It does not envy, it does not boast, it is not proud. It does not dishonor others, it is not self-seeking, it is not easily angered, it keeps no record of wrongs. Love does not delight in evil but rejoices with the truth. It always protects, always trusts, always hopes, always perseveres.

—1 Corinthians 13:4–7 NIV

Love is patient, and love is kind, and as you read through 1 Corinthians 13, you will see all the characteristics of love. If you walk in these virtues and do all these things, you have added to your faith and diligently made your call and election sure.

And now abide faith, hope, love, these three; but the greatest of these is love.

—1 Corinthians 13:13

The last school I attended before my doctorate was my two-year program, where I learned the most about faith and the Scriptures about being in Christ. I was built up strongly. However, I didn't find out until later that the greatest of these was love, not faith, as it says here in 1 Corinthians 13:13. Then I realized Peter was saying that you must add all these things *to* your faith, which had to do with your character. People were moving mountains with their faith and were seeing all these prayers answered, and it was an amazing time back then. Yet most of my friends are not even in ministry anymore.

SATAN CAN COME IN AND GET YOU OFF TRACK IN YOUR CHARACTER

If I go back and think about my time as an undergraduate, I have only met two out of the hundreds in my graduating class still in ministry. That does not mean more aren't in the ministry, but I only know of two people in the ministry to this day. And from the two-year program I attended after my undergrad, I only know two people who are still in the ministry and moving with God. I thought the students from this school would always be in ministry because they were very powerful individuals. The problem is that satan comes in, and he steals from people.

> *Therefore whoever hears these sayings of Mine, and does them, I will liken him to a wise man who built his house on the rock: and the rain descended, the floods came, and the winds blew and beat on that house; and it did not fall, for it was founded on the rock. But everyone who hears these sayings of Mine, and does not do them, will be like a foolish man who built his house on the sand: and the rain descended, the floods came, and the winds blew and beat on that house; and it fell. And great was its fall.*
>
> —Matthew 7:24–27

I find this very thing when I talk to the people who are no longer in ministry and investigate what is happening with them. They did not add all these virtues, which are character traits, to their faith. These virtues place you on a solid foundation so that your house cannot be washed away when the rains come because you are established and strong. I now realize just how important this was the whole time. When studying faith, different supernatural manifestations, and the gifts of the Spirit, we were so excited because we loved it when God used us; we loved to experience the other realm. Unfortunately, satan can come in and get us off track in our character.

> *I do not pray that You should take them out of the world, but that You should keep them from the evil one. They are not of the world, just as I am not of the world.*
>
> —John 17:15–16

BE DILIGENT TO MAKE YOUR CALL AND ELECTION SURE

> *Your eyes saw my substance, being yet unformed. And in Your book they all were written, the days fashioned for me, when as yet there were none of them.*
>
> —Psalm 139:16

We are in this world, but we are not of it, and while I am here, I want to be fortified, lasting to the end. I want to pass all my tests, and I want to stay in there. Jesus established every one of us in our books written in Heaven before we were ever born.

Each one of our days was written in a book before one of them came to pass, yet how many people actually end up fulfilling their destiny? I have seen so many people wash out and fail. I have seen problems come to people I know, and I never guessed that they would lose heart.

We must stay diligent, and if we add all these other virtues to our faith, Peter promises us that we will not be barren or unproductive and will not fail. We have all these promises set before us so that we do not forget we are cleansed from our past sins and are not blind. However, remember that Peter says Christians can be blind and forget they are cleansed from their past sins. Peter says something at the end of this verse in 2 Peter 1:10 that I have never heard talked about or taught, "Therefore, brethren, be even more diligent to make your call and election sure." So what is your call?

God calls people and essentially says, "This is what I have for you, and I am calling you to do it. I have a mission for you, and I am assigning you to it." We all have a calling that God has for us, which God wrote in a book before we were born. If God elected you, chose you, and called you, why did Peter say to do everything you can and be diligent to make that calling sure? Some people think that once saved, you are always saved, and others say you can lose your salvation, and there are many arguments for, against, and between these extremes.

> *Therefore I make known to you that no one speaking*
> *by the Spirit of God call Jesus accursed, and no one*
> *can say that Jesus is Lord except by the Holy Spirit.*
> —1 Corinthians 12:3

1 Corinthians 12:3 says that you cannot say by the Spirit of God that Jesus is cursed because the Spirit would never say that; you cannot do certain things if you are in Christ. If you are doing these things, you need to check to see if you are even in Christ. Paul addressed these kinds of matters in his letters. Similarly, Peter said we must be diligent in making our call and election sure. He is giving us the idea that we could fall away and be lost.

> *Do you not know that those who run in a race all run,*
> *but one receives the prize? Run in such a way that*
> *you may obtain it. And everyone who competes for*
> *the prize is temperate in all things. Now they do it to*
> *obtain a perishable crown, but we for an*
> *imperishable crown. Therefore I run thus: not with*
> *uncertainty. Thus I fight: not as one who beats the*
> *air. But I discipline my body and bring it into*

subjection, lest, when I have preached to others, I myself should become disqualified.

—1 Corinthians 9:24–27

Paul said that after he preached Christ, if he were to live in the flesh, being ruled by his body and not disciplining it and making it listen, he could be eliminated—thrown away—from the race. This saying is hard for some people to accept. This idea of adding these virtues to our faith and that if we do these things, we will never stumble and never fail means that if we do *not* do them, we *could* stumble and *could* fail. And it's the same with many other truths in the Word. So I would not want to test those boundaries and find out.

I know many wonderful people who were wonderful friends who are completely gone now. Either they died early, are out of the ministry, or are struggling now. They were good people who loved God and wanted to serve Him, but satan attacked and targeted them; they did not keep up their temperature spiritually. They did not do all the things we discussed on all these levels that are so important.

I added up every person I went to college with from both universities, which totaled about two thousand graduates. Almost two thousand people on the earth right now, including me, should be walking in what Jesus walked in. I can only name, on one hand, the people I know that are still operating in that from my graduating classes. As I said, there could be more I don't know of, but I should have heard about them.

I know one individual named Roger, who is in India, and from what I understand, he has started over five hundred churches. Roger was very humble, and we spent a lot of time together in college, talking and studying. He was the most amazing man and wasn't trying to be a bigwig or impress anyone.

Roger was sent from another country to college here in America. He fasted, prayed privately, and prayed with me. We sought God and talked about Him, and then Roger returned to his country and did it. He made his call and election sure. I also know another person who is a pastor, and he still believes the same way and continues to serve the Lord. So I know a couple of individuals that continued, but there are so few. That was not God's will at all.

THE GREATER WORKS

Most assuredly, I say to you, he who believes in Me, the works that I do he will do also; and greater works than these he will do, because I go to My Father.
—John 14:12

Jesus was very diligent. I think about what He said in John 14:12, that we would do the works that He did and even greater works. If Jesus were on the earth right now, He would remind us of what He said. When Jesus worked with the disciples, and they failed in doubt, unbelief, or fear, He would say, "How long will I be with you?" (Matthew 17:17). In other words, "I will not be with you very long, and if you don't catch on, how will you be able to carry out the will of the Father? I am training you and getting you ready because I am leaving." Jesus said, "I am going to the Father. So you will do what I am doing, but then you will do even greater works."

> *And they went out and preached everywhere, the Lord working with them and confirming the word through the accompanying signs. Amen.*
>
> —Mark 16:20

People argue about the works of Jesus. Some religious organizations are against speaking in tongues, laying hands on the sick, casting out devils, freeing people from bondages, and preaching that God wants to prosper you. They are against all of that, but that *is* the message of the gospel. These signs and wonders confirm that the Word of God is being preached. They follow those who believe. If the Word is preached and the believing ones do their job doing the works of Jesus, these signs will follow us. However, Jesus would want to coach us right now on the greater works.

What if a whole room of people were healed, received financial freedom, or were delivered from familiar spirits and curses? What if they were delivered from problems that are not of God and should have been taken care of but were not? Jesus would want to mention the number of those receiving miracles and the intensity of the manifestation. However, these religious organizations come against the whole idea of miracles, signs, and wonders because of self-interest. They say, "That is not for this dispensation. That all left with the apostles." It is easier to do that and come against people that believe that way and try to discredit them than manning up and saying, "This is what we should be experiencing."

I do not believe it is God's fault that we are not seeing the greater works or even any works at all. Jesus warned it would be this way; it is a perfect example that God's will is not always done on the earth as it should be. If God's will were done, we would see the works of Jesus in the church and in every believer and even greater works than that. The gates of hell would not prevail against the church.

God's will is *not* always done, yet He is not to blame. He has established His will and let us know what it is. He said we would go beyond faith by adding all these other virtues, characteristics, and personality traits. We will go to that higher level, and then we will not be unproductive and blind; we will not fail but finish our race.

> *Go therefore and make disciples of all the nations, baptizing them in the name of the Father and of the Son and of the Holy Spirit, teaching them to observe all things that I have commanded you; and lo, I am with you always, even to the end of the age." Amen.*
>
> —Matthew 28:19–20

> *Therefore bear fruits worthy of repentance, do not think to say to yourselves, 'We have Abraham as our father.' For I say to you that God is able to raise up children to Abraham from these stones. And even now the ax is laid to the root of the trees. Therefore every tree which does not bear good fruit is cut down and thrown into the fire.*
>
> —Matthew 3:8–10

God's will is that everyone hears the Word of God and produces fruit in keeping with repentance, and I believe that for you. I believe this teaching on holy fire has helped you and given you the proper perspective, and when we all get to Heaven, I will see the fruit that came from this course. I believe I will see all the people you touched and the amazing works of God displayed on the earth because you took what you were taught here. I believe that you will bear much fruit for the kingdom of God.

PRAYER

I thank You, Father, that many, many, many will come into the kingdom because of holy fire. I thank You for fulfilling Your heart in every student's life so that You would produce everything they need inside and outside their lives. Father, I pray that You would bring the finances, that You would bring all the provision that is needed in their bodies and their minds, and bring spiritual wisdom and revelation. I thank You for the finances and deliverance from every type of evil in their lives. In the name of Jesus. Amen.

God bless you.

Salvation Prayer

Lord God,
I confess that I am a sinner.
I confess that I need Your Son, Jesus.
Please forgive me in His name.
Lord Jesus, I believe You died for me and that
You are alive and listening to me now.
I now turn from my sins and welcome You into my heart.
Come and take control of my life.
Make me the kind of person You want me to be.
Now, fill me with Your Holy Spirit,
who will show me how to live for You.
I acknowledge You before men as my Savior and my Lord.
In Jesus's name. Amen.

If you prayed this prayer, please contact us at
info@kevinzadai.com for more information and materials.

We welcome you to join our network at Warriornotes.tv for access
to exclusive programming.

To enroll in our ministry school, go to:
www.Warriornotesschool.com.

**Visit www.KevinZadai.com for additional
ministry materials.**

About Dr. Kevin Zadai

Kevin Zadai, Th.D., was called to the ministry at the age of ten. He attended Central Bible College in Springfield, Missouri, where he received a Bachelor of Arts in theology. Later, he received training in missions at Rhema Bible College and a Th. D. at Primus University. Dr. Kevin L. Zadai is dedicated to training Christians to live and operate in two realms at once— the supernatural and the natural. At age 31, Kevin met Jesus, got a second chance at life, and received a revelation that he could not fail because it's all rigged in our favor! Kevin holds a commercial pilot license and is retired from Southwest Airlines after twenty-nine years as a flight attendant. Kevin is the founder and president of Warrior Notes School of Ministry. He and his lovely wife, Kathi, reside in New Orleans, Louisiana.

CHECK OUT OTHER WORKS ON THIS
SUBJECT BY DR. KEVIN ZADAI

  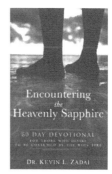

Kevin has written over sixty books and study guides.
Please see our website for a complete list of materials!

www.Kevinzadai.com